Crime Prevention
and
Community Safety

Crime Prevention and Community Safety: New Directions

This text provides some of the set readings for a sixteen-week course (D863 *Community Safety, Crime Prevention and Social Control*) which is offered by the Open University Master's Programme in the Social Sciences. D863 *Community Safety, Crime Prevention and Social Control* is a core course for both the MA in Social Policy and the MA in Social Policy and Criminology.

The Open University Master's Programme in the Social Sciences

The MA/MSc programme enables students to select from a range of modules to create a programme to suit their own professional or personal development. Students can choose from a range of social science modules to obtain an MA in the Social Sciences, or may choose to specialize in a particular subject area by studying modules in one of the offered study lines.

OU-supported learning

The Open University's unique supported ('distance') learning Master's Programme in the Social Sciences is designed to facilitate engagement at an advanced level with the concepts, approaches, theories and techniques associated with a number of academic areas of study. The Social Sciences Master's programme provides great flexibility. Students study in their own environment, in their own time, anywhere in the European Union. They receive specially prepared course materials, benefit from structured tutorial support throughout all the coursework and assessment assignments, and have the chance to work with other students.

How to apply

If you would like to register for this programme, or simply find out more information, please write for the Master's Programme in the Social Sciences prospectus to the Open University, Course Reservations Centre, PO box 625, Milton Keynes MK7 6ZW, UK (telephone +44 (0)1908 858585) (e-mail: ces-gen@open.ac.uk)

Crime Prevention and Community Safety

New Directions

edited by
Gordon Hughes
Eugene McLaughlin
John Muncie

SAGE Publications
London • Thousand Oaks • New Delhi

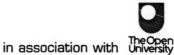

in association with The Open University

First published 2002
Reprinted 2005, 2006

SAGE Publications Ltd
1 Oliver's Yard
55 City Road
London EC1Y 1SP

SAGE Publications Inc
2455 Teller Road
Thousand Oaks, California 91320

SAGE Publications India Pvt Ltd
B-42 Panchsheel Enclave
PO Box 4109
New Delhi 110 017

British Library Cataloguing in Publication data

A catalogue record for this book is available
from the British Library

ISBN-10: 0-7619-7408-3   ISBN-13: 978-0-7619-7408-6
ISBN-10: 0-7619-7409-1 (pbk)   ISBN-13: 978-0-7619-7409-3 (pbk)

Library of Congress Control Number available

Typeset by Mayhew Typesetting, Rhayader, Powys

Contents

Notes on the contributors

Trevor Bradley is an Associate Lecturer at the Institute of Criminology at the Victoria University of Wellington. He is currently completing a PhD dissertation on *The Politics of Crime and Community Safety in New Zealand*. His research interests include neo-liberalism, crime prevention and community safety.

Davina Cooper is Professor of Law and Social Science Research Dean at Keele University. She is the author of *Sexing the City: Lesbian and Gay Politics within the Activist State* (Rivers Oram Press, 1994), *Power in Struggle: Feminism, Sexuality and the State* (Open University Press, 1995), and *Governing Out of Order: Space, Law and the Politics of Belonging* (Rivers Oram Press, 1998). She is completing a book on radical pluralism and normative political theory.

Adam Crawford is Professor of Criminology and Criminal Justice and Deputy Director of the Centre for Criminal Justice Studies, University of Leeds. He is author of *The Local Governance of Crime* (Clarendon Press, 1997), *Crime Prevention and Community Safety* (Longman, 1998), editor of *Integrating a Victim Perspective within Criminal Justice* (Ashgate, 2000, with J. Goodey) and *Crime and Insecurity: The Governance of Safety in Europe* (Willan Publishing, forthcoming). He has worked for the New Zealand Ministry of Justice and the Northern Ireland Office in relation to crime prevention policy, and is part of a research team funded by the Home Office to evaluate restorative reforms introduced into the youth justice system in England and Wales.

Brian Gormally is an independent consultant concentrating on policy analysis and the support of community-based organizations. He was for twenty-five years Deputy Director of Northern Ireland's leading criminal justice voluntary organization. He was heavily involved in the debate around the release of politically motivated prisoners and in helping create alternatives to paramilitary punishment beatings and shootings. He has written widely on prison issues, community restorative justice and the Northern Ireland peace process.

Tim Hope is Professor of Criminology and Director of the Crime Policy Evaluation Research Group, Keele University. He was Director of the

ESRC Crime and Social Order Programme and has worked at the Universities of Manchester and Missouri-St Louis and at the Home Office Research and Planning Unit, where he was principal research officer for community crime prevention. He has published research in the fields of communities and crime, crime prevention, policing, environmental criminology and victimology and has been involved in the design and analysis of the British Crime Survey and in the evaluation of major community crime prevention initiatives. He was a contributor to *Reducing Offending* (Home Office, 1998). His recent publications include *Perspectives on Crime Reduction* (Ashgate, 2000), *Crime, Risk and Insecurity* (Routledge, 2000, co-edited with R. Sparks), and *Housing, Community and Crime* (HMSO, 1993, with J. Foster).

Gordon Hughes is Lecturer in Social Policy at the Open University. Recent publications include *Understanding Crime Prevention: Social Control, Risk and Late Modernity* (Open University Press, 1998), *Ordering Lives: Family, Work and Welfare* (Routledge, 2000, co-edited with Ross Fergusson), *Community Crime Prevention* (Willan Publications, 2001 in press, co-edited with Adam Edwards). He is working on a book of essays, *The Politics of Crime and Community*, for Palgrave/Macmillan. His current research interests lie in the comparative policy field of community safety and urban security, and communitarianism and the contested politics of community in late modernity.

Kieran McEvoy is Reader in Criminology in the School of Law, Queen's University of Belfast. He researches and teaches in the areas of prisons, restorative justice, drugs and human rights. Recent publications include *Ecstasy Use in Northern Ireland* (HMSO, 1999, with Karen McElrath), *Crime, Community and Locale* (Ashgate, 2000, with D. O'Mahony, R. Geary and J. Morison) and *Paramilitary Imprisonment in Northern Ireland* (Oxford University Press, 2001).

Eugene McLaughlin is Senior Lecturer in Criminology and Social Policy at the Open University. His primary research interest is the governance of policing and he is working on the future of the police complaints system. His most recent book is *The Sage Dictionary of Criminology* (Sage, 2001, with John Muncie). He is also co-editor with John Muncie of *The Problem of Crime* (Sage, 2001) and *Controlling Crime* (Sage, 2001).

Harry Mika is Professor of Sociology at Central Michigan University and Adjunct Professor in the School of Law, Queen's University of Belfast. He conducts research and publishes on community-based justice programmes in North America and Northern Ireland, and provides technical assistance on programme implementation, sustainability and performance. His research includes the role of ex-combatants in community regeneration, the evaluator role in justice practice, and the harmonics of restorative justice within conflict transformation.

John Muncie is Senior Lecturer in Social Policy and Criminology at the Open University. Recent publications include *Youth and Crime: A Critical Introduction* (Sage, 1999) and, co-edited with Eugene McLaughlin, *The Problem of Crime* (Sage, 2001), *Controlling Crime* (Sage, 2001) and *The Sage Dictionary of Criminology* (Sage, 2001). His main research interests lie in establishing a distinct, comparative and critical youth criminology.

Tim Newburn is Joseph Rowntree Professor of Urban Social Policy and Director of the Public Policy Research Unit at Goldsmiths' College, University of London. He is the author and editor of numerous books, including *Crime and Criminal Justice Policy* (Longman, 2001) and *Private Security and Public Policing* (Clarendon Press, 1998, with Trevor Jones). He is the co-editor of *Criminal Justice: the International Journal of Policy and Practice* (published by Sage) and general editor of the Longman Criminology Series.

Pat O'Malley is Professor of Law and Legal Studies at La Trobe University, Melbourne. He has served on several state drug commissions, and has been involved with drug law reform for some time. Among his recent publications are *Crime and the Risk Society* (Ashgate, 1998) and *Crime Prevention in Australia* (Federation Press, 1997, with Adam Sutton). Current research includes analysing the implications of the trend toward risk techniques for moralities of justice.

Coretta Phillips is Lecturer in Social Policy at the London School of Economics. In addition to community safety, her main area of interest is race and ethnicity in criminal justice and criminology. She is co-author with Benjamin Bowling of *Racism, Crime and Criminal Justice* (Longman, 2001).

René van Swaaningen is a Reader in Criminology at the Erasmus University, Rotterdam. His work generally relates criminological, criminal justice and penological issues to themes from social theory. His publications include *Critical Criminology: Visions from Europe* (Sage, 1997) and *Tegen de regels: een inleiding in de criminologie* (Ars Aequi, 1999/2001), a Dutch-language introduction to criminology. He is working on a book on community safety politics in a risk society.

Nick Tilley is Professor of Sociology at Nottingham Trent University. He is co-author of *Realistic Evaluation* (Sage, 1997, with Ray Pawson) and co-editor of *Surveillance of Public Space: CCTV, Street Lighting and Crime Prevention* (Criminal Justice Press, 1999, with Kate Painter).

Sandra Walklate is Professor of Sociology at Manchester Metropolitan University. She has written extensively on policing, victims, and communities and crime and has worked with a range of victim support services and police forces in both a voluntary and a training capacity. Her other main publications include *Gender, Crime and Criminal Justice* (Willan Publishing, 2000), *Understanding Criminology* (Open University Press, 1998) and *Zero Tolerance or Community Tolerance? Managing Crime in High Crime Areas* (Ashgate, 1999, with K. Evans).

Reece Walters is a Senior Lecturer at the Victoria University of Wellington. His research areas include state crime, crime prevention, and crime and governance. He has published numerous articles in international journals and books in the areas of crime prevention, community safety and the governance of knowledge. He has also published *The Younger Audience: Children and Broadcasting in New Zealand* (Dunmore Press, 2001). This book explores issues of culture, consumption and regulation. He is also finishing a manuscript on *The Governance of Criminological Knowledge*.

The editors wish to thank the Social Policy Discipline at the Open University for funding a series of seminars which took place at the Walton Hall Campus, Milton Keynes, in 2000. This series of seminars, entitled 'Rethinking Crime Prevention and Community Safety', brought together a genuinely 'inclusive' group of leading researchers, critical theorists and policy advisers in the field. What resulted was an exciting exchange of ideas, perspectives and new directions for research, theory and practice in this increasingly important aspect of the governance of crime control and social order. Much of the content and themes which underpin this collection grew out of this dialogic process. Our thanks go to all the speakers and invited discussants who took part in this collaborative project, namely Roy Coleman, Mary Considine, Adam Crawford, Adam Edwards, Clive Emsley, Janet Fink, Sharon Gewirtz, Daniel Gilling, Barry Godfrey, Lynn Hancock, Tim Hope, Anja Johansson, Paul Lawrence, Gail Lewis, Rachel Lewis, Roger Matthews, Tim Newburn, Coretta Phillips, Alice Sampson, Dick Skellington, Kevin Stenson, Nick Tilley, René van Swaaningen, Sandra Walklate, Rob Whyte and Chris Williams.

This volume is specifically designed for use as a key text for the Open University postgraduate course *Community Safety, Crime Prevention and Social Control* (D863). Beyond this it is designed for a much wider academic audience – of lecturers, researchers and both undergraduate and postgraduate students in Criminology, Criminal Justice Studies, Social Policy, Sociology, Urban Studies and Politics. It will also appeal to the rapidly expanding range of practitioners and policy-makers in this increasingly important and innovative field of professional practice. Although the focus is predominantly on the United Kingdom, the text is international and comparative in scope, in terms of both the range of its material and its authorship, and will be of relevance to academics, students, policy-makers and practitioners across different jurisdictions.

We need to acknowledge the help of many people in putting this collection together, not least the thousands of students who have studied Criminology and Social Policy over the past two decades at the Open University. Although we are named as editors of the book, its development has depended on the contributions of other members of the course team that constitutes the Open University's unique 'collective teacher'. Particular thanks are due to Ken Pease, who acted as external assessor for the

Master's course to which this volume is linked with his usual insightful comments and good humour. We are, of course, especially indebted to the contributors to the volume: thanks to all for their hard work, patience and dedication to this collective endeavour. Thanks, too, to Melanie Bayley, Hilary Canneaux, Donna Collins, Dianne Cook, Liz Freeman, Pauline Hetherington and Nicole Jones. Finally, we are grateful to Sage – and Miranda Nunhofer in particular – for their support and continuing enthusiasm for our collective project.

Gordon Hughes
Eugene McLaughlin
John Muncie

1

The shifting sands of crime prevention and community safety

Gordon Hughes

From the outset it should be noted that this book is not intended either as offering a broad overview of key contributions to the study of the prevention of crime or as a critical introduction to 'the field'. We already have a burgeoning literature which does that work quite satisfactorily (see, for example, Tonry and Farrington, 1995; Gilling, 1997; Crawford, 1998; Hughes, 1998; Rosenbaum, 1998; Hope, 2000). Our brief here is arguably more exciting than that offered in 'state of the art' introductions. Collectively the contributions to this volume assess where we have 'come from' and present a critique of current policy as well as aiming to open up the field of study to new directions and new 'imaginaries'. Within this collection there are voices from both 'within' and 'without' the specialist field of what we may conveniently but problematically term 'crime prevention/community safety studies'.[1] In some cases it is 'insiders' looking out and in others it is 'outsiders' peering into the looking-glass of developments in crime prevention/community safety, with fascinating results. Linguistic awkwardness captured, for example, in the couplet 'crime prevention/community safety', is hard to avoid at times and is itself indicative of the unsettled nature of this fast-changing policy field. The political, practice and policy changes – and cultural developments – which concern us here are difficult to pin down. Instead of trying to define a specialist field or sub-discipline (see, for example, Ekblom, 1996; Tonry and Farrington, 1995; Sherman et al., 1997), our project is to try to do the opposite and to open up and rethink issues in what is possibly the most uncertain and contested terrain where criminology, political theory and social policy analysis collide. Most of the chapters in this book relate the specific developments in the particular 'field' of crime prevention to socio-political thinking about contemporary processes of transformation and reordering of social formations, whilst remaining sensitive to the nuances, specificities and possible hybridizations of particular localities, contexts and examples. Individually and collectively the chapters show that rich analytical insights can develop as a result of stretching the traditional boundaries of the imaginary of criminology. However, the project of rethinking crime prevention and community safety also raises a multitude of complex and unresolved issues and as such it remains an unfinished process.

The new salience of crime prevention, risk management and safety politics

It is hard to avoid the constant reminders and warnings about the seeming growth of crime and disorder, and the breakdown and fracturing of the social order in countries such as the United Kingdom. Such stories make up the staple daily diet of the mass media and the entertainment industry. The nature of these moral tales may vary from that of the depiction of the fears and risks associated with living in the once supposedly bucolic English countryside to the loss of old civilities and the growth of a seemingly 'new' loutism in towns and cities, and to the increased dangers of cross-border organized crime and global drug trafficking. A world of greater uncertainty and increased risks is thus popularly conjured up and is refracted in increasing public concern about fear and risk in both public and private spaces. It would, of course, be ill-conceived to 'write off' these public concerns as merely being expressions of a media-fuelled moral panic. There is a stark, and unevenly distributed, reality to crime-evoked victimization, just like the suffering evoked by, and exclusion embedded in, other 'harms' such as poor housing and inadequate schooling or health provision. Issues of safety and security, and of the prevention and reduction of crime and fear, increasingly provide the focus for many of the most compelling and controversial questions about the nature of criminal justice and allied processes of social control across contemporary societies. Governments now often promote their policies in terms of a commitment to securing 'safer communities' not least through 'the war' on crime and disorder. As Tim Hope (2000, p. xiii) has noted, since 1980 crime prevention has moved from being of marginal intellectual interest to become a significant concern of governments in many countries and regions, with specific practices and politics realized at national, regional and particularly multi-local levels. Overall, the promotion of crime control *in* and *by* the community, and by means of multi-agency partnerships of the agencies of both the state and civil society, represents a major shift in how we think about the governance of crime specifically and social order more generally. With 'partnership' now inscribed as the primary symbolic and organizational means of delivering community safety politics, a broader rearticulation of the responsibilities between national and local government, public and private agencies and groups in local communities has begun to occur.

Alongside these new developments in crime control it has also been noted that by the last decades of the twentieth century nation-states have been increasingly unable to meet their core responsibility to provide citizens with security, not least physical security from criminal attack. Thus we witness a shift from the pursuit of the criminal to the prevention of crime (Stenson, 2000b). And, of course, the 'problems' of the state extend far beyond the specific issues of law-and-order politics, deriving from the interrelated crisis of the 'old' post-war liberal social democratic state and the costs and inefficiencies of traditional criminal justice system responses (Hughes and Lewis, 1998; Clarke et al., 2000). For some commentators, the consequences of these trends have resulted in the so-called 'death of the social' and a loss of faith in the modernist solidarity project of the social democratic state (see, for example, Rose, 1999; Garland, 1996). Others insist that it is more appropriate to think of these shifts in terms of a radical *reconfiguration* of the social (Lewis, 2000). There is no doubt that the decades since the 1980s, particularly in anglophone countries, have seen the rise of neo-liberal modes of governance and the retreat from, or reworking of, 'social' strategies of collective risk management and inclusivist modes of social control. These new modes of governance have instead moved towards a strategy of 'responsibilization' and more restricted and prudentialist (versus collectivist) notions of risk management alongside 'zero tolerance' policing and mass incarceration for the 'dangerous' and 'difficult' members of the excluded 'underclass'. In Bauman's (1998, p. 72) terse comment, 'to be poor is to be criminal'. Such developments have also resulted in a pronounced merging of the previously distinct policy realms of social policy and criminal justice to such an extent that many commentators now write of a heightened process of the 'criminalization of social policy' (Gilling and Barton, 1997; Crawford, 1998). Accordingly, what were once domain issues of social welfare, such as anti-poverty programmes, have become increasingly redefined in terms of their potential contribution to crime control. Poverty thus turns from the subject matter of social policy into a problem for penology, criminal law, policing and, we should add, crime prevention and community safety. At this juncture the main issue to bear in mind is the spaces which the developments described above have created for new strategies of crime control, epitomized by the ideas and practices of crime prevention, community safety and urban security, alongside, and in certain instances 'outside', both the criminal justice system and the social democratic state as traditionally conceived.

The 'new politics' of crime control and the policy debate on 'what works'

We have already noted that the issues of 'prevention' and 'reduction', 'safety' and 'security', present many of the most significant and controversial questions for criminal justice, social control and the 'new' social policy in contemporary societies. Although the study of crime prevention and community safety has been growing over recent years it has been dominated by a focus on evaluating 'what works' in terms of techniques and programmes which can then be transferred and applied from one context to the next (see Sherman et al., 1997; Hough and Tilley, 1998; Goldblatt and Lewis, 1998).

The past thirty years have witnessed recurrent attempts to specify the nature of crime prevention both as policy and practice and as an area of specialist, scientific investigation. Such efforts have not been particularly productive in establishing a specialist field of expertise, although it is difficult to deny the tangible 'success' stories that have emerged around some aspects of crime reduction measures linked with 'primary' and situational crime prevention (Pease, 1997). Much of the existing effort at developing universal, quasi-scientific classifications, typologies and definitions of crime prevention measures has been problematic. This is in no small measure due to the difficulty of arriving at essentialist definitions of a field which is inescapably linked with specific political and normative means and ends in particular socio-historical contexts (Hughes, 1998). Accordingly, those sharing the ambition of defining crime prevention, and even more problematically community safety, across time and space in an *a priori* fashion will be disappointed with the main thrust of the contributions to this volume. Rather it is argued here that the political reality of crime prevention practice is as much part of the subject matter as theory itself; indeed, both appear to be mutually constitutive. Complexity and contextual specificity would appear to be built into any discussion of crime prevention and community safety's scope and nature. The character of crime prevention/ community safety in turn is best understood by an approach which places contemporary perspectives, programmes and practices in terms of their socio-political, cultural, historical and 'scientific' contexts (Hope, 2000).

We acknowledge the importance of engaging with the increasingly dominant 'policy-relevant' focus on 'what works' (see, for example, Chapters 2, 3 and 16 below) but we also aim to move beyond the traditionally narrow, technical boundaries of much previous debate. Many of the chapters in this volume address other challenging issues which have tended to be absent from, or at best marginal to, mainstream enquiry. By exploring the contested definitions and histories of crime prevention and community safety policies and practices we hope to offer new directions in thinking about past, present and future trends in social control as we enter the new millennium. Particular attention is paid to policy developments and emergent practices associated with the reconstruction of the relationship between crime control, communities and the nation-state. An exploration of the diverse and changing sites of conflict, compromise and collusion around these policies and practices will in turn necessitate critical engagement with wider questions regarding historical transformations in degrees of risk, safety and security, and their management. In these ways the book provides a critical rethinking of the traditional ways of thinking within and across both criminology and social policy.

The collection of contributions is inclusive in character, eschewing any rigid adherence to a specific theoretical perspective. If an emergent paradigm is evident, it is an open-ended, cross-disciplinary one, with few, if any, fixed guarantees. Rather the central feature of the collection as a whole is a commitment to exploring new directions for research and analysis, theoretically, empirically and comparatively, which together open up the gates of the supposed 'field' and allow new cross-fertilizations and hybridizations of thought and practice. The book contributes to the process of a radical rethinking of both criminology and allied disciplines in the social sciences, from social policy to sociology and politics. In opening up new insights into the varying and volatile spaces for crime prevention and community safety within the more general politics of social order, the chapters hold the promise of contributing to the rethinking of the social sciences more generally.

Structure and content

The volume is divided into three substantive parts, although the individual chapters also discuss issues of relevance across the three main sections. In Part I, 'Conceptual issues', the primary focus is on the rethinking of the recent history of theory, policy and politics of crime prevention and community safety in the United Kingdom in terms of both its main assumptions and key 'absences'. Chapter 2 by Nick Tilley presents a challenging 'story' of the history of the main developments, in terms of the key policy, practice and intellectual insights in Britain, from the 1970s to the first decade of the twenty-first century. In Chapter 3 Tim Hope examines and critiques the 'what works' approach of much Home Office crime reduction research initiatives since the 1980s. More generally, he addresses the strengths and limitations of the project to try to establish a scientific, 'policy-relevant' paradigm in the social sciences. Chapters 4 and 5, by Sandra Walklate and Eugene McLaughlin respectively, focus on the changing spaces occupied by the discursive figures of 'gender' and 'race' in the practices, policies and politics of crime prevention and community protection in the course of the last three decades of the twentieth century. Both Walklate and McLaughlin alert us to the crucial importance of often 'absent presences' in the articulation of what it is to be constituted (or not) as a legitimate member of the nation and more generally what is the character of 'the social' in the dominant discourses of crime prevention and community safety historically.

Part II, 'Policies, Practices and Politics in the Contemporary United Kingdom', focuses on several recent research studies and critical analyses of community safety and local multi-agency crime and disorder partnerships in the aftermath of 'New' Labour's Crime and Disorder Act 1998. The legislation may be viewed as constituting a radical break with previous crime control strategies, not least by putting into law, for the first time, specific duties and responsibilities for crime prevention. However, at the same time, its managerialist and ideological implications remained closely tied to the neo-liberal tide of governmental reform associated with the new public management (NPM) and the new politics of welfare throughout the 1980s and 1990s (Hope, 2000; Jordan, 1998). Accordingly, Chapters 6 (Tim Newburn), 7 (Gordon Hughes), 8 (John Muncie) and 9 (Coretta Phillips) address the main changes and continuities in England and Wales since 1998 across the increasingly interrelated areas of policing, youth justice and local authority-based crime and disorder partnerships in the wake of this key legislative watershed. In Chapter 10 Kieran McEvoy, Brian Gormally and Harry Mika plot the specific reconstruction of state/ community relations in Northern Ireland around crime control at the beginning of the twenty-first century and in the wake of the 'peace process'. Of particular importance is their conclusion that there are strict limits on the appeal to, and policy transferability of, 'partnerships with the community', given the continued framing of policing and justice in traditional security terms in Northern Ireland.

Taken together, the chapters in Part II present detailed research findings and analytical insights drawn from developments since the election of the 'New' Labour government in 1997 and its national reclamation project. One implication of these studies is that the pronouncement of the death of the 'social state' may be premature (Stenson, 2000a). At the same time the discussions here caution against claiming to have found definitive answers to the questions raised by the new discourses of crime and disorder reduction, community security and safety and the emergent, complex constellations of power which result. Instead these contributions point to the unfinished, contradictory and uneven nature of the political experiment in contemporary crime control in the United Kingdom.

Part III, 'Comparative trends and futures', develops further the comparative approach to studying diverse trends in crime control and community safety. It draws heavily on non-UK case studies as well as research and analysis which fall outside the field of crime prevention, as traditionally conceived. Several of these chapters confirm that crime prevention appears to be achieving a global, if uneven, pre-eminence as a master pattern of crime control, despite growing doubts about the capacity of the 'sovereign' nation-state to guarantee and supply order and security to citizens in their everyday lives (Garland, 1996). Chapter 11 by Adam Crawford provides a critical interrogation of the comparative shifts in crime prevention and the politics of security in France and England since the 1980s. This chapter highlights both the shared dilemmas of the two societies, wrought by the changes associated with 'late modernity', and the crucial differences in their experiences associated with their distinct political cultures and national identities. In Chapter 12 Reece Walters and Trevor Bradley present a detailed case study of crime prevention policies in New Zealand. They critically examine the development and evolution of state-managed community crime prevention in the context of governments' adoption of a radical neo-liberal reform programme. The logic of intense managerialism is emphasized as a crucial explanatory factor of that country's particular trajectory in terms of crime control. Chapter 13 by René van Swaaningen focuses on the lessons to be learnt from the Netherlands' national and local politics and policies of crime prevention and community safety. The chapter also explores the possibility of what abolitionists have termed a 'replacement discourse' around positive notions of safety and mutual tolerance of difference for a more progressive rethinking of safety policies and politics.

In Chapter 14 Pat O'Malley moves us beyond crime *per se* and examines the politics of drug control and harm minimization in several anglophone societies. Drawing particularly on developments in Australia and the United Kingdom as compared with the United States, O'Malley cautions against overly deterministic theories of radical governmental transformation which offer universalistic analyses of how 'the self' might be governed in the context of what has been termed both 'neo-' and 'advanced' liberalism. Arguing against what he has previously termed 'semiologies of catastrophe' (O'Malley, 2000, p. 153), he argues for the important role of relational politics in the new governance of risks and harms. In particular, contemporary fears over 'excess freedoms' and attempts to govern the risks of drug use and abuse (and other penal policies) illustrate the complex tendencies towards hybridity, resistance to change and competing trans-formational tendencies which cannot be 'read off' from supposed universal structural shifts in risk management. Especially significant are the ten-dencies towards the counter-demonization of the drug abuser and the enlisting of users in their own government; in other words a process of normalization. Chapter 15 by Davina Cooper also expands the scope of enquiry beyond that of criminology and crime control. If community safety is no longer part of the sovereign state's guarantee, we may ask what forms of community politics are likely to ensue in its place and with what consequences for justice, tolerance and security in the context of greater cultural pluralism (Hope, 2000)? Cooper's study opens up some key issues regarding the possible nature of this new politics of safety. In particular, she presents a specific case study of a politics of difference and value around the contested construction of a religiously defined boundary (the orthodox Jewish 'eruv') in a borough of the global city of London. In so doing, Cooper opens up new ways of imagining a local politics of safety and cultural protection beyond statist-defined discourses.

In the final chapter Gordon Hughes, Eugene McLaughlin and John Muncie plot some of the possible futures for crime control, and for the new criminologies of everyday life, in the wake of popular dystopian visions of the new world order. In particular they highlight the growth industry in ideas and in policy transfer across the Atlantic between the United States and the United Kingdom. They argue that it is now impossible to deny the increasingly global character of criminology as an 'expert system' with its epicentre in the United States (rather than in Europe as in the late nineteenth and early twentieth centuries). However, it is also wise to be cautious about the likelihood of a crude adoption of the new global criminal justice policies and practices and the 'new architecture of crime control' across different parts of the world. The more likely development and form of policy transfer is one in which specific practices become disembedded from their original contexts and then adapted and re-embedded in new contexts (Chan, 2000, p. 122). Thus, despite the commonality of imagery of the 'frightened city' and the 'anxious citizen', we must remain sensitive to both the converging and the contrasting contours and emphases in specific examples of the new security state.

Note

1 It is not entirely satisfactory to accept the designation of a distinct and separate 'field of study' of crime prevention/community safety studies. Among the other signifiers used in this changing and porous field of study are 'crime reduction', 'risk management', 'politics of (urban) security', 'criminalization of social policy', to name but a few. The so-called field of study remains a particularly problematic one in this fast-moving and hybridized area of politics and practice at the borders of both crime control and social policy, as well as in an area of intellectual investigation which largely defies any simple 'belonging' to such academic disciplines as criminology and social policy analysis. This profoundly unsettled and post-disciplinary character of crime prevention/community safety is nonetheless a source of much of its growing significance in developments in crime control and social welfare in contemporary societies across the world (see Hughes, 2000; Stenson, 2000a).

References

Bauman, Z. (1998) *Work, Consumerism and the New Poor*, Buckingham, Open University Press.

Chan, J. (2000) 'Globalization, reflexivity and the practice of criminology', *Australian and New Zealand Journal of Criminology*, vol. 33, no. 2, pp. 118–35.

Clarke, J., Gewirtz, S. and McLaughlin, E. (eds) (2000) *New Managerialism, New Welfare?*, London, Sage.

Crawford, A. (1998) *Crime Prevention and Community Safety: Politics, Policies and Practices*, Harlow, Longman.

Ekblom, P. (1996) 'Towards a discipline of crime prevention: a systematic approach to its nature, range and concepts' in Bennett, T. (ed.) *Crime Prevention: The Cropwood Papers*, Cambridge, Cropwood.

Garland, D. (1996) 'The limits of the sovereign state: strategies of crime control in contemporary society', *British Journal of Criminology*, vol. 36, no. 4, pp. 445–71.

Garland, D. and Sparks, R. (2000) 'Criminology, social theory and the challenge of our times', *British Journal of Criminology*, vol. 40, pp. 189–204.

Gilling, D. (1997) *Crime Prevention: Theory, Policy and Politics*, London, UCL Press.

Gilling, D. and Barton, A. (1997) 'Crime prevention and community safety: a new home for social policy', *Critical Social Policy*, vol. 17, no. 1, pp. 63–83.

Goldblatt, P. and Lewis, C. (eds) (1998) *Reducing Offending*, Home Office Research Study 187, London, Home Office.

Hope, T. (2000) 'Introduction' in Hope, T. (ed.) *Perspectives on Crime Reduction*, Aldershot, Ashgate.

Hope, T. and Sparks, R. (2000) 'For a sociological theory of situations (or how useful is pragmatic criminology?)' in Garland, D., von Hirsch, A. and Wakefield, A. (eds) *Situational Crime Prevention: Ethics and Social Context*, Oxford, Hart Publishing.

Hough, M. and Tilley, N. (1998) *Getting the Grease to the Squeak: Lessons for Crime Prevention*, Crime Detection and Prevention Series Paper 85, London, Home Office.

Hughes, G. (1998) *Understanding Crime Prevention: Social Control, Risk and Late Modernity*, Buckingham, Open University Press.

Hughes, G. (2000) 'In the shadow of crime and disorder: the contested politics of community safety', *Crime Prevention and Community Safety*, vol. 2, no. 4, pp. 47–60.

Hughes, G. and Lewis, G. (eds) (1998) *Unsettling Welfare: The Reconstruction of Social Policy*, London, Routledge/Open University.

Jordan, B. (1998) *The New Politics of Welfare*, London, Sage.

Lewis, G. (2000) 'Introduction' in Lewis, G. et al. (eds) *Rethinking Social Policy*, London, Sage.

Lewis, G., Gewirtz, S. and Clarke, J. (eds) (2000) *Rethinking Social Policy*, London, Sage.

O'Malley, P. (2000) 'Criminologies of catastrophe? Understanding criminal justice on the edge of the new millennium', *Australian and New Zealand Journal of Criminology*, vol. 33, no. 2, pp. 153–67.

Pease, K. (1997) 'Crime prevention' in Maguire, M., Morgan, R. and Reiner, R. (eds) *Oxford Handbook of Criminolgy* (2nd edn), Oxford, Clarendon Press.

Rose, N. (1999) *Powers of Freedom*, Cambridge, Cambridge University Press.

Rosenbaum, D.P. (1998) *Crime Prevention*, New York, Wadsworth.

Sherman, L., Gottfredson, D., Mackenzie, D., Eck, J., Reuter, P. and Bushway, S. (1997) *Preventing Crime: What Works, What Doesn't, What's Promising*, Research in Brief, National Institute of Justice, Washington DC, US Department of Justice.

Stenson, K. (2000a) 'Crime control, social policy and liberalism' in Lewis, G. et al. (eds) *Rethinking Social Policy*, London, Sage.

Stenson, K. (2000b) 'The new politics of crime control' in Stenson, K. and Sullivan, R. (eds) *Crime, Risk and Justice*, Cullompton, Willan Publishing.

Stenson, K. and Sullivan, R. (eds) (2000) *Crime, Risk and Justice*, Cullompton, Willan Publishing.

Tonry, M. and Farrington, D. (eds) (1995) *Building a Safer Society: Strategic Approaches to Crime Prevention*, Crime and Justice vol. 19, Chicago IL, University of Chicago Press.

Part I

Conceptual Issues

2

Crime prevention in Britain, 1975-2010

Breaking out, breaking in and breaking down

Nick Tilley

What we now think of as crime prevention has antecedents in prehistory. The methods adopted were even quite similar. As Graham Farrell puts it:

> [M]any of the strategies, techniques, tactics, and the mechanisms by which they work to prevent crime in twenty-first-century human society have existed and evolved in various forms since before humankind even existed. Long before we walked the planet, animals protected themselves from each other using preventive mechanisms that are in many ways similar to those used in modern-day crime prevention. Animals protect not just themselves as individuals, but also their kith, kin, and even whole communities, against others of the same species, as well as predators. (Farrell, 2000)

Thomas Hobbes's contention in 1651 that, in a state of nature, life would be 'solitary, poor, nasty, brutish and short' suggests that concerns about organized ways of controlling predatory behaviour in human societies also have a long history.

The category 'crime' is a socially constructed one. It only roughly covers the kinds of predatory behaviour associated with preventive responses in the pre-human animal realm. The strategies, techniques and tactics used there are presumably biologically inscribed as a condition of survival, as is the disposition to behave in predatory ways.

We are now, as Runciman puts it in the title of his book, *Social Animals* (1998). Ours is a largely socially constructed and sustained world. Hobbes's solution to the problems of insecurity produced by the war of all against all, produced in nature as he saw it, was to contract a sovereign to whom power is ceded to regulate behaviour. Order would be imposed by this supreme power. Hobbes's 'just so' story, as Runciman describes it, does violence to the variations in ways in which social order has been and can be maintained in human societies. He was nevertheless right to stress the emergence of humanly constructed social means of trying to prevent interpersonal predation and feelings of insecurity. In particular, the state assumed the role of order maintenance. An important means of order maintenance has been the creation of laws, with criminal justice systems to enforce them. The state's interest until recently in the spontaneous sources of predation reduction has been focused on trying to repress or render unnecessary some of the traditional – but more violent or threatening – means used.

What is distinctive about the past quarter-century is, thus, not the invention of 'crime prevention' (or 'crime reduction' or 'community safety'), but its emergence as a major focus of public policy and criminological research. The purpose of this chapter is to trace those developments, and to try to anticipate their direction over the coming decade.

Three stages are identified: 'breaking in', 'breaking out' and 'breaking down'. The terms used carry deliberately ambiguous normative baggage. One connotation of breaking in is that of invading others' spaces, whilst another is that of overcoming exclusionary practices. Breaking out suggests the spread of a plague as well as an escape from confinement. Breaking down implies both decay and dissolution and the removal of barriers. A positive interpretation of the three phases identified here would have it that crime prevention has been and will continue to be progressive. A negative interpretation would have it that crime prevention has been corrosive and is itself corroding.

Key events from 1975 are picked out in Table 2.1. The developmental steps identified here are those deemed by the author to have been significant in producing present conditions in Britain and to point up what may be expected in the near future. This may suggest a more linear development than in fact occurred. It may also appear to comprise a Whiggish reading of what has happened: a process of continuous progress. Much else occurred in the past, of course, that might have led developments in a different direction. The account here is of what in practice has prevailed,

Table 2.1 *Key developments in crime prevention, 1975–*

The Effectiveness of Sentencing: A Review of the Literature	1976
Crime as Opportunity	1976
Designing out Crime	1980
Co-ordinating Crime Prevention Efforts	1980
'Situational Crime Prevention'	1980
First British Crime Survey report	1983
Crime Prevention Unit set up	1983
Home Office Standing Conference	1983
Home Office Circular 8/84, *Crime Prevention*	1984
First Crime Prevention Unit Paper	1985
Five Towns initiative	1986
Gas and suicide	1988
Getting the Best out of Crime Analysis	1988
Safer Cities	1988
Crime Concern 1988	1988
First Kirkholt report 1988, beginning of repeat victimization focus	1988
Crash helmets and motor-bike theft	1989
Home Office Circular 44/90	1990
Morgan Report	1991
Police Research Group established	1992
Single Regeneration Budget	1993
First CCTV challenge	1995
Repeat Victimization Task Force set up	1996
First issue of *International Journal of Risk, Security and Crime Prevention*	1996
National Training Organization	1998
Home Office Research Study 187	1998
Policing and Reducing Crime Unit established	1998
Crime and Disorder Act 1998, and guidance	1988
Beating Crime	1998
Crime Reduction Programme	1999
Safety in Numbers	1999
Crime Targets Task Force	1999
Foresight Programme	1999
Calling Time on Crime	2000
The Home Office Policing and Crime Reduction Directorate	2000
Appointment of Regional Crime Directors	2000
Preparation and publication of 'Toolkits' to deal with specified problems	2001

sometimes for reasons of happenstance rather than necessity. The recent events that are highlighted refer to what seem to comprise relatively influential developments that point to the directions in which crime reduction is moving. It is quite possible that events which at first sight seem unlikely to shape developments are picked up and take responses to crime elsewhere. Public interest in crime, and the potential it brings for mobilizing political will, mean that high-profile cases may yet produce their own policy consequences (Bottoms and Stevenson, 1992). The (2000) case of Tony Martin, killing an intruder but winning much public sympathy, may, for example, produce a significant policy dividend. Similarly, the decision of the *News of the World* in summer 2000 to publish the names and whereabouts of known paedophiles, and the local public responses to those deemed thereby to be a danger to children, may likewise generate a significant policy legacy. The future will be made by actors in the light of circumstances, interests and understandings, though not in conditions of their own choosing. What is yet to come cannot be predicted with great confidence.

Breaking out, 1975–90

During the 1980s crime prevention moved closer to centre-stage as a response to the problem of rising crime rates (Heal, 1987; Laycock and Heal, 1989). Prior to the 1980s there had been some, albeit limited, interest in crime prevention, and this had initially centred mainly on the work of the police. After all, it had been part of the task of the police as provided for in the Metropolitan Police Act of 1829; there have been police crime prevention officers since the 1950s. The Cornish Report (Home Office, 1965) had examined crime prevention, and made recommendations for it. Local Crime Prevention Panels have been in operation since 1966. Outside the areas of responsibility of the Home Office, community crime prevention had figured in the original aims of the National Association for the Care and Resettlement of Offenders (NACRO) when it was formed in 1966. A Home Office Standing Committee on Crime Prevention was set up in 1975; crime prevention was part of the aim of the Department of the Environment Priority Estates Project in 1979; NACRO established its own Crime Prevention Unit in 1979.

In spite of these earlier concerns, it was not until the 1980s that crime prevention began to 'take off'. The time for crime prevention thinking had come. It appeared to provide a more or less plausible way of responding to the emerging penal crisis. Crime rates were continuing to rise at a rate of 5–7 per cent per annum and it appeared that traditional policing methods could do nothing to affect this. Punishment did not appear to deter; confidence in treatment had disappeared. In relation to the offender, 'Nothing works' (Martinson, 1974) had become the dominant orthodoxy within criminology, and the Home Office in-house community of criminologists, comprising the Research and Planning Unit, had made their own contribution to this thinking (Brody, 1976). In penology, a return to the justice model, fired by 'Nothing works' and the perceived injustices of some 'treatment' programmes had taken place. The prisons were bulging as a consequence. All governments have to address issues of law and order, but for the Conservative Party 'law and order' had become a slogan. Moreover, Conservative economic policies were liable to have the unintended – though for many criminologists predictable – effect of raising crime rates through increasing unemployment, reducing perceived prospects for young people, and producing greater relative deprivation (Field, 1990; Sampson and Laub, 1993). Those same economic policies attempted to limit public expenditure. Where cure appears unavailable, and containment is very expensive, prevention looked extremely attractive in the face of a high-profile problem like crime. Moreover, some threads of criminology, notably within the Research and Planning Unit (RPU) of the Home Office, were beginning to offer some hope of this at the beginning of the 1980s.

The then head of the Research and Planning Unit, Ron Clarke, played an important role in putting crime prevention on the agenda. He expressed disenchantment with the pursuit of what he called 'dispositional' approaches to criminality, and instead focused on situational cues to crime commission, stressing the significance of opportunity and therefore of opportunity reduction. In a series of publications the potential of attention to situational variables for crime prevention was explored and the approach strongly advocated (for example, Clarke, 1980; Clarke and Mayhew, 1980). For the reasons already given, the political ground was fertile for these particular criminological seeds to grow. In addition, it offered an approach to crime prevention which did not entail 'softness' towards offenders, and was consistent with their being held responsible for their acts; it was uncritical of aspects of social structure which might otherwise be seen to create criminality; and it removed responsibility for failure to control crime from the police force. These features were not uncongenial to a Conservative administration. Clarke's own approach was, and remains, strictly and ascetically situational and empirical (see, for example, Clarke and Mayhew, 1988; Mayhew et al., 1989; Clarke, 1995, 1997). First, the clue to crime reduction lies in identifying modifiable features of the situation for offending such that perceived costs exceed perceived benefits for the offender. Second, rather than there being one solution to all crime or to many crimes, attention must be paid to the particularities of the situations for different offences. Third, rigorous efforts must be made empirically to test the consequences of crime reduction measures, including the possibility of displacement, for example to other targets, places, offences or methods.

In 1983 the Crime Prevention Unit was established at the Home Office. Paul Rock refers to this, with some justification, as 'the intellectual progeny of Ron Clarke' (Rock, 1990, p. 265). In practice, there had been an earlier effort to establish the unit, and it was only some tension within the Home Office involving senior civil servants, Ministers and the Research and Planning Unit concerning the direction of the latter's work which allowed the Crime Prevention Unit to emerge. It was headed by Kevin Heal, and its first Principal Research Officer was Gloria Laycock, both of whom had been leading developers of the crime prevention approach conceived and advocated by Ron Clarke. Though crime prevention existed in other government departments and within other divisions of the Home Office, the Crime Prevention Unit was seen as the major driving force.

Notwithstanding the early situational work of its key members, the Crime Prevention Unit at the Home Office and its successor bodies, the Crime Prevention Agency and the Crime Reduction Unit, became very catholic in approach. It came to be believed that rather diverse approaches to crime reduction, rooted in a variety of theoretical traditions, might have something to contribute to crime prevention. Moreover, pragmatically it would be hard to avoid paying attention to the range of agencies which could play a part in crime prevention, for some of which (for example, Probation) rather different theoretical positions from the purely situational would be congenial.

The role of the Crime Prevention Unit was initially to 'light fires', to provoke crime prevention activity as and where it could. It was not a central planning unit, orchestrating a national integrated approach to crime prevention rooted in some universal theory promising a crime prevention panacea. Instead it promoted activity and gave advice about many and varied styles of crime prevention practised by many and varied groups and institutions. In spite of its theoretical heterodoxy, there was a framework to the Crime Prevention Unit approach, and this certainly bore the marks of that unit's origins in Research and Planning.

The Crime Prevention Unit's broad framework had a strong research flavour. In many ways what is described here as a model for crime prevention is simply a description of what could go on in any field of action research. Thus the crime terms could easily be substituted by others to do, for example, with education, environment, health, transport or child abuse. It is notable that for crime prevention the policy is articulated within a quasi-research framework, whilst such is not the case in other policy areas. The framework goes something like this:

1   Crime in general is complex, with many features, causes, motivations and conditions.
2   Given 1, it will not be possible for any agency on its own successfully to address all aspects of all crime prevention problems.
3   It follows from 1 and 2, that inter-agency groups are best suited to do general crime prevention work, though single agencies may be able to deal with specific crimes.
4   Crime problems, patterns, causes, conditions and motivations vary by type of crime, and across space and time.
5   It follows from 3 and 4 that crime prevention strategies will need to be tailored to distinctive local circumstances.
6   Given 5, for crime prevention to work it will be important to find out what the local circumstances are to inform decisions about where crime prevention priorities lie, and to develop possible strategies of ameliora-tion: there is a research dimension.
7   If lessons are to be learned gradually about what works, both locally in order to use resources efficiently, and more widely so that such trans-situational lessons as are possible can be learned, evaluations are needed. Again there is a central research dimension.

This broad framework allowed a variety of content with regard to forms of crime prevention, research and styles of inter-agency working. However, though members of the unit certainly had experience which could inform decisions relative to all these, and were prepared to give advice, there was no unitary line. The main task was to stimulate informed and informative activity. That a sometime researcher was at the tiller, and that the unit had in its heyday a substantial (twelve-person) research element on board, served to give the Crime Prevention Unit something of this character. The period from 1983, when the Unit was established, to 1987 was marked by a number of crime prevention initiatives:

1 The Home Office Standing Conference on Crime Prevention was set up in 1983.
2 Home Office Circular 8/84 enjoined local authorities and other agencies to work together to develop strategies for crime prevention.
3 The 'Five Towns' demonstration project ran for eighteen months from early 1986 to show what could be accomplished if such inter-agency working and planning took place.
4 Neighbourhood Watch was encouraged and grew from one scheme in 1982 to 35,000 in 1987 (Laycock and Heal, 1989).
5 The Ministerial Group on Crime Prevention was established in 1986.
6 The Prime Minister and Home Secretary chaired two seminars on crime prevention at 10 Downing Street in 1986.
7 Eight thousand jobs were attached to crime prevention under the Manpower Services Commission's Community Crime Prevention Initiative in 1987, and many of these were allocated to Home Office-sponsored projects.
8 The first nine of the continuing series of Crime Prevention Unit Papers, disseminating findings from a number of projects illustrating what could be achieved in crime prevention, were published between 1983 and 1987.
9 In addition to these specifically Home Office activities, a variety of projects run from other departments were partly promoted by the Crime Prevention Unit.

The year 1988 saw a crescendo of activity at the Crime Prevention Unit. Eight more Crime Prevention Unit Papers were published, Crime Concern was set up with Home Office core funding, the 'Crack Crime' campaign was launched, and the first report of the highly influential Kirkholt Burglary Prevention Project was published (Forrester et al., 1988). Most important, the Safer Cities programme was initiated (see Tilley, 1993). This programme initially led to the establishment of projects in twenty cities which typically had relatively high crime rates. There were three aims: to reduce crime, to lessen the fear of crime, and to create safer cities in which economic and community life would flourish. The Home Office appointed three staff locally to run each project, and set up a multi-agency steering group in each city including the police, the local authority, Probation, and representatives of the voluntary and private sectors. Each project was provided with £250,000 to allocate to projects, though with a matched funding scheme in practice much more was made available. Projects involving larger expenditure required central approval from the Home Office. All initiatives (of which there came to be about 3,500 in all) were supposed to be evaluated locally. However, the fact that three fairly major initiatives – Safer Cities, Crack Crime and Crime Concern – occurred within a few months of each other did not mark a coherent, organized plan for crime prevention. Rather, it reflected the success of a group of entrepreneurial government researchers in taking advantage of opportunities thrown up by the new (post-1987 election) Parliament, with Ministers sympathetic to such developments, to create a great deal of crime prevention activity along their preferred lines.

It may seem from what has so far been said about the development of the Crime Prevention Unit and its early work that there was no political dimension to the conception of crime prevention that it embodied. This would be a mistake. Several matters which could, in other circumstances, have played a large part in crime prevention were not considered. For example, questions of large-scale social structural change affecting the class, 'race' and gender distribution of power, the decriminalization of some behaviour, and much crime committed by the powerful, did not find a place on the crime prevention agenda, in part because this is set by the political and bureaucratic context in which criminologists in the Home Office work. It was only within a given political framework that there was diversity.

Thus 'modern' state crime prevention began to break out between 1975 and 1990. It was able to do so because of the policy vacuum created by loss of faith in the crime control capacity of rehabilitation, punishment and the criminal justice system more generally. There were continuous crime rate rises, with matching increases in costs and public concern. The form that the new preventive response took was a function of the administrative setting furnished by the Home Office, the research personnel then in post, and their use of the opportunities created to set a radical agenda to deal with crime without making the criminal centre-stage.

Breaking in, 1985–2000

The second stage, 'breaking in', describes the transition from experimentation, opportunism, *ad hoc* development and exhortation to institutionalized practice. It comprises a process of routinization – breaking into existing organizations and ways of working. Once the infrastructure for the preferred pattern of preventive responses was in place, it developed its own impetus. It largely escaped the originating conditions, interests and intentions. The radical agenda of crime prevention was broken in – it was domesticated.

Some of the developments during this stage have already been described: they are transitional points to another stage in the development of public policy and practice of crime prevention. 'Five Towns' marked a first effort to seed crime prevention in an area, and the Safer Cities programme was a more developed, larger-scale effort to do the same. They were both time-limited and involved the expenditure of 'soft money'. The administrative arrangements were *ad hoc*. They were not applied nationally, or according to any transparent needs-based resource allocation model applied across the board. They were still to some degree experimental; they were far from mainstream. Yet they were more than individual projects run from the Home Office. They were intended to have a strategic focus (see Tilley, 1992); an expectation that a legacy would be forthcoming developed; they comprised a step towards normalizing routine attention to crime. Likewise, Crime Concern was set up to stimulate crime prevention, to try to normalize it, to set in motion its routine delivery by multi-agency groups in its local crime reduction programmes. But Crime Concern was not a statutory body; it was not mainstream and was in a position only to try to encourage mainstreaming.

Home Office Circular 44/90 encouraged local bodies, notably the police and local authorities, to develop partnership approaches to crime prevention as a matter of course, though there was no requirement to do so and no money or right to raise money provided to underpin it.

The Morgan Report (Home Office, 1991) explored ways in which inter-agency crime prevention could be made normal business and under what administrative arrangements. The committee reported in August 1991, with the key recommendation that leadership should be placed in the hands of the local authority. This was a clear move towards institutionalizing crime prevention in partnership as part of normal local agency practice and policy. Though Morgan's main recommendation was rejected by the government, the report was popular and continued to be a major point of reference in discussions of the future direction of community safety. In particular, local authorities and local authority organizations saw that community safety was a matter of public concern in which they had a key interest and a significant role.

The secession of the Police Research Group (PRG) from the Crime Prevention Unit in 1992 foreshadowed a change in the complexion of both research and policy. The policy came to lose the experimental/ opportunistic spin it had when informed by researchers' bright ideas, familiarity with academic literature and means of data analysis. It developed instead into a more traditional arm of policy. This was consonant with crime prevention becoming established as a distinct policy area, with its own needs and political interests. The Police Research Group remained part of a policy directorate in the Home Office, separate from the Research and Statistics Directorate. Its structural position and the strong policy/ practice orientation of its first head, Gloria Laycock, maintained a close relationship with policy and practice issues. That said, in a different division, on a different floor of Queen Anne's Gate and with a rather fast turnover of heads of the policy division (see Tilley and Laycock, 2000), the relationship with the crime prevention policy-makers became less immediate.

Research did, nevertheless, continue to play a part in informing policy and practice, particularly in connection with work on repeat victimization. The repeat victimization programme of research, practice and policy was significant in developing routine crime prevention (Farrell et al., 2000). The Kirkholt Project (Forrester et al., 1988, 1990) found high rates of repeat victimization in relation to domestic burglary, and the response to the problem included preventive efforts through targeting victims and their neighbours. A rapid and sustained fall in domestic burglary was achieved. The Kirkholt initiative was followed by others that found repeat victimization patterns across a range of offences, including racial attacks, domestic violence, commercial burglary, school vandalism and so on (Farrell and Pease, 1993; Pease, 1998). The potential for routine prevention was revealed through a series of initiatives: a task force was established within the Police Research Group to promote prevention through attention to victims (Laycock, forthcoming): a Home Office crime prevention performance indicator was devised to assess effectiveness in reducing repeat victimization. Developments relating to repeat victimization both exemplify the process of routinization and were a vehicle for effecting it.

Research was expanding during the 'breaking-in phase', creating an academic community and a body of research literature paralleling, and to some degree informing, the growing policy and practice involvement in crime reduction. Table 2.2 shows the number of Crime Prevention Unit (and successor series) papers in crime prevention over five-year periods up to 1999. 'Normal science' in crime prevention research was taking off, with the establishment of a journal, conference and textbook infrastructure which has been highlighted by Kuhn (1962) as marking the emergence of a research paradigm (see Ekblom and Tilley, 2000). Ten per cent of the £250 million Crime Reduction Programme, running for three years from April 1999, was set aside for research and evaluation, adding a material infrastructure to and amplifying the emerging research interest and activity.

The late 1990s have seen crime prevention breaching specialist walls, breaking into mainstream politics and practice. The most important measure has been the Crime and Disorder Act 1998. This puts partnership crime prevention on a statutory footing. It requires participation by local authorities, police forces, probation services and health authorities. It obliges statutory agencies to draw in and/or consult community groups, the voluntary and private sectors. It attempts to minimize data-sharing obstacles, which can inhibit problem-solving approaches to crime reduction. It requires local authorities, police authorities, joint authorities, National Parks Authorities and Broads Authorities to take crime consequences into account in their practices and policies. It directs partnerships

Table 2.2 *Number of Crime Prevention Unit Papers per five-year period, starting with 1985, the date of the first paper*

1985–9	20
1990–4	36
1995–9	57

towards a triennial cycle of information collection, consultation, strategy development, and monitoring and evaluation. Alongside the legislation has been supportive work by the Audit Commission (1999), HM Inspectorate of Constabulary (HMIC, 1998, 2000), the Local Government Association (HMIC, 2000) and Home Office researchers identifying needs and good practice (see, for example, Hough and Tilley, 1998a, b). Performance monitoring regimes stressing the prevention and reduction of crime have been put in place. Regional Crime Reduction Directors were appointed in 2000 to all nine regional government offices as senior Home Office civil servants whose task it is to facilitate, inform and catalyse increased and improved attention to crime reduction in their areas.

Breaking down, 1995–2010

'Breaking down' has two senses. When linked with barriers it can refer to the removal of obstacles, opening the way to progress. When referring to cars it can mean their ceasing to work.

The developments since 1995, notably the Crime and Disorder Act, *Beating Crime*, the Crime Reduction Programme, *Safety in Numbers*, the Crime Targets Task Force and *Calling Time on Crime*, apply increasing pressure to a widening range of organizations to undertake or organize work that prevents and reduces crime and disorder. They consistently point towards inter-agency collaboration. They signal central state commitment to steering local state agencies towards attention to crime and disorder. They include the assignment of statutory obligations. They amount to an effort to widen responsibility for, and increase capacity to deal with, local crime and disorder problems.

What shape are crime reduction, crime prevention and community safety taking in the light of these developments? Are there any other possibilities? Four major directions can be discerned which encompass both senses of breaking down.

Managerialism and bureaucratization

There is a general move towards increasing managerialism in criminal justice as a means of its oversight and direction (McLaughlin and Muncie, 2000).

Legislation requiring agencies to work together setting targets, the appointment of Regional Crime Reduction Directors, and processes of multi-inspectorate as well as single inspectorate examination of work are providing a context for disciplined and routinized attention to crime and disorder across the country. New rules, roles, committees, tiers of authority, accountability mechanisms and reporting hierarchies are emerging in relation to crime reduction, crime prevention and community safety.

The Crime and Disorder Act's creation of joint statutory responsibility across more than one agency comprises a challenge to traditional ways of working, where single organizations managed service delivery. Structures are thus being created to reproduce intra-organizational bureaucratic controls across agencies. For example, in one large city there is a Responsible Authority Group (including police and local authority), below which is an Executive Partnership Group (including senior members of the probation service, health authority and other invited agencies), below which are divisional Community Safety Co-ordinating Groups, below which are Subdivisional Partnership Groups, below which are Local Action Partnerships, below which are Task Groups comprising those delivering services. This comprises a six-tier multi-agency management and reporting hierarchy. Local councillors are included at the Local Action Partnership level; they are not at the top. This amounts to inter-agency adaptation of a traditional bureaucratic structure with bureaucratic controls. The work will be overseen by the local Regional Crime Reduction Director, who is a Home Office official, as well as by a network of inspectorates.

Local authorities are creating community safety departments and appointing community safety officers. The departments clearly form part of the local authority structure. The National Training Organization is identifying the core competences and training needs required for workers in community safety. A process of accreditation is occurring where those occupying the new roles will have been inducted into the skills needed for them to do their jobs in technically approved ways.

Target-setting and crime reduction-related performance indicators are being widely used by central authorities such as the Home Office, Audit Commission and HMIC as mechanisms to gauge performance levels and to make bodies accountable for the discharge of their crime reduction responsibilities. The publication of performance indicators, with implicit or explicit threats of brickbats and promises of bouquets, is one form of control. The potential threat to resources and autonomy in conducting local affairs is another. This externally imposed system of accountability is being widely mirrored internally, especially in police services, where local divisions, subdivisions and sectors are subject to performance review to attempt to ensure that force objectives are met. The increasing alignment of police basic command units with district/unitary authority boundaries is creating the conditions for joint accountability and joint performance management. There is frustration at the problems of aligning probation and health boundaries with those of the police and local authorities. There is growing interest in maximizing boundary alignment not only for crime reduction but also for pursuing other cross-cutting policy agendas to deal with the so-called 'wicked issues' that lie beyond established individual agency control.

This sedimentation of crime reduction, through adopting and adapting modernized bureaucratic forms of management, organization, accreditation, prescribed good practice, and techniques of accountability, is not without dangers.

Performance indicators as vehicles for achieving accountability and control create difficulties (Tilley, 1995). They are difficult to design without creating perverse incentives. Organizations are apt, for example, to cheat or attend only to that which is measured, or focus only on that which is expected to produce effects in the short term during which measurements are made (Smith, 1990). Performance indicators concerned with outcomes are blind to the actions and mechanisms that produce them, and risk mistaking agency action for other mechanisms generating change. They are thus liable to mislead. Performance indicators imposed centrally are liable to do violence to the varying conditions and needs that obtain in differing communities. As just one example, in the past centrally set performance indicators for policing have not included any reference to traffic, whilst in some areas this is the main problem identified by members of the community.

Action or output-related performance indicators comprise an alternative to those focusing on outcomes. They avoid the dangers of misattributing outcomes to interventions, but they risk creating their own perverse incentives: these have to do with prompting interventions that are irrelevant to local problems or local conditions. For example, the number of Neighbourhood Watch schemes per thousand residents has been used but Neighbourhood Watches have proliferated where they were easiest to establish – in low-crime areas where crime reduction needs were least and where their prospects of reducing crime were slim (Laycock and Tilley, 1995). Output-based performance indicators risk losing sight of the rationale for the measures adopted. They can lead to ritual, by-the-book behaviour at the expense of attention to real local problems and the conditions generating them.

Bureaucratic organizations can be slow in decision-making and resource allocation. They can lead to safe, unimaginative decisions that minimize the risk to agencies or individuals. Enterprise, imagination and innovation can be stifled. Moreover, where there is space for enterprise, imagination and innovation, it can be used to pursue sectional or individual interests rather than the purpose of the organization. Procedures, rules or 'good practice' can become an end in themselves. The value base for community safety work can be forgotten in the discharge of required action. Formal replaces substantive rationality.

Finally, the rigidity of traditional bureaucratic management arrangements inhibits adaptation to changing conditions. In known, well understood, stable, homogeneous and predictable conditions set rules, procedures and methods may make sense. If conditions are uncertain and/or poorly understood and/or changing rapidly and/or they vary widely, these arrangements may not be appropriate (see Ekblom, 1997).

Professionalization and the creation of experts

'Professionalization' describes a second established route to the institutionalization of new practices. Though the potential is as yet less established than that of bureaucratization in relation to crime reduction, crime prevention and community safety, in 2000 there were some embryonic signs that it may develop. One is the course supported by the book in which this chapter is appearing! Additional higher education courses are, of course, being offered. Another example of professionalization is the development of the National Community Safety Network, whose members could form the nucleus of a professional organization.

There is a growing knowledge base of theory and research for crime reduction. The research literature is expanding rapidly. Much has been produced within and published by the Home Office – over 130 crime reduction papers by the year 2000. A sprinkling of specialist journals had been established by the end of the century. Finally, a growing number of texts and edited collections as well as numerous contributions to general journals in criminology have been and are being published (notably Tonry and Farrington, 1995; Clarke, 1997; Gilling 1997; Crawford, 1998; and Hughes, 1998).

The research promises the establishment of evidence-based principles and analytical techniques that can be learned and used by a cadre of crime prevention experts to provide professional advice on dealing with community safety issues. The emerging occupational groups provide an organizational infrastructure for professionalization. Higher education institutions, with an interest in capitalizing on new markets for courses, comprise a ready source of curricula and accreditation.

Paul Ekblom's recent work explains the need for professionalization. Ekblom has pointed out how crime problems change with adaptation by offenders and preventers alike as each tries to adapt to and to thwart the other (Ekblom, 1997; Ekblom and Tilley, 2000). He points also to social and technological changes that create new crime and prevention opportunities. The crime world is, according to Ekblom, not fixed or certain, but is changing and adapting all the time. Fixed methods will not work. Instead well understood principles are needed to analyse crime problem situations and tailor preventive strategies to them. Ekblom's 'conjunction of criminal opportunity' attempts to draw together a comprehensive framework for understanding and planning crime prevention and reduction work (Ekblom, 2000). It is formal in nature and is designed to inform professional development and to catalyse analysis of and thought about preventing crime and disorder problems.

The track record of standard responses to crime and disorder problems is not good. Moreover, much crime reduction has been found to be poorly planned, implemented and evaluated (Audit Commission, 1999; HMIC, 1998; Tilley et al., 1999; Read and Tilley, 2000). Different measures work in different circumstances for different groups (Pawson and Tilley, 1997). Professionalization, in principle, promises practitioners with the specialist understanding to discern relevant differences and to tailor programmes relevant to changing and varying circumstances. It promises a group of experts who will be attentive to new research and the significance it has for improvements in approach.

The problems often associated with professionalization are well known. It can lead to self-interested exclusionary practices that defend members of the group rather than improve public service. It can become complacent, defensive and conservative. It can inhibit the brilliant maverick by the imposition of a panoply of professional regulations. It potentially wrests issues and values from the community to which they belong and pretends that they can become the special preserve of an expert occupational group. It is potentially what the whole crime prevention movement was spurning – crime prevention for everyone, not just the professional few (Laycock, 1996).

Infection and the mutation of institutions and disciplines

A third pattern of development, whose germs can be discerned in current developments, comprises a process of desegregation from other areas of scholarship, policy and practice. Crime reduction may in this way infect or be infected by other areas of activity, incorporating its agenda into them or mobilizing them for its own purposes.

The Section 17 provisions of the Crime and Disorder Act 1998 are the clearest expression of this development so far, where local agencies are required to take unintended crime consequences into account in policy and practice. Fear of litigation where this has not taken place (see Moss and Pease, 1999) may incentivize systematic attention to the requirement. The government is also requiring individual government departments to consider ways in which they too might be enabling or encouraging crime and disorder and to attend to this. The Foresight programme is highlighting the many ways in which developments in science and technology are creating changed potential for crime and for crime prevention (Foresight Crime Prevention Panel, 2000).

Routine activities theory (Cohen and Felson, 1979; Felson, 1998) highlighted how the conditions for crime (co-presence of likely offender, suitable target and absence of capable guardian) are brought about as the unintended consequence of changes in everyday life. Hence, for example, changes in patterns of mobility and work affect the guardianship of residences; changes in technology affect the supply of lightweight, anonymous, high-value goods suitable for theft; and changes in family life reduce the time those most likely to offend (young men) are tied to their families through domestic chores. Administrative practices, notably housing allocation criteria, have been shown to produce unintended crime impacts (Bottoms and Wiles, 1992). At a more micro level, in Britain water-based franking ink led to stamps being wiped and reused, and the shipment of silver in small ingots in the old west enabled them to be shared out and carried away by robbers on horseback (see Rogerson et al., 2000; Hough and Tilley, 1998b). There are now grounds for seeing crime patterns at any point largely as the crystallized side-effects of past changes, some of which were introduced for their own good reasons (Tilley, forthcoming). If this is the case, generalizing sensitivity to the potential crime legacy of new developments makes sense, not necessarily to inhibit those developments, but where possible to implement them in ways that avoid or minimize their crime-generating effects. Building new housing estates clearly always brings potential crime targets into an area. There is now strong evidence that considering the varying crime potential offered by differing designs has a major effect on the level of crime (Armitage, 1999). Likewise, product design inadvertently produces potentially hot objects of theft, but they could also be rendered less attractive to thieves (Clarke, 1999, 2000).

There are good research grounds for seeing crime patterns as avoidable or modifiable side-effects of changing policies, practices and technologies. These may, of course, lead to reductions in problem behaviour as well as increases. The unintended effect of switching from (toxic) town gas to (less toxic) natural gas was substantially to reduce the number of suicides by making it less easy to kill oneself painlessly and without disfiguration (Clarke and Mayhew, 1988). The unintended effect of requiring motor cyclists to wear crash helmets, and enforcing the requirement, was to reduce motor-cycle theft by making it more risky to steal a motor bike on the spur of the moment or without carting a helmet about (Mayhew et al., 1989).

There are some indications of a 'greening' of crime prevention, that is to say, routine sensitivity and attention to the crime impacts of changing products, practices and policies. This is in part consequent on statutory requirement or other forms of incentivization. It is also to do with a changing consciousness. In this sense the process is analogous to other developments where changed awareness, in part stimulated by legislation, is leading to changed ways of thinking about acting. Equal Opportunities and environmental concern are two areas where the kind of consciousness and routine consideration that may be occurring in regard to crime prevention seem already largely to be in place.

A more general crime production and prevention consciousness would take crime research away from its traditional roots in criminology and the social science theoretical foundations in which it has been rooted. Computer science, management science, engineering, genetics, materials science, telecommunications, marketing and so on become central to understanding crime patterns and to crime control. The Jill Dando Institute of Crime Science at University College London, which was launched in 2001, represents an institutional expression of this direction of change.

The benefit of 'greening' would be routine attention to emerging crime potential. It would pre-empt the need for catch-up where new patterns became sedimented before reaching *post hoc* attention with efforts to reduce or eliminate the problem. It would avoid the need for what Ken Pease has termed 'retro-solutions' (Rogerson et al., 2000). In fast-changing, late modern conditions, habits of crime foresight may have particular value (Friedman, 2000).

There are, as yet, no signs of widespread pressure on or grass-roots support for a greening of crime prevention. Moreover the discourse of offender responsibility for crime is likely to inhibit pressure on those not actually committing the crimes to accept the costs that may be incurred by taking the generation of crime risks into account in making plans and adjusting to changing market conditions. Unless attention to crime is backed by effective levers, the greening of crime prevention is unlikely to emerge. It is, as yet, not easy to see what will prompt the production of those levers.

It is striking that the mass media, though paying a great deal of attention to crime, show very little interest in crime reduction issues, reflecting as well as contributing to fairly low levels of public and political concern. A joint inspectorate report on crime reduction which made some critical points about what is being achieved across the country, as well as suggestions for improvements, was published in July 2000 (HMIC, 2000). A press notice was issued and Ministers launched the report. It received not a single mention in the national media. It was a substantial piece of work running to 160 pages. It involved several major agencies, including HMIC, the Social Services Inspectorate, the Office for Standards in Education, the Local Government Association, the Home Office and the Audit Commission. Its disregard is an indication of the level of public interest in and consciousness of crime reduction.

Though there may be germs of a growing crime and crime prevention consciousness, it is far from present now. Unlike equal opportunities and environmentalism, it lacks social movements promoting change. Whilst crime may be high on people's lists of worries, it appears more generally to be construed as a problem of bad people and their social conditions than one of side-effects of everyday life, and as a responsibility of government and specialist criminal justice agencies rather than all of them.

Evaporation of crime reduction from the policy agenda

The three potential lines of development highlighted so far all suggest a growing place for crime prevention, crime reduction and community safety. Though there are few signs of major moves to reverse them, there are critical voices that speak out against crime prevention. They are not yet numerous, but could grow. The critiques refer, for example, to:

1 Overestimation of the nature of the crime problem, the real problem being one of tolerance, not crime.
2 The creation of a 'fortress society' organized around risk reduction.
3 The use of techniques which exclude those deemed to be a risk to others.
4 The creation of a society divided into safe and unsafe spaces, preserves of different sections of the community.
5 The development of discriminatory and privacy-invading surveillance.
6 The subversion of trust as a condition of good community life.
7 Neglect of the social conditions in local areas generating criminal behaviour.
8 The stigmatization of communities, families and individuals picked out for their risks of becoming involved in crime.
9 The attachment of responsibility to agencies and individuals for crime control, which is the proper preserve of the criminal justice system, thereby skewing the agendas of agencies whose proper concern is not crime reduction.
10 Subversion of the justice agenda for criminal justice agencies in favour of utilitarian crime-reducing ones.
11 The imposition of social engineering on free agents, undermining free-market mechanisms.
12 The displacement of crime on to those least able to reduce their own crime risks and poorly placed to take advantage of state support for crime reduction.
13 The displacement of crime to more serious offences.
14 Disregard of fundamental problems (contradictions, inequalities or inequities) in social structure or culture, generating patterns of problems, including among others, crime.
15 Rewarding feckless and irresponsible offenders (and victims).
16 The treatment of moral issues as if they were purely technical.
17 The ineffectiveness of piecemeal crime reduction in the face of the social forces producing crime.
18 Misconstruing crime reduction as a specific policy issue, since it will be achieved only as a by-product of high-quality and inclusive social policy more generally.
19 Misconstruing crime reduction as a potential policy issue, since crime is a result of individual wickedness.
20 Abandonment of the pursuit of the good society in favour of harm reduction.

There is not space to go through these in detail here. Clearly some of the criticisms are mutually inconsistent (for example, 3 and 15). Many are unsupported by evidence (for example, 12 and 13). Several relate to specific measures or approaches rather than to crime reduction as such (for example, 2 and 5). Some would be easily refuted (probably 7 and 17). Most show crime reduction implicitly to involve value judgements of various kinds, and some are expressions of value judgement (for example, 1 and 10). They add up to scepticism about the value and direction of efforts at crime reduction.

If crime rates go up significantly, confidence may be lost in the potential of crime reduction policies. If crime rates fall significantly, and crime control drops off the policy agenda, crime reduction policy and practice may wither. If the public come to embrace significant elements of the criticisms that have been made – for example, that crime reduction is ineffective or simply displaces crime at an unacceptable rate or in dramatically undesirable directions – public investment in it may be withdrawn on political grounds.

None of this looks very likely. Being seen to be involved in crime reduction is deemed important, even if the public is generally uninterested in what is being done. Indeed, public indifference to the detail is likely normally to extend to the criticisms, which have also received muted attention. Moreover, with regard to impact there is strong evidence that some crime prevention is, indeed, effective (see, for example, Clarke, 1997). There would be real losses to the public were the preventive agenda to be abandoned.

Whilst it is possible that crime reduction will evaporate, that looks unlikely in the short to medium term, whatever doubts may be held about some or all of it. What is more likely is that those elements of crime reduction that are vulnerable to serious criticism will survive and thrive because it is politically inexpedient to abandon them and there are vested interests in their maintenance. Whilst the public may take little interest in what is done by way of crime reduction, or in detailed arguments about it, that is not to say that they could not be mobilized to defend what they deem to protect them. A report which suggested that there might be limited value in allocating resources to support for Neighbourhood Watch in affluent low-crime areas was roundly condemned by the late Alan Clark in his *Mail on Sunday* column, as the author of this piece knows to his cost! (See Laycock and Tilley, 1995; Clarke, 1995.)

A fifth way?

None of the four directions for state-sponsored crime reduction is without sense and none is without difficulty. In terms of the 'breaking down' metaphor, bureaucratization and managerialism break down resistance by individuals and organizations to taking responsibility for crime prevention, but they also risk breaking down the imagination and adaptability needed for creative responses. Professionalism breaks down the mechanical, rule-bound, thought-free responses that tend to come with bureaucratization, but it also risks breaking down collective, routine, commonsense action and commitment across agencies and communities. Infection and mutation promise to break down disciplinary, occupational and organizational boundaries, but risk misreading the level and nature of public and agency interests in crime and disorder. Moves towards evaporation comprise reminders that there are irreducible moral choices in crime prevention. The risk is that the public will lose the enhanced safety that public crime prevention provides. Abandoning public sector crime prevention would risk leaving the weak prey to displacement effected by the strong (see Barr and Pease, 1990). It would have (mal)distributive implications.

There may be scope to shape a fifth way, drawing on what is of value in the directions that have been identified, but sidestepping the potential perils. Key principles for a fifth way might include:

1   Recognition that there are important moral dimensions to the various means used in crime reduction that need to enter any discourse on their adoption.
2   Recognition that there are distributive justice dimensions to the inputs and outcomes that need to enter any discourse on the selection of means and allocation of effort.
3   Acknowledgement that members of communities know something about their own crime and disorder problems, and are necessarily implicated in their definition and responses to them (even though not all crime problems are community-based).
4   Recognition that there are contextual variations in the ways in which problems are generated, hence in the responses that will be effective.
5   Sensitivity to the mechanisms through which crime problems change fundamentally over time with new crimes, new types of criminal and new methods requiring new preventive responses; sensitivity, too, to emergent opportunities to reduce and prevent crime with changes in technology and social practice.
6   Acceptance that our knowledge of the ways in which crime problems are generated and changed is patchy and partial and is likely to remain so, as is our knowledge of the causal efficacy of intended preventive measures.
7   Realization that crime reduction decisions require judgement; they cannot be recipe-book matters.
8   Recognition that common sense has limitations for crime reduction. There are unacknowledged and unrecognized conditions for problems and unintended consequences from preventive action. There is a growing body of specialist theory and analytic technique and substantive findings that can usefully be deployed to inform preventive work.
9   Acceptance that a variety of agencies at a variety of levels have contributions to make to reducing and preventing crime and disorder.

10 Acceptance that problems can be construed at varying levels and that they can be addressed at those varying levels, from the incident to the repeat incident to the vulnerable group in the parish to the vulnerable groups in the local authority to the national generators of patterned problems.

Policies and practices consonant with these principles might include:

1 Continued investment in multidisciplinary programmes of basic research on the generation of crime events, and on mechanisms for their prevention or reduction.
2 The adoption of a problem-solving approach at the local and national levels, attuned to variations and changes in what problems emerge and how problems are generated.
3 The involvement of members of the community in community-focused crime prevention and reduction.
4 The provision of educated cross-disciplinary researchers/advisers with an understanding of relevant theory, research techniques and methods of engagement with others to help understand and anticipate problems.
5 The creation of research-literate local and national policy-makers and practitioners, able to interpret and make appropriate use of research findings.
6 Provision for the collection of reliable data that can be shared across agencies and routinely analysed in aggregate form.
7 The creation of a context, through legislation or publicity campaigns making or enforcing expectations, that 'crime harvests' from developments and routine practices are normal across the public, private and voluntary sectors at national and local levels.
8 Provision for problems emerging in local settings to be subjected to broader analysis and attention at regional or national level to identify emerging needs and preventive opportunities.
9 Arrangements to ensure that the major normative issues surrounding crime reduction ends and means are attended to by both practitioners and policy-makers, with provision for democratic accountability for the decisions made.

Conclusion

Individual interest and engagement in efforts to avoid becoming victims of predatory behaviour are, as was stated at the start of this chapter, a normal part of being members of the species *Homo sapiens*, as they are a normal part of belonging to many other animal species also. This chapter has mainly been about recent state involvement in prevention and reduction, informed by collective choice rather than by instincts for self-preservation.

This history is past, and hence closed. The future, of course, is open – there for the making. The latter part of the chapter has tried to tease out the emerging directions for policy and practice that can be discerned in current developments, and to suggest a preferred, though not necessarily probable path that might be taken instead.

What actually happens is likely to be largely a function of the range of possible options and the contingencies at work when decisions are taken by actors pursuing their own interests. What 'opportunity theory' has to say about crime goes also for policy and practice. The space to create a preferred crime prevention future will not be of our choosing. Given the space, alternatives are possible.

References

Anderson, D., Chenery, S. and Pease, K. (1995) *Biting Back: Tackling Repeat Burglary and Car Crime*, Crime Detection and Prevention Series Paper 58, London, Home Office.

Armitage, R. (1999) 'An Evaluation of Secured by Design Housing Schemes Throughout the West Yorkshire Area', mimeo., University of Huddersfield.

Audit Commission (1999) *Safety in Numbers*, London, Audit Commission.

Ballintyne, S., Pease, K. and McLaren, V. (eds) (2000) *Secure Foundations: Key Issues in Crime Prevention, Crime Reduction and Community Safety*, London, Institute for Public Policy Research.

Barr, R. and Pease, K. (1990) 'Crime placement, displacement and deflection' in Morris, N. and Tonry, M. (eds) *Crime and Justice: A Review of Research*, vol. 12, Chicago, IL, University of Chicago Press.

Bottoms, A. and Stevenson, S. (1992) 'What went wrong? Criminal justice policy in England and Wales, 1945–70' in Downes, D. (ed.) *Unravelling Criminal Justice*, Basingstoke, Macmillan.

Bottoms, A. and Wiles, P. (1992) 'Explanations of crime and place' in Evans, D., Fyfe, N. and Herbert, D. (eds) *Crime, Policing and Place: Essays in Environmental Criminology*, London, Routledge.

Bridgeman, C. and Sampson, A. (1994) *Wise after the Event: Tackling Repeat Victimization*, London, National Board for Crime Prevention.

Brody, S. (1976) *The Effectiveness of Sentencing*, Home Office Research Study No. 35, London, HMSO.

Chenery, S., Holt, J. and Pease, K. (1997) *Biting Back II, Reducing Repeat Victimization in Huddersfield*, Crime Detection and Prevention Series Paper 82, London, Home Office.

Clarke, R. (1980) 'Situational crime prevention: theory and practice', *British Journal of Criminology*, vol. 20, no. 2, pp. 136–47.

Clarke, R. (1995) 'Situational crime prevention' in Tonry, M. and Farrington, D. (eds) *Building a Safer Society*, Chicago, IL, University of Chicago Press.

Clarke, R. (ed.) (1997) *Situational Crime Prevention: Successful Case Studies*, New York, Harrow & Heston.

Clarke, R. (1999) *Hot Products: Understanding, Anticipating and Reducing the*

Demand for Stolen Goods, Police Research Series Paper 112, London, Home Office.

Clarke, R. (2000) 'Hot products: a new focus for crime prevention' in Ballintyne, S. et al. (eds) *Secure Foundations*, London, Institute for Public Policy Research.

Clarke, R. and Mayhew, P. (1980) *Designing out Crime*, London, HMSO.

Clarke, R. and Mayhew, P. (1988) 'The British gas suicide story and its criminological implications' in Tonry, M. and Morris, N. (eds) *Crime and Justice*, vol. 10, Chicago, IL, University of Chicago Press.

Cohen, L. and Felson, M. (1979) 'Social change and crime rate trends: a routine activity approach', *American Sociological Review*, vol. 44, no. 4, pp. 588–608.

Cornish, D. and Clarke, R. (eds) (1986) *The Reasoning Criminal: Rational Choice Perspectives on Offending*, New York, Springer-Verlag.

Crawford, A. (1998) *Crime Prevention and Community Safety*, London, Longman.

Ekblom, P. (1988) *Getting the Best out of Crime Analysis*, Crime Prevention Unit Paper 10, London, Home Office.

Ekblom, P. (1997) 'Gearing up against crime: a dynamic framework to help designers keep up with the adaptive criminal in a changing world', *International Journal of Risk, Security and Crime Prevention*, vol. 2, pp. 249–65.

Ekblom, P. (2000) 'The conjunction of criminal opportunity' in Ballintyne, S. et al. (eds) *Secure Foundations*, London, Institute for Public Policy Research.

Ekblom, P. and Tilley, N. (2000) 'Going equipped: criminology, situational crime prevention and the resourceful offender', *British Journal of Criminology*, vol. 40, pp. 376–98.

Farrell, G. (forthcoming) 'Crime prevention' in Bryant, C. (ed.) *Encyclopaedia of Criminology and Deviant Behaviour*, London, Taylor & Francis.

Farrell, G., Edmunds, A., Hobbs, L. and Laycock, G. (2000) *RV Snapshot: UK Policing and Repeat Victimization*, Crime Reduction Series Paper 5, London, Home Office.

Farrell, G. and Pease, K. (1993) *Once Bitten, Twice Bitten: Repeat Victimization and its Implications for Crime Prevention*, Crime Prevention Unit Paper 46, London, Home Office.

Felson, M. (1998) *Crime and Everyday Life: Insights and Implications for Society* (2nd edn), Thousand Oaks, CA, Pine Forge Press.

Field, S. (1990) *Trends in Crime and their Interpretation: A Study of Recorded Crime in Post-War England and Wales*, Home Office Research Study 119, London, HMSO.

Foresight Crime Prevention Panel (2000) *Just Around the Corner: A Consultation Document*, London, Department of Trade and Industry.

Forrester, D., Chatterton, M. and Pease, K. (1988) *The Kirkholt Burglary Prevention Project, Rochdale*, Crime Prevention Unit Paper 13, London, Home Office.

Forrester, D., Frenz, S., O'Connell, M. and Pease, K. (1990) *The Kirkholt Burglary Prevention Project: Phase II*, Crime Prevention Unit Paper 23, London, Home Office.

Foster, J. and Hope, T. (1993) *Housing, Community and Crime: The Impact of the Priority Estates Project*, Home Office Research Study 131, London, HMSO.

Friedman, T. (2000) *The Lexus and the Olive Tree*, New York, Anchor Books.

Gilling, D. (1997) *Crime Prevention: Theory, Policy and Politics*, London, UCL Press.

Goldblatt, P. and Lewis, C. (eds) (1998) *Reducing Offending: An Assessment of*

Research Evidence on Ways of Dealing with Offending Behaviour, Home Office Research Study 187, London, Home Office.

Heal, K. (1987) *Crime Prevention in the United Kingdom: from Start to Go*, Home Office Research and Planning Bulletin 34, pp. 9–15.

Heal, K. and Laycock, G. (eds) (1986) *Situational Crime Prevention: From Theory to Practice*, London, HMSO.

HM Inspectorate of Constabulary (1998) *Beating Crime*, London, HM Inspectorate of Constabulary.

HM Inspectorate of Constabulary (2000) *Calling Time on Crime*, London, HM Inspectorate of Constabulary.

Hobbes, T. (1651) *Leviathan, or The Matter, Form and Power of a Commonwealth Ecclesiastical and Civil*, ed. Richard Tuck, Cambridge, Cambridge University Press, 1996.

Home Office (1965) *Report of the Committee on the Prevention and Detection of Crime* (Cornish Report), London, Home Office.

Home Office (1984) *Crime Prevention*, Home Office Circular 8/84, London, Home Office.

Home Office (1990) *Crime Prevention: The Success of the Partnership Approach*, Home Office Circular 44/90, London, Home Office.

Home Office (1991) *Safer Communities: The Local Delivery of Crime Prevention through the Partnership Approach* (Morgan Report), London, Home Office.

Home Office (2000) *Annual Report 1999–2000*, London, Home Office.

Hough, M. and Mayhew, P. (1983) *The British Crime Survey: First Report*, Home Office Research Study 85, London, HMSO.

Hough, M. and Tilley, N. (1998a) *Auditing Crime and Disorder: Guidance for Local Partnerships*, Crime Detection and Prevention Paper 91, London, Home Office.

Hough, M. and Tilley, N. (1998b) *Getting the Grease to the Squeak: Research Lessons for Crime Prevention*, Crime Detection and Prevention Paper 85, London, Home Office.

Hughes, G. (1998) *Understanding Crime Prevention: Social Control, Risk and Late Modernity*, Buckingham, Open University Press.

Kuhn, T. (1962) *The Structure of Scientific Revolutions*, Chicago, IL, University of Chicago Press.

Laycock, G. (1985) *Reducing Burglary: A Study of Chemists' Shops*, Crime Prevention Unit Paper 1, London, Home Office.

Laycock, G. (1996) 'Rights, roles and responsibilities in the prevention of crime' in Bennett, T. (ed.) *Preventing Crime and Disorder: Targeting Strategies and Responsibilities*, Cambridge, Cambridge University Press.

Laycock, G. (forthcoming) 'Hypothesis-based research and the RV story', *Criminal Justice: The International Journal of Policy and Practice*.

Laycock, G. and Heal, K. (1989) 'Crime prevention: the British experience' in Evans, D. (ed.) *The Geography of Crime*, London, Routledge.

Laycock, G. and Tilley, N. (1995) *Policing and Neighbourhood Watch: Strategic Issues*, Crime Detection and Prevention Series Paper 60, London, Home Office.

Martinson, R. (1974) 'What works? questions and answers about prison reform', *Public Interest*, vol. 35, pp. 22–54.

Mayhew, P., Clarke, R., Sturman, A. and Hough, M. (1976) *Crime as Opportunity*, Home Office Research Study 34, London, HMSO.

Mayhew, P., Clarke, R. and Elliott, D. (1989) 'Motorcycle theft, helmet legislation, and displacement', *Howard Journal*, vol. 28, pp. 1–8.

McLaughlin, E. and Muncie, J. (2000) 'The criminal justice system: New Labour's new partnerships' in Clarke, J., Gewirtz, S. and McLaughlin, E. (eds) *New Managerialism, New Welfare?* London, Sage.

Moss, K. and Pease, K. (1999) 'Crime and Disorder Act 1998: wolf in sheep's clothing?', *Crime Prevention and Community Safety*, vol. 1, no. 4, pp. 15–19.

Nee, C. and Taylor, M. (1988) 'Residential burglary in the Republic of Ireland: a situational perspective', *Howard Journal*, vol. 27, pp. 105–16.

Newman, G., Clarke, R. and Shoham, S. (eds) (1997) *Rational Choice and Situational Crime Prevention*, Aldershot, Ashgate.

Pawson, R. and Tilley, N. (1997) *Realistic Evaluation*, London, Sage.

Pease, K. (1997) 'Predicting the future: the roles of routine activities and rational choice theory' in Newman, G. et al. (eds) *Rational Choice and Situational Crime Prevention*, Aldershot, Ashgate.

Pease, K. (1998) *Repeat Victimization: Taking Stock*, Crime Detection and Prevention Paper 90, London, Home Office.

Read, T. and Tilley, N. (2000) *Not Rocket Science: Problem-solving and Crime Reduction*, Crime Reduction Research Series Paper 6, London, Home Office.

Rock, P. (1990) *Helping Victims of Crime*, Oxford, Oxford University Press.

Rogerson, M., Ekblom, P. and Pease, K. (2000) 'Crime reduction and the benefit of foresight' in Ballintyne, S. et al. (eds) *Secure Foundations*, London, Institute for Public Policy Research.

Runciman, G. (1998) *The Social Animal*, London, HarperCollins.

Sampson, R. and Laub, J. (1993) *Crime in the Making*, Cambridge, MA, Harvard University Press.

Sherman, L., Gottfredson, D., MacKenzie, D., Eck, J., Reuter, P. and Bushway, S. (1997) *Preventing Crime: What Works, What Doesn't, What's Promising*, Research in Brief, National Institute of Justice, Washington, DC, US Department of Justice.

Smith, P. (1990) 'The use of performance indicators in the public sector', *Journal of the Royal Statistical Society A*, vol. 153, pp. 53–72.

Sutton, M. (1996) *Implementing Crime Prevention Schemes in a Multi-agency Setting: Aspects of Process in the Safer Cities Programme*, Home Office Research Study 160, London, Home Office.

Tilley, N. (1992) *Safer Cities and Community Safety Strategies*, Crime Prevention Unit Paper 38, London, Home Office.

Tilley, N. (1993) 'Crime prevention and the Safer Cities story', *Howard Journal*, vol. 32, pp. 40–57.

Tilley, N. (1995) *Thinking about Crime Prevention Performance Indicators*, Crime Prevention and Detection Paper 57, London, Home Office.

Tilley, N. (forthcoming) 'Crime and safety in Nottingham', Nottingham.

Tilley, N. and Laycock, G. (2000) 'Joining up research, policy and practice about crime', *Policy Studies*, vol. 23, no. 3, pp. 213–27.

Tilley, N., Pease. K., Hough, M. and Brown, R. (1999) *Burglary Prevention: Early Lessons from the Crime Reduction Programme*, Crime Reduction Research Series Paper 1, London, Home Office.

Tonry, M. and Farrington, D. (eds) (1995) *Building a Safer Society: Strategic Approaches to Crime Prevention*, Crime and Justice vol. 19, Chicago, IL, University of Chicago Press.

The road taken[†]

Evaluation, replication and crime reduction

Tim Hope

The pursuit of 'what works'

The ghost of the possibility that, in the end, 'nothing works' continues to haunt governments in their pursuit of crime prevention. This is not surprising, since the contemporary interest in preventing crime – particularly by means that lie outside the 'sovereign state's' criminal justice system – itself sprang from evident failures and public concern about the latter's efficacy in protecting its citizens (Hughes, 1998; Garland, 1996). Indeed, in Britain, the specific failures of penal treatment (Brody, 1976) or policing (Clarke and Hough, 1980), identified in evaluation research, provided not only an evidential basis but also a theoretical stimulus for government-sponsored thinking about crime prevention (Clarke and Cornish,1983). Nevertheless, since its emergence during the 1970s the doctrine that 'nothing works' in the reduction of crime (Martinson, 1974) has continued to be anathematized as unduly or unwarrantedly pessimistic (Ekblom and Pease, 1995).

In the face of such lingering doubt, a review of the scope for crime reduction commissioned as part of the British government's 1998 Comprehensive Spending Review more confidently asserted that:

> it had become increasingly clear that research evidence produced over the previous 40–50 years indicated that certain approaches to reducing crime would be more effective than others. *It was not true that 'nothing works'.* (Goldblatt and Lewis, 1998, p. 1; emphasis added)

Yet, although it is hardly surprising that policy-makers should want to make a success of what they do, the political pursuit of 'what works' in crime prevention is animated by a rather more profound set of needs that, in turn – and this is the subject of my chapter – have consequences for the conduct and status of social scientific 'evaluation research' of crime prevention programmes.

The 'Martinson problem'

Pessimism about crime prevention – and the pursuit of optimism by governments in response – has both cultural and methodological origins. Reasons for cultural pessimism, and its accompanying and simplifying set of punitive responses (Beckett and Sasson, 2000; Garland, 1996), can be found in the salient features and transformations of late modern society (see Garland, 2000; Young, 1999). In the risk society, a focus on crime prevention can be regarded both as a necessary response to new forms of emergent risk and as an exemplar of a new mode of managing and governing risk and hazard (Hughes, 1998). Nevertheless, because contemporary social risks, such as crime, are in a sense 'manufactured' out of our everyday social organization (Felson, 1998), there remains a profound sense of unease about our capacity to cope with them (Hope and Sparks, 2000). As socially manufactured risks become more central to everyday life our capacity to manage them becomes increasingly more necessary for our own well-being (Giddens, 1990). The growing public importance of crime victimization surveys such as the British Crime Survey attests, increasingly, to the demand for scientific assistance to help us understand the risks we face in our everyday lives. Nevertheless, at the same time, our faith in science's capacity to eradicate hazard and deliver progress has diminished (Beck, 1992).

Yet, despite the cultural pessimism of the risk society, it is nevertheless noteworthy that the new governmental project of crime prevention has been accompanied by renewed assertiveness amongst criminologists that their work does indeed provide a rationale for a new, optimistic response to crime risk (Felson, 1998). The new theories of crime prevention –

whether 'situational' (Clarke, 1992) or 'developmental' (Farrington, 1996) – are imbued with a sense of progress and practicality, particularly a belief that the application of scientific knowledge and rational planning, if done properly, will help us to find 'what works' in crime prevention. A similar spirit of scientific optimism now also infuses those social scientists who have enlisted to help 'evaluate' governments' new crime reduction project:

> Many crime prevention programs work. Others don't. Most programs have not yet been evaluated with enough scientific evidence to draw conclusions. Enough evidence is available, however, to create provisional lists of what works, what doesn't and what's promising. *Those lists will grow more quickly if the Nation invests more resources in scientific evaluations to hold all crime prevention programs accountable for their results.* (Sherman et al., 1998a, p. 1; emphasis added)

For such evaluators the great selling point of social scientific research lies less in the ideas and explanations emerging from research studies than in the *application of scientific method itself* – 'the major strength of scientific evaluations is that rules of science provide a consistent and reasonably objective way to draw conclusions about cause and effect' (Sherman, et al., 1998a, p. 3). These rules essentially codify those that are inherent in the application of the 'experimental paradigm' – that is, the treatment of social programmes as if they were social experiments and the attempt to design social research on those programmes that emulate the rules and precepts of scientific experimentation (Cook and Campbell, 1979).

The classic statement about the application of the 'experimental paradigm' to social policy is that of Donald. T. Campbell in his celebrated paper 'Reforms as experiments' (1969). The recent foundation of a '"Campbell" Crime and Justice Collaboration' (Petrosino, 2000) – modelled on the 'Cochrane Collaborations' in medicine and health care (see Oakley, 2000) – is an example of his legacy. Campbell's implicit assumption was that the 'experimenting society' would be the 'good society' because social and political learning would be advanced by the application of scientific method; the use of scientific criteria to inform political choice would consequently lead to progress in the social policy sphere just as it had done in the fields of medicine and economic life. Yet, more recently, particularly with reference to the reduction of crime, we find Pawson and Tilley (1997) referring to this endeavour as the 'Martinson problem':[1] 'why, from the "nothing works" days to the present, has experimental evaluation continued to produce inconsistent findings?' (p. 30). For them, inconsistency is worthless for policy; moreover, inattention to the detailed 'reality' of successful programmes will not guide practitioners towards better practice. At the root of the problem are the epistemological premises of the 'experiment' that undermine the validity of its advocates' claims to utility. A different evaluation research philosophy is needed – one resting upon the causal logic of *scientific realism* – which will help us to get at the more essential truths about social interventions so as to find out not simply 'what works' but 'what works, for whom and in what circumstances' (Pawson and Tilley, 1997).

Yet, whatever else divides them, the two evaluation paradigms still aim to be useful – especially, *useful to government*. For the 'scientific realists', just as for the 'experimentalists', the task is to provide governments with 'useful knowledge' on what works (with the additional practical benefits of 'for whom, in what circumstances') so that policy-makers can initiate, modify and fine-tune their interventions in pursuit of the common goal of progress towards crime reduction. The paradigm wars concerning the evaluation of crime reduction that have been waged so heatedly (see, for example, Pawson and Tilley, 1994; Bennett, 1996) have been for the ear of government. Which version of science can provide the most useful and usable knowledge? Which version can provide the best technology for crime control? And the occasion and application of these campaigns have been prompted by an avowed commitment on the part of the Labour government generally to 'evidence-led policy' and, particularly, by its application to the task of reducing crime in community settings (Goldblatt and Lewis, 1998).

Evaluation and political accountability

Yet, returning for the moment to the nature of Campbell's (1969) call for social interventions to be treated as if they were experiments, we find him addressing a rather different notion of utility from that espoused subsequently. While there is, indeed, an aspiration to provide useful knowledge in the furtherance of social progress, Campbell also saw the need to establish an essential condition for attaining this goal – namely, the creation of an *experimental ethos in public administration*. The chief obstacle to establishing this ethos was not the absence of knowledge to experiment with, nor even the practical difficulties of implementing scientific methods of evaluation (considerable though they might be) but the political obstacles in the way of informed social learning and choice stemming from the nature of government itself. Rather than placing science as a methodological tool for governments to *use*, in Campbell's vision of the reform society, science would also need to be a methodological tool with which to hold government *accountable* for its actions to a wider public interest.

The reason why Campbell took this view was that without an external (publicly accessible) method of accounting for political choice, public administrators have built-in incentives not only to avoid critical scrutiny of their public record and achievements,[2] but also to make political capital by claiming success for what they have purportedly done:

It is one of the characteristic aspects of the present situation that *specific reforms are advocated as though they were certain to be successful*. For this reason, knowing outcomes has immediate political implications . . . If the political and administrative system has committed itself in advance to the correctness and efficacy of its reforms, it cannot tolerate learning of failure. (Campbell, 1978, p. 80; original emphasis)

Campbell's methodological contribution lay in advocating research design solutions to the many various 'threats' to the validity of programme evaluation research (Cook and Campbell, 1979; Campbell and Stanley, 1963). Many of these threats stem from the practical difficulties of implementing valid experiments with human subjects in field settings. However, there is a set of threats or biases that stem from the fact that the subjects of study *are* also part of purposive interventions organized by interested agents (usually governments). In Campbell's terminology, these consist chiefly of regression artefacts – 'pseudo-shifts occurring when treatment units have been selected upon the basis of extreme scores' (Campbell, 1978, p. 82) – and *selection biases* resulting from the differential selection of subjects, groups or treatments.

Both are threats to validity because in a sense they capitalize on chance: the former does so by virtue of theoretical statistical properties inherent in time-series data, including 'regression to the mean' – the greater probability that cases with extreme scores will become less extreme than more extreme over time – and excessive instability, noise and aberration in the series. The greater our lack of understanding of the 'causes' and processes determining the statistical series, the less our ability to detect such 'spurious' or chance decreases (or increases). Selection bias is also a matter of chance, though this time more akin to a wager in which one endeavours, on the basis of available information ('form'), to predict outcomes, usually to pick winners, in advance. However, in political sweepstakes, the 'races' are usually organized by those (i.e. governments) who have a stake in winning, since they have already staked (political) capital on their particular horse (i.e. reform project). Hence the problem of evaluation, as posed by Campbell, lies not just in how to organize a race so that we can distinguish 'winners' from 'losers' (so that we would be able to tell 'what worked' from 'what didn't', for instance) but also in how to organize a fair contest on behalf of the ordinary punter (i.e. citizen) who is, after all, putting up the stake (i.e. political legitimacy) in the first place. For Campbell, in as much as these biases were 'games of chance', the chief technique to guard against them in order to ensure a fair contest was to build chance into the game itself – mainly through the use of techniques and procedures of randomization, which he saw as the essential ingredient for replicating the controls of an 'experiment' in field settings (Cook and Campbell, 1979; see also Oakley, 2000, especially chapter 7). Why it was necessary to take such steps in the first place was not just to guard against threats to explanation but also to guard against the possibility of the manipulation of the results, for *a priori* political purposes.

Campbell (1969) was acutely aware that his discussion of such possibilities would become what we would now call *reflexively available*. That is to say, through publication of his views he felt he was giving advice not only to the 'experimental administrator' – who deserved to be protected from threats to the accumulation of valid and useful knowledge about programmes – but also to the 'trapped administrator' (see also Ekblom and Pease, 1995) – 'whose political predicament requires a favourable outcome whether valid or not' (Campbell, 1978, p. 87). For the latter, (reflexive) knowledge of the 'rules of chance' would greatly help in the task of engineering favourable outcomes and thus at least preserving, if not accumulating, political capital.

More generally, then, the version of scientific validity proposed by Campbell constitutes an admittedly stringent set of criteria that is offered to the political public to help them to assess the claims of policy-makers. The stringency was necessary because, as policy-makers became more sophisticated in their use of data and statistics, they would be able to make claims that appeared more convincing than mere assertions of conviction. And they would also become more sophisticated in capitalizing on some of the rules of chance in order to support their claims to efficacy. Thus the kind of evaluation research suggested by Campbell was to be carried out in the service of the public interest so that genuine claims could be assessed and real progress attained for the overall public good. The problem for the public in having these criteria implemented is well known – such 'quasi-experiments' may be difficult to set up, individual experiments may become unrepresentative, or may involve unethical choices affecting 'subjects', such as the random administration of penalties or the denial of beneficial treatments (Oakley, 2000). The problem for policy-makers, though, is a different one – the Martinson problem or, in other words, that programmes may not always be judged to be successful despite the ambitions of their sponsors.

For the policy-maker the 'threat' posed by evaluation research is also different from that for the social scientist (assuming the latter is acting in the 'public interest'). An important and well established aim in the design of explanatory social research is to optimize the acceptance of the validity of findings between two types of 'error' – that is, how best to weigh up the risk of making a 'Type I error' – i.e. concluding that a finding is true when it is false – against that of making a 'Type II error' – that is, concluding that a finding is false when it is true. Because its main focus is upon producing generalizable knowledge, social scientific enquiry is oriented towards the avoidance of 'Type I error'. For the policy-maker, however, the situation is reversed. Although policy-makers who make 'Type I errors' may well incur opportunity costs to the wider public interest (e.g. by diverting resources towards ineffectual programmes and away from desirable policies), the direct 'political' costs to themselves of making alternative 'Type II errors' may weigh just as heavily – that is, that they may be induced to throw away their programmes, and consequently their own credibility, needlessly. Thus evaluation research potentially threatens the political capital vested in social programmes (Oakley, 2000, p. 312).

In this sense, then, the experimental paradigm poses a political dilemma, since the price to be paid for insisting on scientific rigour on the grounds of democratic accountability may well be a lack of 'utility' for policy-makers (if it tends to throw up 'nothing works'-type findings). What may serve the public interest in one way – by holding government accountable – may hinder it in another – by inhibiting government from finding out 'what works'. There would thus be considerable advantage to be gained if we were able to preserve the safeguards of validity inherent in 'scientific method' – perhaps by suggesting alternative criteria of validity and research designs to implement them – while at the same time producing useful results. Indeed, this is what Pawson and Tilley (1997) promise with 'realist' evaluation.

Replication

Notwithstanding battles about the nature of scientific experimentation, all sides of the contemporary paradigm wars agree that valid knowledge about policies is likely to develop only through the accumulation of findings from the replication of projects. Indeed, notwithstanding their criticism of the inability of the experimental paradigm to explain its own findings, Pawson and Tilley (1997, p. 115), as foremost advocates of the alternative approach of (scientific) realist evaluation, see the replication of results in other circumstances as the essence of their vision of utility. Replication is to be carried out through the process of establishing plausible context–mechanism–outcome configurations (CMOCs) and thence to find or engineer other CMOCs which differ in various ways in one or more of their constituent elements (C, M, O) in order eventually to identify the specific ways (i.e. the particular CMOCs) in which things work, for whom and in what contexts.

Nevertheless, the problem with this approach is that – unlike those quasi-experimental designs intended to guard against threats to validity – there seems to be no apparent guarantee or safeguard in realist evaluation methodology which would ensure not only fair and unbiased findings at the end of the process of replication but also that the course of enquiry pursued during the process of replication was itself valid and unbiased. In short, despite the avowed intention of realist replication to generate external validity (Pawson and Tilley, 1997, p. 128), and hence the utility for government which flows from generalizability, the scientific realist approach contains no externally available methodology to guard against selection bias (conscious or not) in the accumulation of case studies and, as important, in the selection and interpretation of evidence.

I will try to demonstrate this with regard to the example cited frequently and in detail by Pawson and Tilley (1997; and Tilley, 2000) – 'the hugely esteemed and famously successful' Kirkholt Burglary Prevention Project (Pawson and Tilley, 1997, p. 117) and the political emphasis on reducing *repeat victimization* that followed (see also Forrester et al., 1988, 1990; Tilley, 1993b; Farrell and Pease, 1993; Pease, 1998). Even though the 'Kirkholt Project' was carried out during the 1980s, it has achieved subsequently an iconic status in worldwide contemporary thinking on crime prevention and is still given prominence in compendia of 'what works' in crime prevention (Goldblatt and Lewis, 1998; Sherman et al., 1998a), especially that which is claimed to be 'cost-effective' (Welsh and Farrington, 1999; Ekblom et al., 1996).[3]

Replication and selection bias: 'Kirkholt and after'

What was Kirkholt?

The problem, as we shall see, is that with any programme like Kirkholt there is, potentially, an 'infinitely large number of descriptions of an infinitely large number of social transactions . . . all of the stakeholders' views could be spelled out in greater detail. All of them could hold the key to the success of the program' (Pawson and Tilley, 1997, p. 130). Thus, to avoid staring relativism and social constructivism in the face (see *ibid.*, chapter 1), the realists must set out – indeed, impose – some analytical framework on to their narrative of the past. Unfortunately, the extraction of the 'essence of Kirkholt', as it were, provides space for policy selectivity and bias.

Over and above the lists provided of what 'Kirkholt' was about (Tilley, 2000; Pawson and Tilley, 1997; Tilley, 1993a), we might add or re-emphasize the following:

1 'It' was an 'intervention' on the Kirkholt estate, Rochdale – an area of local authority-owned housing in north-west England – comprising some 2,280 dwellings. Between 1986 and 1990 researchers sponsored by the Home Office were engaged in action research and the evaluation of a set of crime prevention measures – known together as the Home Office Burglary Prevention Project. The accounts reveal that the researchers were also involved in 'directing' the preventive 'action' on the estate (Forrester et al., 1988, 1990). The cost of the research component was put at around £84,000 (Safe Neighbourhoods Unit, 1994).

2 The Home Office Burglary Prevention Project on the estate (the subject of the above research) was itself a multi-agency initiative, involving a

range of different expertise, capacities, interventions, etc., over the reporting period. These included upgrading the security of recently victimized dwellings, property marking, and the removal of pre-payment utilities meters (Forrester et al., 1988). Latterly the local probation service organized group work and community service programmes for local offenders, which were accompanied by the establishment of a credit union for residents and a school-based programme for local youth (Forrester et al., 1990). A particular innovation was to establish 'cocoon' watching groups – small groups consisting only of the immediate neighbours of recently victimized households. Considerable success in organizing cocoon groups was reported (Forrester et al., 1990). The total cost of these interventions (including the Home Office research) was estimated at around £298,000 (Welsh and Farrington, 1999; Safe Neighbourhoods Unit, 1994). The published Home Office reports on the Kirkholt Project make little mention of other potential crime prevention measures, processes and funding sources being implemented on the estate (see 3 below) and, where these are mentioned obliquely, we are given the impression that they were 'co-opted' into the Burglary Prevention Project interventions (see Forrester et al., 1988, p. 15; 1990, p. 7).

3   Nevertheless, the Home Office Burglary Prevention Project was, it seems, part of a bigger programme of work on the estate launched in 1984 and recognized by the local authority as the Kirkholt Development Project (Safe Neighbourhoods Unit, 1994). A considerable number of interventions and practices had been and were being undertaken on the estate, funded or implemented by a range of public agencies (including the central government Department of the Environment), preceding or concurrent with the Home Office initiative. These interventions included improvements to dwellings, local estate-based management and repair services, some of which were assisted by the Priority Estates Project (cf. Foster and Hope, 1993), community development, youth work and so on (Safe Neighbourhoods Unit, 1993) – some or all of which may conceivably have had some (direct or indirect) bearing on burglary reduction (Hope, 1995a).[4] The total cost of these initiatives between 1985 and 1990 (including those described under the rubric of the Burglary Prevention Project) was estimated at around £1.5 million (Safe Neighbourhoods Unit, 1994).

In most of the accounts of developments at Kirkholt – including those of the original researchers (Forrester et al., 1988; 1990) – prominence has been given to the most innovative feature – the prevention of repeat victimization. Clearly, this promised to be a new 'big idea' in crime prevention (Bridgeman and Sampson, 1994), and the apparent success in reducing burglary rates on the estate seemed to vindicate the actions of the Home Office Burglary Prevention Project. Between 1986/87 and 1989/90 the recorded residential burglary rate on the estate fell by 75 per cent;

there was a 40 per cent reduction within five months of the start of the programme and, importantly, repeat victimizations fell to zero over the same period (Forrester et al., 1990). Given these effects, it is not surprising that most reviewers have inferred that the actions of the Home Office Burglary Prevention Project, which claimed to have impacted directly upon repeat victimization, had in fact brought the burglary rate down (Farrell, 1995). Thus we may formulate our first hypothesis about the 'Kirkholt effect':

1   The reduction in the burglary rate on the Kirkholt estate was brought about by a reduction in the risk of repeat victimization which, in turn, was the result of the interventions of the Home Office Burglary Prevention Project.

Nevertheless, there remains a difficulty about the attribution of causes to effects, particularly to the effects of the Home Office project as distinct from the effect of the Kirkholt Development Project, whether taken separately or in total. The presence of a co-ordinated estate improvement programme on Kirkholt may have provided a framework for the project to fit into, as well as a substantial pool of resources already targeted on the estate's burglary problem (Safe Neighbourhoods Unit, 1994, p. 70). Many general and specific prevention measures were implemented during the period. Arguably, it may have been the multiplicity of interventions on the Kirkholt estate which achieved the effect rather than those specifically targeted at repeat victims, even if the chief beneficiaries turned out to be those who might otherwise have been repeatedly victimized (Hope, 1995b). The overall scale of resources brought to bear on the estate during the Kirkholt Development Project suggests a considerable intensity of investment and activity. We may then formulate a second hypothesis about the Kirkholt effect:

2   The reduction in the burglary rate on the Kirkholt estate was brought about by the multiplicity of interventions and the intensity of preventive effort brought to bear on the estate by a multiplicity of agencies.

Unfortunately, by no stretch of the imagination could the evaluation research design employed at Kirkholt reach the kind of experimental 'gold standard' envisaged by Campbell's followers.[5] Nor could subsequent retrospective attempts at data analysis provide conclusive and unequivocal attribution of effects to the Home Office initiative specifically.[6] So a replication 'offers another and classic way of arbitration' (Tilley, 1993b, p. 2). Tilley (2000) describes a course of replication that subsequently led to (or arguably legitimized) a policy of seeking to intervene in the 'time course' of repeat victimization.

Replication: the road taken

As it has been described in 'realist' evaluation accounts,[7] the process of replication and development from the Kirkholt Project took a number of turns, some thought to be false (Tilley, 2000), but eventually claiming to have arrived at valid and usable knowledge, not only about crime reduction but also about the specific approach of reducing crime by focusing effort on the reduction of repeat victimization (Pease, 1998; Pease and Laycock, 1996; Farrell, 1995; Farrell and Pease,1993). Nevertheless, if we go 'back and back again to puzzle over present findings about the effectiveness of current practices', as Pawson and Tilley (1997, p. 115) enjoin us to do, we may find different starting points and different roads to be taken. My point in suggesting this is not to argue for an even more 'real' account but merely to suggest that, despite its good intentions, realist evaluation is perhaps as – and may be even more – vulnerable to manipulation and selection bias, as other more overtly politicized accounts.

First, we shall consider the road taken by realist accounts. This focuses primarily on the efficacy of those measures claimed in the evaluators' account to have had a bearing on repeat victimization on the assumption that measures to reduce repeat victimization (i.e. the crime concentration rate) would bring about reductions in the crime (incidence) rate (see Pawson and Tilley, 1997, pp. 127–47). Tilley (2000) selects two replication studies (deriving from the Safer Cities programme: see below) which produced ambivalent results: the case '?R1' generated a 74 per cent increase in incidence; the other case, '?R2', saw a 66 per cent reduction. Clearly, neither of these is a satisfactory result, yet nor, as Tilley argues, is exact replication possible. Case ?R1 did some but not all the things done at Kirkholt, but burglary increased dramatically. Case ?R2 produced similar dramatic reductions but its context and mechanisms were not at all similar (Tilley, 2000). The lesson taken from these findings, however, was to carry on replicating, selecting out and refining particular context and mechanism configurations until (at last!) similar outcome patterns could be achieved – though never quite as dramatic as originally achieved at Kirkholt (see Pease, 1998). That ultimate policy replication path is not my concern here. My concern is with illustrating alternative replication paths that might have led in a different direction and with different results. Was the selection of things to be replicated focusing on that which might have been replicable about Kirkholt? And what things were not selected for replication? Here there is other 'replication' evidence germane to both the 'hypotheses' about the Kirkholt effect noted above.

Replication road not taken (hypothesis 1)

It is widely acknowledged in all the accounts that there was a dramatic reduction in the rate of domestic burglaries on the estate. But what does that mean? Here it is helpful to clarify what can be meant by a 'crime rate' and how it may decrease. A programme of research work has sought, in part, to 'unpack' what is meant by the crime victimization rate (Trickett et al., 1995; Hope, 1995b; Trickett et al., 1992), employing the heuristic idea of 'crime flux' (Barr and Pease, 1992). The simple idea behind the notion of crime flux is that the crime rate can be decomposed into two distinct statistics, measuring two empirically different phenomena that combine together in the commonplace definition of the crime rate. That is,

1   the crime incidence rate = the number of victimization events *per capita* of population,

Which can be broken down into:

2   the crime prevalence rate = number of victims/population,
3   the crime concentration rate = number of victimization events/number of victims.
4   Thus, incidence = prevalence × concentration.

It follows, logically, that change in an observed crime rate can be due to any combination of change in prevalence or concentration. With our present state of knowledge we know little or nothing about the circumstances of changes in crime flux, nor what our expectations of these patterns of outcomes may be (Hope, 1995b; Trickett et al., 1992).

The hypothetical assumption about the mechanism inherent in Kirkholt (hypothesis 1) was that measures aimed at preventing revictimization had an effect on reducing concentration and that it was, implicitly, the reduction in concentration that caused the reduction in incidence – hence the justification for the policy of focusing on repeat victimization. One logical course to be taken by replication, then, would be to see if we can find other examples where the Hypothesis 1 effect occurred – that is, where a 'dramatic' reduction in incidence was produced by a reduction in crime concentration.

Kirkholt was not the only evaluation-based study of interventions and burglary rate changes going on in the 1980s and 1990s. From three studies it is possible to compile information on burglary rate changes for twenty-six identifiable CMOCs where, in each case, the context was a residential area, the majority comprising local authority-owned housing. The advantage of these data is that they allow calculation of the relevant rates from information drawn from household victimization sample surveys utilizing broadly similar definitions of burglary and representative, random samples of relevant populations. In each case the data consist of two-wave cross-sectional surveys, separated by at least a twenty-four-month period. In brief, the studies are:

1   *The 'DICE evaluation'*. As part of an evaluation of the impact of radical design improvement schemes on selected council housing estates in England (see Price Waterhouse, 1997), survey data were collected

from samples of residents on five estates subject to the redesign. For each 'experimental' estate, a comparable sample was collected from about three other estates within the same urban area. In all, this yielded ten CMOCs, that is, the five experimental estates and the five separate 'control' samples. The surveys were conducted on both experimental and control estates prior to the start of the improvement scheme and again twelve months following the completion of the physical works.[8]

2   *The PEP evaluation study.* Survey data were collected in this study as part of an evaluation of the impact of 'Priority Estates Project' interventions in two 'experimental' areas of local authority housing in, respectively, the London borough of Tower Hamlets and the city of Kingston upon Hull (see Foster and Hope, 1993; Glennerster and Turner, 1993). For each estate a comparable 'control' area within the respective city was selected. For the purposes of this analysis, these four areas have been further subdivided into eleven CMOCs, separated primarily on the basis of physical–spatial differences (some of which have been reported in Foster and Hope, 1993). Household surveys were carried out in all areas in 1987 and 1990.[9]

3   *The Safer Cities (Phase I) evaluation.* Burglary rates for these CMOCs are calculated directly from Ekblom et al. (1996, tables 2.1 and 2.2). The report evaluates the impact of Phase I of the Safer Cities programme, funded and managed by the Home Office, which ran from 1988 to 1995. Household surveys were carried out in sampled neighbourhoods (defined as census enumeration districts) with the areas covered by Safer Cities projects in 1990 and 1992, and also in a set of comparison cities. Four CMOCs were formed in terms of a 'burglary action intensity score' applicable to the Safer Cities areas in terms of 'none' (control), 'low' (experiment), 'medium' (experiment) and 'high' (experiment). A further CMOC comprised the sample from the comparison cities (control).

In this collection of CMOCs, for which we have burglary rates at two time periods, there is a substantial range of differences in terms of demography, culture, social structure, events occurring and purposive crime prevention interventions. For the purposes of this analysis, however, such differences are largely irrelevant, though they are not, of course, for purposes of explanation, as the various studies of the data, cited above, make abundantly clear. Rather, however, the concern here is to look at the changing patterns of 'crime flux' in each CMOC between two time periods; specifically, to identify whether similar patterns of outcomes can be found to that hypothesized to have occurred at Kirkholt – namely a change (reduction) in burglary incidence accompanied by a change (reduction) in burglary concentration (hypothesis 1). Nevertheless, the 'experimental' or 'control' status of each area has been identified in the analysis, primarily to indicate whether they had been subject to any purposive or 'intentional' burglary reduction effort. One point, though, is

Table 3.1 *Findings from twenty-six 'context–mechanism–outcome configurations': changes in burglary rates [%]*

'Experimental' or 'control'	Change in incidence	Change in concentration	Change in prevalence
Biggest reductions in incidence			
Control	−86	−29	−80
Control	−78	−33	−67
Experiment	−71	−16	−66
Control	−67	0	−67
Experiment	−66	+18	−71
Experiment	−59	−14	−52
Biggest reductions in concentration			
Control	−43	−90	+470
Control	+130	−39	+230
Control	−78	−33	−67
Control	−86	−29	−80

'Experimental' or 'control' denotes the status of the surveyed area during the original programme. *Incidence*: number of victimization incidents per head of population. *Prevalence*: number of victims per head of population. *Concentration*: number of victimization incidents per victim. The table shows percentage changes between the wave 1 (pre-intervention) and wave 2 (post-intervention) surveys.

Sources: Tabulations by the author; by kind permission of the Home Office and the Department of the Environment, Transport and the Regions; Ekblom et al. (1996, tables 2.1 and 2.2).

worth noting, that – with the partial exception of three CMOCs from Safer Cities I – none focused specifically on preventing repeat victimization and, even in the former, other preventative initiatives were also implemented (Ekblom et al., 1996).

Table 3.1 arranges some of the CMOCs in terms of their (crime flux) relationships between incidence and concentration. The general conclusion is that we cannot find any patterns of outcome (hypothesis 1) similar to those found at Kirkholt. Yet this is not to suggest that outcomes of the magnitude of Kirkholt cannot be found. Table 3.1 shows that we can find at least some bigger reductions in either incidence or concentration compared with those attained at Kirkholt, but that in none of the results can we find combinations where big reductions in both the incidence and the concentration go together. Nor, it might be added, are reductions exclusively the property of areas designated as the subject of purposive crime prevention experiments; similar reductions occurred in so-called 'control' areas as well. Table 3.2 suggests that, across the twenty-six CMOCs, change in prevalence may have a stronger relationship (0.773) with change in incidence than does change in concentration (0.439). What is more, there seemed to be no relationship across the CMOCs between changes in prevalence and changes in concentration.

Table 3.2 *Findings from twenty-six 'context–mechanism–outcome configurations': correlations between changes in incidence, prevalence and concentration*

	Change in incidence	Change in concentration
Change in concentration	0.439 (0.025)	
Change in prevalence	0.773 (0.000)	−0.042 (0.837)

The table shows correlations between changes in pre- and post-intervention rates of, respectively, incidence, concentration and prevalence for each of the twenty-six areas with 'context–mechanism–outcome' configurations. Correlation coefficients are calculated as Spearman's, non-parametric, rank order coefficients (rho). The statistical significance (p) of the correlation coefficient is given in parentheses.

Sources: Tabulations by the author; by kind permission of the Home Office and the Department of the Environment, Transport and the Regions; Ekblom et al. (1996, tables 2.1 and 2.2).

Across the – admittedly limited – range of examples available here it would seem that the outcome pattern achieved by the Kirkholt Project has been unique. Yet does this suggest that Kirkholt itself is uniquely successful in crime prevention, and that only close replications of Kirkholt – or its most salient feature – will produce similar outcomes? The answer might be 'yes' if only hypothesis 1 was entertained – that Kirkholt was really about reducing burglary incidence only through reducing repeat victimization. The answer, however, might be 'no' if we asserted that Kirkholt was commendable simply because it brought about huge reductions in burglary – similarly large reductions in incidence, concentration and prevalence can be found to have occurred in other places – sometimes not even as a result of purposive prevention efforts (Table 3.1). In any event, the jury remains out on the main verdict on hypothesis 1. Though there are examples in these CMOCs where reductions in burglary incidence and concentration rates have been greater than at Kirkholt, there is none where these have gone together.

None of this is to deny the major burglary reductions that occurred at Kirkholt. Yet we do know from these examples that burglary incidence can decline, sometimes by dramatic amounts. Pawson and Tilley (1997) are right in pointing out that without some kind of informed method to guide the selection of future replications, or the interpretation of similar ones, we shall not know what it is we are looking for when we look for replications. Equally, though, the experimentalists may also be right in saying that unless we ensure that the expected outcomes from the original experiment are clear and unambiguous such that we know what works sufficiently well in order to replicate it, then we have no way of ensuring that the selection of either interventions or candidate trials will not be open to selection bias – in this case, a bias towards a particular theory of crime reduction.

Replication: the road not taken (hypothesis 2)

As noted above, the Kirkholt Project stands out also as an intensive, large-scale, multiplex intervention brought to bear upon a single residential area. A reasonable, alternative hypothesis about the 'Kirkholt effect' would be that the scale of burglary reduction is proportionate to the scale of the investment made and to the efficiency with which the various agencies worked together (hypothesis 2). Curiously, though, evaluations have been at pains to avoid such a conclusion – it was unacknowledged in the original reports (Forrester et al., 1988; Forrester et al., 1990) and has been denied by others in terms suggesting that the (unnamed) critics were motivated merely by envy at the success of the Burglary Prevention Project (see Pawson and Tilley, 1997, p. 128; Farrell, 1995, p. 493). A more charitable view – and one that is perhaps somewhat less *parti pris* – would be that such 'critics' had different concerns, particularly to assess the significance of the Kirkholt Development Project as a *housing-related* crime prevention programme (Safe Neighbourhoods Unit, 1993) in more holistic 'comprehensive community initiative' terms (cf. Connell et al., 1995). The full cost of the Development Project has also been ignored in efforts to use Kirkholt in comparative cost–benefit analyses (Welsh and Farrington, 1999), largely, it seems, 'because of the many difficulties presented in assessing the validity of the criticisms' (*sic*) (Welsh and Farrington, 1998, p. 358), though including them would also have altered the favourable benefit–cost ratio attributed to the Kirkholt Burglary Prevention Project (Welsh and Farrington, 1999).

Yet, in contrast, a key conclusion of Ekblom and colleagues' highly internally reliable evaluation of Safer Cities Phase I burglary reduction initiatives seems particularly relevant – 'the more intense the [preventive] burglary action, the greater the additional drop in risk' (Ekblom et al., 1996, p. xvi). Intensive prevention schemes were the more costly ones (as were ones which concentrated resources in small areas), and to achieve a greater reduction in the intensive-activity areas cost disproportionately more than the average cost per burglary reduced. Finally, the strongest and most reliable effect on burglary was when all the various elements of crime prevention were present, suggesting that 'a comprehensive approach is best' (Ekblom et al., 1996, p. 42). Not only does this study represent a highly reliable replication, capable by virtue of its 'quasi-experimental' research design of yielding generalizable conclusions, but also we actually seem to have found – via hypothesis 2 – a generalizable replication road leading from Kirkholt: a road seemingly more reliable than that taken in pursuit of hypothesis 1. Thus, rather than simply extracting the repeat victimization story – in the belief that it was what was most useful about Kirkholt – it might have been equally 'useful' to policy-makers to find out what would be involved in organizing intensive, efficient and sustainable multiple interventions to bring about the kind of dramatic reduction noticeable at Kirkholt and some of the other estates noted above (see Stafford and Silverlock, 2000). But that was a road not taken (so far).

Conclusion

It remains an historical puzzle – and probably part of the explanation of the particular selection bias involved – as to why the *ex post facto* replication narratives about Kirkholt did not seek additional tests of the basic hypothesis 1 effect (i.e. that the reduction in the incidence rate was due solely to efforts to reduce the concentration rate) and denied the possibility of hypothesis 2 (that Kirkholt achieved its effect through its intensity of action). Whatever the reason, though, the ability to posit alternative replication narratives underscores the potential *vulnerability to selection bias* of the scientific realist approach to replication. Campbell (1969) prioritized avoidance of the possibility of administrators perpetrating selection biases (wittingly or unwittingly) in the presentation to the wider public of information about public programmes. He recognized that this might be a difficult task to achieve *politically*. To move towards realizing his aspiration of the 'experimenting society' it would be necessary not only to impose the rigour of the experiment but also to educate the public as to why designs of such rigour – or adherence to the rationale of science underpinning them – were needed, difficult though they might be to implement properly. For Campbell, then, the proper stance for the evaluator was as a 'scientist' – a public custodian of a *method of reasoning*, whose application would advance the public good. Yet, in the years that have followed, both Campbell's followers and their opponents have shared a different expectation – that in order to be useful it is necessary to produce useful knowledge that purports to be of practical assistance to policy administrators.

Judged by this standard, the scientific realist case has been that, in most actual circumstances, the experimental paradigm is neither practicable to implement nor useful as a generator of practical knowledge. Yet in advocating an alternative the realists may have thrown out the external methodological checks that would save them from perpetrating selection biases of various kinds on behalf of their political sponsors, albeit with the best of intentions of contributing to the public good. The closeness achieved by social-scientists-cum-policy-entrepreneurs in gaining access to the policy process (see also Tilley, 1993a), though it may have helped to advance the contribution of criminology to public policy, may not have helped to maintain the scientific rigour necessary to avoid becoming 'trapped' in particular policy predicaments and claims, not unlike their more overt political colleagues. Writing about 'experimentation and criminal policy development in Britain', Nick Tilley notes the institutional advantages of having research managers within government:

> This direct, in-house relationship between policy maker and researcher brings significant advantages. *The research agenda can be tailored to the policy-making one* . . . Informed researchers can steer research programs in directions likely to be fruitful for future policy making. (Tilley, 2000, p. 205; emphasis added)

But the disadvantage is perhaps not just that, as Tilley further notes, 'there may be some loss of an independent, critical edge' (2000, p. 205), but that abandonment of the methodological checks which might safeguard some degree of independence of results renders such researchers-cum-policy-entrepreneurs all the more vulnerable to the pressures and temptations of their political environment. And if, at the end of the day, the results become misleading or partial, the Faustian bargain that social scientists may be tempted to make in the pursuit of 'what works' may not be worth it.

Notes

†   The title of this chapter makes reference to the poem *The Road Not Taken* by Robert Frost which contains the following passage 'Two roads diverged in a wood, and I- / I took the one less travelled by / and that has made all the difference'. The relevance of the ideas in this poem to the recent history of crime reduction and evaluation research will become apparent as the argument of the chapter develops.

An earlier version of this chapter was presented at the British Society of Criminology Conference 2000, Leicester, July 2000.

1   Named after the researcher who carried out an influential American 'what works' review of the effectiveness of penal treatment (Martinson, 1974).

2   'The facts relevant to experimental program evaluation are also available to argue the general efficiency and honesty of administrators' (Campbell, 1978, p. 80).

3   As a simple illustration of its impact, a 'Boolean' word search on the internet search engine AltaVista.co.uk on 13 November 2000 yielded seventy-three pages of web links making reference to the project.

4   'More detailed investigation as part of this case study, however, has found evidence of many other security measures which are equally likely to have had an effect on burglary and which were overlooked in the original assessment of the burglary demonstration project' (Safe Neighbourhoods Unit, 1994, p. 67).

5   There is a peculiar set of inconsistencies here. On the one hand, Sherman et al. (1998a) rate the 'Kirkholt Project' at the highest level of their scale of scientific rigour (p. 11); on the other hand, elsewhere they rate it only at an intermediate 'level 3' (in table 7-2 in Eck in Sherman et al., 1998b; see Sherman et al. 1998a, p. 5, for an explanation), consistent with other interpretations of the source material (see also Welsh and Farrington, 1999, p. 357; Hope, 1995a, pp. 62–64). In particular, an analysis comparing the Kirkholt estate with another produced inconclusive results for the specific effect on repeat victimization (Forrester et al., 1988, appendix B) and was not pursued in the Kirkholt Phase II report (Forrester et al., 1990).

6   Again, there are inconsistencies here: Pawson and Tilley (1997), Tilley (1993b) and Farrell (1995) refer to an 'unpublished study' by Farrington (1992) entitled 'Was the Kirkholt Burglary Prevention Project effective?' which, according to Tilley (1993b), 'has attempted independently to referee between . . . interpretations of the burglary reduction by reanalysing data from Kirkholt

itself. Its results were favourable to the conclusion of the original report, *though this has failed to satisfy all sceptics*' (p. 2; emphasis added). Nevertheless, the author does not encourage citation of this report (Farrington, 2000).
7 My account here is based on Tilley (2000).
8 Burglary rates were calculated directly from the survey data.
9 Again, burglary rates have been calculated directly from the survey data.

References

Barr, R. and Pease, K. (1992) 'A place for every crime and every crime in its place: an alternative perspective on crime displacement' in Evans, D.J., Fyfe, N.R. and Herbert, D.J. (eds) *Crime Policing and Place: Essays in Environmental Criminology*, London, Routledge.

Beck, U. (1992) *Risk Society: Towards a New Modernity* (trans. M. Ritter) London, Sage.

Beckett, K. and Sasson, T. (2000) *The Politics of Injustice: Crime and Punishment in America*, Thousand Oaks, CA, Pine Forge Press.

Bennett, T. (1996) 'What's new in evaluation research?', *British Journal of Criminology*, vol. 31, no. 1, pp. 1–14.

Bridgeman, C. and Sampson, A. (1994) *Wise After the Event: Tackling Repeat Victimization*, London, National Board for Crime Prevention.

Brody, S. (1976) *The Effectiveness of Sentencing*, Home Office Research Study 35, London, HMSO.

Campbell, D.T. (1969) 'Reforms as experiments', *American Psychologist*, vol. 24, pp. 409–29.

Campbell, D.T. (1978) 'Reforms as experiments' in Bynner, J. and Stribley, K.M. (eds) *Social Research: Principles and Procedures*, London, Longman/Open University.

Campbell, D.T. and Stanley, J.C. (1963) *Experimental and Quasi-experimental Designs for Research*, Chicago, IL, Rand McNally.

Clarke, R.V. (ed.) (1992) *Situational Crime Prevention: Successful Case Studies*, New York, Harrow & Heston.

Clarke, R.V. and Cornish, D. (1983) *Crime Control in Britain: A Review of Policy Research*, Albany, NY, SUNY Press.

Clarke, R.V. and Hough, M. (eds) (1980) *The Effectiveness of Policing*, Farnborough, Gower.

Connell, J.P. et al. (1995) *New Approaches to Evaluating Community Initiatives*, Washington, DC, Aspen Institute.

Cook, T.D. and Campbell, D.T. (1979) *Quasi-experimentation: Design and Analysis for Field Settings*, Boston, MA, Houghton Mifflin.

Ekblom, P. and Pease, K. (1995) 'Evaluating crime prevention' in Tonry, M. and Farrington, D.P. (eds) *Building a Safer Society*, Chicago, IL, University of Chicago Press.

Ekblom, P., Law, H. and Sutton, M. (1996) *Safer Cities and Domestic Burglary*, Home Office Research Study 164, London, Home Office.

Farrell, G. (1995) 'Preventing repeat victimization' in Tonry, M. and Farrington, D.P. (eds) *Building a Safer Society*, Chicago, IL, University of Chicago Press.

Farrell, G. and Pease, K. (1993) 'Once bitten, twice bitten: repeat victimization and its implications for crime prevention', Crime Prevention Unit Paper 46, London, Home Office.

Farrington, D.P. (1996) *Understanding and Preventing Youth Crime*, York, Joseph Rowntree Foundation.

Farrington, D.P. (2000) Personal communication, 14 July.

Felson, M. (1998) *Crime and Everyday Life* (2nd edn), Thousand Oaks, CA, Pine Forge Press.

Forrester, D., Chatterton, M. and Pease, K. (1988) *The Kirkholt Burglary Prevention Project, Rochdale*, Crime Prevention Unit Paper 13, London, Home Office.

Forrester, D., Frenz, S., O'Connell, M. and Pease, K. (1990) *The Kirkholt Burglary Prevention Project: Phase II*, Crime Prevention Unit Paper 23, London, Home Office.

Foster, J. and Hope, T. (1993) *Housing, Community and Crime: The Impact of the Priority Estates Project*, Home Office Research Study 131, London, HMSO.

Garland, D. (1996) 'The limits of the sovereign state: strategies of crime control in contemporary society', *British Journal of Criminology*, vol. 36, no. 4, pp. 445–71.

Garland, D. (2000) 'The culture of high crime societies: some preconditions of recent "law and order" policies', *British Journal of Criminology*, vol. 40, no. 3, pp. 347–75.

Giddens, A. (1990) *The Consequences of Modernity*, Cambridge, Polity Press.

Glennerster, H. and Turner, T. (1993) *Estate Based Housing Management: An Evaluation*, Department of the Environment, London, HMSO.

Goldblatt, P. and Lewis, C. (eds) (1998) *Reducing Offending: An Assessment of Research Evidence on ways of Dealing with Offending Behaviour*, Home Office Research Study 187, London, Home Office.

Hope, T. (1995a) 'Community crime prevention' in Tonry, M. and Farrington, D.P. (eds) *Building a Safer Society*, Chicago, IL, University of Chicago Press.

Hope, T. (1995b) 'The flux of victimization', *British Journal of Criminology*, vol. 35, pp. 327–42.

Hope, T. and Sparks, R. (eds) (2000) *Crime, Risk and Insecurity: Law and Order in Everyday Life and Political Discourse*, London, Routledge.

Hughes, G. (1998) *Understanding Crime Prevention: Social Control, Risk and Late Modernity*, Buckingham, Open University Press.

Martinson, R. (1974) 'What works? Questions and answers about prison reform', *Public Interest*, vol. 35, pp. 22–54.

Oakley, A. (2000) *Experiments in Knowing: Gender and Method in the Social Sciences*, Cambridge, Polity Press.

Pawson, R. and Tilley, N. (1994) 'What works in evaluation research?', *British Journal of Criminology*, vol. 34, pp. 291–306.

Pawson, R. and Tilley, N. (1997) *Realistic Evaluation*, London, Sage.

Pease, K. (1998) *Repeat Victimization: Taking Stock*, Crime Detection and Prevention Series Paper 90, London, Home Office.

Pease, K. and Laycock, G. (1996) 'Revictimization: reducing the heat on hot victims', *Research in Action*, National Institute of Justice, Washington, DC, US Department of Justice.

Petrosino, A. (2000) Personal communication, 10 November, Co-ordinator Campbell Crime and Justice Group, American Academy of Arts and Sciences and Harvard University, Cambridge, MA.

Price Waterhouse (1997) *The Design Improvement Controlled Experiment (DICE): An Evaluation of the Impact, Costs and Benefits of Estate Re-modelling*, Regeneration Research Report, London, Department of the Environment.

Safe Neighbourhoods Unit (1993) *Crime Prevention on Council Estates*, Department of the Environment, London, HMSO.

Safe Neighbourhoods Unit (1994) *Housing Safe Communities: An Evaluation of Recent Initiatives*, Department of the Environment, London, HMSO.

Sherman, L., Gottfredson, D., McKenzie, D., Eck, J., Reuter, P. and Bushway, S. (1998a) *Preventing Crime: What Works, What Doesn't, What's Promising*, Research in Brief, National Institute of Justice, Washington, DC, Department of Justice.

Sherman, L., Gottfredson, D., McKenzie, D., Eck, J., Reuter, P. and Bushway, S. (1998b) 'Preventing crime: what works, what doesn't, what's promising', National Criminal Justice Referencing Service (http://www.ncjrs.org/works/wholedoc.htm).

Stafford, J. and Silverlock, L. (2000) 'What works and what makes what works work?' in Ballintyne, S., Pease, K. and McLaren, V. (eds) *Secure Foundations: Key Issues in Crime Prevention, Crime Reduction and Community Safety*, London, Institute for Public Policy Research.

Tilley, N. (1993a) 'Crime prevention and the safer cities story', *Howard Journal*, vol. 32, pp. 40–57.

Tilley, N. (1993b) *After Kirkholt: Theory, Method and Results of Replication Evaluations*, Crime Prevention Unit Series Paper 47, London, Home Office.

Tilley, N. (2000) 'Experimentation and criminal justice', *Crime and Delinquency*, vol. 46, pp. 194–213.

Tonry, M. and Farrington, D.P. (eds) (1995), *Building a Safer Society: Strategic Approaches to Crime Prevention*, Crime and Justice vol. 19, Chicago, IL, University of Chicago Press.

Trickett, A., Osborn, D.R., Seymour, J. and Pease, K. (1992) 'What is different about high crime areas?', *British Journal of Criminology*, vol. 32, no. 1, pp. 81–9.

Trickett, A., Ellingworth, D., Hope, T. and Pease, K. (1995) 'Crime victimization in the eighties', *British Journal of Criminology*, vol. 35, pp. 343–59.

Welsh, B.C. and Farrington, D.P. (1998) 'Assessing the effectiveness and economic benefits of an integrated developmental and situational crime prevention initiative', *Psychology, Crime and Law*, pp. 341–68.

Welsh, B. and Farrington, D. (1999) 'Value for money? A review of the costs and benefits of situational crime prevention', *British Journal of Criminology*, vol. 39, pp. 345–68.

Young, J. (1999) *The Exclusive Society*, London, Sage.

4

Gendering crime prevention

Exploring the tensions between policy and process

Sandra Walklate

> . . . the state alone is not, and cannot effectively be, responsible for preventing and controlling crime. Property owners, residents, retailers, manufacturers, town planners, school authorities, transport managers, employers, parents and individual citizens – all of these must be made to recognize that they too have a responsibility in this regard, and must be persuaded to change their practices in order to reduce criminal opportunities and increase informal controls. In effect, central government is, in this field of policy as in several others, operating upon established boundaries which separate the private from the public realm, seeking to renegotiate the question of what is properly a state function and what is not. (Garland, 1996, p. 445)

> The first duty of government is to protect the lives and property of all citizens, and thus by definition, reduce the citizen's likelihood of becoming a victim of crime. (Editorial, *Police*, vol. xxxi, no 4, April 1999)

The quotations above allude to the way in which not only has the public come to expect to be protected by the criminal justice system (freedom from risk) but also the extent to which governments have increasingly seen it as part of their responsibility to put in place mechanisms whereby such protection can be delivered. However, part of Garland's thesis is to note that the criminal justice system has gradually adapted to its failure to control rising crime rates and by implication failed in providing protection. This process of adaptation is characterized by Garland as a process of 'responsibilization' in which we are all encouraged to share actively the increasing burden posed by the problem of crime. Indeed, it is now almost commonplace to observe that crime prevention has to all intents and purposes become victimization prevention (Karmen, 1990). We are increasingly encouraged to protect ourselves. Yet, as we shall see, there are evident tensions in the processes of change that these observations imply. The purpose of this chapter is to offer a critical exploration of this process of responsibilization and to ask whether or not a more meaningful understanding of the crime prevention dimensions to it might be better constructed if it were examined through a gendered lens.

This chapter then discusses crime prevention under four main headings: a public sense of well-being; a private sense of well-being; a gendered sense of well-being and a structured sense of well-being. These headings are intended to alert us to both the presences and the absences in the debates around crime prevention by identifying the differing focus, strategy and style of various crime prevention policies. In so doing it is hoped that the terms 'crime', 'prevention' and 'gender' associated with these different headings will be rendered more problematic, not just as a rhetorical device but as a way of encouraging more critical thinking about what is knowable and doable about crime. These labels have also been adopted to highlight the value of situating the specific issues relating to crime prevention in the broader historical context of the risk society and the demand for protection. But, first, some general observations about the changing nature of crime prevention.

Changing directions in crime prevention policy

In some respects the headings adopted in this chapter reflect in and of themselves the way in which discussions concerning crime and its prevention have altered in emphasis over the last thirty years. The current focus is not only on the prevention of (recurring) criminal behaviour but also on securing a sense of feeling safe both in public and in private for everyone in society. In this latter respect both Garland and Karmen, referred to above, are correct in the observations they have made about the changing nature of crime prevention activity. Crime prevention activity is no longer seen as the preserve of the police. Since the 1970s policy in this area has shifted from an exclusive emphasis on the police through notions of inter-agency working, multi-agency working and the more currently popular idea of partnership. Indeed, this latter notion has been made a legal requirement under the Crime and Disorder Act 1998. Moreover these same policy orientations have had different foci of activity – the offender, the victim, the community, respectively – and have had different styles of implementation – top-down or bottom-up – all of which renders the crime prevention scene a relatively complex one. In addition, the absence of a clear and consistent understanding of what would count as a sound evaluation of such policies has contributed to the uncertainty concerning what is prevented, where, when and how.

However, in general terms, prevention is seen to be a 'good' thing because social problems are a bad thing (Freeman, 1992). This is the case whether or not the issue is public health or crime. It is clear that any understanding of prevention entails two strategies: predicting an outcome and being able to intervene in (that is, alter) a predicted outcome. In the context of crime this presumes that we can identify the cause(s) of crime and subsequently prohibit its commission. If this were indeed the case, the discipline of criminology would look somewhat different. Moreover the positive connotations associated with the prevention industry reflect more deeply held societal concerns. Those concerns, as Douglas (1992) has argued, can be articulated as a view of risk management as being equated with risk avoidance. Walklate (1997) has identified the problems that such deeply held assumptions hold for criminology. Such problems, however, are present in crime prevention policy and arguably reflect more fundamental (generative) mechanisms which underpin the nature and structure of contemporary social relations. Such relations are to a greater or lesser degree informed by our sense of 'ontological security' (Giddens, 1990), our sense of well-being, hence the use of the term in this chapter as a way of making some critical sense of the complexity of the contemporary nature of crime prevention activity.

A public sense of well-being

As this section heading suggests, there is a clear dimension within crime prevention policy that focuses on public space. Much of the crime prevention activity of the 1980s, whether it be situational crime prevention or social crime prevention, had as its focus of concern public space. How public space might be rendered safer can take different forms. Interventions can centre on the offender, the victim, the environment, the community or any combination of these. We shall therefore briefly discuss each in turn.

Some policy initiatives centre on the offender and can be 'hard' or 'soft'. In October 1993, for example, Michael Howard, then Home

Secretary, made an impassioned plea to the Conservative Party conference that 'Prison works!' Such a way of dealing with offenders, especially recidivists, is neither novel nor cheap but invokes a presumed deterrent effect of the criminal justice system. However, 'enforcement crackdowns' (Elias, 1986) can have a softer edge. Initiatives such as the introduction of Intermediate Treatment in the late 1970s and early 1980s for (potential) juvenile offenders, and latterly mediation and reparation projects under the auspices of the Crime and Disorder Act 1998, are also designed with preventive goals in mind. Initiatives such as these presume that offenders are educable and, through targeting, their behaviour can be redirected.

Whether hard or soft, offender-centred policies assume that the cause of offending behaviour lies within the individual. And whilst there is some evidence that factors such as personality, attitude and moral sense predispose some individuals to criminality, an exclusive focus on the individual in this way offers only part of the picture of the causation of crime. Other policies designed to focus on public space address the contribution that the victim may make to the production of criminal behaviour.

Victim-centred policies, rather like offender-centred policies, can also take different forms. The victim of crime can, of course, be an individual property or an individual human being and different crime prevention activity (here, clearly, read victimization avoidance activity) has been developed. So the individual victim is exhorted to fit the appropriate window locks to reduce the likelihood of burglary, or to use an approved steering-wheel lock to avoid car theft, or to avoid putting themselves in public situations where they might be at risk. This latter theme has been particularly directed towards women. As Stanko observes:

> Crime prevention advice revolves around public crime. And while the police and criminal justice system are slowly becoming involved, private violence is still seen as something different than public violence. Crime prevention advice, including much of the advice about avoiding sexual assault, focuses on the public domain. It is easier to give advice about checking the back seat of your car for intruders, or advising against standing at dimly lit bus stops, than finding ways of advising women not to trust so-called 'trustworthy' men. (Stanko, 1990, p. 4)

We shall discuss crime prevention in the private domain shortly, but Stanko's comment tells us much about the questions of crime, responsibility and avoidance with which this chapter began. Whilst the individualistic approach presumed by offender-centred and victim-centred policies may be seen as problematic in different ways, it can be argued that the focus on the environment, which is the concern of some policies addressing public space, is less contentious.

Environment-centred crime prevention policy can target specific crimes or can be of the more general approach of 'designing out' crime. The overall purpose of this kind of activity is to manipulate the environment in such a way as to reduce the overall opportunity for crime to occur. This focus on the environment presumes that the cause of crime lies in the physical structures/opportunities made available to the offender (rather than the risk/reward ratio for the offender) and assumes that offenders engage in a rational decision-making process, choosing how and under what circumstances to offend. The extent to which offenders actually do this is a moot point, but there is no doubt that the presence of opportunities to commit crime can increase the likelihood of its occurrence. So, the problems of displacement notwithstanding (see Barr and Pease, 1992), reducing opportunity reduces facilitation (though not necessarily causation).

There is one final theme that can be identified in the search for a public sense of well-being; that policy theme has differently endeavoured to harness the idea of community. As Crawford (1995, p. 98) has pointed out, the concept of community is 'both a signifier and a referent around which complex and contradictory effects, meanings and definitional struggles coalesce'. And as a concept it certainly has contemporary relevance in governmental concern to 'Bring Britain together' (Social Exclusion Unit, 1998). It is important to note that since the early 1980s much effort has been put into harnessing the 'community' towards an improved public sense of well-being. This has taken two main forms: that which invokes the community as a citizen watcher (Neighbourhood Watch through to crime prevention patrols); and that which invokes the community as agency-led co-operation (from Safer Cities to more current notions of partnership). Each of these strands raises different though related questions: the first about who watches, where, when and with what resources; the second about who works with whom, how and with what resources. Nonetheless each has a similar crime focus: property crime, street crime or nuisances.

All these versions of enhancing a public sense of well-being may have something to offer in the limited context of our understanding what works, where, when and how. They share a focus on public space; they share in an individualistic and/or opportunistic view of the cause of crime; they presume equality of citizenship; and for the most part they share in a 'top-down' policy implementation style. But what crime prevention couched in these terms lacks is what Currie (1988) has called 'structural awareness'. This lack of awareness renders invisible the questions of whose crime, whose offenders, whose community? A consideration of questions such as these is one route into considering the second strand to the nature of crime prevention under consideration here: a private sense of well-being.

A private sense of well-being

In this section we shall consider the nature and extent of activity which has been directed towards the issue of 'domestic' violence during the 1990s. Home Office Circular 60/1990 constituted a landmark in directing policy energy to crime behind closed doors. The two-dimensional attack on 'domestic' violence of supporting the 'victim' and arresting the offender, borrowed from North America and enshrined in that circular, heralded an increase in police resources and responsiveness to this issue.

Home Office Circular 60/1990, which was issued to all chief constables (and other chief executives of various service delivery agencies), urged police forces to treat 'domestic' violence as seriously as violence occurring between strangers in the street. The circular reminded chief constables in particular of the range of statutory and common law powers available to them to arrest perpetrators of violence, and encouraged them to consider the establishment of dedicated 'domestic' violence units as part of their policy response to support the victims. The circular offered a twofold approach to domestic violence: a presumption-of-arrest policy, backed by a policy framework supportive of the victim.

In some respects this has been a very influential Home Office circular. As Radford and Stanko (1991) have commented, police forces appear to have been competing with one another to see which can put into practice the most imaginative policy response to the issue. This is not the place, however, to discuss the strengths and weaknesses of such a policy document in relation to 'domestic' violence. Suffice it to say that this policy constitutes a partial translation to the United Kingdom of an essentially North American response to 'domestic' violence. This in itself poses some difficulties without addressing whether or not as a policy it constituted an adequate or effective way of responding to the needs of women. The central concern here is what such a policy response represents in relation to the question of crime prevention.

In many ways, as a preventive response, the strategies recommended and subsequently adopted following Circular 60/1990 represent an offender-centred 'enforcement crackdown' policy (see above and Elias, 1986). It rests on the assumption that treating 'domestic' violence like other incidents of violence will have a preventive effect. In other words, it is presumed that treating such behaviour as an offence and using the available legal framework to arrest the perpetrator will have two consequences. First, it will convey the general message that such behaviour is no longer acceptable. Second, the act of arresting the perpetrator will deter that individual from engaging in similar behaviour in the future. A number of questions follow from this kind of policy stance on this issue.

First, the policy rests on the presumption that arrest does have a deterrent effect in such circumstances. The evidence for this is partial and inconclusive, and in some circumstances an arrest may actually make the situation worse for the victim (Berk and Sherman, 1984; Sherman, 1992). Second, the policy also presumes that the normative response of police officers is to arrest the offender in non-domestic incidents of violence. As Chatterton (1983) and others have shown, the decision to arrest is a far more complex process. Moreover, these presumptions are particularly interesting given the patent failure of arrest to deter persistent offenders from committing other kinds of crime. Why, then, should it be presumed that arrest is a reasonable deterrent strategy in 'domestic' incidents?

Asking questions such as these is not intended to imply, of course, that such a strategy should be either abandoned or not taken seriously. Any strategy which affords some protection for a woman (or anyone else) in a violent relationship, for however short a period, has to be acknowledged as offering her something and, perhaps more important, conveys the message that her needs are being taken seriously. What this discussion is intended to draw our attention to is the individualistic offender-centred nature of this policy as a crime prevention policy, policy in which the rhetoric of the community is notable for its absence. This absence is all the more remarkable given the sheer weight of its presence in policy response across a broad spectrum of other issues since the early 1980s. In addition, the North American evidence on which policies in this area appear to draw so heavily indicates that a presumption-of-arrest policy is at its most effective when put in place alongside a range of other community-based initiatives such as refuge facilities for women and children, counselling initiatives for men and so on (see, for example, Jaffe et al., 1986), making this absence perhaps all the more surprising. What has not been absent from these developments, as this policy initiative has unfolded in practice, has been a focus on a multi-agency approach to co-ordinate common local practice on the issue.

The foregoing discussion presumes that one of the goals of this policy initiative on 'domestic' violence was indeed crime prevention, which may, of course, not necessarily be the case. Indeed, there is some evidence to suggest otherwise. It may make some sense, for example, to view this particular kind of policy as constituting part of a range of processes occurring within policing to do with 'value for money', efficiency and securing consent, rather than as a crime prevention policy. Yet the policy does convey a preventive message: arrest the offender and support the victim. This is a preventive message that raises some fundamentally contradictory questions for crime prevention policy in relation to women in particular.

Whilst the focus of concern on the nature and extent of 'domestic' violence makes the maleness of the crime problem more visible, the question remains as to why, for example, so much crime prevention literature focuses on the threat to women from strangers, when women know that those most likely to be troublesome to them are so-called 'trustworthy' men, i.e. men they know and/or live with. On the other hand, raising awareness of the maleness of the crime problem raises other questions about the viability of devising community responses to this, or any other, crime problem. In other words, to what extent is it possible to presume that any community into which a preventive initiative might be introduced is a coherent one in which all individuals share the same or similar concerns about the same or similar law-breaking activity? So what this pursuit of a private sense of well-being has achieved is to encourage us to think much more carefully about what is both visible and invisible in the community crime prevention industry. In so doing it also encourages us to think about communities in relation to crime as experienced differently by men and women.

In summary, recent initiatives focusing on private space as opposed to public space share some of the same characteristics as those focusing on public space. The main message has reflected concern to criminalize the offender, and to support the victim through inter-agency or multi-agency co-operation, characterized for the most part by a 'top-down' policy implementation style. This has resulted in policy proceeding again with little sense of what might actually work, for whom, where, when and how, though it does succeed in recognizing the maleness of much criminal behaviour. However, what has been remarkably absent from much of the policy discourse and practice in this area is the notion of community. How might communities be harnessed to tackle the issue of 'domestic' violence? Communities are, of course, layered (Massey, 1994): in other words, it is a mistake to presume that all members of a community will share the same concerns and will want to respond to the same concerns. This question leads us to consider a much deeper understanding of what a genuinely gendered approach to crime prevention (or well-being) might look like.

A gendered sense of well-being

The early 1990s were marked by other events that have subsequently fuelled some aspects of the crime prevention debate. The murder of James Bulger contributed to emotional debate not only about the evil nature of such a crime but also about the more general propensity of young males to engage in crime. On the one hand this debate contributed to the further demonization of the single-parent family (Tuck, 1993), and, on the other, Campbell's (1993) analysis of the civil disturbances of 1991 offered the conclusion that: 'Crime and coercion are sustained by men. Solidarity and self-help are sustained by women. It is as stark as that.'

Of course, as Campbell goes on to recognize, it is not quite as stark as that, but the comment leads us to think about who does what in communities and how community life is actually experienced and structured. This is part of what Massey (1994) refers to as understanding the layering of communities. In furthering our understanding of the gendered nature of communities, this discussion will draw on the findings of a longitudinal study of two, predominantly white, high-crime areas conducted from 1994 to 1996 (see Walklate and Evans, 1999). The two areas involved in this study are referred to as Oldtown and Bankhill. This study covered a number of issues but was primarily concerned with understanding how people routinely manage their sense of well-being (their ontological security) and makes some interesting observations about the gendered nature of such security as well as the gendered nature of crime. But first I shall make some general observations about the concerns of the people living in these two localities.

The 1994 British Crime Survey showed that people worried more about burglary than any other crime and that people living in the inner city tend to report higher levels of fear of all crimes. In the study Evans and I asked similar questions in a survey of people living in our two research areas. We found the fear of crime to be gendered in Oldtown. In that area women taking part in the survey did say that they worried more about a whole range of crimes than did the men. Similar numbers of men and women said they worried about most property crime but significantly more women than men said that they worried about their personal safety, both during daylight hours and after dark. In fact, men worried more than women about only one crime – that of having their car stolen. In Bankhill, where stated fear of crime was generally higher than in Oldtown, these gender differences were far less apparent. So whilst it is not possible directly to compare these survey findings with those of the British Crime Survey, it is clear that the gendered nature of the fear of crime in Oldtown compared more directly with that highlighted by the British Crime Survey.

Women in Oldtown generally worried more than men in a range of different situations – being home alone, being attacked by a stranger, being harassed in the street, being robbed in the street, and in addition, after dark they worried about walking past pubs and about using public transport – though again locality was an important variable in these expressed concerns. Certainly in Canalside, a small area within Oldtown, in discussion groups much of the talk relating to the fear of crime was different for the men than for the women. Women in these focus groups shared an experience of feeling threatened both inside and outside the home, whereas a male resident of the locality expressed this view: 'maybe because I'm male, I don't know what it feels like to be threatened in this area'.

But in the Triangle, another small area within Oldtown, most people talked about feeling safe most of the time. In the Triangle women were more clearly involved in local networks, perhaps based around their family or local commitments. Some of the women talked here of feeling uncomfortable in the park or the shopping precinct where young men congregate, but other women said that they felt safe everywhere. This latter group tended to be the women with the longest-standing links and social networks within the community, who knew the young men who were hanging around. In the south end of the Triangle residents said they felt safer than anywhere else in the ward. People here felt that the community had been able to take control of some of its problems (for example, young people had been actively involved by other community members to think about the consequences of their actions) and, as a result, expressed levels of fear of crime were much lower than elsewhere in the ward.

To summarize, whilst much is made in the general literature of sex differences in relation to crime and the fear of crime, in Oldtown the relationship is neither simple nor straightforward. It is clear that overall the women in the area expressed worries about crime to a greater degree than the men, but what is also clear is that these expressed differences were mediated by locality and involvement in the locality. Again the assertion of locality or some sense of local identity and belonging seems to influence how people manage their routine construction of well-being. Indeed, interestingly enough, when people were asked in discussion groups who they thought were most likely to be the victims of crime and the offenders in the area, people in Canalside thought that people living in the Triangle were most likely to fit both categories and people in the Triangle thought it would fit those living in Canalside. On the other hand, differences such as these could not be discerned in the data gathered from Bankhill. For people in Bankhill age rather than sex seemed to be the salient variable (see below). Having become sensitive to some of the general features of the views expressed by people in these areas, the question remains of how it is possible to understand them. One way of progressing our understanding is by appreciating the way in which people in each of the areas understood and related to the problem of crime in their district.

Both areas are known as high-crime areas. The locations in the survey are part of the Salford Division of the Greater Manchester Police. The recorded crime rate for Salford as a whole was, at the time of the study, significantly higher than the national average: for example, in 1992 the incidence of recorded crime in England and Wales was 10,500 offences per 100,000 population, and in Salford it was 16,660. The two areas in the survey did not correspond with police boundaries, but the recorded burglary rate, for example, for the subdivision in which Bankhill was situated was 70.3 per 1,000 population in 1993, and was 88.4 per 1,000 population for the subdivision which included Oldtown. Moreover, police officers believe that there is significant underreporting of crime in each of these areas. Indeed, our own criminal victimization survey, conducted in August 1994, reported that 23.7 per cent of people in Oldtown and 36.9 per cent of people in Bankhill had been victims of crime in the previous year. Analysis of command and control data covering the beats relevant to these two localities for the month of January 1995 suggests that on a daily average twenty-one incidents are reported in Oldtown (one per eleven residents) and twenty-four in Bankhill (one per twenty-four residents) – though, of course, it must be remembered that not all these incidents are necessarily crime-related nor are they necessarily recorded as crimes.

Sources of data such as command and control data and criminal victimization survey data provide one way of constructing an understanding of the crime problem in each of these localities and, consequently, one way of formulating policy responses to that problem. Indeed, the policy implementation process suggested by the Morgan Report (Home Office, 1991) recommended that such sources of data should be used to inform community safety initiatives, and similar data sources have been used in local crime audits undertaken as part of the implementation process of the Crime and Disorder Act 1998.

Using data sources such as these, it could be taken that the crime problem in these two localities is of a fairly conventional nature, that is, burglary, car crime and criminal damage. Consequently practitioners may be persuaded that policy can also be conventionally informed, as, for example, the introduction and resourcing of Neighbourhood Watch schemes as a means of tackling burglary. However, reliance on such data sources alone would address only the surface manifestation of the crime problem in localities such as Oldtown and Bankhill. These data do not penetrate its deep structure. Other sources of information afford a better insight. One place where clues to this deep structure can be found is in the discussions which took place in the local Police/Community Consultative Forums in each of these areas.

Police/Community Consultative Group meetings, held monthly, were attended regularly by around thirty people from Oldtown and towards sixty in the Bankhill area. Analysis of the minutes of these meetings from February 1994 to July 1996 reveals that there were four recurring themes in both areas: how to deal with troublesome youth, the problem of intimidation, the impact of force restructuring, and the slow response to 999 calls. In addition, in Bankhill frequent concern was expressed about the possible closure of the local police station and the rapidity of turnover of local police personnel.

So whilst what went on in police/community consultative meetings does not match exactly the concerns highlighted in other sources of data, there is enough similarity in the concerns expressed to suggest that such meetings were not just giving a voice to those who chose to attend, but were tapping more widely held community concerns. What is particularly interesting in respect of those more widely held community concerns is the expressed problem of intimidation. In-depth interview and focus group data gathered in both of these areas facilitated a deeper understanding of what this more qualitative talk about crime was articulating.

Depending upon where you live in Oldtown the experience of crime can be very different. In the Canalside and The Way (where the incidence of home ownership is at its highest), people were concerned that their houses or sheds might be broken into or objects taken from their garden. In discussion groups in these areas we found that people were much more likely to talk about taking preventive measures against crime, by planting prickly shrubs near fences or buying alarms for houses and cars. Crime here was talked about as a nuisance rather than a major threat to peace of mind. However, in other parts of the ward, commonly known as the Triangle, the central talk about crime focused on groups of young males who gathered in particular parts of the estate and were seen to be involved in a good deal of antisocial behaviour. It is here that we can begin to get a feel for the problem of intimidation.

The problem of intimidation has been discussed in the context of Oldtown in greater detail elsewhere (see Evans et al., 1996). Indeed, in 1994 the area was chosen as part of a Home Office-sponsored survey dealing with the question of intimidation but the survey was left incomplete as the interviewers were 'asked' to leave the area after two days! Here the idea that 'You're all right round here if you're local' has considerable force; and such 'being local' has less to do with length of residence than sticking to a particular code of conduct. This code includes not 'grassing to the police' and not openly working against the interests of the criminal gang which has a significant local presence. In return the gang offers to cut down on the number of local people who will be victims of crime by letting people know that crime against local people will not be tolerated and by punishing those who break this code.

The gang (all male) therefore can and does intimidate local residents, many of whom keep quiet and do not 'grass' to the authorities rather than incur the displeasure of the gang. Indeed, in the middle of Oldtown there is an area where nearly all the local amenities are located. In this area the names of 'grasses' are often daubed on walls, acting as a very public reminder of the alternative structures of control on the estate. Moreover, even those residents who had called the police reported feeling undermined by the length of time it took for the police to respond; this further marginalized them and fostered reliance on the view that local people would sort things out. The underlying mechanisms highlighted by these processes have been discussed elsewhere in relation to the question of trust (Walklate, 1998).

Walking around Bankhill, the pedestrian can encounter areas that differ in their appearance and their 'feel'. Some areas look well cared for and are largely clear of rubbish and the effects of vandalism, whereas others are heavily painted with graffiti and may have other signs of disorder. Such places may amount to 'hot spots' for crime, and indeed in discussion groups a number of people said that they found it easier to cope with burglary than the petty crime engendered by such locations. But such signs of disorder also signalled a more general deterioration and loss of faith in the neighbourhood. The view was frequently expressed that 'This area is going downhill rapidly'. This view, alongside the construction of young people as 'people to be feared', had an enormous impact in Bankhill.

As the survey data cited above for Bankhill indicated, a substantial percentage of people living in the area worried about young people hanging around on the streets. Indeed, in many parts of the area groups of young people, primarily male but not solely, are very visible. And whilst a proportion of these young people will be involved in criminal activity, such activity (at the time of the study) was not as well organized as in Oldtown. As a consequence, local residents appeared to see all young people as people to be feared, avoided and mistrusted.

Such views have an enormous impact on old and young in this neighbourhood. They have not as yet, however, undermined the willingness of people living in the area to work with the official agencies to try to improve matters and to look to such agencies for guidance and solutions.

To summarize, in Oldtown people feel they know who the criminals are, and feel that they know who will solve local 'disputes': the local criminal gang. They also know something about the highly organized nature of crime in their area. Based on this knowledge they know who to trust, who not to trust, when and how. Police officers managing and working in the area also know some of these things. They also know that they are, for the most part, marginal to these processes unless the equilibrium between them, the community and the criminals becomes unbalanced in some way. In these circumstances Oldtown becomes a policing problem for both the police and the residents alike. They both 'know' that targeting troublesome youth, in and of itself, would not begin to penetrate the organized nature of crime in the area.

In Bankhill people also know who the criminals are: 'young people'. What they do not know is who is going to sort out their local 'disputes'. What they do know is that they would like the 'officials' to do something, whilst at the same time they lack the belief and level of sociability to know how or what to do for themselves. Crime in this area is prevalent, but relatively disorganized, and people know who they want to trust ('the officials') and whom they distrust (young people). However, because of the relative disorganization of criminality and community relationships in the area, this knowledge remains fragile. Such fragility – alongside the belief that 'This area is going downhill rapidly' – means that there is little for people to rely on in terms of community and/or social infrastructure. Targeting the troublesome behaviour of young people in this area, which a simple aggressive policing style like zero tolerance would do, *might* have an effect on the local fear of crime (Hope and Hough, 1988) but would not solve the other problems of people in the area (for example, vandalism, neglect of properties, absence of community relationships, etc.).

Putting all these observations together, the data are clearly suggestive of the need for a finely nuanced policy response based on an understanding of the specific difficulties faced by the agencies working within an area *and* the potentially variable community dynamics of the area. To reiterate, the areas under discussion were less than two miles apart, yet the question of what might work in each of them looks potentially very different. That question of what might work is rooted in the lived reality of the crime problem in these areas and how the people living there are responding to it, and it is not necessarily penetrated by reliance on more formal sources of data alone. So where does this evidence lead in respect of the notion of crime prevention?

'Partnership' has become the new buzzword of the crime prevention industry. Indeed, there is an argument that it is no bad thing that the responsibility for the 'crime problem' is owned by an increasingly diffuse variety of individuals and organizations. There is a point of view, for example, which would render rational the demand from insurance companies that people living in certain postcode areas must fit particular types of door and window lock before becoming eligible for household insurance. On the other hand Crawford (1998) has alluded to some of the dangers inherent in this diffusion of responsibility, especially at an organizational level. He situates the appeals to 'community' and 'partnership' as part of the wider process of the governance of crime: that is, as part of the increasingly shifting and opaque boundaries between the state and other intra-organizational networks (the public, the private, the voluntary sector) who have become ever more involved in managing the crime problem.

Analyses of the strengths and weaknesses of the partnership approach are more than viable if researchers and policy-makers alike insist on looking for solutions to the crime problem from the top down. What about looking from the bottom up? Can community safety partnerships prevent, reduce or manage crime in areas like Oldtown and Bankhill? If so, what kind of crime, how and under what circumstances, and with what kinds of partnership?

At the time the research was conducted in Bankhill there was great willingness on the part of the community to work for change. Such willingness was expressed in the desire to work with the 'authorities' and in the trust and expectation invested in them to be able to make things happen. In return, people in Bankhill wanted their concerns, which may appear petty and trivial (criminal damage and vandalism), to be taken seriously by the 'authorities'. Consequently, in an area like this, the local authority and the police may be able to take a lead in local developments and will find support for such in the local community, support that may be best harnessed by exploring interpretations of the notion of partnership above and beyond the more normatively prescribed multi-agency approach.

This kind of strategy implies the view that crime is a local problem to be *managed* locally, not necessarily prevented or reduced. So the result may not be crime prevention, or even crime reduction, but management: that is, ensuring that people feel better about, and more in control of, what is going on. By implication, this vision of the relationship between partnership and crime embraces the importance of managing incivilities as highlighted by the much maligned 'broken windows' thesis (Wilson and Kelling, 1982), with perhaps a rather different focus on who is responsible for that process.

The construction of young people as 'people to be feared' in Bankhill might demand a different response again. On a longer-term basis this is, arguably, the most pressing problem in the area. At present Bankhill offers little to young people and they in return are hesitant to go out of 'their area' to use what facilities there are. This may well be the space in which partnerships between teachers, youth workers, private enterprise, parents and the young people themselves (and other relevant agencies) might work most effectively.

On the other hand, in Oldtown the crime problem is already being managed, not by a community safety partnership strategy, but through the (fragile) equilibrium between the police, the local community and the organized nature of crime in the area. A very different conception of what might constitute a partnership! Yet the processes underpinning these relationships, in allowing people to feel all right about living in their locality, seem to work for most of the people living there most of the time. Of course, relationships such as these make agency-led intervention a difficult prospect in areas such as Oldtown. Moreover in different localities within the area, local residents working together, sometimes with official aid coming afterwards, sometimes with such aid not being forthcoming at all, have managed very local problems.

In other words, partnerships in areas like Oldtown might well be formed but they may not have any of the characteristics of conventional organizational allegiances; such partnerships may be with strategically placed individual residents, for example. Again, understanding the problem to be managed may be primarily about just that: management; the desired result may not be crime prevention or crime reduction but restoring local equilibrium and the opportunity to discover what such an equilibrium may look like.

So a gendered sense of well-being has led us to consider communities not only in terms of how they may or may not be sustained or threatened by the different levels of involvement and activities of the different sexes who people communities, but also in terms of the effect of other structural properties. This results in a series of further questions. When does gender count and when is age, class or ethnicity the salient variable in under-standing how communities work? To reiterate, gender relations seemed to matter more in Oldtown, and age relations seemed to matter more in Bankhill. When do these different groups have interests in common, and about what, and when do they differ? What may crime prevention look like in a community in which to some extent crime is functional to its survival? How might partnerships be differently structured to take account of this kind of nuanced understanding?

In some respects this discussion returns to the whole question of crime prevention and/or crime reduction, since without an understanding of the nature of the crime problem in any locality no strategy of intervention is going to have much effect. Such an understanding would truly constitute a bottom-up approach and leads us into the final heading under which to consider these issues: a structured sense of well-being.

A structured sense of well-being

The previous section raised some important questions of contemporary relevance. The questions are not peculiar to Oldtown and Bankhill. Each large city – and increasingly every rural area – will have its equivalent of Oldtown and Bankhill. It is also important not to assume that the ques-tions posed are pertinent only to high-crime areas. Wealthier rural areas also have legitimate questions to ask about their access to protection from crime (see Walklate, 2000). But if we were to take an understanding of the structure of local communities seriously and feed it into a crime prevention/crime reduction agenda, what would that look like?

First, it would mean not assuming that there is an appropriate package which can be taken off the shelf and applied to all communities. This is the case whether one is considering a particular crime prevention initiative, a focus on a particular crime problem, or a particular style of implementation. If this first observation is the case, then what follows is the requirement to develop quite a sophisticated understanding of how particular localities are structured: who is powerful and why; what kind of intervention might solicit support and why. This, of course, may result in quite different crime reduction agendas in different localities, and they may need to be differently negotiated between, for example, local businesses, young people and residents' associations. In some areas this may also require the recognition of the role that organized crime actually plays in a locality. Such a role may not be just in terms of intimidation but may also be in providing an alternative job structure, for example, from (illegitimate) criminal gang activity to (legitimate) security work.

Crime prevention informed by a structured sense of well-being would, as a consequence, take people's 'lived realities' very seriously indeed. This may mean transcending debates about the relevance of the public and the private (though not necessarily ignoring them) and moving towards taking on board the things that concern people. This would require a genuine dialogue between those who are charged with policy implementation and those who are not. Such a dialogue might find it necessary, at a minimum, to understand the important role that is played within any community by the locally powerful and, at a maximum, targeting resources towards them. It may also mean recognizing and accepting that in some communities, increasingly marked by the withering away of the state, their vested interests may lie with already well established ways of managing their ontological security. All of which raises fundamental questions about the role of the state, legitimacy and social justice.

Conclusion: crime, market, risk and trust

It is clear that whilst the relationship between the citizen and the state has changed in emphasis in the United Kingdom since 1945, there are also strong historical continuities in that relationship, such as notions of a distinction between the deserving and the undeserving, the principle of less eligibility, and the 'dangerous classes'. These dangerous classes, of course, provide the criminal justice system with much of its work, so for that reason alone it is important to grasp a clear understanding of how and why these processes happen in the way that they do.

In a different context Currie (1997) has discussed the 'marketization' of violence, by which he means the processes whereby the 'pursuit of private gain' is 'likely to breed high levels of violent crime'. In this context, that same pursuit seems to have produced communities which, when left to devise their own management strategies, have found ways of making life all right for themselves: namely what we may term the 'marketization of trust' (see Walklate and Evans, 1999). The consequences of these processes are to be seen (*inter alia*) in the report by the Social Exclusion Unit (1998). That report highlights communities for whom not only crime, but health, education, housing, etc., still constitute issues of serious concern. In the foreword to that document the Prime Minister stated: 'Our goal is simple: to bridge the gap between the poorest neighbourhoods and the rest of Britain. Bridging that gap will not be easy. It will require imagination, persistence, and commitment.'

The argument presented here certainly supports the view that bridging the gap will not be easy. Those who are socially excluded, and have found ways of managing their exclusion, will not easily be persuaded that it is in their interest to manage differently.

If the lived experiences of people living in high-crime areas are taken into account, there is clearly another layer of questions to be considered concerning what works, for whom, how, why, where and when. However, in order for such accounting to occur it is important that academics, politicians, policy-makers and the locally powerful pay constant vigilant attention to the questions of whose policy and whose community. As Giddens (1998, p. 8) states:

> In order to work, partnerships between government agencies, the criminal justice system, local associations and community organizations have to be inclusive – all economic and ethnic groups must be involved. . . . To be successful, such schemes demand a long-term commitment to social objectives.

As Giddens goes on to point out, such an approach does not necessarily mean that any link between unemployment, poverty and crime is denied; but it does mean that policies need to be co-ordinated with common goals and objectives. They also need to be resourced – an issue remarkably absent from the implementation process of the Crime and Disorder Act 1998.

In conclusion, above all else a genuine desire for policy to work for change needs to be cognizant of the importance of the local context in which the policy is set. In some settings this may mean taking gender into account; in others it may mean that other structural variables are more important. But, above all, policy needs to work with rather than against the historical and socio-economic circumstances which structure any local context. This does demand imagination, commitment and persistence. It also requires that the desire for policy to work must be both authentic and genuine for the communities themselves. This may also require a closer critical examination of what we understand by protection, who is responsible for the delivery of protection, and how it may be implemented.

References

Barr, R. and Pease, K. (1992) 'The problem of displacement' in Evans, D.J., Fyfe, N.R. and Herbert, D.T. (eds) *Crime, Policing and Place: Essays in Environmental Criminology*, London, Routledge.

Berk, R.A. and Sherman, L.W. (1984) 'The specific deterrent effects of arrest for domestic assault', *American Sociological Review*, vol. 49, pp. 261–72.

Campbell, B. (1993) *Goliath: Britain's Dangerous Places*, London, Virago.

Chatterton, M. (1983) 'Police work and assault charges' in Punch, M. (ed.) *Control and the Police Organization*, Cambridge, MA, MIT Press.

Crawford, A. (1995) 'Appeals to community and crime prevention', *Crime, Law and Social Change*, vol. 22, pp. 97–126.

Crawford, A. (1998) *Crime Prevention and Community Safety*, London, Longman.

Currie, E. (1988) 'Two visions of crime prevention' in Hope, T. and Shaw, M. (eds) *Communications and Crime Reduction*, London, HMSO.

Currie, E. (1997) 'Market, crime and community', *Theoretical Criminology*, vol. 1, no. 2, pp. 147–72.

Douglas, M. (1992) *Risk and Blame: Essays in Cultural Theory*, London, Routledge.

Elias, R. (1986) *The Politics of Victimization*, Oxford, Oxford University Press.

Evans, K., Fraser, P. and Walklate, S. (1996) 'Whom do you trust? The politics of grassing on an inner city housing estate', *Sociological Review*, vol. 44, no. 3, pp. 361–80.

Freeman, R. (1992) 'The idea of prevention: a critical review' in Scott, S., Williams, G., Platt, S. and Thomas, H. (eds) *Private Risks and Public Dangers*, Aldershot, Avebury.

Garland, D. (1996) 'The limits of the sovereign state', *British Journal of Criminology*, vol. 36, no. 4, pp. 445–71.

Giddens, A. (1990) *Modernity and Self Identity*, Cambridge, Polity Press.

Giddens, A. (1998) *The Third Way*, Cambridge, Polity Press.

Home Office (1991) *Safer Communities: The Local Delivery of Crime Prevention through the Partnership Approach* (Morgan Report), London, Home Office.

Hope, T. and Hough, M. (1988) 'Area, crime and incivility: a profile from the British Crime Survey' in Hope, T. and Shaw, M. (eds) *Communications and Crime Reduction*, London, HMSO.

Hope, T. and Shaw, M. (eds) (1988) *Communications and Crime Reduction*, London, HMSO.

Jaffe, P., Wolfe, D.A., Telford, A. and Austin, G. (1986) 'The impact of police laying charges in incidents of wife abuse', *Journal of Family Violence*, vol. 1, pp. 37–49.

Karmen, A. (1990) *Victimology: An Introduction*, Belmont, CA, Brooks Cole.

Massey, D. (1994) *Space, Place and Gender*, Cambridge, Polity Press.

Police (1999) Editorial, vol. xxxi, no 4, April.

Radford, J. and Stanko, E.A. (1991) 'Violence against women and children: the contradictions of crime control under capitalism' in Stenson, K. and Cowell, D. (eds) *The Politics of Crime Control*, London, Sage.

Sherman, L.W. (1992) *Policing Domestic Violence: Experiments and Dilemmas*, New York, Free Press.

Social Exclusion Unit (1998) *Bringing Britain Together: A National Strategy for Neighbourhood Renewal*, London, Cabinet Office.

Stanko, E.A. (1990) 'When precaution is normal: a feminist critique of crime prevention' in Gelsthorpe, L. and Morris, A. (eds) *Feminist Perspectives in Criminology*, Buckingham, Open University Press.

Stanko, E.A. (1992) Plenary address, 'Violence against Women' conference, Manchester, May.

Tuck, M. (1993) 'Research and public policy' in Coote, A. (ed.) *Families, Children and Crime*, London, Institute for Public Policy Research.

Walklate, S. (1997) 'Risk and criminal victimization: a modernist dilemma?', *British Journal of Criminology*, vol. 37, no. 1, pp. 35–45.

Walklate, S. (1998) 'Crime and community: fear or trust?', *British Journal of Sociology*, vol. 49, no. 4, pp. 550–69.

Walklate, S. (2000) 'For Whom does the Bell Toll? Crime, Fear and Community Safety', paper presented to conference on 'Crime and Insecurity', University of Leeds, May.

Walklate, S. and Evans, K. (1999) 'Zero tolerance or community tolerance?' in *Managing Crime in High Crime Areas*, Aldershot, Avebury.

Wilson, J. and Kelling, G. (1982) 'Broken windows: the police and neighborhood safety', *Atlantic Monthly*, March, pp. 29–38.

The crisis of the social and the political materialization of community safety

Eugene McLaughlin

The many meanings of community

Despite the many difficulties that have been identified with the use of the concept of 'community' as the basis of policy formulation, the 1990s saw its growing centrality in debates about crime prevention. Certain social theorists seem to have made it their life's work to produce a precise 'work-able' definition of 'community' and scrutiny of the literature identifies: community as a spatially bounded locality/territory; community as cultural sentiment and attachment; and community as common interest. Sceptics have argued, however, that community should be treated as a 'non-concept' precisely because it is incapable of exact definition and its vagueness serves more to confuse than to illuminate, concealing all kinds of contradictions. Liberals and left-wing commentators have also voiced very specific concerns about using 'community' as an organizing concept.

> I don't much like the word community. I am not even sure I like the thing. If by community one implies, as is often the case, a harmonious group, consensus, and fundamental agreement beneath the discord or war, then I don't believe in it very much and I sense in it as much threat as promise. There is doubtless this irrepressible desire for a 'community' to form but also for it to know its limit and for its limit to be *opening*.
> (Derrida, quoted in Caputo, 1997, p. 107)

A strong version of 'community' has a long tradition of respectability within right-wing thought, sitting comfortably alongside ideas about an exclusionary, racialized, authoritarian, imagined national community.

In this chapter I want to explore the cultural constructions and patterns of inclusions and exclusion embedded in two specific contemporary articulations of 'community'. I shall examine, first, the role that community played in the post-war period in policy debates about immigration, 'race', crime and policing and, second, how it re-emerged in debates from the late 1980s about the threat posed by a 'white' underclass. In both instances I shall argue that debates centre on 'community' in the United Kingdom at moments of social or national crisis and take the form of 'loss of community', a 'fear of community' and/or a desperate 'quest to rediscover, reconstruct and/or re-imagine community'. In the final section I detail how community is central to New Labour's governmental project of reclaiming the social.

There goes the neighbourhood: the emergence of community safety

Nikolas Rose (1999, p. 175) argues that although the term 'community' has 'long been salient in political thought' it only becomes 'governmental when it is made technical'. 'Community' began to feature prominently in UK public policy debates in the 1960s as part of the social democratic state's response to the problems of inner cities, marked by deepening poverty, low levels of educational achievement, problem families and the decline of conventional forms of political representation and participation. From this period the discourse of community was the means whereby certain forms of state intervention and regulation were organized:

> Communities become zones to be investigated, mapped, classified, documented, interpreted, their vectors explained to enlightened professionals-to-be in countless college courses and to be taken into account in

numberless encounters between professionals and their clients, whose individual conduct is not to be made intelligible in terms of the beliefs and values of 'their community'. (Rose, 1999, p. 175)

The social groups subjected most comprehensively to the new community initiatives were Britain's West Indian and Asian immigrants. Racism, their structural role within the post-war British economy, and their location within the declining inner cities, all meant that the new immigrants were located on the margins – or indeed the outside – of the edifice of British citizenship. A particular version of 'community' was vital to the political management of Britain's unfolding race relations crisis because it was the means whereby the colonial 'Other' was to be articulated into the 'host' society in the context of a debate about post-colonial citizenship (Phillips and Phillips, 1998).

Special 'community liaison' and 'consultative' structures were formalized at the highest levels of state policy in the legislative measures passed during the 1960s to curb immigration and encourage integration or assimilation. The process was completed when Labour's Race Relations Act 1968 established a statutory Community Relations Committee. Supporters of the new community initiatives argued that the state was recognizing the need to provide 'extra' mechanisms of representation to compensate for the under- or non-representation of immigrant interests in the established political structure; that it was constructing channels through which community discontent and concerns could be articulated; and it was creating an infrastructure for future community formation.

However, critics have argued that a series of negative consequences resulted from the institutionalization of forms of governance that had been originally used in the native quarters of British colonial cities. Non-democratically constituted community liaison and consultation were substituted for equal rights of citizenship within the 'imagined nation'. Such sponsorship also cultivated an unaccountable 'buffer zone' of self-appointed community leaders and representatives who, in exchange for recognition and influence, were required to approve decisions taken by state departments and to maintain social and political control over 'their' communities. Furthermore, funding and official recognition went to the least militant and most multi-racial organizations, effectively marginalizing important strands of ethnic minority views. What is clear is that irresolvable long-term problems were built into the arrangements. The 'representativeness' of the arrangements was open to constant questioning and challenge. The arrangements could not deliver the 'consent' of the community and nor could they address the routine institutionalized racism to which the new immigrants were being subjected.

Paul Gilroy (1987) argues that during this period a process of cultural reconstruction and reassemblage was taking place that forged an alternative version of the 'black community' which was interpretative and participative in nature. Intimate collision and conflict with 'white' society produced evolving and eclectic understandings of the forms of racial prejudice and discrimination in play and also created counter-discourses 'through which to articulate their own experiences and make sense of their common exclusion from Britain and Britishness':

> Community is as much about difference as it is about similarity and identity. It is a relational idea which suggests, for British blacks at least, the idea of antagonism – domination and subordination between one community and another. The word directs analysis to the boundary between these groups. It is a boundary which is presented primarily by symbolic means and therefore a broad range of meanings can co-exist around it, reconciling individuality and commonality and competing definitions of what the movement is about. (Gilroy, 1987, p. 235)

Gilroy illustrates how policing and criminal justice played a crucial role in the construction of post-war black communities in Britain. Conflict over policing, in particular, produced new forms of political organization and methods of grass-roots political campaigning, as well as new police and Home Office understandings of their relationship with the emergent communities. Roach, in his inside history of the Metropolitan Police Community Relations Branch, confirms the crucial role that 'race' played in the establishment of the initiative:

> The first tentative move to respond to a growing recognition that community relations needed to be put on a firmer basis was, therefore, to appoint, in 1959, a Chief Superintendent to be responsible for co-ordinating and developing police activity in the field of race relations. The significance of this appointment is amply illustrated by noting that he was the first officer ever specifically employed to work solely in community relations in the preceding 129 years history of the Metropolitan Police force. (Roach, 1978, p. 18)

Roach argues that past waves of 'white' immigration had not posed a problem for the police because integration into the 'host' community within a few generations had brought a solution to any problems of culture clash. However, because of prejudice and discrimination from the host population and the failure of government programmes, the assimilation of immigrants 'distinguished by skin colour' was presenting the police and other government agencies with more intractable problems.

During the first half of the 1970s the Home Office took a more active role in the co-ordination of community relations and the fashioning of its remit. However, various Inspectorate of Constabulary reports on the revamped 'community relations' narrate the deteriorating state of police relations with minority ethnic groups and the emergent explanations for the conflicts. So, for example, the 1973 report notes that the standard community liaison approach:

does, however, presuppose that coloured people are to some extent organized and have 'representatives' with whom the police may forge links. With the rise of the British 'second generation' there is less likelihood of this and the police are now frequently faced with real difficulties in establishing contact with younger coloured people who very often are outside such 'representative' organizations. (HMIC, 1973, p. 57)

This is the moment when 'criminality' surfaced as the central police concern and young black people came to be constructed as a 'problem presence'. Intensive news coverage of 'mugging' as a particular form of racialized crime exaggerated its seriousness; it accentuated the 'otherness' of young black men as 'a race apart' and the inner cities as 'a place apart'; and suggested that the problem of racial violence in Britain was one of black-on-white street crime; this all generated demands for firm police action. Popular and professional depictions of the 'disorganized', pathological black family, as the source of a culture of poverty, welfare dependence, criminality and a lack of respect for the law, explain why black people came to be seen as 'lesser breeds without the law', as the 'Other' who stood outside of what (ever) it meant to be English or British (Gilroy, 1987). Hence there are several overlapping discourses of 'family', 'places', 'culture' and 'community' tied together in diverse ways to mark out boundaries of inclusion and exclusion, citizen and criminal.

The other notable feature of Inspectorate reports is that they also detail the emergence of 'community policing' as a specific police philosophy. The Home Office viewed a 'low-key' version of 'community policing' as the vehicle to deliver situational crime prevention strategies, victim support schemes and police community race relations training. However, for John Alderson, then Chief Constable of Devon and Cornwall, it was the basis of a paradigm shift in policing appropriate to changing social and cultural realities:

> The purpose of preventive policing in the broad sense is to find ways of bringing joint resources to bear in times of social change and economic deterioration. Without new ideas and the will to fly in the face of tradition, we may witness a police service beginning to feel unable to cope and having to rely more and more on technologies, 'coppery' and response-time evaluation for self-esteem. The fusion of social policing and legal policing has a better chance of success than either would enjoy separately. The necessary change must begin in police culture, attitudes and habits and these changes should reflect and be reflected in policies. Police efforts to harness 'society against crime' would exhibit care, education, persuasion, and ultimately enforcement. (Quoted in Brown, 1990, p. 227)

For sections of the left the joining of 'community' with 'policing' heralded the coming of an authoritarian mode of urban governance. According to critics, it masked the paramilitarization of policing, allowed the intensification of information-gathering and surveillance, and co-opted other agencies into the policing function. In sum, 'community policing' was being promoted because of the recognition that in the context of socio-economic crisis whole groups and neighbourhoods rather than just individuals now needed to be policed and disciplined (see State Research, 1980).

The nationwide riots of 1980–81 and the report of the Scarman inquiry (1981) intensified the debate about community, 'race', crime and policing. Multidimensional, overlapping representations of 'the black community' arose out of the ashes of Brixton, St Paul's, Southall, Moss Side, Liverpool 8, Chapeltown and Handsworth. For commentators such as Sivananden, Howe and Gilroy the riots indicated 'community' first and foremost as a site of resistance and as self-defence; for the police and many newspapers the riots represented 'community' as lawless, pathological no-go areas. Lord Scarman's overriding task was to square a series of circles by re-imagining police/community relations and thereby reordering the relationship between black communities and the state and society (Hall, 1982). To do so, Lord Scarman acknowledged the grievances of black communities about coercive, racially discriminatory policing practices and the lack of police protection from racist attacks. His recommendations on 'community policing' foregrounded the fundamental policing principles appropriate to a multi-racial society: that policing by consent must inform all aspects of police work and that crime control was a responsibility of the whole community. Scarman also formalized 'community consultation' in the formulation of all policing policy and operations:

> If a rift is not to develop between the police and the public as a whole (not just members of the ethnic minority), it is in my view essential that a means be devised of enabling the community to be heard not only in the development of policing but in the planning of many, though not all, operations against crime. (Scarman, 1981, para. 5.56)

Post-Scarman, 'community' become a crowded and contested space. For the Home Office 'crime prevention' could be moved from the margins to the centre via Scarman's proposals for community consultation:

> These could have simply been taken as a means of obliging the police to take account of the wishes of the community, which would have been a distorted view . . . The consultative arrangements should also be seen as a way of ensuring that the community see it as a duty to support and help the police . . . These groups can have a constructive and practical purpose. The Home Secretary regards this as a crucial element of crime prevention in its broadest sense: that is, harnessing the community's good will towards the police, in the interest of its own protection. I can assure you that any statutory provision for consultation will reflect this thought. (Sir Brian Cubbon, quoted in Heal and Burrows, 1983, p. 3)

The community was to be left in no doubt as to its responsibility for crime reduction and the contribution it could make to it (*ibid.*, p. 28).

In terms of future developments, the Home Office identified 'situational crime prevention' initiatives and addressing 'neighbourhood decline':

> The second concept – less systematically researched . . . is the theory that as neighbourhoods decline, those living there become less willing to control the uncivil and anti-social activities of others and that in time this breeds an atmosphere where crime is acceptable. The idea of areas undergoing 'cycles of decay' is significantly different from the more long-standing, traditional view that poverty, poor education and living conditions lead to criminality. What is important, however, about these developments is that while the police cannot abrogate their duty to prevent crime, they require the assistance and support of others holding positions of responsibility to be effective. (Quoted in Heal and Burrows, 1983, p. 33)

The Home Office's newly established Crime Prevention Unit disseminated its message through input into interdepartmental circulars, crime surveys, the Five Towns and Safer Cities programmes, Crime Concern and Victim Support. Located at the centre of the various initiatives was the insistence that crime reduction was beyond the organizational capacity of the police and the formal criminal justice system. The Home Office was also involved in a number of schemes activated by the Department of Trade and Industry and the Department of the Environment that also had a 'designing out crime' dimension, such as the Inner City Task Forces and the City Action Teams. The final set of Home Office anti-crime initiatives occupying the post-Scarman space of community related to racial violence and harassment. Evidence from a variety of initiatives collated in the aftermath of the publication of the influential Home Office *Racial Attacks* report in 1981 revealed both high levels of harassment and intimidation and the inadequacy of the police response. The interdepartmental Racial Attacks Group which was convened in 1987 subsequently presented detailed proposals for proactive multi-agency responses to the problem of racial violence.

For Sir Kenneth Newman, who was appointed Commissioner of the Metropolitan Police in 1982, the Scarman Report provided the opportunity to reconceptualize the problem of policing multi-ethnic communities. Drawing upon his experience of policing in Northern Ireland, he constructed a theory of 'symbolic locations' to explain the legal, political and moral challenges facing the police in coping with what he described as London's black 'underclass':

> Throughout London there are locations where unemployed youths – often black youths – congregate; where the sale and purchase of drugs,

the exchange of stolen property and illegal drinking and gaming is not unknown. The youths regard these symbolic locations as their territory. Police are viewed as intruders, the symbol of authority – largely white authority – in a society that is responsible for all their grievances about unemployment, prejudice and discrimination. They equate closely with the criminal rookeries of Dickensian London. If allowed to continue, locations with these characteristics assume symbolic importance, a negative symbolism of the inability of the police to maintain order. Their existence encourages law breaking elsewhere, affects public perceptions of police effectiveness, heightens the fear of crime and reinforces the phenomenon of urban decay. (Quoted in Gilroy, 1987, p. 108)

Newman achieves a remarkable double racialization in this statement by making the connection between contemporary symbolic locations which are black and nineteenth-century rookeries which were overwhelmingly Irish. He insisted that the crime and social problems generated by and concentrated within these areas were so extreme and multi-faceted that they could not be addressed by the police acting on their own. According to Newman, it was no longer sufficient to think of framing policy responses in terms of traditional crime control. The police and the civil authorities needed as a matter of urgency 'to lift the problems to a higher level of generality, encompassed by the expression "social control", in a benign sense, in order to provide a unifying concept within which the activities of police and other agencies can be co-ordinated' (*ibid.*). The police would also have to deploy new intelligence-gathering, surveillance and targeting techniques in these localities and develop contingency plans in the event of large-scale violent disorder. Hence Newman allied himself with chief police officers such as John Alderson (communitarian) and James Anderton (authoritarian) who were also conceptualizing the future policing of a multi-ethnic United Kingdom in governmental terms.

Local authority police monitoring units contested the post-Scarman agendas pursued by the Home Office and the police. Some of them gained local and national notoriety for their attempts to block police-led multi-agency initiatives and police/community consultative committees and their campaigns for greater police accountability. However, although politically controversial, many of these units also played an important role in establishing that local authorities had a central role to play in tackling neighbourhood crime problems. As a result of their local audits and group-based surveys and project work, the units gave voice to the special needs of the victims of sexual, domestic, racial and homophobic violence and confirmed that sustained investment was needed to address the complex social and communal factors producing and/or concentrating high levels of crime, delinquency, disorder and fear in particular localities and estates. It is not surprising that these units tended to opt for the phrase 'community safety' rather than 'crime prevention' to encompass the interrelated range of issues they were dealing with (McLaughlin, 1994).

Thus by the end of the 1980s a large number of anti-crime projects and programmes were in place across the country and a 'quiet consensus' had emerged that multi-agency partnerships were essential to developing and supporting a comprehensive crime prevention framework. There was also broad agreement that such a framework could not be created until central government acknowledged that investing in prevention was more cost-effective than squandering resources on traditional criminal justice approaches, formalized the role of local authorities, halted the proliferation of 'ad hoc' agencies and criss-crossing short-term initiatives, and established mechanisms for systematic information-gathering and the dissemination of good practice (see AMA, 1990; Home Office, 1991; NACRO, 1989; Hope and Shaw, 1988).

'Lawless Britain', the underclass and anti-communities

During the early 1990s the terms of the debate about 'community' shifted as a result of the well publicized interventions of Charles Murray, the right-wing US political scientist who argued that the liberal principles underpinning post-war social policy had changed the incentives and penalties governing human behaviour. In the UK context, Murray (1990) 'discovered' the existence of a 'new' 'underclass' whose defining feature was not its economic marginality or disadvantage but its moral and cultural 'otherness' and self-exclusion. Murray's anthropological journey to the 'heart of darkness' in the United Kingdom uncovered a growing population of healthy people of working age 'who live in a different world from other Britons, who are raising their children to live in it, and whose values are now contaminating the life of entire neighbourhoods – which is one of the most insidious aspects of the phenomenon, for neighbours who don't share those values cannot isolate themselves' (1990, p. 27).

Murray argued that the early-warning signals of underclass neighbourhoods were the trend lines of rising rates of illegitimacy, refusal to participate in the labour market and high levels of violent crime. What was also significant in the UK context, according to Murray, was that, unlike in the United States, this 'underclass' was overwhelmingly 'white' and growing at a significant rate. In his analysis, rising crime levels were a key indicator of how far the underclass was entrenched in UK society. The crime levels and patterns within certain neighbourhoods evidenced the presence of a substantial number of habitual criminals who were living off mainstream society without participating in it. High levels of criminality were also indicative of communal disorganization and social disintegration:

> The key issue in thinking about an underclass is how the community functions, and crime can devastate a community in two especially important ways. To the extent that the members of a community are

victimized by crime, the community tends to become fragmented. To the extent that many people in a community engage in crime as a matter of course, all sorts of the socialising norms of the community change, from the kind of men that the younger boys choose as heroes to the standards of morality in general. (Murray, 1990, p. 31)

Young men choosing not to work and young women choosing to have children outside stable traditional family relationships were devastating certain neighbourhoods:

As many have commented through the centuries, young males are essentially barbarians for whom marriage – meaning not just the wedding vows, but the act of taking responsibility for a wife and children – is an indispensable civilizing force. Young men who don't work, don't make good marriage material. Often they don't get married at all; when they do, they haven't the ability to fill their traditional role. In either case, too many of them remain barbarians. (Murray, 1990, p. 39)

In terms of what should be done to address the problem of the 'undeserving underclass', Murray argued that radical social policies were needed to stimulate 'a new spirit of family and community values'. The state should enable law-abiding and respectable citizens to reclaim their neighbourhood and resist the incursions of the underclass. Murray stressed that criminal justice policies should be more deterrent and punitive, illegitimacy should be re-stigmatized and state benefits withdrawn from unmarried mothers and from young men who refuse to work. Murray warned that, without action, the value systems of the 'underclass' would engulf culturally unstable neighbourhoods.

An extensive debate was triggered by Murray's 'reculturing' of the crime debate. Since virtually all parts of the political spectrum agreed that an 'underclass' existed, the debate focused on establishing its defining features, the nature of its value system, and the appropriate policy response (for an overview, see Levitas, 1998). The underlying concern for social democrats and 'one-nation Tories' was the nature of the threat that such an 'underclass' might pose to the United Kingdom's fragile social order, given that these crime-ridden neighbourhoods stood outside the national culture and the authority of the state.

During 1991–92, in the context of steeply rising official crime rates, headline-grabbing murders, escalating fear of crime, serious rioting and new forms of disorder associated with 'hedonistic' and 'nihilistic' youth cultures, the debate about the threat posed by the 'white underclass' took on a sharper focus. The intensity and nature of the 'white riots' in 'sink estates' seemed to provide proof of the underclass thesis:

What was new in the eighties and nineties was that riot became routine. Its persistent resurgence demands that we ask questions about community, solidarity, law and disorder among men and women living in desperate local economies. Fissured by gender and generation, race and class, the riots of the nineties are so much against the community as they are about it; indeed, they render the very concept of 'community' problematic. (Campbell, 1993, p. xi)

It is in this context that a public debate about the state of 'the social' and of 'the nation' coheres. Among the condemnations of 'mindless' violence and yobbery many commentators juxtaposed the emergence and spread of forms of antisocial behaviour associated with ethnically mixed, inner-city ghettos with the stoic response of the traditional, white, working-class communities in the past, which had suffered greater deprivation and unemployment but did not riot. The traditional, white working class had lived in cohesive communities where family separation was rare and social institutions, such as the Church and the trade unions, were valued (see Dennis, 1993).

Towards the end of 1992 news media coverage of the seemingly inexorable rise in crime began to focus on a hard core of persistent offenders who were deemed to be out of control and defiant of all attempts to control them. This was the context within which the abduction and murder of two-year-old James Bulger by two ten-year-old boys from 'broken homes' occurred in Liverpool on 12 February 1993. The murder triggered an anguished public debate about the moral and spiritual malaise that had produced such a monstrous crime:

Some deaths are emblematic, tipping the scales, and little James's death . . . seemed like the murder of hope: the unthinkable thought of the undoable done. If child killings are the worst killings, then a child killing a child must be worse than worst, a new superlative in horror. In that spring of cold fever, it was as if there'd been a breach of nature: the tides frozen; stars nailed to the sky; the moon weeping far from sight. (Morrison, 1997, p. 21)

Commentators across the political spectrum warned of the dreadful implications of the escalating number of 'edge' and 'sink' estates where law and order and virtually all notions of civil society had broken down and where crime, violence and disorder had become endemic. For the right, institutions – such as family, school and community – which traditionally provide children with a sense of discipline and morality were now seen to have declined in their ability to impart these values: 'the result is the social anarchy and squalor of today's estates, inhabited by a largely white underclass which has come to resemble in crime, violence, illegitimacy, benefit dependency and work aversion the black ghettos of urban America' (*Sunday Times* editorial, 21 February 1993, News Review, p. 3).

The left proclaimed that the United Kingdom was reaping the whirl-wind of the shift to a neo-liberal society. There had been a breakdown in the cultural mechanisms which had inculcated self-responsibility and mutual obligations:

> The social consequences of driving through the market principle have been social disorganisation, unleashing attitudes of violence, a kind of callousness towards human life . . . a lack of care and sensitivity, a lack of respect for human beings, and the abolition of social reciprocity as an organizing principle of life. In trying to organize society entirely according to market principles all those intricate complex social and cultural ties which make it possible for a society of different people with different interests to survive together and function will be dismantled. (Hall, 1993, p. 7)

Geoff Mulgan, one of the key advocates of a 'new' Labour Party, also expressed concern about the fall-out of consumer-driven, over-individualistic societies. They:

> seemed to lose out on personal responsibility and the everyday morals and mutual respect that make it possible to live in densely packed cities and nations. As societies seemed to fall apart many began to fear that the cult of choice was not only a symptom but also a cause of fragmentation. (1993, p. 1)

Throughout 1993 the news media presented numerous stories of 'lawless', 'battered' Britain, a country where the law-abiding were living under a self-imposed curfew, and crime had spread from the inner city and the 'sink estates' to suburbia and the village. There was also an increasing number of incidents reported where the law-abiding – frustrated with the inability or willingness of the authorities to deal with local criminals – had taken matters into their own hands, set up their own forms of DIY protection or hired private security companies. Equally disturbing were the reports that, as a result of the activities of resurgent extreme right-wing political groupings, racist harassment and violence (including murder) had reached unprecedented levels and racial tensions were running so high in some localities that race wars were a distinct possibility. This triggered renewed campaigns, most notably that of the families of Rolan Adams, Stephen Lawrence and Quddus Ali, to force the authorities to acknowledge and act upon the problem of racist violence (see Home Affairs Committee, 1994; Bowling, 1999).

New Labour, community safety and governance of the social

As panic raged about the deepening law-and-order crisis, Tony Blair, Labour's newly appointed spokesman on home affairs, moved centre-stage with a series of carefully crafted statements that he presented as both a 'restatement' and a 'modernization' of his party's traditional position on crime and punishment. He had already warned that the issue of crime was so serious that it had become a test 'not just of law and order, but of our ability to function as a coherent democracy' (Blair, 1993, p. 27). Blair's belief that the dangerous social tensions and levels of violent alienation on many council estates posed a strategic threat to the very possibility of governance was shared by many who would play a key role in constructing New Labour's political project (see Mulgan and Wilkinson, 1995; Mandelson and Liddle, 1996). This was the context within which Blair forged and popularized the 'tough on crime and tough on the causes of crime' soundbite both to reconnect Labour with its traditional heartland constituencies and to convince the broader electorate of 'middle England' that the party could be trusted on law and order. If successful, Blair's position on crime would play a pivotal role in the construction of 'New' Labour and accelerate the collapse of the Conservatives at a moment when their broader 'New Right' political project was straining under the weight of its own contradictions (Gould, 1998, p. 213).

This was the moment when Labour's political interest in the 'third way communitarian' writings of Amitai Etzioni was coming to the fore. United States society, according to Etzioni, was facing an unprecedented crisis of values and loss of virtue because the moral infrastructure had been neglected and undermined as a result of relativization and pluralization, the social policies of the liberal left and the New Right's privileging of self-interest over the needs of the social order. High levels of criminality and antisocial behaviour were very obvious outcomes of a culture of rampant individualism and the quest for instant gratification. The urgent political task for the communitarians was the need to rebuild – or indeed reimpose – a resilient moral infrastructure by emphasizing that strong rights presume equally strong responsibilities. The 'good society' could be restored only if individuals were re-embedded in a dense web of communal responsibilities, reciprocal obligations, self-restraint and shared moral values. For Etzioni, levels of crime were a strong indication of the health or otherwise of the 'total community fabric' and crime rates in the United States indicated that the country was not just disintegrating but sliding into moral anarchy. Urgent steps had to be taken to strengthen the traditional civic institutions (the family, schools, voluntary associations), neighbourhood values and public standards of conduct that facilitated the re-creation of a strong communal infrastructure (Etzioni, 1993a, 1995).

The core messages of 'communitarianism', particularly the renewed emphasis on 'family', 'responsibilities' and 'obligations', and the need for a return to 'core moral values', chimed almost perfectly with the resurgent ethical and Christian socialist wing of the Labour Party, presenting themselves, for example, in the deliberations of Labour's commission on social justice (Hughes, 1996). Tony Blair and Gordon Brown foregrounded the concept of 'community' as part of their efforts to forge a distinctive 'third way' between what they defined as the 'failed' political philosophies of state-centred social democracy and free-market individualism. Brown, for example, signalled that the reinvention of government was dependent on the 'reconstruction of community' (Brown, 1994). However, it was in a speech to the Wellingborough constituency Labour Party, one week after the murder of James Bulger, that Blair pulled together the various strands of his thinking on community not just to offer a perspective on the question of crime but to moralize the near-hysterical debate about the state of the nation. The news headlines of the previous week, he declared, had been like 'hammer blows against the sleeping conscience of the nation' and he insisted that the murder of James Bulger should act as a catalyst for the remoralization of society. Blair reiterated that the crime was directly related to the disintegration of standards of conduct necessary to sustain community:

> A solution to this disintegration . . . must come from the rediscovery of a sense of direction as a country and most of all from being unafraid to start talking once again about the values and principles we believe in and what they mean for us, not just as individuals but as a community. We cannot exist in a moral vacuum. If we do not learn and then teach the value of what is right and what is wrong, then the result is simply moral chaos which engulfs us all . . .

> The importance of the notion of community is that it defines the relationship not only between us as individuals, but between people and the society in which they live, one that is based on responsibilities as well as rights, on obligations as well as entitlements. Self-respect is in part derived from respect for others, the notion that we are not just buyers and sellers in some market place, or individuals set in isolation, but that we are members of a community that owes obligations to others as well as ourselves and that depend on others to succeed and prosper. It is easy to deny the idea of community and some may feel unhappy with it. But call it community values, family values, or even spiritual values: what they all have in common is something bigger than me. (Quoted in Gould, 1998, pp. 234–5)

The enthusiastic news media coverage of the speech, alongside extensive criticism of the Conservative government for its abdication of responsibility and failure to address public anxieties, enabled Blair to underline his 'new' approach to crime. He insisted that there was an urgent political need to go beyond the existing 'individual responsibility versus social causes of crime' debate. Blair's approach emphasized that protecting citizens from crime required the state to hold criminals morally responsible for their actions and bring them to justice, and to deal with the underlying social problems that contributed to the growth of crime. This in turn required a new relationship between individual, community and state.

The rebuilding of community was premised on three important themes. First, attention needed to be paid to strengthening the family. During 1993–

94 the Conservatives' ill-fated 'Back to basics' campaign provided Blair with the political space to insist that the family was the most important mechanism for transmitting moral values and social discipline and the place where a sense of individual responsibility and 'community' was nurtured. The breakdown in law and order was, according to Blair, intimately linked with the break-up of strong, cohesive communities, and this 'loss of community' was a result of the stresses in contemporary family life (Blair, 1994; see also Utting et al., 1993). Proposals were subsequently presented to provide child-rearing education and advice for all parents to enable them to provide effective socialization and supervision; additional state support would be given to families experiencing difficulty in coping with their children and guaranteed places for pre-school education for disadvantaged children were also pledged (Labour Party, 1996).

Tackling youth crime was Blair's second theme. In order to toughen the Labour Party's image on law and order, he launched a raft of 'tough on youth crime' policy reviews to tackle 'persistent young offenders' and break the cycle of antisocial and petty criminal behaviour. *Getting a Grip on Youth Crime*, launched in February 1993, indicated how Labour would strengthen the capacity of the youth justice system to tackle crime effectively. Blair backed compulsory programmes to force offenders to confront the nature and consequences of their criminal behaviour and he acceded to the need for secure accommodation for the 'hard core' of young offenders. The need for a co-ordinated partnership approach to tackle escalating levels of truancy was also highlighted in his anti-youth crime proposals, as was the need to provide 'welfare to work' programmes for the young unemployed (Muncie, 1999).

Finally, Blair championed the need for a strategic framework to nationalize and institutionalize crime prevention. At a very practical level the debate about tackling crime effectively had moved, as a result of the recommendations of the Morgan Report (Home Office, 1991), from 'crime prevention' to 'community safety'. As was noted previously, the notion of 'public safety' and 'community safety' had already acquired a powerful resonance for Labour local authorities from the mid-1980s, because it was deemed to be a more expansive and inclusive framework than 'crime prevention', which focused primarily on target-hardening techniques. The concept of 'community safety' embraced consideration of the social aspects of crime, the fear of crime and victim support. Equally important, it facilitated recognition that in many localities there was concern and anger about high levels of non-criminal forms of public disorder and antisocial behaviour. 'Community safety' affirmed that local authorities should act as the strategic body to co-ordinate all the statutory agencies and ensure that they worked in partnership to stimulate the development of those features of neighbourhood life which were deemed by residents to be significant in inhibiting crime, fear and insecurity and in building confidence.

What we also need to note about Blair's proposals was his recognition that multi-agency community regeneration initiatives needed to integrate an equality perspective so that it could address the crime and safety concerns of sections of the community and specific groups, most notably women and minority ethnic communities, who were vulnerable to particular forms of victimization and/or were traditionally underrepresented in policy formulation:

> This entails clear recognition of the diversity of the community and diverse range of needs within it. It means above all ensuring that crime prevention strategies are responsive and relevant to the needs of the entire community and, in particular, providing equity in crime prevention strategies for those groups in the community who are doubly disadvantaged by crime and discrimination. (Labour Party, 1994, p. 18)

Blair signalled, for example, that a future Labour government would make racially motivated violence a specific criminal offence and would criminalize racial harassment and intimidation.

I would argue that what is politically significant in New Labour's evolving communitarian position on crime is the assertion of the right of the state to intervene in 'the social'. High-crime localities would be 'disciplined' in order to encourage desirable social behaviour, thereby recreating or strengthening local communities and families and improving the quality of life. Under a future Labour government there would not be any 'no-go areas' or 'taboo issues' in terms of the reach of the state's social and criminal justice policies.

When Tony Blair succeeded John Smith as leader of the Labour Party in 1994, it fell to Jack Straw to consolidate Labour's 'tough on crime' stance and deepen the determination to re-moralize and re-responsibilize the social:

> Some people would deny that any government can achieve such changes. But the government have at their disposal more effective levers than are available to any private individual or agency. The government also have the responsibility – the moral duty – to use the power that they have for the good of all . . . For the past eighteen years, Britain had a government who preached the value of self-interest above everything else. It should therefore come as no surprise that some people then choose to ignore their responsibilities to other people; when 'there is no such thing as society', there can be no shared standards of behaviour. Where there is a steady erosion of community of shared values, links between individuals collapse and people become fearful and distrustful of others. It's 'Get what you can, don't worry about anyone else' – the instincts of those who commit crime. Crime is the ultimate selfish act. It results from the breakdown of rules and from an evasion of responsibility for other people. (Straw, quoted in Anderson and Mann, 1997, p. 230)

To the consternation of civil rights pressure groups, Straw unveiled a batch of headline-grabbing plans to convince the electorate that New

Labour had finally discarded its 'soft on crime' image. Many of these initiatives foregrounded what New Labour described as the need for a 'zero tolerance' approach to tackling the rising tide of public disorder and antisocial behaviour. These highly controversial 'defining deviance up' initiatives provide further evidence of the breadth of New Labour's unfolding anti-crime agenda and attestation of its readiness, if elected, to use the legislative powers of the national and local state to intervene in 'disorderly' communities and 'dysfunctional' families in order to shift the balance of power from the 'criminal' and 'antisocial' to the 'law-abiding' and respectable.

Reclaiming the council estates and the streets and families

In June 1995 Jack Straw proposed community safety orders to enable police forces and local authorities to crack down on 'noisy neighbours' and 'families from hell' who indulged in chronic criminal, antisocial, threatening or disruptive behaviour. Breaches of the community safety order, which would be based on civil evidence, and thus require a lower level of proof than criminal evidence, could lead to eviction or imprisonment (Labour Party, 1995). In June 1996 Straw announced plans to provide local authorities with the power to introduce US-style night-time curfews on children and teenagers as part of his 'zero tolerance' stance on antisocial behaviour. Straw claimed that he was responding to a tide of complaints about estates plagued with under-age drinking, vandalism, noise, joy-riding and the threatening behaviour associated with gang culture. For Straw a key source of disorder was a hard core of parents who did not know how – or were unwilling – to discharge their parental responsibilities and a generation of children who were inadequately socialized and supervised. Later in 1996 Straw launched a strategy document to promote 'tough love' parenting as part of New Labour's policies to address the root causes of juvenile delinquency and criminality. The strategy document affirmed his intention to introduce child protection curfews to keep young children off the streets at night (Labour Party, 1996). Local consultation between residents, the local authority and the police would establish how the curfew should work. Straw also recommended that courts should have the power to impose a Parental Responsibility Order on parents who refused to accept responsibility for their children's delinquent actions. Under the order, parents would be required to attend counselling and guidance sessions to help them to control their children effectively. Straw used a classic 'child-saving' discourse to reject accusations that his proposals were authoritarian:

> Such intervention is surely better than allowing these children to decline into delinquency through neglect and disinterest . . . Giving children the chance to grow up in a secure and orderly way, in which adults take

responsibility for them, is one of the greatest freedoms we can secure for
the young and for our future. (1996, p. 29)

In the course of a speech launching Lewisham's Community Safety
Strategy in September 1995, Straw promised that Labour would also
authorize the police and local authorities to reclaim the increasingly
brutalized streets by cracking down on aggressive beggars, drug addicts,
drunks, louts, vandals, graffiti artists and 'squeegee merchants'. This
speech was inspired by the high-profile 'zero tolerance' or 'quality of life'
policing strategy implemented in New York by William J. Bratton, the
NYPD Commissioner, and Mayor Rudolf Giuliani. Underpinning this
approach was the 'broken windows' thesis of Wilson and Kelling, which
claimed that low-level disorder and serious crime were inextricably linked:
'if a window in a building is broken and is left unrepaired, all the rest
would soon be broken' (Wilson and Kelling, 1982, p. 31; see also Kelling
and Coles, 1996, and Bratton, 1997).

In October 1996 Straw pulled together the previous three years'
'tough on crime and tough on the causes of crime' policy proposals in
Tackling the Causes of Crime, declaring that 'securing people's physical
security, freeing them from the fear of crime and disorder, is the greatest
liberty government can guarantee' (Straw and Michael, 1996, p. 1). The
document trailed many of the proposals that would eventually appear in
the Crime and Disorder Act 1998 and the Youth Justice and Criminal
Evidence Act 1999, put on the statute book by the New Labour government elected in 1997.

The policy proposals stated that communal disorder and antisocial
behaviour would be a priority if New Labour was elected because:

> It is not just specific crimes which affect our quality of life. The rising tide
> of disorder is blighting our streets, neighbourhoods, parks, town and city
> centres. Incivility and harassment, public drunkenness, graffiti and
> vandalism all affect our ability to use open spaces and enjoy a quiet life
> in our homes. Moreover, crime and disorder are linked. Disorder can
> lead to a vicious circle of community decline in which those who are able
> to move away do so, whilst those who remain learn to avoid certain
> streets and parks. This leads to a breakdown in community ties and a
> reduction in natural social controls tipping an area into decline,
> economic dislocation and crime. Crime and disorder strike not only
> individuals – they can affect whole communities and the commercial
> success of town and city centres. (Straw and Michael, 1996, p. 4)

If elected, New Labour would place a statutory duty on local authorities and the police to use the findings of crime audits to develop
community safety and crime prevention programmes. In keeping with its
belief that the family was the key to crime prevention. New Labour also
committed itself to establishing programmes to: re-educate 'irresponsible'

and 'incompetent' parents; support 'malfunctioning' families; provide pre-school education for 'disadvantaged' children; and reinforce parental responsibility via school-home contracts. *Tackling the Causes of Crime* also committed New Labour to reintegrating truants into the education system, the young unemployed into the labour market, and the young homeless, mentally ill and drug addicts into mainstream society. Sitting alongside this agenda were proposals inspired by the Audit Commission (1996) for new multi-agency youth justice teams whose function would be to intervene earlier in the lives of potential young offenders and ensure that they – and their parents – took responsibility for their antisocial behaviour. To reinforce moral responsibility, New Labour also confirmed that children aged under ten years would no longer be exempt from prosecution. Overlaying all this were emergent antisocial exclusion plans to resocialize work-deprived, welfare-dependent, 'hard to hear' multi-problem estates and localities which were deemed to be 'outside' conventional society. This meant that particular communities were going to be subjected to the attentions of managerialized governmental agencies operating with new powers and techniques and new forms of co-ordinated intervention.

Conclusion

Throughout this chapter I have argued that 'community' has played a central imaginary role in debates about the state of crime, the state of society and the state of the nation. Nikolas Rose (1999, pp. 189-90) argues that 'governing through community' necessitates making communities 'real'. To do so, boundaries and distinctions have to be put in place and spaces have to be visualized, mapped and represented via surveys, audits, market research, opinion polls, focus groups, citizens' juries and so on. New experts emerge who operationalize these techniques, who construct theories and conceptualizations and who advise on 'how communities and citizens might be governed in terms of their values, and how their values shape the ways they govern themselves' (*ibid.*, p. 189). Equally significantly, 'governing through community' requires a new political status to be given to the 'indigenous' authorities of community, such as 'community representatives' and 'community leaders': 'In the name of community, political programmes, both at the micro-level and macro-level, disperse the tasks of knowing and governing through a myriad of micro-centres of knowledge and power' (*ibid.*).

These features are present in Labour's policies to deal with the social consequences of post-war immigration from former colonies and more recently in New Labour's attempts to tackle crime and disorder. New Labour utilizes 'the community' not just to bemoan fragmentation and breakdown but to signal its determination to use the organizational powers available to the state to reclaim and reactivate the social and thereby draw the feared 'underclass' back into mainstream society. Tackling not just crime but restoring order and pro-social behaviour are the acid tests for New Labour and represent the defining difference between New Labour and previous New Right administrations. For New Labour to succeed, it has to construct a more holistic, preventive and *interventionist* model of governance. The scale and intensity of New Labour's national reclamation project can be visualized only when one realizes that certain 'hard to hear' and 'hard of hearing' localities are being subjected to multiple cross-cutting interventions. The Crime and Disorder Act 1998 and allied social policy legislation are generating new discourses of 'order' and 'control', constructing new criminal subjects and 'new model citizens', and rewriting the script of local governance.

Why is New Labour so attracted to communitarian ideas of 'governing through community'? I would argue that its determination to strengthen community bonds is intimately connected with its 'third way' understanding of the future of the nation-state under globalization. It is, to use a favourite New Labour soundbite, 'both a strategy and a necessity'. Globalization for New Labour provides new opportunities and new choices and brings the threat of 'new inequalities and automization, straining or severing bonds of family, community and nation and traditional mechanisms of mutual support and values' (Straw, 2000, p. 4). New Labour also believes that diverse societies like the United Kingdom have to pay particular attention to the potential for division: 'The core values need to be stated and affirmed so that everyone understands what they are, so that we can speak the same moral language' (*ibid.*). 'Core values' are to be institutionalized through New Labour's programme of constitutional reform and the establishment of a human rights culture which emphasizes rights *and* responsibilities.

Central to all this is the determination to construct 'active communities' 'in which the commitment of the individual is backed by the duty of all organizations – in the public sector, the private sector and the voluntary sector – towards a community of mutual care and a balance of rights and responsibilities' (Straw, 1998, p. 16). For New Labour, mechanisms have to be found to strengthen the bonds between individuals and to create local communities, and nation-states, that are not just active but robust and responsibilized enough to withstand the challenges thrown up by the new global economy – hence the attempts to strengthen the family and parenting. New Labour is also trying to resurrect 'volunteering', which 'brings people together and helps create a sense of citizenship that is often missing from communities today' (Straw, 2000, p. 7) and revalorize the voluntary sector because it 'builds and strengthens community life like nothing else' (*ibid.*). Equally important, for New Labour's communitarians the fight against crime and disorder also provides opportunities for communal solidarity. Various policy initiatives and aspirational declarations provide a governmental imaginary where communities are encouraged to strengthen their moral and physical boundaries; to be intolerant of and censure antisocial behaviour; to set police priorities; to participate in broader policing and surveillance; to determine the nature of punishment and restitution; and to stigmatize or expel unrepentant, hard-core criminals. Communities that demonstrate active willingness to tackle their crime and disorder problems will receive investment for further 'crime-proofing'. Such an imaginary offers the intriguing possibility of moving from 'governing through community' to governing through a community of remoralized, responsibilized and decriminalized local communities.

References

Anderson, P. and Mann, N. (1997) *Safety First: The Making of New Labour*, London, Granta Publications.

Association of Metropolitan Authorities (1990) *Crime Reduction: Framework for the 1990s*, London, AMA.

Audit Commission (1996) *Misspent Youth*, London, Audit Commission.

Blair, T. (1993) 'Why crime is a socialist issue', *New Statesman and Society*, 29 January, pp. 27–8.

Blair, T. (1994) 'Sharing responsibility for crime' in Coote, A. (ed.) *Families, Children and Crime*, London, Institute for Public Policy Research.

Blair, T. (1996) *New Britain: My Vision of a Young Country*, London, Fourth Estate Books.

Bowling, B. (1999) *Violent Racism*, Oxford, Clarendon Press.

Bratton, W. (1997) 'Crime is down in New York: blame the police' in Dennis, N. (ed.) *Zero Tolerance: Policing a Free Society*, London, Institute of Economic Affairs.

Brown, G. (1994) 'The politics of potential: a new agenda for Labour' in Marquand, D. (ed.) *Reinventing the Left*, Cambridge, Polity Press.

Brown, J. (1990) *Insecure Societies*, London, Macmillan.

Campbell, B. (1993) *Goliath: Britain's Dangerous Places*, London, Methuen.

Caputo, J.D. (1997) *Deconstruction in a Nutshell: A Conversation with Jacques Derrida*, New York, Fordham University Press.

Dennis, N. (1993) *Rising Crime and the Dismembered Family*, London, Institute of Economic Affairs.

Etzioni, A. (1993a) *The Spirit of Community*, London, Fontana.

Etzioni, A. (1993b) *The Parenting Deficit*, London, Demos.

Etzioni, A. (1995) 'Nation in need of community values', *The Times*/Demos Lecture, *The Times*, 20 February.

Gilroy, P. (1987) *There Ain't No Black in the Union Jack: The Cultural Politics of Race and Nation*, London, Hutchinson.

Gould, P. (1998) *The Unfinished Revolution: How the Modernizers Saved the Labour Party*, London, Little Brown.

Hall, S. (1982) 'The Scarman Report', *Critical Social Policy*, vol. 2, no. 2, pp. 66–72.

Hall, S. (1993) 'Backing away from basics', *New Times*, 27 November, pp. 6–7.

Heal, K. and Burrows, J. (eds) (1983) *Crime Prevention: A Co-ordinated Approach*, London, Home Office.

HM Inspectorate of Constabulary (1973) *Annual Report*, London, Home Office.

Home Affairs Committee (1994) *Third Report: Racial Attacks and Harassment*, London, House of Commons.

Home Office (1981) *Racial Attacks: Report of a Home Office Study*, London, Home Office.

Home Office (1991) *Safer Communities: The Local Delivery of Crime Prevention through the Partnership Approach* (Morgan Report), London, Home Office.

Hope, T. and Shaw, M. (eds) (1988) *Communications and Crime Reduction*, London, HMSO.

Hughes, G. (1996) 'Communitarianism and law and order', *Critical Social Policy*, vol. 16, no. 4, pp. 17–41.

Kelling, G. and Coles, C. (1996) *Fixing Broken Windows*, New York, Touchstone Books.

Labour Party (1994) *Partners against Crime: Labour's New Approach to Tackling Crime and Creating Safer Communities*, London, Labour Party.

Labour Party (1995) *A Quiet Life: Tough Action on Criminal Neighbours*, London, Labour Party.

Labour Party (1996) *Parenting*, London, Labour Party.

Levitas, R. (1998) *The Inclusive Society?*, London, Macmillan.

Mandelson, P. and Liddle, R. (1996) *The Blair Revolution: Can New Labour Deliver?*, London, Faber.

McLaughlin, E. (1994) *Community, Policing and Accountability*, Aldershot, Ashgate.

Morrison, B. (1997) *As if*, London, Granta.

Mulgan, G. (1993) 'Preface' in Etzioni, A., *The Parenting Deficit*, London, Demos.

Mulgan, G. and Wilkinson, H. (1995) *Freedom's Children*, London, Demos.

Muncie, J. (1999) *Youth and Crime*, London, Sage.

Murray, C. (1990) *The Emerging British Underclass*, London, Institute of Economic Affairs, Health and Welfare Unit.

National Association for the Care and Resettlement of Offenders (1989) *Crime Reduction and Community Safety*, London, NACRO.

Phillips, M. and Phillips, T. (1998) *Windrush: The Irresistible Rise of Multi-racial Britain*, London, HarperCollins.

Rentoul, J. (1995) *Tony Blair*, London, Warner Books.

Roach, L. (1978) 'The Metropolitan Police Community Relations Branch', *Police Studies*, September, pp. 17–21.

Rose, N. (1999) *Powers of Freedom: Reframing Political Thought*, Cambridge, Cambridge University Press.

Scarman, Lord (1981) *The Scarman Report: The Brixton Disorders, 10–12 April 1981*, Harmondsworth, Penguin Books.

State Research (1980) *Policing the Eighties: The Iron Fist*, London, State Research.

Straw, J. (1996) 'I have a dream – and I don't want it to be mugged', *Guardian*, 8 June, p. 29.

Straw, J. (1998) 'Building social cohesion, order and inclusion in a market economy', Nexus conference on 'From Principles to Policies: Mapping out the Third Way', 3 July, King's College, London (http://www.netnexus.org/events/july98).

Straw, J. (2000) 'Human rights and personal responsibility: new citizenship for a new millenium', London, Home Office (http://www.homeoffice.gov.uk/hract/).

Straw, J. and Michael, A. (1996) *Tackling the Causes of Crime: Labour's Proposal to Prevent Crime and Criminality*, London, Labour Party.

Utting, D., Bright, J. and Henricson, C. (1993) *Crime and the Family: Improving Child-rearing and Preventing Delinquency*, London, Family Policy Studies Centre.
Wilson, J.Q. and Kelling, G. (1982) 'Broken windows', *Atlantic Monthly*, March, pp. 29–38.

Part II

Policies, Practices and Politics in the Contemporary United Kingdom

Community safety and policing

Some implications of the Crime and Disorder Act 1998

Tim Newburn

Crime prevention and the police: a brief review

The principal duty of the 'new' police when they were first established in London in 1829 was declared to be the prevention of crime. This was the core of the Peelian vision of policing in the early nineteenth century. At the heart of the new force was the uniformed constable – the bobby on the beat – who not only formed the bedrock of the police in the nineteenth century, but who remains central, if only on an ideological level, to modern philosophies of policing (Reiner, 1992). Uniformed patrol – the visible presence of the police on the street – was seen as the key to crime prevention: the 'scarecrow function', as it has been characterized, aided by the deterrent value of investigation and detection of those crimes that did take place.

Whilst the Peelian vision may never have been fully realized, this rather narrow 'model' of crime prevention persisted in large part until at least the mid-twentieth century. Indeed, Bottoms and Wiles have argued that:

> Until the middle of the twentieth century crime prevention, both in fact
> and in public policy debates, was necessarily tied to the existence of the
> new public police. In the public domain public policing was accepted as
> having a monopoly; whilst in the private domain crime prevention either
> did not involve the use of manpower or, where it did, this was of a
> primitive form (i.e. nightwatchman), and a very junior partner to public
> policing. (1996, p. 2)

Although this case is rather overstated (see Jones and Newburn, 1999)
it nonetheless captures the rather limited way in which crime prevention
was conceived in relation to policing in this period. It was not until the
1960s that the practice and the discourses of crime prevention began a
process of fundamental change. In relation to the internal organization of
the police service, it was not until after the publication of the report of the
Cornish Committee on the Prevention and Detection of Crime (Home
Office, 1965) that specialist crime prevention departments began to come
into being in any number. The committee recommended, *inter alia*, the
need for specialist police officers who would be experts in crime prevention
technology; that an officer of at least the rank of inspector should take on
the role of force crime prevention officer; and that a more professional
approach was needed in respect of the publicity material used by the
police.

Perhaps anticipating one of the potential problems with this approach,
the committee pointed out that the creation of the specialism should not be
taken to imply that the responsibility of other officers with regard to crime
prevention had lessened. Furthermore, in what has by now become a
standard crime prevention argument, it emphasized the importance of
building relations with organizations outside the police, and as part of this
process of eliciting such support it recommended the setting up of 'crime
prevention panels'. Such panels had no formal status and have generally
been chaired by the police themselves (Home Office, 1971). Because of
their lack of status and the fact that there has never been any requirement
to set them up in local areas, crime prevention panels developed in a
largely *ad hoc* way and, following the lead taken by the nascent crime
prevention departments, which exercised a strong influence over them
(Home Office, 1971), tended to focus fairly narrowly on physical security
(Gladstone, 1980).

Despite the apparent rise in the stock of crime prevention within
central government, responsibility *within* police forces for crime prevention work remained the domain of specialist crime prevention units and
crime prevention officers (CPOs). In the main, crime prevention remained a
small-scale police specialism, with crime prevention officers usually rep-
resenting less than 1 per cent of a force's establishment (Harvey et al.,
1989) and rarely occupying a rank higher than chief inspector. The relatively narrow focus of crime prevention panels was largely replicated
within police forces, and research has suggested that the tasks actually

undertaken by crime prevention officers have, in practice, been very limited (Harvey et al., 1989; Johnston et al., 1993), being largely reactive and dominated by 'situational prevention' (Clarke and Mayhew, 1980; Clarke, 1992). When more socially based or 'community' initiatives have been undertaken the basis on which they were being encouraged has often been unclear.

Though initially treated as a peripheral specialism of low status and interest when placed alongside crime fighting (Graef, 1989), the 1980s saw increasing emphasis on crime prevention. There was a concomitant rise in the visibility of such work (or at least the publicity given to the work) within the police, to the point at which Reiner (1992, p. 99) even felt able to assert that crime prevention departments had become the 'belles of the ball'. Though this is a considerable overstatement, a number of very significant changes did take place during the 1980s which put crime prevention on the map. In his review of these developments Bottoms (1990) highlights the setting up of the Crime Prevention Unit in the Home Office in 1983, the issuing of the 1984 interdepartmental circular on crime prevention (Home Office, 1984, followed by a Scottish Office circular), the two seminars on crime prevention held at 10 Downing Street in 1986, the 'Five Towns' initiative, followed by the Safer Cities programme and the launch of the charity Crime Concern. To this list one might add the reconstituting of the Home Office Standing Conference on Crime Prevention, the second Home Office circular (44/90), which updated 8/84, and the formation of the ACPO sub-committee on crime prevention.

Not only did crime prevention activity proliferate in this period, but the discourses and practices of what was then generally referred to as 'social crime prevention' came further to the fore. The origin of these shifts, as several authors have argued, is largely to be found in the progressive rejection of the 'impossible mandate' of central government responsibility for social order and crime control (Manning, 1977; Garland, 1996). The 'rise' of crime prevention represented, according to some, a paradigm shift in criminal justice (Tuck, 1988). The emerging paradigm emphasizes 'partnership', 'community' and 'prevention' and in doing so places decreasing emphasis upon the role of formal criminal justice agencies and on the power of the 'sovereign state' to solve the problem of crime or to guarantee security (Garland, 1996).

The post-war period was the high point of public support for, and belief in, public policing. The past thirty years or so, however, have seen a dramatic reversal of the process of increasing legitimization. Numerous factors underpin this change in fortune, including the controversial use of paramilitary tactics in public order policing, corruption scandals and miscarriages of justice (Reiner, 1997). Perhaps most important, however, has been the growing visibility of the limitations of the crime control capacity of the police. By the early 1980s the police themselves had begun to respond explicitly to this problem. Thus as crime continued to rise, despite the increase in resources devoted to policing in the early 1980s, one of the key messages emanating from the police was that they could not be expected to carry responsibility for the prevention of crime unaided. As a result, increasing emphasis came to be placed upon the 'community' both in relation to policing generally and, more specifically, in relation to crime prevention (cf Willmott, 1987). Indeed, the impetus for this had begun even earlier, crucial in this regard being a Home Office circular (211/1978, which became known as the Ditchley Circular) which recommended improved co-ordination between criminal justice agencies, together with community-based initiatives, as a solution to what was perceived at that time to be the piecemeal approach to dealing with juveniles.

The so-called 'community policing' approach that developed is most closely associated with John Alderson, the one-time Chief Constable of Devon and Cornwall, who emphasized the importance of close relations between police and public and, consequently, the broad service role of his constabulary (Alderson, 1979). Community-focused policing initiatives were many and varied during the 1980s and included such developments as community constables (Brown and Iles, 1985), directed patrolling (Burrows and Lewis, 1988), focused patrolling (Chatterton and Rogers, 1989), neighbourhood policing (Irving et al., 1989) and Neighbourhood Watch (Husain, 1988; Bennett, 1990; McConville and Shepherd, 1992). Community policing came to be seen 'as the collective answer to abuses of power, lack of effectiveness, poor public confidence, and concerns about legitimacy' (Crawford, 1997, p. 47).

The main issue affecting, and arguably inhibiting, the development of crime prevention at this time was the unwillingness of government to task any one agency with taking lead responsibility for such measures. Numerous commentators have suggested that this was merely the Home Office ducking the issue (see Crawford, 1998b) with the consequence that responsibility tended to fall to the police. There were clearly also significant ideological inhibitors at play, particularly central government reluctance to invest responsibility or resources in local government. This was increasingly problematic, given a certain 'dampening of enthusiasm' (Gilling, 1997, p. 92) for purely situational prevention and the increasing emphasis upon a hybrid of situational and social approaches – increasingly referred to as 'community safety' – a move signalled as early as Home Office Circular 8/1984. This phase of crime prevention policy tended to rely upon a dual strategy: 'First there was a concerted effort to pass the responsibility down through the community to the individual citizen, and secondly there was an attempt to locate it within multi-agency structures. The concept of partnership linked the two' (Gilling, 1997, p. 95).

Indeed, this very terminology was incorporated in the terms of reference of what has subsequently become known as the Morgan Committee. The Morgan Committee's final report (Home Office, 1991) recommended that a statutory responsibility should be based on local authorities (alongside the police) for the 'stimulation of community safety and crime prevention programmes, and for progressing at a local level a multi-agency approach to community safety'. It also sought to encourage further voluntary and private sector involvement in community safety. There was widespread support for the Morgan Report's recommendations from within local government and academic circles. However, this consensus coincided within an exceedingly unsympathetic government. The Conservative administration was at that time in the run-up to a general election. It was concerned about too great an emphasis on the socio-economic bases of crime, and was heavily engaged in attempting to decrease – not increase – the powers and responsibilities of local authorities.

During the course of the 1990s the stock of 'community safety' continued to rise and pressure increased on government to establish clear lines of accountability. Within police forces, however, there continued to be mixed messages about crime prevention. Successive governments had stressed the importance of crime prevention initiatives and programmes and, at least at a rhetorical level, argued that the prevention of crime should be considered a central part of the standard policing function. Similarly, the police themselves had generally been quick to support the idea that this area of work remained fundamental. The reality was that it remained for the most part a fairly narrowly defined specialism. With the passage of the Crime and Disorder Act 1998 this is all set to change. The remainder of this chapter focuses on the Act and speculates on its likely implications for the future of policing.

The Crime and Disorder Act 1998 and policing

In its pre-election publications and pronouncements the Labour Party made it clear that community safety and crime prevention were to be key elements in its criminal justice strategy once elected. They made a manifesto commitment to implement the major recommendations of the Morgan Report and soon after the election published precise details of their plans, first in a consultation document (Home Office, 1997) and subsequently in the Crime and Disorder Bill.

The degree of difference between the outgoing Conservative government and the new Labour administration in relation to community safety was well illustrated in the first paragraphs of the consultation document, *Getting to Grips with Crime*. The document opened with a discussion of the Morgan Report and, in particular, the key strategic role of local authorities. The document stated:

> Even though the previous administration chose not to implement the Report, many of Morgan's key findings have in fact been taken on board spontaneously by partnerships all over the country, to their benefit and – most importantly – that of local communities . . . The years which have elapsed since Morgan have seen a complete acceptance of the partnership concept at all levels of the *police service*. The service now explicitly

recognizes that it cannot cope with crime and disorder issues on its own
. . . The Government accepts the principle set out in Morgan that the
extent, effectiveness and focus of existing local activity would be greatly
improved by clear statements in law as to where responsibility for this
work lies. (Home Office, 1997, pp. 3–5)

What it then went on to say, however, was that in its forthcoming
Crime and Disorder Bill the government proposed to include provisions
to give local authorities *and* the police new duties to develop statutory
partnerships to help prevent and reduce crime. This approach neatly
sidestepped the issue of a 'lead' agency in crime prevention. The government said that it was not persuaded that the Morgan view of giving local
authorities lead responsibility would be workable in practice. Its views,
rather, were that the 'principles of partnership' required joint working and
collective responsibility. Consequently, they proposed that responsibility
should lie jointly with the chief constable and the district or unitary
authority (or London borough) or, where two-tier structures still existed,
with the county council.

The new structures and requirements are set out in detail in the Crime
and Disorder Act 1998. Sections 6 to 8 are key. Sections 5 and 6 place the
statutory duty on chief police officers and local authorities, in co-operation
with police authorities, probation committees and health authorities, to
formulate and implement a 'strategy for the reduction of crime and
disorder in the area'.

The Act is also specific about what the strategy should contain. Not
surprisingly in these managerialist times, at the top of the list comes
'objectives to be pursued by the responsible authorities' followed by 'long-
term and short-term performance targets for measuring the extent to which
such objectives are achieved'. Once a strategy has been formulated, it is to
be published by the responsible authorities. The publication should include
details of: the bodies involved in the strategy; the results of the local audit;
and the objectives and performance targets. In this way it parallels in many
respects the nature of local policing plans, published annually by local
police authorities, as a requirement of the Police and Magistrates' Courts
Act 1994 (now consolidated by the Police Act 1996).

The final element in the Act which is of particular relevance to this
chapter is Section 17 which imposes on every local authority a duty 'to
exercise its various functions with due regard to the likely effect of the
exercise of those functions on, and the need to do all that it reasonably can
to prevent, crime and disorder in its area'. The consultation paper, *Getting
to Grips with Crime*, which preceded the new legislation, described this
new duty in the following manner:

The proposals are not about requiring local government to deliver a
major new service, or to take on substantial new burdens. Their aim is to
give the vital work of preventing crime a major new focus across a very

wide range of local services . . . It is a matter of putting crime and disorder considerations at the heart of decision-making. (Home Office, 1997, p. 6)

Where does all this leave us? What are the implications of the Act for policing? The arguments and speculations offered below are organized around three themes:

1   The implications for the role of the police in the 'community' and, in particular, the implications of working in partnership.
2   The implications for the police organization and, in particular, its culture and values.
3   The implications for policing more broadly.

The police role in community safety

Under New Labour the idea of things being 'joined up' has become a key organizing idea in how social policy should be designed in response to the challenge posed by contemporary levels of crime and disorder. There are two fairly simple ideas at the heart of this formulation. First, there is the assumption – supported by a wealth of rigorous academic research – that the problems which the government has to tackle are multidimensional in character (Farrington, 1996; Walker, 1997). Whatever the problem – unemployment, poverty, crime, social exclusion – its causes are various and unlikely to fall solely within the remit of one government department or to be amenable to a single 'solution'. The second assumption, which follows logically from the first, is that the responses to these problems need, equally, to be multidimensional and multi-agency in character. Community safety is a good example.

As an approach, community safety has three key elements. It tends to be localized, to have a broad focus on social problems beyond simply crime and disorder and to be delivered via 'partnership' (Crawford, 1998b). The first set of implications flowing from the Crime and Disorder Act 1998 that I wish to consider concerns both the police working in partnership with other agencies and the relationship between the police and the communities they serve. In fact there appear to be (at least) three sets of issues here. First, there are the problems of 'inter-agency' working or 'partnership' working. Second, there is the question of relations with local communities, particularly where these are in some way 'problematic', and, finally, there is the 'role' of the police after the Crime and Disorder Act 1998. I shall deal with each briefly in turn.

The problems of partnership   In discussing partnership Crawford (1998b) distinguishes between 'multi-agency' and 'inter-agency' relations. The former, he suggests, involve agencies coming together in relation to a particular problem without this unduly affecting the way in which they work. Inter-agency relations, by contrast, 'interpenetrate and thus affect normal internal working practices of the agencies involved'. The challenges in inter-agency working are greater for the police (and all organizations) than they are in multi-agency working. The benefits of properly 'joined up' working are also likely to be greater. Given the results-oriented nature of the Crime and Disorder Act the pressure will be on the police service to become involved not only in collaborative but in interdependent activity. Doing so, however, will once again highlight some of the difficulties and tensions in such work. Without going into detail, it is worth briefly revisiting some of these problems, for the implication of the Act is that the police service will be forced to confront them and to attempt to identify means for their mitigation or resolution.

First, there is the problem of inter-organizational conflict. It may arise over ideology, purpose and aims, interests and, notwithstanding the planning process set up by the Act, priorities. It is also possible that tensions over goals and priorities may be exacerbated by some aspects of managerialism currently dominating much public service provision. As Rhodes (1997) has summarized it, the problem with New Public Management is that it may encourage an intra-organizational focus rather than developing structures for the management of inter-organizational networks.

Second, there is the issue of differential power relations between the partners. This may be exhibited in material and human resources, access to, and the sharing of, information and expertise, and in legal powers. Third, there is the problem of blurred boundaries between the roles and functions of partners with a possible concomitant loss of autonomy. Finally, there is the danger of confusion over responsibility and accountability. In particular, responsibility may become fragmented and thus accountability blurred. This may be particularly acute in relation to the central goal of all this activity: that is, reductions in the level of crime and disorder.

Police-community relations Through a variety of means, the Crime and Disorder Act seeks to 'reinsert' the community into policing. The key elements of the process are the local audit of crime and disorder (taking into account the views of those who live and work in an area), the determination of priorities, followed by the publication of a consultation document. The aims of consultation at this stage are to:

1 Confirm that the audit has construed problems accurately.
2 Check that it does not contain crucial omissions.
3 Ensure that it is not based on misconceptions about the communities to which it relates.
4 Canvass opinion about proposed priorities and options.

The guidance in the Act specifies a wide range of organizations, agencies and community groups or representatives who it is intended should be sent copies of the audit document and invited to comment. In addition, partnerships are encouraged to consult bodies that represent or promote the interests of, or provide services to, women, the young (including children), the elderly, the physically and mentally disabled, and those of different racial groups within the meaning of the Race Relations Act.

Additionally, where they are working well, partnerships are encouraged to build on existing consultation arrangements. In relation to existing consultation, two pieces of legislation here are key. First is the Police and Magistrates' Courts Act 1994, consolidated in the Police Act 1996. This requires police authorities 'before the beginning of the financial year to determine objectives for the policing of the authority's area during that year'. The local policing plan shall include a statement of 'any objectives determined by the Secretary of State', 'objectives determined by the authority' and 'performance targets established by the authority'. The Police and Magistrates' Courts Act consequently places greater emphasis on police–community consultation than had previously been the case. At the end of the year the police authority is required to produce an annual report, giving performance against the objectives. Second, as part of the government's drive to modernize local government, the 'Best Value' initiative is aimed at achieving economy, efficiency, effectiveness and quality in the delivery of local services. This agenda has highlighted the need to extend the involvement of the public, both as consumers of local services and as local taxpayers, via more effective consultation arrangements (DETR, 1998). The Local Government Act places a central duty upon local authorities to consult local people in the planning and delivery of public services. As a key local service, the police are required to respond to the Best Value initiative, not least by reviewing and improving consultation mechanisms.

Finally, partnerships are required to involve in the consultation process groups who may be considered 'hard to reach'. Though clearly mechanisms for public participation in discussions about both community safety and policing policy are vital, there are continuing limits to the extent to which the outputs of such consultation represent the view of the 'public' or the 'community'. As Smith (1987) has argued, there are many 'publics', and they may often hold conflicting views about the priorities for local public bodies such as the police and others involved in community safety.

Several recent reports have drawn attention to some of the limitations of current consultation mechanisms – particularly in relation to policing. Two Constabulary Inspectorate reports (HMIC, 1997, 1999b) on the policing of plural communities, though providing examples of 'good practice', have been critical of the formal and informal links developed by forces for consulting the harder to reach sections of some communities. Perhaps most critically, the Macpherson inquiry (1999) into the death of Stephen Lawrence has once again highlighted the gulf between the police service and some ethnic minority communities.

The guidance provided to Crime and Disorder Partnerships notes the importance of involving groups that are 'hard to reach' and specifically mentions in this regard young men, the homeless, drug users, the gay community, members of ethnic minority communities, children, those who suffer domestic abuse and the elderly. A number of problems in the general area of police–community consultation may be identified. I will outline five briefly here.

Hard to reach groups. Despite the current emphasis on such groups, there remains considerable confusion about which groups may be considered 'hard to reach' and why. There is considerable variation between police forces and a lack of clarity about the nature and purpose of consultation in this area. The terminology is perhaps unhelpful, for it appears, for example, that groups or communities may, for example, become considered to be 'hard to reach' for a broad range of reasons (see Jones and Newburn, 2000). These include:

1 They are small and difficult to locate.
2 They are large and not well organized (consequently finding community representatives is difficult).
3 They are large yet diffuse (consequently finding community representatives is difficult).
4 They are hostile to the police.
5 They are largely 'invisible'.
6 They wish to minimize contact with the police.
7 Their needs are not recognized or understood.
8 There are cultural or language barriers.
9 There is simply little history of consultation with this group.

Means and ends. Police forces and communities are often confused about, and frequently confuse, the means and the ends of consultation. 'Consultation' is now widely recognized to be a 'good thing' by police forces. However, there are several potential areas of confusion associated with the 'means' and 'ends' of consultation:

1 The reasons for engaging in consultation are often not spelt out, or are unclear – i.e. the anticipated 'ends' may be at best implicit.
2 The reasons for engaging in consultation may vary and, at worst, may be confused.
3 The 'means' and 'ends' of consultation may become confused – consultation may simply become an end in itself.
4 The primary ends of consultation may be different for hard to reach groups and police managers.

Un-coordinated consultation. There is the danger of a lack of co-ordination, of overlap and duplication (within and without the police organization) in relation to consultation activities in general, and in connection with 'hard to reach groups' in particular. Thus, for example, responsibility for consultation activities associated with the Police and Magistrates' Courts Act and the Crime and Disorder Act tends often to lie in a different part of the police organization from responsibility for consultation around Best Value. Some forces have recognized the dangers here and are working on methods for streamlining and co-ordinating these activities; others, however, are some way behind.

Consultation overload. Certain groups or community representatives are repeatedly bombarded with requests to participate in consultation exercises, and there is a danger of provoking knee-jerk responses which rush to establish mechanisms without properly thinking through their fundamental purpose. Because of the perceived need to locate public policing within forms of democratic accountability, and because of the increasing political desire to 'include' the public in policing activities (what Garland, 1996, calls 'responsibilization') the demands on the police organization to 'consult' have increased exponentially. There is a real danger that both the police themselves, and the communities they are meant to serve, will both suffer 'consultation overload'.

Sustainability. This problem arises, in part, from the confusion surrounding the purpose(s) ('ends') of consultation. Lack of clarity about why some forms of consultation are being undertaken means that the rationale becomes short-term (it is a current priority). Consequently there are occasions where long-term commitment to sustaining consultation is not as visible as it might be. Sustainability is anyway a problem. Consultation, by its very nature, depends in part on the individual representatives (police and 'community') involved. For differing reasons there is often a relatively high turnover among representatives. This makes long-term strategic thinking all the more important.

The role of the police The Crime and Disorder Act 1998 prioritizes community consultation, partnership working and problem-solving as a strategy. It would appear, on the surface at least, that one of the implications of the Act is that the role of the police will be subjected to increased scrutiny and public debate and, moreover, that as a result the fundamental role of the police may undergo some alteration. There are a number of directions in which change is possible. In considering the possible alternatives, a model provided by David Bayley (1994) is useful, if not entirely accurate (see Morgan and Newburn, 1997, for a critical review). He offers five options.

The first he calls 'dishonest law enforcement', wherein the police claim to prevent crime, but actually only provide 'authoritative intervention and symbolic justice'. This, he argues, is roughly what happens now. The second is 'determined crime prevention', in which the police move centre-stage to become 'society's official criminologists', identifying both the causes of, and the solutions to, crime. Third is 'honest law enforcement' in which the police disavow responsibility for, and the capacity to provide, primary crime prevention on the basis that it is something they cannot deliver. The fourth model he calls 'efficient law enforcement', which involves the scrapping or radical reorganization of those aspects of law enforcement that contribute little to crime prevention, perhaps via civilianization or privatization, and reallocating resources to reinforce community or 'problem-solving' policing. Finally, there is 'stratified crime prevention', in which responsibility for crime prevention is limited to the activity of front-line uniformed neighbourhood officers, i.e. those most closely in touch with communities.

Of course, it is not yet clear how the police service in England and Wales will respond to the type of question Bayley poses. On the surface some of the options he outlines would appear to be non-starters. First, we would already appear to have moved beyond stratified crime prevention. Second, 'honest law enforcement' is unrealistic: implying that the police can engage in effective law enforcement without promoting aspects of community policing is surely mistaken. Third, even if Bayley were right, and contemporary policing could be characterized as 'dishonest law enforcement' (and I do not think he is), the Crime and Disorder Act ought to make maintaining such a stance all but impossible. The same may be said of 'determined crime prevention', though this may still be a role some senior police managers covet. That leaves 'efficient law enforcement' and, indeed, it seems plausible that some aspects of this role will be visible in policing during the next period of its history.

Bayley's own solution to the problem he poses involves a three-pronged strategy. On the ground, neighbourhood police officers would deliver crime prevention; above that 'basic police units' would develop operational strategies from the bottom up; finally, police forces would provide resources, management and evaluation from the centre. The major problem with this view is that Bayley's analysis concentrates disproportionately on police responsibility for policing. There are two aspects to this. First, in an obvious but rather narrow sense Bayley's model cannot readily incorporate the central role that local authorities will play in formulating, managing and implementing community safety strategies. Second, and I return to this below, he treats the police as if they operated in a policing vacuum. That is, what he offers is a police solution to the problem of contemporary policing. In reality, of course, the police are part of an increasingly complex and diffuse patchwork quilt of policing activity. This, I will argue later, rather than being inhibited is likely to be further stimulated by the provisions of the Crime and Disorder Act.

Nonetheless, the somewhat narrower question of the role of the police remains important. What seems clear is that the public police will, at a general level, be pushed increasingly towards what is generally thought of as 'community policing'. Though difficult to define or pin down, 'community policing' 'relies upon organizational decentralization and a reorientation of patrol in order to facilitate two-way communication between police and the public. It assumes a commitment to broadly focused, problem-oriented policing, and requires [the] police [to] be responsive to citizens' demands when they decide what [the] local problems are and set their priorities. It also implies a commitment to helping neighbourhoods solve crime problems on their own, through community organizations and crime prevention programmes' (Skogan and Hartnett, 1997, p. 5).

As many authors have noted, it is not difficult to see that this is a far from unproblematic model of policing. Writing over a decade ago, Smith (1987) outlined a number of problems associated with the community policing model that are just as pertinent to policing after the Crime and Disorder Act as they were then. I want to focus briefly here on three issues raised by Smith.

First, police-initiated activity is mostly adversarial; consensus-building activity is hard to plan. It is in response to immediate demands that most consensus-building activity by the police occurs. Police activities that are most easily planned are mostly adversarial. In what ways, therefore, and to what extent, can the police plan for increased involvement in consensus-building activities?

Second, policing impinges on different sections of the community, or on different communities, in contrasting ways and this may be a considerable source of friction and conflict. Appeals to community do not necessarily solve the problem. As Crawford (1997, p. 294) notes, 'An assertion of community at a local level can be beautifully conciliatory, socially nuanced and constructive but it can also be parochial, intolerant, oppressive and unjust.' This raises the question of how the conflicting demands on the police are to be solved in a just and democratic manner. Third, decentralization conflicts with the universal framework of law. The issue of police discretion comes to the fore in community policing models and means for the proper democratic governance of policing become all the more important.

The culture of the police

Crime prevention has occupied a relatively marginal and secondary position within public policing over the bulk of the last century and a half. It has been 'ghettoized' (Crawford, 1998a). Though one should never underestimate the ability of the constabulary to appear to change without really changing at all, it seems unlikely, given the requirements of the Crime and Disorder Act, that crime prevention and community safety can remain ghettoized. At the heart of the Act there is an attempt to bring policing and communities closer together to plan, manage and implement crime and disorder strategies.

Assuming the Act is even partially successful in its aim of radically empowering local people, it will have implications not only for the way in which problems are identified and priorities set, but also for the way in which they are tackled. Put a different way, it will not be simply a question of identifying and prioritizing local problems and then pointing the police (with partners) in the right direction. Rather, it is likely to require the police to move (further) towards 'community' or 'problem-oriented' policing methods and styles, and this has implications for the internal cultures of policing.

One does not have to have been a particularly avid student of recent British policing to see some of the challenges that lie ahead in such a process of reorientation. It is still the case that much 'preventive' policing work is undertaken by specialists who are, in many cases, marginalized within their forces, and whose ability to effect change is hampered by a police culture which is resistant to the 'service' ethic that is central to much of this type of work. It is not just the style of this form of policing which poses a challenge, but also the context in which it takes place. Community policing in a multicultural society in which there are very significant, and perhaps growing, social divisions also poses a very real challenge to the internal culture of the police service. Indeed, rather than talking of 'police culture' here, it is perhaps more satisfactory to think instead in terms of what Chan (following Bourdieu) has referred to as the 'habitus' of policing: 'the institutionalized perceptions, values, strategies and schemas' of police work (Chan, 1997, p. 92), and to distinguish this from the 'field' (the formal rules that govern policing) in which it takes place.

My second contention about the likely implications of the Act is therefore a very simple one. It may be summarized in three points. First, the Act seeks to bring a significant reorientation of the way in which police services are managed and provided. Second, and more particularly, it seeks to bring the police and local communities, however they may be defined, closer together. Third, such a reorientation requires changes not only in the objectives, management and provision of policing services (the field), but crucially also in the internal culture of the organization itself (the habitus).

That this is so may be illustrated by considering the experiments in 'community policing' that have already taken place. In describing one of the best known of these, in Chicago, Skogan and Hartnett suggest that community policing required:

> that officers do many of their old jobs in new ways, and that they take on tasks that they never imagined would come their way. They are asked to identify and solve a broad range of problems; reach out to elements of the community that previously were outside their orbit; and put their careers at risk by taking on unfamiliar and challenging responsibilities. (1997, p. 71)

The findings of the Chicago study are of considerable relevance to post-Crime and Disorder Act policing in the United Kingdom. The Chicago Police Department invested heavily in the business of attempting to capture 'hearts and minds'. Officers were consulted about their concerns and fears – these included worries over potential loss of autonomy, the diversion of resources from the traditional core functions of policing, the imposition of unrealistic goals by local citizens and out-of-touch management. Police officers' jobs were changed to enable them to spend more time on the beat and in the community generally. Significant investment in training was made, as were attempts to change the department's management style, from the top of the organization to the bottom, and with particular emphasis on the role and involvement of first-line managers. Now, unlike many experiments in 'community policing', Chicago's would appear to have been a success. The extent of the investment and effort required to make it so should not be underestimated, just as the extent of its successes should not be exaggerated.

Without doubt, then, the Crime and Disorder Act poses challenges to police culture. Together with the Macpherson Report, inquiries into integrity and standards in public life, and the arrival of the Human Rights Act 1998, it raises questions about values, attitudes and appropriate conduct. In a parallel manner, Walklate (1996) has argued that Equal Opportunities policies, if taken seriously, also have the potential to change not only the internal dynamics and relationships of police organizations, but also relations with the public. She also argues that recognizing these links, and acting on them, constitutes a 'fundamental challenge' to what is understood as proper police work: 'Once anti-discriminatory practices are seriously embraced within an organization . . . that embrace, by definition, demands a critical examination of how that organization delivers its central tasks and the appropriateness of those tasks' (p. 204).

The police role in policing

The issues that arise under this heading do not simply emanate from the Crime and Disorder Act. Rather they are associated with the significant changes occurring in relation to policing which are the product of, or at least are associated with, the deeper social processes often summarized as 'late modern social change'. Nonetheless, the Act is both part of these processes and, simultaneously, serves to reinforce and give impetus to some of the key changes taking place.

Reiner described the social transformation I am referring to in the following way:

> the deeper social changes of postmodernity are transforming the role of the police institution within the whole array of policing processes. The rise of *the* police – a single professional organization for handling the policing function of regulation and surveillance, with the state's monopoly of the legitimate use of force as its ultimate resource – was itself a paradigm of the modern. It was predicated upon the project of organizing society around a central, cohesive notion of order . . . The changes in social structure and culture which have been labelled

postmodern render this conception of policing increasingly anachronistic
... In short, policing now reflects the processes of pluralism, disaggrega-
tion and fragmentation which have been seen as the hallmark of the
postmodern. (1992, p. 779)

The characteristics of such 'postmodern' or 'late modern' change can
be summarized as follows:

1 Developments in economics, communication and transport technology
   have created a global metropolitan culture and consumer market that
   offers a wide range of choices of self-identity and lifestyles, and leads to
   increasing material and social polarization.
2 The social geography of the city has been transformed, often through a
   radical process of 'hollowing out', by the combined influence of
   international capital and changes in the nature of production and
   consumption.
3 Linked with this has been the 'privatization' of public space, the rise of
   'mass private property' and the development of 'zones of private
   governance' and defensive crime prevention strategies and a consequent
   decline of civil society.
4 One of the consequences of the contemporaneous processes of globalization and localization, together with the rise of new technologies of
   surveillance, is the segmentation of social control.
5 The disembedding of social activity from local contexts, changing the
   sources of trust from local systems to abstract systems, with a resulting
   heightening of 'ontological insecurity' (Giddens, 1990) and consequen-
   tial impact on expectations of policing and the police as 'symbolic
   tokens of trust'.
6 The rise of 'systemic', 'consumerist' and 'actuarial' forms of managerialism (Bottoms, 1995) and the tensions between these.
7 The rising visibility of differentiated moral value systems (Newburn,
   1991).

The consequences of these changes for policing have been:

1 The contemporaneous and linked processes of globalization and
   localization have increasingly 'stretched' public policing, resulting, in
   part, in increasing levels of public dissatisfaction.
2 Increasingly, security has become commodified: 'Once "security"
   ceases to be guaranteed to all citizens by a sovereign state, it tends to
   become a commodity, which, like any other, is distributed by market
   forces rather than according to need' (Garland, 1996, p. 463).
3 New technologies of surveillance have expanded rapidly. (Indeed, this
   is the most rapidly expanding part of the private security industry.)
4 Increasing emphasis on setting performance objectives and targets, and
   measuring outputs and outcomes.

5   Perhaps most crucially of all, the falling into disrepute of the modern
    criminal justice state. This is what Garland (1996) has otherwise
    referred to as the increasing visibility of 'the limits of the sovereign
    state', signalling the end of belief in the possibility of a police solution
    to the problem of crime control. In respect of policing, the effects of
    this can most visibly be seen in the increasingly complex policing
    division of labour (Jones and Newburn, 1998).

    The Crime and Disorder Act 1998 has to be understood in the context
of these broader and deeper changes that are taking place. Simultaneously,
however, the Act itself is likely to serve to stimulate and intensify the
transformation of policing we are witnessing as a result of these changes.
The logic of the Act is such that, in tandem with other changes taking
place, local policing is set to become increasingly plural. There are a
number of reasons for this. First, it is the case that the Act places a
significantly increased emphasis on the identification of local problems and
local responses to them. Second, it encourages local choice and is likely
therefore to stimulate competition. Third, it explicitly encourages
partnerships between public, private and municipal providers and,
additionally, Best Value requirements will further reinforce this 'marketization' of criminal justice. Perhaps crucially in this regard, Best Value
requires reviews of service provision to be undertaken according to what
are known as the 'Four Cs': Challenge why and how a service is being
provided; invite Comparison with others' performance across a range of
relevant indicators, taking into account the views of both service users and
potential suppliers; Consult local taxpayers, service users and the wider
business community in the setting of new performance targets; and
embrace fair Competition as a means of securing efficient and effective
services. Together, therefore, the Crime and Disorder Act and Best Value
not only make explicit the impossibility of a 'police solution' to policing,
they are likely to stimulate competition and change.
    On one level I see little problem with some of these developments. As
Reiner (1997) has argued, the existence of a public police service with an
omnibus mandate is increasingly anachronistic under late modern
conditions. Many of the likely changes are therefore to be welcomed. At
the very least it is important that the increasingly complex policing division
of labour is recognized and, in some respects, accommodated. Nonetheless,
it would be shortsighted to ignore some of the dangers ahead. The
increased marketization of crime control does raise some important issues.
Among these, three appear to be key.
    First are the dangers associated with inequalities in the provision of
protection and the problem of 'majoritarianism'. One of the greatest
dangers in the marketization of protection is that the material and social
polarization that already exists will be exacerbated by the addition of
further 'security differentials'. This may occur in a number of ways,
including the simple purchasing of security and policing services by those

who can afford them and, because of differences in the ability to articulate needs, the drawing away of public policing services from areas of greatest need to areas of least need. The potential for the emergence, or extension, of such inequalities raises the second important issue, the problem of governance.

There are at least three aspects to the problem of governance that need consideration. The first is the question raised about how the public police are to be held accountable in an environment in which pluralism is encouraged. One potential positive outcome of a renewed focus on questions of police governance is that the issue of 'operational independence' will come under critical scrutiny. The second is the related question about how the private security industry, and all its component parts, is to be regulated or otherwise governed. Finally, there is the issue of the governance of security networks. With the recognition that plural policing is already with us, numerous authors have already paid some attention to the question of how such networks may be governed (Jones and Newburn, 1998; Johnston, 2000; Blair, 1998; Loader, forthcoming). Of all these, it is the case put forward by Ian Blair that has received the greatest discussion. Focusing on the opportunities provided by the Crime and Disorder Act, Blair argues that plural policing and, in particular, plural patrolling should be provided within what he calls a 'police-compliant system', i.e. a system in which many providers are possible, but where standards, training and accreditation would be overseen by the public police. Now, given what has been said already about choice and competition under the new system, it is difficult to see how such a 'regulatory role' could be undertaken by one of the organizations which is supposed to be subject to such competition. We are probably therefore forced to reject such a role for the police. The important points to note here are, first, the dangers of the absence of 'proper' governance and, second, the need for a normative debate about what form such governance should take (Loader, forthcoming).

The final issue I wish to focus on is the dual one of the future of 'populist punitiveness' and 'punitive segregation'. Garland (2000) argues that, despite the encouragement of new 'preventive strategies' associated with crime prevention and community policing, governments are actually ambivalent about such strategies and frequently retreat from their implications.

> Under certain circumstances, or with respect to certain kinds of offences and offenders, they respond to the predicament by denying it; by reactivating the old myth of the sovereign state; and by engaging in a more expressive and more intensive mode of punishment that purports to convey public sentiment and the full force of state authority. (p. 349)

The symbolic reassertion of state sovereignty tends to involve, as Jock Young (1999) has pointed out, two fallacies: a 'cosmetic fallacy' (crime is a superficial problem rather than a chronic problem) and the idea of the 'social as simple' (where problems have a small number of readily identifiable causes). In policing, the key recent example of such processes at work would be the relatively crude 'zero tolerance' model embraced by some officers in recent years. Despite the dangers and difficulties – not the least of which will be the likely continued attractiveness of 'populist punitiveness' (Bottoms, 1995) and 'punitive segregation' (Garland, 2000) to governments – the Crime and Disorder Act potentially provides the basis upon which more constructive forms of policing may be established. As Les Johnston (2000) has argued, the challenge facing us now is how we can embrace diversity in policing to bring about an optimal system that is neither 'quantitatively excessive' nor 'qualitatively invasive'.

References

Alderson, J. (1979) *Policing Freedom*, Plymouth, Macdonald & Evans.

Bayley, D. (1994) *Police for the Future*, New York, Oxford University Press.

Bennett, T. (1990) *Evaluating Neighbourhood Watch*, Aldershot, Gower.

Blair, I. (1998) 'Where do the police fit into policing?', speech to the Association of Chief Police Officers' conference, 16 July.

Bottoms, A.E. (1990) 'Crime prevention: facing the 1990s', *Policing and Society*, vol. 1, no. 1, pp. 3–22.

Bottoms, A.E. (1995) 'The philosophy and politics of punishment and sentencing' in Clarkson, C. and Morgan, R. (eds) *The Politics of Sentencing Reform*, Oxford, Oxford University Press.

Bottoms, A.E. and Wiles, P. (1996) 'Crime and policing in a changing social context' in Saulsbury, W., Mott, J. and Newburn, T. (eds) *Themes in Contemporary Policing*, London, Policy Studies Institute.

Brown, D. and Iles, S. (1985) *Community Constables: a Study of Policing Initiative*, Research and Planning Unit Paper 30, London, Home Office.

Burrows, J. and Lewis, H. (1988) *Directing Patrolwork: a Study of Uniformed Policing*, Home Office Research Study 99, London, HMSO.

Chan, J. (1997) *Changing Police Culture: Policing in a Multicultural Society*, Cambridge, Cambridge University Press.

Chatterton, M. and Rogers, M. (1989) 'Focused policing' in Morgan, R. and Smith, D. (eds) *Coming to Terms with Policing*, London, Routledge.

Clarke, R. (1992) *Situational Crime Prevention*, New York, Harrow & Heston.

Clarke, R. and Mayhew, P. (1980) *Designing out Crime*, London, HMSO.

Crawford, A. (1997) *The Local Governance of Crime: Appeals to Community and Partnerships*, Oxford, Clarendon Press.

Crawford, A. (1998a) *Crime Prevention and Community Safety: Politics, Policies and Practices*, Harlow, Longman.

Crawford, A. (1998b) 'Community safety and the quest for security: holding back the dynamics of social exclusion', *Policy Studies*, vol. 19, pp. 237–53.

DETR (1998) *Modernizing Local Government: Improving Local Services through Best Value*, Department of the Environment, Transport and the Regions, London, HMSO.

Farrington, D. (1996) *Understanding and Preventing Youth Crime*, York, Joseph Rowntree Foundation.

Garland, D. (1996) 'The limits of the sovereign state: strategies of crime control in contemporary society', *British Journal of Criminology*, vol. 35, no. 4, pp. 445–71.

Garland, D. (2000) 'The culture of high crime societies: some preconditions of recent "law and order" policies', *British Journal of Criminology*, vol. 40, no. 3, pp. 347–75.

Giddens, A. (1990) *The Consequences of Modernity*, Cambridge, Polity Press.

Gilling, D. (1997) *Crime Prevention: Theory, Policy and Politics*, London, UCL Press.

Gladstone F.J. (1980) *Co-ordinating Crime Prevention Efforts*, Home Office Research Study 62, London, HMSO.

Graef, R. (1989) *Talking Blues*, London, Collins.

Harvey, L., Grimshaw, P. and Pease, K. (1989) 'Crime prevention delivery: the work of crime prevention officers' in Morgan, R. and Smith, D. (eds) *Coming to Terms with Policing*, London, Routledge.

HM Inspectorate of Constabulary (1997) *Winning the Race: Policing Plural Communities*, London, Home Office.

HM Inspectorate of Constabulary (1999a) *Police Integrity: Securing and Maintaining Public Confidence*, London, Home Office.

HM Inspectorate of Constabulary (1999b) *Winning the Race Revisited*, London, Home Office.

Home Office (1965) *Report of the Committee on the Prevention and Detection of Crime* (Cornish Report), London, HMSO.

Home Office (1971) *Crime Prevention Panels*, Home Office Circular 48/1971, London, Home Office.

Home Office (1978) Home Office Circular 211/1978 (the 'Ditchley Circular'), London, Home Office.

Home Office (1984) *Crime Prevention*, Home Office Circular 8/84, London, Home Office.

Home Office (1991) *Safer Communities: The Local Delivery of Crime Prevention through the Partnership Approach* (Morgan Report), London, Home Office.

Home Office (1997) *Getting to Grips with Crime*, London, Home Office.

Home Office (1998) *The Crime and Disorder Act: Guidance on Statutory Crime and Disorder Partnerships*, London, Home Office.

Husain, S. (1988) *Neighbourhood Watch in England and Wales*, Crime Prevention Unit Paper 12, London, Home Office.

Irving, B., Bird, C., Hibberd, M. and Willmore, J. (1989) *Neighbourhood Policing: The Natural History of a Policing Experiment*, London, Police Foundation.

Johnston, L. (2000) *Policing Britain: Risk, Security and Governance*, Harlow, Longman.

Johnston, V., Shapland, J. and Wiles, P. (1993) *Developing Police Crime Prevention: Management and Organizational Change*, Crime Prevention Unit Paper 41, London, Home Office.

Jones, T. and Newburn, T. (1997) *Policing after the Act: Police Governance after the Police and Magistrates' Courts Act 1994*, London, Policy Studies Institute.

Jones, T. and Newburn, T. (1998) *Private Security and Public Policing*, Oxford, Clarendon Press.

Jones, T. and Newburn, T. (1999) 'Urban change and policing: mass private property reconsidered', *European Journal on Criminal Policy and Research*, vol. 7, pp. 225–44.

Jones, T. and Newburn, T. (2000) *Widening Access: Improving Police Relationships with 'Hard to Reach' Groups*, London, Home Office.

Jones, T. and Newburn, T. (forthcoming) 'The transformation of policing? Understanding current trends in policing systems', *British Journal of Criminology*.

Loader, I. (forthcoming) 'Plural policing and democratic governance', *Journal of Law and Society*.

Macpherson, Sir W. (1999) *The Stephen Lawrence Inquiry*, London, Stationery Office.

Manning, P (1977) *Police Work*, Cambridge, MA, MIT Press.

McConville, M. and Shepherd, D. (1992) *Watching Police, Watching Communities*, London, Routledge.

Morgan, R. and Newburn, T. (1997) *The Future of Policing*, Oxford, Oxford University Press.

Morgan, R. and Smith, D. (eds) (1989) *Coming to Terms with Policing*, London, Routledge.

Newburn, T. (1991) *Permission and Regulation: Law and Morals in Post-war Britain*, London, Routledge.

Reiner, R. (1992) *The Politics of the Police*, Brighton, Harvester.

Reiner, R. (1997) 'Policing and the police' in Maguire, M., Morgan, R. and Reiner, R. (eds) *The Oxford Handbook of Criminology*, Oxford, Clarendon Press.

Rhodes, R. (1997) *Understanding Governance: Policy Networks, Governance, Reflexivity and Accountability*, Milton Keynes, Open University Press.

Skogan, W.G. and Hartnett, S.M. (1997) *Community Policing, Chicago Style*, Oxford, Oxford University Press.

Smith, D.J. (1987) 'The police and the idea of community' in Willmott, P. (ed.) *Policing and the Community*, London, Policy Studies Institute.

Tuck, M. (1988) *Crime Prevention: a Shift in Concept*, Home Office Research Bulletin 24, London, Home Office.

Walker, R. (1997) 'Poverty and social exclusion in Europe' in Walker, A. and Walker, C. (eds) *Britain Divided*, London, Child Poverty Action Group.

Walklate, S. (1996) 'Equal opportunities and the future of policing' in Leishman, F., Loveday, B. and Savage, S. (eds) *Core Issues in Policing*, Harlow, Longman.

Weatheritt, M. (1986) *Innovations in Policing*, London, Croom Helm.

Willmott, P. (ed.) (1987) *Policing and the Community*, London, Policy Studies Institute.

Young, J. (1999) *The Exclusive Society: Social Exclusion, Crime and Difference in Late Modernity*, London, Sage.

Crime and disorder reduction partnerships

The future of community safety?

Gordon Hughes

The 1950s and 1960s were characterized by a cross-party consensus regarding law and order and the belief that the criminal justice system was fit for its intended purpose, with fine-tuning being all that was required. Since the 1970s many have claimed that we have seen a crisis of legitimacy, or what we may term the 'unsettling' of the political consensus around criminal justice, the details of which need not concern us here. However, after a prolonged period of 'failure' and of 'Nothing works' in prevention and rehabilitation, recent years have seen what Gilling (1999, p. 1) terms a 'remarkable air of optimism' blowing through parts of the criminal justice system. The new optimism challenges the claim that nothing can be done about crime (and its reduction) with case studies of success. Gilling (1999, p. 1) again notes a convergence of commitment and perspective among agencies around the ideologies of 'preventionism' and 'community': 'there is a new-found belief that something can be done about crime if it is done early, in the name of prevention, and if it is done by and with the support of the community'. Allied to this is a growing consensus over the intolerance of disorder and its control through 'zero tolerance' policing and the rise of another ideology, that of partnership: 'Where discourses of crime control were once discordant, there is now a sense of harmony' (Gilling, 1999, p. 1). This development is epitomized most powerfully by the rallying call and policy of community safety partnerships.

Of course, these developments are not unique to the United Kingdom. The rhetoric and practice of community crime prevention, multi-agency partnerships and the mixed economy of community safety characterize developments in crime control across many contemporary societies. Internationally there is also evidence of a declining role of the state – a 'hollowing out' – as the direct provider of crime prevention activities. Crime prevention is increasingly organized at global and local levels rather than the national level. Whilst acknowledging the international context of community safety developments, this chapter adopts a UK focus, since Britain has been a pioneer and useful exemplar of the mix of local authority and police action and central direction, and of the 'mixed economy' approach, involving statutory, voluntary, community and business 'partners'. It is possible, then, to make a case for some cautious comparative lesson-drawing from the United Kingdom. Post-1998 developments appear to represent a watershed in crime control policy, with events moving fast for 'an area of social policy and practice which is more accustomed to incremental rather than rapid change' (Ballintyne et al., 2000, p. 1).

Future trends in community safety are by no means certain or easily amenable to technical fixes. This is not to deny the laudable concern with trying to answer the question 'What works?' In turn we have seen the emergence of the increasingly ascendant discourse of 'evidence-based' policy and practice drawing on 'rigorous', measurable research findings across the whole range of social, health and criminal justice policy fields. Such pragmatic, problem-oriented and outcome-focused concerns are crucial to understanding current trends in community safety and crime reduction. But equally important is the fostering of a critical and reflexive culture around this 'wicked issue' of community safety, not least to encourage a stepping back from the headlong rush to action. Community safety may be said to be a 'wicked issue' in more senses than one. Most researchers in the field know that it is a 'wicked issue' for practitioners and agencies in that it is not a sequestered activity: it does not fall into the neat compartments of the criminal justice system or into established local authority lines of organizational division. Whilst the Home Office's concerns relate to the problem that insufficient local practice has been evaluated, an equally important concern is the insufficient knowledge of what local practice is or, very important, why it takes the shape it does (Gilling, 1999, p. 6).

Community safety thus remains a contested terrain, not just for the challenges it raises for not being easy to compartmentalize the practices and policies of crime prevention and related forms of harm reduction, but also for the conceptual, moral and political challenges associated with its nascent agenda which may move us beyond the traditional boundaries of both social policy and crime control. Arguably the central question to bear in mind throughout the following discussion is the extent to which community safety should be viewed as synonymous with crime reduction and the control of social disorder (as embodied in the Crime and Disorder Act 1998 in Britain) or whether it should be linked with wider concerns about both hazards and safety in communities from both criminal and *non-criminalized* harms. The latter has been termed a 'pan-hazard' approach to community safety (Wiles and Pease, 2000).

Community safety and the academy

Throughout the 1980s and 1990s community safety occupied the dubious status of being a Cinderella subject in the fields of both criminology and social policy analysis (see Hughes, 2000). Community safety has been viewed as a vacuous, at best 'feel good', term but, as policy and practice, not something that is amenable to quantifiable evaluation in terms of 'what works'. Nor does community safety fit easily into the persistent, if embattled, modernist project of 'dispositional' criminology being constituted as a science of crime, in terms of the study of its causation and control. Furthermore, community safety – when viewed as concerning pan-hazard harm reduction rather than crime and disorder reduction – may not be easily accommodated into criminology's at times collusive relationship in the United Kingdom with the criminal justice system. Put briefly, it has not been easily reconciled with the traditional 'business' of the discipline of criminology.

So what is all the chatter and international hive of activity about community safety in the 'crime prevention industry at the present time'? With the statutory institutionalization of community safety strategies in the Crime and Disorder Act, it is now on the policy agenda of central government and local authorities and also on the research agenda of mainstream criminology in the United Kingdom. Viewed cynically, money and rewards are now available for researching community safety strategies, given their prominence in the aforementioned policy. Viewed less cynically, the growing interest in 'all things community safety' may also be indicative of the increasingly post-disciplinary thinking in the academy generally (Muncie, 2000). Whatever interpretation is taken, community safety is unlikely to disappear from the criminological landscape as either an evolving policy field or a rhetorical political discourse.

Key moments in the history of a capacious concept

The term 'community safety' first emerged around the radical left politics of police monitoring groups in the metropolitan police authorities in the mid to late 1970s. It was deployed to try to challenge the police's self-defined 'ownership' of the problem of crime and disorder and to give members of often embattled communities greater say and involvement in what constituted safety and order. Never fully articulated, this concern was explicitly taken up and modified by the National Association for the Care and Resettlement of Offenders (NACRO). In various 'high crime' localities during the 1980s NACRO promoted some important local developments in crime prevention which involved the active participation of communities in the articulation of perceived solutions to the problems they were facing and which also fused situational and social crime prevention techniques (Bottoms, 1990).

Throughout the 1980s community crime prevention and multi-agency partnerships – alongside the technical 'fixes' of situational crime prevention – became increasingly associated with the Conservative governments' use of community safety for legitimacy purposes and as a counterweight to the crisis of criminal justice and law and order. This approach involved a dual strategy, namely passing responsibility down through the community to the individual citizen and being located within multi-agency structures. In turn, both features were linked by the crucial concept of partnership.

The next key moment in the life of community safety was associated with the Home Office's 1991 report *Safer Communities: The Local Delivery of Crime Prevention through the Partnership Approach* (known as the Morgan Report). The main thrust of the Morgan Report was that the concept of 'crime prevention' is somewhat limiting in scope and has generally been police-driven, with other agencies having only a marginal stake in it. In the words of the report:

> The term *'crime prevention'* is often narrowly interpreted and this reinforces the view that it is solely the responsibility of the police. On the other hand, the term *'community safety'* is open to wider interpretation and could encourage greater participation from all sections of the community in the fight against crime. (Home Office, 1991, p. 3)

The Morgan Report also supported the notion that local authorities should be given the statutory duty (and therefore the resources) to co-ordinate crime prevention strategies for their locality. The report also argued that sufficient resources to make this change must be forthcoming from central government.

The recommendations of the Morgan Report were taken up quite selectively by the Conservative governments of the 1990s. This is not, however, to deny its significant effect on local authorities since its publication. Although the governments of the 1990s were not keen to play up the leadership role of the local authority, much of the thrust of the report was accepted and the major central government policy vehicle of this period, the Safer Cities programme, provided a means of promoting community safety at the local level, especially in the cities and bigger towns across the country (Gilling, 1999, p. 2). Here, then, is the moment when the discourse of community safety spread across the terrain of local government. By the mid-1990s many local authorities had 'signed up' to the new rhetoric of the 'mixed economy' of crime prevention involving statutory and voluntary agencies, business and 'responsibilized' community participants in multi-agency partnerships.

Adam Crawford's (1997) and Daniel Gilling's (1997, 1999) work in particular has alerted us to some of the dangers inherent in this approach to crime prevention. Multi-agency 'community' crime prevention is viewed as being vague and open-textured, with a vision that is largely pragmatic and managerial and with forms of intervention tending to be short-term and situational in character. More tellingly, it is argued that there is a potential for such initiatives becoming co-opted on to the broader right-wing law-and-order agenda in an attempt to regain public confidence. This process of co-option means that the 'social crisis' is managed in such a way that we see the 'criminalization of social policy', as a result of which fundamental public issues are marginalized except in so far as they are defined in terms of their criminogenic qualities. Finally, there is a tendency for community safety to be associated with an exclusivist impulse and the promotion of a fortress mentality among communities towards those seen as 'the Other'.

The broad thrust of the above thesis may be too certain and totalizing in its conclusions. Other empirical research has highlighted a complex picture whereby, under the umbrella of 'community safety' and 'multi-agency partnerships', some politically progressive and inclusivist practices were also generated in specific localities (Edwards and Hughes, 2001). For example, some authorities have used community safety as a conduit for the political reconstruction of the issue of crime prevention as one of social regeneration. Gilling (1997, p. 204) himself argues that 'power is productive as well as negative or repressive, and there is always some scope or arena for its exercise that renders reductionist accounts unwise and inaccurate'. It would, of course, be misguided to view any community safety strategy, however well conceived and implemented, as a panacea for the historical shifts associated with post/late modernity and globalization. However, the very looseness of the concept of community safety perhaps provided a space and an opportunity for creative ideological appropriation by local alliances and networks which could challenge, or at least negotiate, the terms of the regressive local and central tendencies.

By the late 1990s the Labour administration was proposing a statutory partnership between the police and local authorities, rather than Morgan's recommendation of a leadership role for local authorities. This noted, much of the Morgan Report's managerialist philosophy of partnerships, multi-agency collaboration and its quasi-communitarian promotion of the active participation of the 'community' – themes also close to the heart of neo-liberalism's critique of 'old' criminal justice responses – has been to the fore in 'New' Labour's crime reduction policy. The deciphering of this key moment preoccupies the next section of this chapter.

In the shadow of crime and disorder? Community safety and the Crime and Disorder Act 1998

As a result of the recent legislation, for the first time crime prevention is an acknowledged purpose of civil government in Britain. Perhaps most important, the Crime and Disorder Act 1998 represents a watershed in the politics of crime control in sponsoring what Tim Hope (1998, p. 6) terms 'the civilianization of crime prevention, to be devolved to the community through local government and its voluntary partners alongside the statist services of the police and criminal justice'. Other commentators have praised aspects of the new legislation for 'its long overdue recognition that the levers and causes of crime lie far from the traditional reach of the criminal justice system' (Crawford, 1998, p. 4). It is difficult to argue with the Act's calls for more efficient co-ordination and management of multi-agency partnerships and the tackling of people's worries over crime and disorder. However, despite some positive features, there are few reasons to feel optimistic about the prospects of a progressive agenda on community safety in the wake of the Act.

Community safety or crime and disorder reduction?

Despite the existence of Section 17, which requires all local authorities to 'mainstream' community safety issues in all areas of local government policy, the logic of the Act drives community safety policy into an obsession with 'managing' the measurable reduction of certain types of crime and disorder that local authorities may find difficult to resist. It is telling to note that we have community safety in a Crime and Disorder Act rather than crime and disorder in a Community Safety Act. Indeed, it is instructive to listen to the supporters of the legislation who generally lapse into a form of linguistic slippage by which 'community safety' becomes synonymous with 'crime reduction' or 'anti-crime and disorder' strategies.

On the basis of the first local crime and disorder/community safety audits and strategies which appeared in 1999, it would seem that many local authorities may also fall into the not so tender trap of equating community safety with a narrow brief of certain types of crime reduction (and certainly not corporate crime reduction). (For a fuller discussion see Hughes, 2000.)

Authoritarian welfarism

Perhaps the most significant new feature of the Act has been the 'civilianization of law' as a result of which civil law gets mobilized as an instrument of regulation of antisocial but not necessarily criminal behaviour, whether it be rowdy neighbours or young people on the street. 'New' Labour's law and order agenda has thus seen the resurgence of 'tough' reparative and rehabilitative measures in the Act, geared towards the resocialization of offenders. According to Hope (1998), this dangerous moralizing tendency is closely related to the problem of controlling the consequences of the long-term residualization of social housing in the most deprived and poorest areas since the 1980s. The attraction for 'New' Labour of what has been called the 'strategy of responsibilization' (Garland, 1996) may represent a further undermining of the post-war solidarity project based on the collective management of risks and harms. However, it may also be argued that leading figures in 'New' Labour see themselves as involved in a communitarian revitalization of solidarity (Hughes and Little, 1999).

It has been widely noted that much of the new legislation is both welfarist and moralizing in tone. New Labour's broad social policy 'project' shares this moralizing logic, aided and abetted by a conservative variant of communitarianism. The diktat seems to be 'You will be socially included, if necessary through the coercive responses of a "tough love" state' (Hughes and Little, 1999). Accordingly, as well as being efficient managers, the 'moral' task for local authorities may be that of reforming disorderly people into orderly citizens or potential future productive citizens. There appears to be a strong elective affinity between this trend and Wilson and Kelling's (1982) massively influential thesis of 'broken windows' and their celebration of zero tolerance community policing of incivilities and minor disorders.

New governance and the cult of partnerships

The Crime and Disorder Act 1998 is underpinned by the ethos of solving problems through partnership and joint ownership. At the same time the responsibilities of local agencies are circumscribed by central directives and statute. As in the field of youth justice, developments in crime reduction appear to be highlighting the simultaneous centring and decentring of criminal justice policy and practice.

Supporters of the partnership approach tend to note that it has the advantages of affording a holistic approach to crime and related issues, is problem-oriented rather than bureaucratically premised, allows the systematization and co-ordination of effort, expertise and information (given that diverse agencies have a different purchase on a given crime problem), enables the pooling of resources, and disrupts 'cosy cultures' of professional interest groups (Crawford and Matassa, 2000, p. 89). It is clear that the implementation of the Act requires extensive changes in the working practices and thinking of all the criminal justice and partner social policy agencies. Because the partnerships are expected to work across a series of institutional barriers, and further blur and mix the boundaries between private, public, voluntary and community spaces, they have the potential to produce entirely new organizational networks within a managerialized framework. Furthermore, the communities 'on' which the partnerships are working are being subjected, in the words of Edwards and Stenson (1999), to unprecedented 'weeding and seeding' strategies. As a result of the recognition that effective crime control strategies must be rooted in the dynamics of local communities, and 'New' Labour's fixation with clamping down on disorder, we are witnessing an intensive reterritorialization and remoralization of highly localized crime control strategies. The outcome of devolved partnerships working within statutory requirements and subject to centralized monitoring is to:

1   Produce new conceptualizations and discourses of crime control.
2   Construct new criminal subjects and new, 'model', law-abiding citizens.
3   Rewrite the script of local governance and civil liberties (Muncie et al., 2001).

Managerialism and the audit culture

In the new criminal justice settlement at the start of the twenty-first century, it is already clear that the modernization of criminal justice is to be achieved not by the diminution but through the *intensification* of managerial disciplines and techniques as they work their way through the various parts of the policy environment.

This managerialist culture has been most significantly promoted by the increasingly influential policy evaluator, the Audit Commission. The commission's own report (1999) on 'measuring' the success of community safety across Britain in terms of performance indicators and outputs ran in tandem with the auditing drive of the Crime and Disorder Act 1998. Cope and Goodship (1999, p. 10) see the Audit Commission as one of the significant links between 'central steering agencies and local rowing agencies'. In fact this view underestimates its significance, since the commission has achieved the status of a super-regulatory body, acting not so much as a pliant myrmidon but rather as a key mentor to government bodies at both central and local levels. The Audit Commission's recommendations (in tandem with the findings of Home Office researchers) have emphasized the need to act primarily on evidence-based research that reveals 'what works' and to ignore alternative approaches considered uneconomic, ineffective and inefficient.

In the area of community safety there has been a massive transformation in the importance attached to local audits and evidence-led strategies. Since 1998 all 376 statutory Crime and Disorder Partnerships in England and Wales have had to produce and publish a strategy to reduce these problems, based on the evidence drawn from an audit of crime and disorder in the specific locality. In developing such local strategies, partnerships have been guided extensively by the increasingly synergetic services and materials provided by what may be termed the 'supra-local' partnerships of the Home Office, Audit Commission, Local Government Association, NACRO and Crime Concern. Such local strategies are driven by a performance management agenda in which cost-effective measures for the realization of specific outcome reduction targets are prioritized. This is neatly captured in the promotion of what is termed 'SMART' targets, i.e. targets which are 'Specific', 'Measurable', 'Achievable', 'Realistic' and 'Timetabled' (Audit Commission, 1999). In over half of all local strategies produced in 1999, these specific crime reduction targets were those for vehicle crime, burglary and violent crime (Phillips et al., 2000). This clearly reflects the national priorities of central government and the recommendations of the Audit Commission. It is also likely that these targets represent more easily achievable reduction aims than those associated, for example, with domestic violence and hate crimes, the targeting of which may result in an increase rather than a reduction in recorded crime in the locality. From the evidence to date from local Crime and Disorder Partnership strategies, there is a clear danger that what can be reduced in crime and disorder is largely synonymous with what can be counted and audited, and easily targeted.

As a consequence of this managerialist logic, there is now a statutory requirement for all local authorities to produce crime and disorder audits which must generate clearly measurable performance indicators. On the positive side, this may result in more strategic thinking on crime prevention and greater pressure to show 'what works' with measurable evidence in an area of policy and practice previously noted for its lack of tangible successes. However, there is also a potential down side to the establishment of a culture of audit around 'crime reduction', never mind 'community safety'. There is, of course, a long history of auditing as a process of financial accounting in relation to the provision of public services. Nevertheless, the 1980s and 1990s have seen both an intensification and a transformation of such processes. Auditing has become increasingly concerned with issues of organizational achievement (for example, 'performance indicators', 'outputs'). Services are viewed as auditable objects and providers need to be self-auditing subjects in their turn (Clarke et al., 2000). This project has been much informed by the New Right's critique of the old public sector and its questioning and dissolution of the assumed homological relationship between the public, public services and the social democratic state. A question that remains after this neo-liberal assault on the public is: how may the vacuum be filled? Here enter 'audit', inscribed as the new incarnation of the public interest in relation to public services, enabling government to supervise and direct services 'at a distance'.

Like Thatcherism, the Blairite project of reforming government has been able to portray itself as on the side of the people against the entrenched interest groups of the state and public services. At this moment in late modernity, then, we are seeing the production of auditable organizations, driven not just by the need to show procedural compliance but also performance evaluation and success in competition with each other. Audit now occupies a key normative and evangelizing role in the new governance of services for the public. In turn, auditing and evaluative agencies appear to lay claim to being the embodiment of the sceptical citizen/consumer in terms of whose interests they represent and promote.

There are dangers with this obsession with measuring success in terms of outputs. An output-fixated approach is likely to prioritize narrowly defined and easily measured activity at the expense of broader objectives and less easily 'measured' goals. Bottoms and Wiles (1996) also note the likely tendency for self-monitoring organizations to produce 'paper' tales of achievement and success which need bear little relationship to 'real', on-the-ground developments outside the institution's own criteria. Indeed, Crawford (1998) suggests that we are likely to see a fixation on outputs (organizationally defined and thus potentially stage-managed) at the cost of an engagement with the much more important but less predictable issue of the 'outcomes' of policy and practice, in other words the consequences of outputs on the wider community and environment. Finally, we may ask ourselves whether the 'democratic deficit' is spiralling into free fall in the crime control 'business', with the new modes of governance through partnerships and the seemingly 'hands off' but vice-like grip of a staggeringly complex, chameleon-like and evolving range of evaluation–consultancy–audit–inspection bodies. Labour's modernization project of government in the first decade of the twenty-first century should not therefore be confused with greater democratization.

It would appear from the above overview of trends that community safety is being structured in quite specific ways, including a heady brew of managerialization, moralization and the push towards social exclusion rather than inclusion. Is this too bleak a picture of the post-1998 world of community safety and crime and disorder reduction strategies? My own earlier research on local community safety initiatives in the early to mid-1990s (Hughes, 1996, 1998) inclines me to question the account outlined immediately above. Even in the chilling culture of severity promoted by the Conservative government's 'Tough on crime' and 'Prison works' agenda from the mid-1990s onwards, there was evidence of local resistance to this centralizing law-and-order project. Resistance, negotiation and compromise are thus likely to take place in the currently evolving local strategies of crime and disorder reduction. For example, there have been signs in the first years of legislative implementation that local authorities have been wary of introducing the child curfew orders and antisocial behaviour orders despite their power to do so since 1999. Indeed, community safety strategies as projects for the empowerment of marginalized and disadvantaged communities under the umbrella of social regeneration may not be drowned in the dangerous sea of law-and-order politics, obsessed with street crime and disorder and the remoralization of the 'underclass'. Practitioners such as Mills and Pearson (2000, p. 189), for example, have argued that community safety strategies are about improving people's quality of life and this necessarily encompasses measures which are not specifically aimed at reducing crime, such as those targeted at social and economic regeneration. They go on to contend that community safety practitioners and strategists should be wary of the 'success imperative' and the tendency to be driven by outputs. As they note sanguinely, outputs 'may be easy to measure but they will not necessarily either reflect quality of input or lead to a desired outcome' (Mills and Pearson, 2000, p. 199).

At the same time, we also need to be aware of the possible tension between local democratic control (however defined) and the goal of social inclusion. The danger of 'punitive populism' invading community safety at the local level needs to be acknowledged. Community safety partnerships may have the potential to encourage a stronger and more participative civil society; however, they may also encourage a 'defended exclusivity' among communities (Crawford, 1997). In part we must wait for the findings from detailed empirical research into the long-term policy implementation processes of the legislative powers. In this context, it is also crucial to note the confirmed arrival of a 'new kid' on the crime and disorder reduction 'block' who will play a potentially pivotal role in the implementation and realization of the Crime and Disorder Act, namely the community safety officer/ manager. What follow are some speculations about the possible fate of the new institution of community safety expertise and its officers and managers.

Futures of community safety: institution-building and the rise of a new expertise

Much of what follows in this section is necessarily speculative in character, given the open-ended and fundamentally unfinished nature of the processes of institutional change around community safety policies and practices. In introducing some theoretical insights into the debate, it is important to remember the following cautionary advice from Douglas Shearing (1998) with regard to the status of theorizing: the latter 'should take place in ways closely tied to empirical digging and political practice and contestation. The theoretical, the empirical and the normative are, at their best, mutually reinforcing activities.' In other words, be wary of compelling, totalizing grand narratives and intellectual foreclosures of processes, both optimistic and pessimistic, which in many ways remain embryonic, complex and contested across the myriad of localities and sites within the fast developing policy field of community safety and crime and disorder reduction.

A new institutional complex and body of expertise around community safety and crime and disorder reduction practices is being created. In 1991, at the time of the Morgan Report, there were eighty community safety partnerships across the country; by 2000 there were approximately 400 (Stafford and Silverlock, 2000, p. 97). Community safety officers, co-ordinators or managers represent a nascent 'quasi-professional' occupation by the beginning of the twenty-first century, to be found in virtually every local council. There is also a growing division of labour and hierarchical co-ordination of tasks. As part of this process of institution-building, the Home Office's Crime Prevention College, the Community Justice National Training Organization, several universities, NACRO, Crime Concern and the Audit Commission have all been involved in 'advising' the budding occupation and its sponsors in central and local government on the training and educational needs of what should constitute community safety 'expertise'. We have also seen the rapid growth of the National Community Safety Network, by 2000 made up of over 200 members, the overwhelming majority of whom are employed as local community safety officers/managers/co-ordinators. In the context of this flurry of training and monitoring and a headlong rush to action (Ballintyne et al., 2000, p. 1) there is a battle between different institutional players to 'govern the soul' of the new occupational complex, its practitioners/managers and their 'habitus' (Gilling and Hughes, 2000).

At present there are certainly more questions than answers regarding the likely future of this emerging occupational complex. What will crime and disorder partnerships evolve into? Have the prospects of a social inclusivist and empowering politics of community safety been sunk by the Crime and Disorder Act? Is community safety already fatally inscribed in the rigid managerialist and auditing discourse noted above? How will practitioners be positioned as part of what appears to be an increasingly fragmented, demoralized, cost-controlled and 'performative'-oriented public service class (Webb, 1999)? What are the aspirations of the community safety 'quasi-profession'? It seems unlikely that community safety experts will aspire to the professional or quasi-professional model of occupational culture and control (see Johnson, 1972). Indeed, claims by sociologists such as Heraud (1970) at the start of the 1970s that 'the movement of occupations toward professional status is one of the features of modern societies' now come across as a relic of the modernist faith in, and celebration of, the expert. Since the neo-liberal assault on the public sector throughout the 1980s and 1990s, the figure of the professional/ bureaucratic 'hero' has largely been replaced by, or transmogrified into, that of the manager. Community safety 'managers' are just the latest incarnation of a seemingly never-ending assembly line of managerialized subjects in the post-welfare state.

Taking bets on the 'moral career' of community safety officers

We are supposedly living in the era of the 'risk society' (Beck, 1992). Bauman (1999) has claimed that the most powerful cultural expression of this culture of fear is the heightened sense of *Unsicherheit*, a term difficult to translate simply into English, but which conveys a potent mix of a heightened sense of unsafety, uncertainty and insecurity. The stakes for a safe and secure future seem increasingly uncertain for most of us. Let's embrace this cultural shift and indulge in some 'risky' bets on the possible futures facing community safety practitioners and experts located in statutory, multi-agency partnerships. In particular, I wish to outline three different, if interrelated, scenarios for community safety experts in the local state. However, before doing this, several qualifications are in order. First, these are deliberately exaggerated ideal-typical models of what may happen. Furthermore they seriously downplay the importance of the very different local histories and contexts of community safety work across the country. And, most important, they are largely speculative, given the absence to date of detailed empirical research findings which might open up the complex and multiple lived realities of 'doing' community safety and crime reduction work. Finally, this concentration on the future of state-based experts should not lead us to downplay the crucial growth of other experts in crime reduction and community safety 'outside' the state and located in the growth industry around risk management as epitomized in private businesses and consultancies.

Bet 1: the technicist risk manager
There is a burgeoning intellectual debate on the apparent rise of the risk society and its implications for crime control, not least the rise to prominence of actuarialist risk management (Feeley and Simon, 1994). It is possible that the chief role of community safety managers will increasingly be that of making the risks of crime and disorder, and insecurity more generally, more identifiable and visible and of advising and instructing others on their successful management (rather than eradication and pre-vention). The expertise of such managers would thus reside in discovering, gathering and processing knowledge about (in)security and risks of crime and disorder. This thesis has been most famously applied to the police by Ericson and Heggarty (1997). They see the police as occupying a key strategic position as risk knowledge brokers, gathering risk-related infor-mation, sorting and interpreting such information, and forwarding it to relevant institutions and agencies in the public–private mix. In the risk society the key work of the police is about 'informational transactions concerned with risks'. If this diagnosis is viewed as being applicable to the public police, it could also be applied to the emergent role of the com-munity safety manager in multi-agency, and increasingly intersectoral, partnerships. It is evident that Crime and Disorder Reduction Partnerships are routinely and centrally involved in the collection of vast amounts of information and data. Much of the co-ordination of the collection of the data, the setting of realistic targets for the management of risks and the calculative assessment of success resides in the office of the community safety manager. Given this key position in the pluralized arrangements for

policing crime and disorder, surely community safety managers will be increasingly central as risk knowledge brokers (perhaps challenging the police's past and current ascendancy in crime prevention partnerships)? Indeed, we may speculate on the chances of community safety teams being seen as the 'favoured children' – heroes, even – of the central state's modernization project for both local government and criminal justice, given their remit to address 'wicked issues' through 'joined up', Best Value-oriented and targeted 'problem-solving' approaches which carry none of the 'old baggage' of bureau-professional compartmentalization.

Less heroically, the odds appear to be on the community safety officer of the first decade of the twenty-first century being a mix of 'jobbing' auditor/evaluator, networker/facilitator of never-ending partnership loops, and competitive and entrepreneurial bidder for project funding from central government. Much of the routine work of the community safety manager may reside in developing increasingly bureaucratized audits and output-based strategies. The non-heroic twist here would be the absorption of community safety teams in the production of 'safe option', 'easy win' measurable performance indicators of success in crime reduction strategies.

The first 'bet' is that of community safety practitioners being cast largely as amoral managers and 'technicians' caught up in actuarial risk management. However, there are some doubts as to whether community safety can remain untouched by moral and political debates in crime control and social order, as the second 'bet' makes clear.

Bet 2: the promoter and manager of the new moral hygiene
Nikolas Rose (1999) suggests that we are witnessing the rise of a new 'ethico' politics in which the responsibilization of individuals, families and communities, as causes of and solutions to crime and disorder, has come to the fore. Given the emphasis on the targeting of 'at risk'/dangerous groups and localities (alongside the appeal to protecting the 'vulnerable', majoritarian community) in local crime and disorder reduction strategies, it may be that community safety officers and managers are unlikely to operate, or be viewed, as purely technical, apolitical experts in risk knowledge brokerage. Instead it is possible that they may be dragged into, or collude in, the local politics of public sanitization and exclusivist impulses towards late modernity's 'difficult' and 'dangerous' people and places, now ideologically framed as 'the underclass'. Community safety managers may thus be cast in the guise of 'tough love' facilitators in the attempts to impose compulsory social inclusion on society's disaffected minorities if possible, or social exclusion if necessary, through such powers as antisocial behaviour orders. Should this scenario be realized, partnerships in community security, and community safety experts themselves, will face mounting problems of legitimacy. In particular, they may face increasingly intractable conflict with those citizens and localities designated as 'antisocial', 'disorderly' and 'criminal' (Stenson, 2000). However, it is also possible that Community Safety Partnerships may never be able to 'do

enough' in the eyes of those citizens in areas which are 'fearful', 'outraged', 'law-abiding' and 'orderly' and so on.

In the light of these possible developments, there is also a danger that the wider ambitions of some local authorities to promote social regeneration through community safety may get lost. Given the statutory requirement of a local crime and disorder audit and strategy (rather than a community safety audit and strategy), the hazards of street crime and certain forms of anti-social behaviour (particularly of young people) are likely to be prioritized over other hazards, such as pollution levels, transport dangers, food risks, corporate fraud, and unsafe housing and working conditions.

Is there any antidote to this last depressing, dystopian scenario? This leaves us with the final 'bet' – and rank outsider.

Bet 3: radical cadres of transformative power

It is difficult to arrive at a working title for our third, 'long odds' bet on the future career of community safety practitioners/managers. Given that the majority of community safety officers and managers have been recruited from local government rather than criminal justice occupational back-grounds, it is likely that the emergent community safety expertise will be influenced by a significant number of practitioners' experience in local government of radical debates regarding anti-discriminatory practices and policy, multiculturalism and diversity. What chances, then, of community safety managers – in some places, on certain issues – occupying an embattled role as radical cadres promoting the cause of collective yet diverse well-being and safety in the uncertain conditions of late modernity? The vision of community safety here would be that of an inclusive public good (rather than an exclusive 'club' good). Such radical practitioners in multi-agency partnerships would need to remain vigilant with regard to the relationship of community safety to broader, yet critical, social issues, particularly the potential of community safety to exacerbate social exclusion and the creeping 'criminalization of social policy' which community safety may herald. 'In this context, crime may not be the best vehicle around which to foster open and tolerant communities as the mainstay of civil society' (Crawford and Matassa, 2000, p. 96). The dominant place and role that 'crime' and 'disorder' occupy in community safety thus need to be held in 'a deliberately precarious position' (*ibid.*, p. 97). As Crawford and Matassa (2000, p. 96) note, there is scope for creative expropriation of this trend:

> as the boundaries between social policy and crime prevention become more blurred, one could argue for the potential development of an inverse relationship – the 'socialization of criminal policy' – whereby the traditional direction and funding of criminal policy is reoriented towards proactive prevention through social welfare.

This may lead community safety practitioners and managers towards involvement and engagement with a progressive 'replacement discourse' (see Chapter 13 below).

For such a replacement discourse to be developed there may need to be a lively and critical debate about the nature of the values underpinning the work of community safety officers/managers, not least in the contexts of the coexisting pragmatic 'what works' paradigm and the 'populist punitive' agenda promoted by key players in both central and local governmental circles. Kevin Stenson (1998) has noted that social scientists function in part as agents of 'governmental *savoir*', contributing to the forms of knowledge which are part of the apparatus of government and at times contributing to the constitution of the realities which we describe. As Stenson goes on to argue, those social scientists involved in researching and analysing trends in crime control may be seen as harbingers of a new 'police science' – helping to formulate and legitimate new strategies of control and management of crime and disorder. But, of course, as governmental 'savants', social scientists – in their dialogue with practitioners, policy-makers, politicians and communities – may also help to develop alternative, counter-discourses of justice, safety and the 'crime problem' to the dominant 'law and order' and managerialist/pragmatic discourses. Such developments are possible not least in the struggles of practitioners in the messy realities where 'crime and disorder' strategic work meets, and at times confronts, alternative 'community safety' thinking and practice.

Of the three bets waged, the third looks on the surface the least likely to emerge in full-blown fashion across the country. Other forces associated with the first two bets appear to be in the ascendancy over more progressive counter-tendencies. It is, however, unlikely that we shall see a pure manifestation of any one 'ideal type'. Instead hybridization of elements from all three hypothesized figures may be more likely. Another possible future career route for community safety experts, for example, may be that of being technical managers absorbed in the production (or manufacture) of measurable performance indicators of success in the 'war against crime and disorder'. Since the 1980s crime prevention has been politicized. As Gilling (1997, p. 104) notes,

> this politicization has meant that in addition to its projected role as a form of crime control, crime prevention policy has often had as much to say about such matters as the respective roles and responsibilities of state and citizen, the balance of powers between central and local government, and the proper limits of the state's welfare responsibilities.

This reality appears unlikely to change in the foreseeable future.

Conclusion

We have seen a dramatic growth of income inequality in the United Kingdom since the 1970s. And such inequalities coincide with the growth in inequality in the distribution of harm from crimes: for example, one-fifth of all communities in England and Wales suffer over 50 per cent of the total recorded property crime in the British Crime Survey, while half the country experiences just 15 per cent of crime recorded. For those communities most prone to both criminalization and criminal victimization the adverse circumstances ratchet together to produce social dislocation with damaging knock-on effects on the institutions of community and civil society (Hope, 1998). Addressing these problems lies beyond a narrow law-and-order agenda associated with the Crime and Disorder Act and would require long-term, seriously 'joined up' interventions regarding the causes of neigh-bourhood destabilization in the struggle for greater social justice.

What, then, are the possibilities for a 'pan-hazard', harm reduction (and less crime-driven) approach to community safety involving co-ordinated or 'joined up' efforts in specific localities? This paradigm of community safety may offer an alternative vision to hold on to in the context of the currently dominant crime and disorder discourse. Com-munity safety here is understood as a multi-agency and community-based strategy guided by the principle of harm reduction where the notion of harm extends beyond the actions proscribed by criminal law. As Wiles and Pease (2000, p. 21) note, 'community safety is the phrase to be preferred only if safety refers to the likely absence of harms (particularly serious harms) from all sources, not just from human acts classifiable as crime'. If the definition is narrowed (as in the Crime and Disorder Act), a double standard results whereby we are 'protected from attack by others, while choking gently on polluted air' (*ibid.*). Words count, and the struggle to give meaning to key rhetorical devices is one which needs to be continued in the contested politics of community safety. Participants in this contested politics need to think through how community safety might be rethought in terms of the goals of social justice as well as those of criminal justice.

References

Audit Commission (1999) *Safety in Numbers*, London, Audit Commission.
Ballintyne, S., Pease, K. and McLaren, V. (eds) (2000) *Secure Foundations: Key Issues in Crime Prevention, Crime Reduction and Community Safety*, London, Institute for Public Policy Research.
Bauman, Z. (1999) *In Search of Politics*, Cambridge, Polity Press.
Beck, U. (1992) *Risk Society: Towards a New Modernity*, London, Sage.
Bottoms, A. (1990) 'Crime prevention: facing the 1990s', *Policing and Society*, vol. 1, no. 1, pp. 3–22.
Bottoms, A. and Wiles, P. (1996) 'Crime prevention and late modernity' in Bennett, T. (ed.) *Crime Prevention: The Cropwood Papers*, Cambridge, Cropwood.
Clarke, J., Gewirtz, S., Hughes, G. and Humphrey, J. (2000) 'Guarding the public interest: the rise of audit' in Clarke, J., Gewirtz, S. and McLaughlin, E. (eds) *New Welfare, New Managerialism*, London, Sage.
Cope, S. and Goodship, J. (1999) 'Regulating collaborative government: towards

joined-up government?', *Public Policy and Administration*, vol. 14, no. 2, pp. 3–16.

Crawford, A. (1997) *The Local Governance of Crime: Appeals to Community and Partnerships*, Oxford, Clarendon Press.

Crawford, A. (1998) 'Community safety partnerships', *Criminal Justice Matters*, No. 33, pp. 4–5.

Crawford, A. and Matassa, M. (2000) *Community Safety Structures: an International Literature Review*, Research Report 8, London, Stationery Office.

Edwards, A. and Hughes, G. (2001) *Community Crime Prevention: Research, Theory, Methods and Politics*, Cullompton, Willan Publishing.

Edwards, A. and Stenson, K. (1999) 'Crime Control and Liberal Government: the Third Way and the Shift to the Social', paper delivered at the 'Crime, Neo-liberalism and Risk Society' conference, John Jay College of Criminal Justice, New York, 14–16 April.

Ericson, R. and Heggarty, K. (1997) *Policing the Risk Society*, Oxford, Clarendon Press.

Feeley, S. and Simon, J. (1994) 'Actuarial justice: the emerging new criminal law' in Nelken, D. (ed.) *Futures of Criminology*, London, Sage.

Garland, D. (1996) 'The limits of the sovereign state: strategies of crime control in contemporary society', *British Journal of Criminology*, vol. 36, no. 4, pp. 445–71.

Gilling, D. (1997) *Crime Prevention: Theory, Policy and Politics*, London, UCL Press.

Gilling, D. (1999) 'Community safety: a critique' in Brogden, M. (ed.) *British Criminology Conferences: Selected Proceedings*, vol. 2 (http://www.lboro.ac.uk/departments/ss/bsc/bccsp/vol02/07GILLI.HTM).

Gilling, D. and Hughes, G. (2000) 'A National Survey of Community Safety Officers: Preliminary Findings', paper delivered at the British Criminology Conference, University of Leicester, July.

Heraud, B. (1970) *Social Work and Sociology*, Oxford, Pergamon.

Home Office (1991) *Safer Communities: The Local Delivery of Crime Prevention through the Partnership Approach* (Morgan Report), London, Home Office.

Hope, T. (1998) 'Letting social policy off the hook', *Criminal Justice Matters*, No. 37, pp. 5–6.

Hughes, G. (1996) 'Strategies of crime prevention and community safety in contemporary Britain', *Studies on Crime and Crime Prevention*, vol. 5, no. 2, pp. 221–44.

Hughes, G. (1998) *Understanding Crime Prevention: Social Control, Risk and Late Modernity*, Buckingham, Open University Press.

Hughes, G. (2000) 'In the shadow of crime and disorder: the contested politics of community safety', *Crime Prevention and Community Safety*, vol. 2, no. 4, pp. 47–60.

Hughes, G. and Little, A. (1999) 'The contradictions of New Labour's communitarianism', *Imprints*, vol. 2, no. 2, pp. 37–62.

Johnson, T. (1972) *Professions and Power*, London, Macmillan.

Mills, A. and Pearson, S. (2000) 'From audit to strategy: a practice view' in Ballintyne, S. et al. (eds) *Secure Foundations*, London, Institute for Public Policy Research.

Muncie, J. (2000) 'Decriminalizing criminology' in Lewis, G., Clarke, J. and Gewirtz, S. (eds) *Rethinking Social Policy*, London, Sage.

Muncie, J., McLaughlin, E. and Hughes, G. (2001) 'Modernizing criminal justice: New Labour, crime reduction and New Public Management', *Journal of Criminal Justice* (forthcoming).

Phillips, C., Jacobson, J., Considine, M. and Lewis, R. (2000) *A Review of Audits and Strategies produced by Crime and Disorder Partnerships in 1999*, Briefing Note, London, Home Office.

Rose, N. (1999) *Powers of Freedom: Reframing Political Thought*, Cambridge, Cambridge University Press.

Shearing, D. (1998) 'Theorizing *sotto voce*' in Holdaway, S. and Roche, P. (eds) *Thinking Criminologically*, London, Macmillan.

Stafford, J. and Silverlock, L. (2000) 'What works and what makes what works work' in Ballintyne, S. et al. (eds) *Secure Foundations*, London, Institute for Public Policy Research.

Stenson, K. (1998) 'Displacing social policy through crime control' in Hänninen, S. (ed.) *Displacement of Social Policies*, Jyväskylä, SoPhi Publications.

Stenson, K. (2000) 'Crime control, social policy and liberalism' in Lewis, G. et al. (eds) *Rethinking Social Policy*, London, Sage.

Webb, J. (1999) 'Work and the new public service class', *Sociology*, vol. 33, no. 4, pp. 747–66.

Wiles, P. and Pease, K. (2000) 'Crime prevention and community safety: Tweedledum and Tweedledee' in Ballintyne, S. et al. (eds) *Secure Foundations*, London, Institute for Public Policy Research.

Wilson, J. and Kelling, G. (1982) 'Broken windows', *Atlantic Monthly*, March, pp. 29–38.

Young, J. (1999) *The Exclusive Society: Social Exclusion, Crime and Difference in Late Modernity*, London, Sage.

8

A new deal for youth?

Early intervention and correctionalism

John Muncie

Though not always fully acknowledged, young people are the implicit target of much of the current crime prevention and crime reduction initiative. The prevailing discourse is of 'nipping crime in the bud' by targeting certain identified 'risk factors' such as inadequate parenting, truancy and lack of training and employment. As a result, all manner of misbehaviours, incivilities and disorders are being drawn into conceptions of the 'problem of crime'. And increasing numbers of social policy agencies – health, education, welfare – are being drawn into formal networks of crime control as partners in crime reduction. When this 'safety net' fails, an expansive array of pre-court initiatives, community sentences and secure facilities await the young offender. A rhetoric of crime prevention, restorative justice and inclusion underlies much of this reforming zeal, but it is also characterized by a reworking of a familiar series of 'old' correctional, retributive, punitive and parent-blaming values. This chapter explores the traces of welfare, children's rights, diversion and authoritarian populism that can be found in the emergent new youth justice of England and Wales. By analysing in some detail the legal powers and procedures ushered in by the Crime and Disorder Act 1998 and the Youth Justice and Criminal Evidence Act 1999 it examines how far the new domain assumptions of youth justice are capable of activating a shift away from an exclusionary punitive justice and towards an inclusionary restorative justice.

From welfare, diversion and justice to 'what works'

In crucial respects the separate systems of youth justice that were developed in most Western jurisdictions from the mid-nineteenth century onwards have always sought legitimation for their existence in the rhetoric of crime prevention. The means through which such an endeavour is to be achieved has, however, never remained constant and always appears subject to dispute and expansion. What may have begun as an attempt to prevent the 'contamination of young minds' by separating the young from the adult offender in prison has evolved into a complex of powers and procedures that penetrate deep into the everyday lives of young people and their families. Typically, systems of youth justice are beset by the ambiguity, paradox and contradiction of whether young offenders should be cast as 'children in need of help, guidance and support' or as 'corrupt, undisciplined and evil beings' who fully deserve their 'just deserts'. Traditionally this confusion has played itself out along the axis of whether the philosophical justification of a separate justice system for young people is one of delivering welfare or justice.

Much of the welfare principle in youth justice derives from the reforming zeal of philanthropists and 'child savers' in the 1850s. Youth crime was thought best deterred by confining children in reformatories and subjugating them to disciplined labour and religious re-education. Such intervention was legitimized in the language of care. As a result, it was able to draw not only the offender but also those thought likely to offend – the orphan, the vagrant, the runaway, the independent and those with a 'deviant' street lifestyle – into its remit. This prevailing argument that age and the neglect and vice of parents should be taken into account when adjudicating on juveniles subsequently opened the way to a plethora of welfare-inspired legislation in the twentieth century. In England and Wales the Children Act 1908 created a separate and distinct system of justice based on the juvenile court; the Children and Young Persons Act 1933 formally required the court to place welfare considerations paramount; and the Children and Young Persons Act 1969 advocated the phasing out of criminal, in favour of civil, proceedings. By the 1960s custodial and care institutions were also being criticized as stigmatizing, dehumanizing and criminogenic, rather than being seen as agencies capable of preventing further offending. In their place a range of preventive and rehabilitative treatment units located in the community was advocated: 'What is needed is a mobilization of the whole community in a new drive for the *positive prevention* of crime . . .' (Labour Party Study Group, 1964, p. 70).

Welfarism, though, has never been universally accepted as the most propitious means of preventing youth crime. A strong law-and-order lobby has also ensured that a range of punitive custodial options – borstals, detention centres, youth custody centres – have remained firmly in place. Consequently, it has been argued that the fate of welfarism has been one of simply adding to the range of interventions and disposals available to the courts. Indeed, during the 1970s welfarism was generally employed with a younger age group of, for example, low school achievers, 'wayward girls' and truants from 'problem' families designated as 'pre-delinquent', whilst the courts continued their old policy of punishing offenders. The two systems became vertically integrated (Thorpe et al., 1980). Moreover the concept of welfare in law was, and remains, characteristically narrow and circumscribed. At best it may allow acknowledgement of the reduced culpability of children, but this in turn has been used to justify early intervention against those considered to be 'at risk'. Rarely, if ever, has it meant that children are dealt with more leniently (King and Piper, 1995).

By the 1980s liberal lawyers, civil libertarians and radical social workers were also becoming increasingly critical of 'welfare-based' procedures and sentencing. They argued that 'meeting needs' acted as a spurious justification for placing excessive restrictions on individual liberty, particularly for young women, which were out of proportion either to the seriousness of the offence or to the realities of being in 'need of care and protection'. It was also maintained that social work involvement not only preserved explanations of individual pathology but also drew young people into the judicial process at an ever earlier age, with rarely any prospect of escape. Young people were placed in double jeopardy – sentenced for their background as well as for their offence – and as a result their movement up the sentencing tariff tended to accelerate (Morris et al., 1980).

In the wake of these criticisms a justice-based model of correction emerged that was founded on the principles of proportionality of punishment to crime, determinacy of sentencing, an end to judicial, professional and administrative discretion, protection of rights through due process and the diversionary principle of 'least interference'. These notions of the normality of much youth offending and of punishing the crime, not the person, had clear attractions for those seeking an end to the abuse of discretional power and the contagion of institutional confinement. Initially this approach did appear to be remarkably successful. From the mid-1980s the recorded number of young offenders reduced quite dramatically, as did the number of those sent to custody. Diversion from prosecution was encouraged through informal police cautioning (rather than prosecution) and diversion from custody was secured by the development of intensive community-based intermediate treatment schemes. Notions of 'just deserts' through proportionate sentencing were formalized by the Criminal Justice Act 1991. A focus on 'deeds' rather than 'needs' formally expunged many of the last vestiges of welfarism from the system and did indeed appear to be successful in preventing initial offending and in reducing re-offending rates (Rutherford, 1989).

However, the liberal critique of welfare also coalesced with the concerns of traditional retributivists that rehabilitation was a 'soft option' and that its 'successes' were far from clear-cut; for them, tougher sentencing would also enable criminals to get their 'just deserts'. In the political climate of the 1980s notions of 'just deserts' and 'anti-welfarism' began to be politically mobilized by the right. The language of 'justice and rights' was appropriated as a matter of 'individual responsibility and obligation'. Accordingly, Hudson (1987) has argued that the 'just deserts' or 'back to justice' movements that emerged in many Western jurisdictions in the 1980s were evidence of a 'modern retributivism' rather than necessarily heralding the emergence of new liberal regimes and a positive rights agenda. The Criminal Justice Act 1991 may have helped to expand non-custodial measures, but their retributive edge was considerably sharpened. The favoured rhetoric and practice became that of delivering *punishment in the community* rather than prioritizing community-based preventive measures. Moreover, renewed fears of persistent young offenders, and in particular the political fall-out from the murder of James Bulger by two ten-year-olds in 1993, enabled the youth justice system to take a decisively retributive turn. Custody was once more promoted as the key means to prevent reoffending through the incapacitive slogan 'Prison works'. As a result, it has been argued that, particularly in England and Wales, a legal discourse of guilt, responsibility and punishment has always tended to surface and resurface as the dominant position in the definition and adjudication of young offending (Muncie, 1999b). In addition, Fionda (1998) has noted how a series of legislative changes and reformulations of policy from the 1980s onwards has constructed a system that now has 'an almost stubborn blindness' to welfare principles and the mitigating circumstances of age. This 'adulteration' of youth justice became most marked in the abolition of *doli incapax* in 1998 through which ten-to-thirteen-year-olds now face almost the same sentencing tariffs as were previously restricted to those aged fourteen or over. As a result, by the end of the 1990s the youth justice system was offering neither welfare, nor diversion, nor progressive justice to those who came before it (Goldson, 2000). In their place has emerged the rather less philosophically defensible aim of preventing offending by any pragmatic means possible. The viability of such means rests primarily on prior assessments of risk. A policy can be shown to 'work' only when it can be substantiated either through the tools of evidence-based research or through those of the fiscal audit. Moral debate about the purpose and *process* of intervention has been shifted to the sidelines in the search for 'value for money' and cost-effective, measurable *outcomes*. Young offending, it seems, has simply become another risk to be managed.

Targeting youthful disorder: 'nipping crime in the bud'?

This emergent strategy was first formalized in the Crime and Disorder Act 1998, whereby it was claimed that 'The principal aim of the youth justice system is to prevent offending by children and young persons and requires those involved in the youth justice system to have regard to that aim' (Home Office, 1997b, p. iii). It was also the first piece of criminal justice legislation in England and Wales (at least since the vagrancy statutes of the early nineteenth century) to act explicitly against legal *and* moral/social transgressions. The prevailing contention was that crime runs in certain families and that antisocial behaviour in childhood is a predictor of later criminality. Such notions opened the door to a range of legislative initiatives targeted at 'disorderly' as well as criminal behaviour. It was also designed to draw children below the age of criminal responsibility into formal networks of social control. Much of this early intervention (as distinct from diversion) became justified through notions of 'child protection' or 'nipping crime in the bud' . It was made possible by giving local authorities and newly formed youth offending teams a statutory obligation to reduce crime by establishing partnerships between the police and criminal justice, health, education and welfare agencies.

The family and remoralization strategies

Tony Blair first coined the 'realist' slogan 'Tough on crime, tough on the causes of crime' in January 1993 in an attempt to wrest the law-and-order agenda from the Conservatives. Since then New Labour has continually promised that its policies would be based on recognition of the underlying causes of crime, which could then be addressed by a raft of legal, social and economic measures. These 'causes' were first spelt out in detail in the consultation document *Tackling the Causes of Crime* (Straw and Michael, 1996). The key social and economic conditions of crime were considered to be parenting, truancy, drug abuse, lack of facilities for young people, homelessness, unemployment, low income and recession. However, a year later, when the White Paper *No More Excuses* was published, these 'causes' were significantly contracted to provide a more limited focus on parenting, truancy and peer groups. Now the key factors were deemed to be: being male, being brought up by criminal parents, living in a family with multiple problems, poor parental discipline, school exclusion and associating with delinquent friends (Home Office, 1997b, p. 5).

A major preoccupation with the family and crime has dominated Labour's legislative initiatives. This rather narrow interpretation of crime causation is in no small part derived from multivariate correlational analyses, which have identified the quality of parent/child relationships as a key 'risk factor' in the onset of offending (Graham and Bowling, 1995; Utting, 1996; Graham, 1998). A major influence has been the empirical longitudinal study of 'delinquent families' conducted by the Cambridge Institute of Criminology since the 1960s (Farrington and West, 1990; Farrington, 1996). Six variables have been consistently suggested as predictors of future criminality:

1   Socio-economic deprivation (e.g. low family income/poor housing).
2   Poor parenting and family conflict.
3   Criminal and antisocial families.
4   Low intelligence and school failure.
5   Hyperactivity/impulsivity/attention deficiency.
6   Antisocial behaviour (e.g. heavy drinking, drug taking, promiscuous sex).

Within this seemingly broad range of social and personality 'risk factors', a particular reading of 'failed families' has become crucial:

> children from poorer families are likely to offend because they are less able to achieve their goals legally and because they value some goals (e.g. excitement) especially highly. Children with low intelligence are more likely to offend because they tend to fail in school. Impulsive children . . . are more likely to offend because they do not give sufficient consideration and weight to the possible consequences. Children who are exposed to poor child rearing behaviour, disharmony or separation on the part of their parents are likely to offend because they do not build up internal controls over socially disapproved behaviour, while children from criminal families and those with delinquent friends tend to build up anti-authority attitudes and the belief that offending is justifiable. The whole process is self-perpetuating . . . (Farrington, 1994, pp. 558–9)

Farrington (1996) went on to suggest that the 'most hopeful' methods of tackling crime and antisocial behaviour (derived from experimental research in the United States and Canada) were those designed to counter 'specific risk factors', such as:

1   Home visiting by health professionals to give advice on infant development, nutrition and alcohol and drug avoidance in order to reduce parental child abuse.
2   Pre-school programmes to stimulate thinking and reasoning skills in young children.
3   Parenting education programmes.

4 Cognitive and social skills training to teach children to consider the
   consequences of their behaviour.
5 Teacher training and anti-bullying initiatives in schools.

   This analysis coalesced with that of such self-styled 'ethical socialists'
as Norman Dennis and George Erdos. They argued that children from
'fatherless families' would grow up without appropriate role models and
supervision and would thus reduce their own chances of becoming com-
petent parents. For Dennis and Erdos (1992) it is 'common sense' that
family breakdown and rising crime will go hand in hand. A breakdown of
the nuclear family unit, high divorce rates and increases in single parenting,
it was argued, were the root causes of a moral decay epitomized by
increased crime rates, homelessness and drug-taking. In addition, excessive
welfare dependence had encouraged families to rely on state benefits rather
than each other. In the process, children's moral development had been
eroded.
   Whilst such notions of 'responsible parenting' and the dangers of a
'parenting deficit' might be usually associated with Conservative ideo-
logues, on coming to power Tony Blair argued:

> We cannot say we want a strong and secure society when we ignore its
> very foundations: family life. This is not about preaching to individuals
> about their private lives. It is addressing a huge social problem . . .
> Nearly 100,000 teenage pregnancies every year; elderly parents with
> whom families cannot cope; children growing up without role models
> they can respect and learn from; more and deeper poverty; more crime;
> more truancy; more neglect of educational opportunities, and above all
> more unhappiness. Every area of this government's policy will be
> scrutinized to see how it affects family life. Every policy examined, every
> initiative tested, every avenue explored to see how we strengthen our
> families. (*The Guardian*, 1 October 1997)

   In this rhetoric, strong families fit the traditional image of conjugal,
heterosexual parents with an employed male breadwinner. Single parenting
and absent fathers are key harbingers of social disorder. Indeed, one of
Labour's key formative influences in defining a 'third way' – Etzioni's
communitarian agenda – also emphasizes that the root cause of crime lies
within the home and that it is in the domestic sphere that the shoring up of
our moral foundations should begin (Etzioni, 1995, p. 11). It is such a
communitarianism which speaks of parental responsibility and moral obligation that continually resurfaces in the new reforming agenda (Hughes,
1996, p. 21). The single most important factor in explaining and preventing
criminality is deemed to be the quality of a young person's home life,
including parental supervision:

> We will uphold family life as the most secure means of bringing up our
> children . . . [Families] should teach right from wrong. They should be

the first defence against antisocial behaviour. (Tony Blair, April 1997, cited by Cook, 1997, p. 2)

Children under ten need *help* to change their bad behaviour just as much as older children. (Home Office, 1997a, p. 18; emphasis added)

It should be noted, however, that, whatever the precise form such 'help' may take in the prevention of crime, it has rarely been promoted as an alternative, but more as an adjunct, to situational measures. In practice it has been realized through a series of programmes which seek either to remove young people from the street or to provide special skills training. Akin to Farrington (1996), Utting (1996) recites numerous 'promising' projects (largely American) that may be effective in reducing criminality. These are directed at parents as well as 'at risk' youth and include pre-school programmes, parental skills training, holiday play schemes, truancy watch schemes and anti-bullying campaigns. Much of this was to be mirrored in both the Audit Commission's (1996) and the Home Office's (Goldblatt and Lewis, 1998) assessments of 'what works'. Parental training and a range of behavioural and cognitive interventions are considered to be most effective. (In contrast, counselling, therapy, shock incarceration and corporal punishment are deemed 'not to work'.) As a result concern over irresponsibility and lack of parental discipline dominates the powers of the 1998 Act. For example, new powers were introduced to require a parent or guardian of a convicted young person to attend counselling or guidance sessions and to comply with certain specified requirements (such as ensuring the child goes to school each day and is indoors by a certain hour in the evening). The stated aim is to 'encourage' parents to address a child's antisocial and offending behaviour, but breach is a criminal offence with a liability of up to a £1,000 fine.

In such ways the targets of early intervention have invariably become individualized and behavioural. Primary attention is paid to responding to the symptoms, rather than the causes, of young people's disaffection and dislocation. The social contexts of offending are bypassed. The disadvantages faced by young people (e.g. lack of income support, accommodation and leisure facilities) are obscured by a narrow focus on 'at risk' and troublesome behaviour (Muncie et al., 1995). Throughout this remoralization strategy lies the objective of compelling parents to take 'proper' care and control of their children, whilst by the age of ten children will be held fully responsible themselves (Goldson, 1999).

Early intervention and responsibilization strategies

One of the most radical initiatives of the Crime and Disorder Act 1998 is the availability of new orders and powers that can be made other than as a sentence following conviction. Child safety orders, local child curfews, antisocial behaviour orders and sex offender orders do not necessarily require either the prosecution or indeed the commission of a criminal offence.

Child safety orders can be made by a family proceedings court on a child below the age of criminal responsibility if that child is considered 'at risk'. Justified as a 'protective' measure, it places the child under the supervision of a social worker or a member of a youth offending team for a period of up to twelve months. The court can specify certain requirements such as attending specified programmes or avoiding particular places and people. Breach may result in the substitution of a care order under the powers of the Children Act 1989. In addition local authorities can, after consultation with the police and local community, introduce a local child curfew – from 9.00 p.m. to 6.00 a.m. – to apply to *all* children under the age of ten in a specific area. In these ways children can be targeted as 'offenders' before they are old enough to be criminally responsible. Similarly an antisocial behaviour order (ASBO) is a civil order which can be made by the police/local authority on anyone over the age of ten whose behaviour is *thought* likely to cause alarm, distress or harassment. The order lasts a minimum of two years and breach is punishable by up to five years' imprisonment. Though justified as a means to control 'nuisance neighbours', there is increasing evidence that ASBOs are targeted primarily at youthful 'rowdy and unruly' behaviour. Sex offender orders may be less applicable to young people but can be imposed on anyone over the age of ten. Again it is a community-based order, applied for by the police, against any sex offender whose present behaviour is considered to be a cause of serious harm. It lasts for a minimum of five years and breach is punishable by imprisonment.

In addition the Crime and Disorder Act 1998 replaced the previous practice of police cautioning with a system of reprimands and a final warning. In 1994 guidelines had already been issued to discourage the use of second cautions, even though they had been successful in diverting many young people out of the system altogether. Now on a second offence a final warning (akin to caution-plus schemes that had previously operated in some parts of the country) usually involves some community-based intervention whereby the offender is referred to a youth offending team for assessment and allocation to a programme designed to address the causes of offending, even though no formal prosecution has taken place. Non-compliance with a programme may be announced in court on the committing of future offences. The danger, as frequently voiced, lies in young people being consistently 'set up to fail'.

Most significantly, referral orders, introduced by the Youth Justice and Criminal Evidence Act 1999, are designed to be the *mandatory*, standard sentence imposed on all young offenders, no matter how relatively minor the offence, as long as there are no previous convictions and the offender pleads guilty. It bypasses the possibility of giving a conditional discharge. Offenders are referred to a youth offender panel, established by a local youth offending team, to agree a programme of behaviour to address their offending. There is no provision for legal representation. It is not a formal community sentence but does require a contract to be agreed to last from a minimum of three months to a maximum of twelve. The programme may include victim reparation, victim mediation, curfew, school attendance, staying away from specified places and persons, participation in specified activities, as well as general compliance with the terms of the contract for supervision and monitoring purposes. Failure to agree a contract or breach of conditions results in the case being referred back to court for the young offender to be sentenced afresh.

What is noticeable in this gamut of legislative reform is that virtually any intervention, monitoring and scrutiny of young people's lives can be justified in the name of crime prevention. Moreover it is a scrutiny which not only penetrates more deeply but also more widely, by targeting younger children and those below the age of criminal responsibility. As Haines and Drakeford (1998, p. 238) warned, this 'repressive intent' may not only fail to prevent offending but instead amplify and distort young people's misbehaviour 'by drawing them ever earlier and ever closer into a system which cannot but do more harm than good'.

In formulating these new powers New Labour is well aware that the key formal principle underlying all work with young offenders remains that of ensuring their general welfare. For instance, the UN Convention on the Rights of the Child requires that in all legal actions concerning those under the age of eighteen, the 'best interests' of the child shall prevail. However, the 1998 Act gives no direction to the courts or youth offending teams that child welfare should be a primary consideration. Instead New Labour's reform programme, often involving action against non-criminal behaviour, is couched in the language of crime prevention, child protection and responsibilization.

> Recognizing that there are underlying causes of crime is in no way to excuse or condone offending. Individuals must be held responsible for their own behaviour, and must be brought to justice and punished when they commit an offence. (Straw and Michael, 1996, p. 6)

Erosion of age differences and civil liberties is, however, presented as an enabling new opportunity and, even more paradoxically, as an 'entitlement' (Scraton, 1999). In the 1997 White Paper *No More Excuses*, and in response to the UN Convention on the Rights of the Child in 1999, Labour has claimed that:

> The government does not accept that there is any conflict between protecting the welfare of the young offender and preventing that individual from offending again. Preventing offending *promotes* the welfare of the individual young offender and protects the public. (Home Office, 1997b, para. 2.2; emphasis added)

If a child has begun to offend they are *entitled* to the earliest possible intervention to address that offending behaviour and eliminate its causes. The changes will also have the result of putting all juveniles on the same footing as far as the courts are concerned, and will contribute to the *right* of children appearing there to develop responsibility for themselves. (HM Government, 1999, para. 10.30.2; emphasis added)

This representation of criminalizing measures – that penetrate deep into the everyday lives of young people and their families – as progressive is clearly designed to ward off criticism and conflict with the Human Rights Act 1998, which was implemented in 2000. This Act incorporates the European Convention on Human Rights into British law. Article 6 provides for the right to a fair trial with legal representation and a right of appeal. Youth offender panels deliberating on referral orders would appear to be in denial of such rights. Article 8 confers the right to respect for private and family life and protects families from arbitrary interference. Parenting orders, child curfews and antisocial behaviour orders, in particular, would again appear to be in contempt (Dinham, 1999). Moreover, many of the principles of the new crime prevention, in particular the powers of the Youth Justice and Criminal Evidence Act, only confer a right on the victim or the community to receive reparation, but 'does not confer, nor does it appear to even recognize, that children have rights and that these are protected in law. [It] establishes only that children have responsibilities' (Haines, 2000 p. 64). The contractual language of referral orders masks their fundamentally coercive, compulsory and potentially authoritarian nature (Wonnacott, 1999; Ball, 2000).

Targeting young offenders: preventing reoffending?

Youth justice pressure groups have long argued that the 'justice' afforded to young people should move beyond narrow interpretations of the due process, fairness or impartiality of modern Western legalism to connect with conceptions of respect, reconciliation, community and restoration. Proponents of restorative justice have maintained that justice should be primarily a process of reconciling conflicting interests and healing rifts in communities resulting from harm committed.

Such notions are derived in part from the rediscovery, to varying degrees, of the systems of justice of indigenous peoples as in Canada and New Zealand. But there is also a much wider 'abolitionist' body of literature on restorative justice (Christie, 1977; De Haan, 1990) which suggests that crime is not the object but the product of crime control philosophies and institutions. Social problems, conflicts and trouble are an inevitable part of everyday life and therefore should not be delegated to professionals and specialists claiming to provide 'solutions'. When professionals and state agencies intervene, the essence of social problems and conflicts are 'stolen' and re-presented in forms that only encourage their perpetuation. Formal and legalistic court proceedings based on adversarial justice reduce both the victim and the offender to passive spectators. In contrast restorative initiatives hold a greater potential to achieve redress through the individual and collective ownership of dispute.

Ironically, however, such notions have come to surface alongside a simultaneous renaissance of correctionalism and a retributive model of justice.

Restorative justice

Much has been made of the principles of restorative justice – responsibility, restoration, reintegration – that ostensibly underpin some of New Labour's legislative initiatives. For some, such principles hold a potential to transform a system that in other major respects is governed by punitive values (Dignan, 1999). Restorative principles are typically cited as being present in referral, reparation and action plan orders and the stated general aim of providing opportunities for victims and offenders to meet and make amends. The often quoted reference points are the experience of Family Group Conferences (FGCs), pioneered in New Zealand in 1989, and the children's hearing system established in Scotland in 1971.

Family Group Conferences based on traditional systems of conflict resolution within Maori culture, involve a professional co-ordinator, dealing with both civil and criminal matters, who calls the young person, their family and victims together to decide whether the young person is 'in need of care and protection' and, if so, what should be provided. The outcome is usually some form of apology or community work. The key element of progressive restorative practice is that the offender is not marginalized but accepted as a key contributor to decision-making (Hudson et al., 1996). Children's hearings in Scotland are similarly a lay, welfare-based tribunal which decide on future action rather than determining matters of guilt or innocence. They deal with those up to the age of sixteen and have been lauded by many of their advocates as 'an object lesson' in ensuring that welfare, individualized attention and the child's own opinion remain at the centre of decision-making (McAra and Young, 1997).

Such notions have long been an aspiration of youth justice pressure groups in England and Wales, and New Labour has been remarkably successful in bringing some of these (for example, NACRO) on board. However, as Morris and Gelsthorpe (2000) point out, the restorative elements of the new youth justice in England and Wales appear partial and peripheral when compared with their New Zealand counterparts. They are additions to, rather than core defining components of, a system that is also intent on punishment and retribution. In Scotland, too, welfarism tends to be reserved for less serious offences and some routes into adult justice

– particularly for those aged sixteen and over – remain unchallenged. Throughout the potential of restorative initiatives is circumscribed by their dovetailing with neo-liberal discourses of remoralization, discipline and individual responsibility. The lack of accountability and the absence of protection for the offender in terms of appeals to legality and due process remain major areas of concern. Restorative justice can easily be sidelined as a set of alternatives *within* formal systems, for example by siphoning off less serious cases or those that might previously have not been acted upon (Daly and Immarigeon, 1998). As a result, the question remains of the extent to which restorative justice initiatives, administered in a governmental context – and subject to bureau-professional capture – may simply act to extend the net of social control deeper into the community. Whilst none of the above criticisms can negate the progressive potentialities of restorative justice *per se*, they do demonstrate both the pitfalls of poor implementation and the subversion of restorative justice's principles in specific 'projects'. A more general difficulty with restorative justice concerns its assumption – alongside correctionalism – that young people are always autonomous, rational individuals able to make free moral choices for which they can be held to account.

The new correctionalism and repenalization

For many years the standard custodial provision available to the youth court in England and Wales for those aged fifteen to seventeen years was detention in a young offender institution. Following the Criminal Justice and Public Order Act 1994 the maximum sentence was increased from twelve to twenty-four months. The same Act also introduced secure training orders for twelve- to fourteen-year-olds who had been convicted of three or more offences which would be imprisonable in the case of an adult. By 2000 three such centres were available. However, the Crime and Disorder Act 1998 abolished the sentences of secure training and detention in a young offender institution and replaced them with a generic sentence of a detention and training order (DTO). A DTO can be given to fifteen- to seventeen-year-olds for any offence considered serious enough to warrant a custodial sentence; to twelve- to fourteen-year-olds who are considered to be 'persistent offenders'; and to ten and eleven-year-olds at the discretion of the Home Secretary. The orders are for between four and twenty-four months. Half the order is served in the community under the supervision of a social worker, a probation officer or a member of a youth offending team. These age reductions in the detention of young people coupled with increases in maximum sentence appear directly at odds with the UN Convention on the Rights of the Child. The convention states at Article 37 that imprisonment of a child 'shall be used only as a measure of last resort and for the shortest appropriate period of time'. Moreover, as there are no separate young offender institutions for girls, they are held in adult prisons, often sharing the same facilities as adults. The DTO raises the possibility that twelve- to fourteen-year-old girls could now also find themselves in adult jails. Again this is in contravention of the UN Convention, which states that 'every child deprived of liberty shall be separated from adults unless it is considered in the child's best interests not to do so' (Howard League, 1999).

There are other grounds for considering that restorative justice and the principal aim of youth justice to 'prevent offending' are being bypassed. Whilst it is acknowledged that crime prevention and reduction are best achieved through community-based intervention, any communitarian rationale is made to work with and through a series of authoritarian measures. The 1998 and 1999 legislation claims to be supportive of parents and protective of children but its preventive rhetoric is backed by coercive powers. Civil orders are backed up by stringent criminal sanctions. Similarly, by equating 'disorder' with crime it significantly broadens the reach of criminal justice to take in those below the age of criminal responsibility and the non-criminal as well as the known offender. Above all, the number of young offenders incarcerated has continued to grow since 1993 and there is evidence to suggest that detention and training orders are accelerating, rather than reversing, this trend (Nathan, 2000). Growing penal populations inevitably undermine any commitment to promoting rehabilitation and preventing reoffending. Moreover in the two years following the passing of the 1998 Act, New Labour moved further to substantiate its authoritarian credentials by advocating the withdrawal of benefit for those who fail to comply with community sentences; extending electronic monitoring to ten- to fifteen-year olds; implementing the 'three strikes and you're out' rule for burglars; introducing mandatory drug testing of all those arrested; increasing fines for the parents of truanting children; urging greater use of antisocial behaviour orders; extending blanket curfews to include ten- to fifteen-year-olds; advocating on-the-spot fines for drunken, noisy, loutish and antisocial behaviour; and imposing 'lifestyle' sentences, such as driving licence confiscation, for public order offences.

As a result New Labour's preventive rhetoric has done nothing to undermine the pivotal position of youth custody. Inclusion is sanctioned only if exclusion is retained for particular groups of young offenders. This authoritarian mood has persisted despite compelling evidence of custody's harmful effects. The numbers sent to young offender institutions have continued to grow since 1994. England and Wales not only have one of the lowest ages of criminal responsibility, but also lock up more young people than most other countries in Western Europe. For reasons which appear political rather than pragmatic, the example followed is usually that of the United States, whose punitive values are legendary. As numerous campaign groups have maintained, vengeance and retribution through custody are demonstrable failures in preventing reoffending. Reconviction rates in England and Wales are well established and if anything are worsening. Up to 90 per cent of young people leaving custody reoffend within two years.

Young offender institutions are beset with brutality, suicide, self-harm and barbaric conditions – so much so that the Chief Inspector of Prisons has urged their closure forthwith (*Observer*, 19 November 2000). Moreover custody diverts considerable resources from community provision to high-security institutions. It is clear that the great majority of young people sentenced to custody pose no serious risk to the community and, indeed, by leading to broken links with family, friends, education, work and leisure, they may become a significantly greater danger on their return (Children's Society, 1993; Goldson and Peters, 2000).

Limitless intervention: inclusion and exclusion

The new youth justice has been described as a 'melting pot of principles and ideologies' (Fionda, 1999), as 'institutionalized intolerance' (Muncie,1999a) and as a 'misconceived and misguided' overreaction (Gelsthorpe and Morris, 1999). It is clear that any number of inclusionary and exclusionary practices can be legitimated within the general rubric of crime prevention. The new legislation has, in the main, augmented, rather than overturned, existing legislation. Youth justice is now an amalgam of:

1 *Just deserts* – the erosion of age considerations by focusing on the gravity of the offence and formulating a proportionate response.
2 *Risk assessment* – acting on the possibility of future crime and on the non-criminal as well as the criminal, thus again drawing younger populations into formal systems of control.
3 *Managerialism* – the rewriting of the purpose of youth justice to achieve measurable and cost-effective outcomes that are amenable to audited accounting.
4 *Community responsibilization* – maintaining that certain families and communities are implicated in criminality and that they have a responsibility to put their own house in order. If they 'fail', stringent and intrusive community penalties are warranted.
5 *Authoritarian populism* – the resort to overtly punitive measures to respond to and channel perceptions of public punitiveness for the purposes of short-term political expediency and electoral gain.
6 *Restorative justice* – the attempt to increase offender awareness and ensure they make amends to victims and communities.

(Gelsthorpe and Morris, 1999; Newburn 1998; Muncie, 1999a; Bottoms, 1995; Garland, 1996.)

This mélange of measures reveals the fundamental contradictions underlying a youth justice system cemented around loosely defined notions of 'crime prevention and reduction'. First, it undoes the complexities of crime by prioritizing a moral debate about the nature of 'responsible' families and 'proper' parenting. Any claim to recognizing broader social contexts is subjugated to a much narrower discourse which tends to demonize particular parents and their children and implies that 'choice' has no material basis. Second, in the formulation of policy the emphasis on inclusionary crime prevention is used to mark a significant departure from punitive justice, yet a commitment to an ethos of individual responsibility and penal custody is retained and seems actively to promote exclusion. Significantly, the principles of inclusion are frequently backed by coercive powers. Third, radical reform of youth justice organizations has been achieved only by introducing the techniques of public sector managerialism into how the system should be run. In the guise of 'modernization' welfare, justice and rights have been eclipsed by the imprecise science of risk assessment and the statutory responsibility to meet performance targets.

At the heart of much of this reimagining of youth justice is a fear of an undisciplined underclass. For observers on the right the underclass is young, homeless, criminal and welfare-dependent, but for some of those on the left the 'underclass' is a pejorative label to describe those who have been systematically excluded from the labour market. They point out that a succession of such labels has been consistently attached to the poorest members of society in order to mark them out as either politically danger-ous or as marginal outsiders – from the 'undeserving poor', 'dangerous classes' and 'social outcasts' of the nineteenth century to the 'culture of poverty', 'scroungers' and 'work-shy' of the twentieth (Mann, 1991). It is not welfare dependence but cuts in welfare provision, the widening of class differentials and the exclusion of the poor that lie at the heart of the 'youth problem' (Jordan, 1996).

There are limited traces of such acknowledgement in New Labour discourse and policy (Charman and Savage, 1999, p. 197; Brownlee, 1998, pp. 318–21). Measures to assist single parents back to work, to tackle social exclusion, to provide universal nursery education, to prevent drug use through education classes in primary schools and to ensure that all eighteen- to twenty-four-year-olds are in work, education or training have all been justified as 'ways of helping to tackle the roots of juvenile crime' (Home Office, 1997b, p. 10). But, as Hope (1998) notes, Labour's crime prevention legislation generally 'fails to acknowledge, let alone provide a means to tackle the social roots of disorder'. The risks associated with poverty, poor housing and income inequality are significant in their absence. New Labour appropriates only one part of the dictum that crime involves 'moral choice in certain restricting circumstances' (Young, 1994, p. 109). Moreover Labour's logic of 'compulsory inclusion' has strong coercive and authoritarian undertones. The welfare-to-work 'new deal' is designed to take a quarter of a million under twenty-five-year-olds off the dole. It has always been touted as 'as much an anti-crime as it is an economic policy' (Straw and Michael, 1996, p. 9). But it also stipulates that if claimants refuse to take up the proposed employment and training options they will lose all right to claim welfare benefit. The general right to welfare benefit for sixteen- to eighteen-year-olds had of course already been removed in 1988. Moreover the withdrawal of benefit from those who fail to comply with community sentences (announced in the 1999 Queen's Speech) heralds a further negation that poverty and immiseration may be significant factors in continued offending.

It may well be that crime will be endemic in societies built on principles of competition, conflict and individualism. In which case for some it can be obviated only by controlling relative deprivation and perceptions of inequality (and thereby crime) and by opening up opportunities through developing a 'radical meritocracy' (Young, 1999). Or, as Currie argues, to attack the roots of the crime problem 'we must build a society that is less unequal, less depriving, less insecure, less disruptive of family and community ties and less corrosive of co-operative values' (1985, p. 225). In short an effective crime prevention strategy lies outside the criminal justice system and in the fields of education and employment, through which fundamental economic, social and political inequalities can be challenged. In contrast Labour's limited attempts to bring the excluded 'back in' fail to recognize that their inclusion would only be to a world that continues to be dominated by market exploitation, discrimination and a widening gap between rich and poor (Levitas, 1996). Labour's rhetoric of community also provides for the exclusionary targeting not just of identified offenders but of entire 'dangerous' underclass groups (Hughes, 1998, p. 113). Ill-defined notions of the ' antisocial' are more than capable of simply being used to restrict those engaged in minority cultural or political activities, or others who are unpopular with local councils (Ashworth et al., 1998). By institutionalizing intolerance towards the 'different', the regular production of structures of exclusion, inequality, discrimination and oppression can be ignored (Muncie, 1999b).

Conclusion

The exact nature of crime prevention has always been an ill-defined affair – so much so that almost any element of social policy and criminal justice can be justified on these grounds. Theoretically it should be able to recognize that socio-economic inequalities (poor housing, lack of community facilities, unfair income differentials) can promote a disposition to known offending. But in practice, despite the rhetoric of restoration, a particularly narrow and draconian version of what crime prevention and youth justice entail usually comes to the surface. Because of their ill-defined and kaleidoscopic nature, preventative strategies are readily co-opted and added into existing youth justice discourse. New Labour's 'modernization' of youth justice and crime prevention holds authoritarian, responsibilization and remoralization discourses firmly in place. Pragmatism, efficiency and the continual requirement to 'get results' by any means necessary take precedence over any commitment to due process, justice and democratic accountability.

Youth justice over the 1990s has become more and more dominated by 'evidence-based' research. But a policy of 'what works' tends to focus only on the immediate problems of individual young people and their parents. Whilst it is possible to view some of these initiatives with guarded optimism (Anderson, 1999; Hester, 2000), it is unlikely that any can be simply transferred from one jurisdiction to another, or indeed from one locality to another, with the same results. Moreover these programmes of individual adaptation or of managerial partnership encourage the dissolution of any long-term objectives and are reflective of a failure to impact on the broader social contexts of disadvantage, disaffection, discrimination and criminalization. Radical readings of the potential of youth crime prevention and restorative strategies for social justice ultimately require a commitment to long-term change, tolerance and respect that cannot simply be reduced to the statistical artefacts produced by short-term trial assessments of 'what works' (Muncie et al., 1995; White, 2000).

And, of course, it is always worth reminding ourselves that for all the 'talk' of a new social inclusion, countervailing tendencies remain in the ascendant. The most ostensible forms of crime prevention, those firmly grounded in defensive principles of zero tolerance, target hardening, rational choice, privatized security, fortified communities and electronic surveillance, still take precedence over any initiative which may promise a more lasting settlement.

References

Anderson, B. (1999) 'Youth, crime and the politics of prevention' in Goldson, B. (ed.) *Youth Justice: Contemporary Policy and Practice*, Aldershot, Ashgate.

Ashworth, A., Gardner, J., Morgan, R., Smith, A., Von Hirsch, A. and Wasik, M. (1998) 'Neighbouring on the oppressive: the government's Antisocial Behaviour Order proposals', *Criminal Justice*, vol. 16, no. 1, pp. 7–14.

Audit Commission (1996) *Misspent Youth*, London, Audit Commission.

Ball, C. (2000) 'The Youth Justice and Criminal Evidence Act 1999: a significant move towards restorative justice or a recipe for unintended consequences?', *Criminal Law Review*, April, pp. 211–22.

Bottoms, A. (1995) 'The philosophy and politics of punishment and sentencing' in Clarkson, C. and Morgan, R. (eds) *The Politics of Sentencing Reform*, Oxford, Clarendon Press.

Brownlee, I. (1998) 'New Labour – new penology? Punitive rhetoric and the limits of managerialism in criminal justice policy', *Journal of Law and Society*, vol. 25, no. 3, pp. 313–35.

Charman, S. and Savage, S. (1999) 'The new politics of law and order: Labour, crime and justice' in Powell, M. (ed.) *New Labour, New Welfare State?*, London, Policy Press.

Children's Society (1993) *A False Sense of Security: The Case against Locking up More Children*, London, Children's Society.

Christie, N. (1977) 'Conflicts as property', *British Journal of Criminology*, vol. 17, no. 1, pp. 1–15.

Cook, D. (1997) *Poverty, Crime and Punishment*, London, Child Poverty Action Group.

Currie, E. (1985) *Confronting Crime: An American Challenge*, New York, Pantheon.

Daly, K. and Immarigeon, R. (1998) 'The past, present, and future of restorative justice: some critical reflections', *Contemporary Justice Review*, vol. 1, no. 1, pp. 21–45.

De Haan, W. (1990) *The Politics of Redress*, London, Unwin Hyman.

Dennis, N. and Erdos, G. (1992) *Families without Fatherhood*, London, Institute of Economic Affairs.

Dignan, J. (1999) 'The Crime and Disorder Act and the prospects for restorative justice', *Criminal Law Review*, January, pp. 48–60.

Dinham, P. (1999) 'A conflict in the law?', *Youth Justice Matters*, December, pp. 12–14.

Etzioni, A. (1995) *The Spirit of Community*, London, Fontana.

Farrington, D. (1994) 'Human development and criminal careers', in Maguire, M., Morgan, R. and Reiner, R. (eds) *The Oxford Handbook of Criminology*, Oxford, Clarendon.

Farrington, D. (1996) *Understanding and Preventing Youth Crime*, Social Policy Research Findings 93, York, Joseph Rowntree Foundation.

Farrington, D. and West, D. (1990) 'The Cambridge study in delinquent development' in Kerner, H.J. and Kaiser, G. (eds) *Criminality: Personality, Behaviour and Life History*, Berlin, Springer-Verlag.

Fionda, J. (1998) 'The age of innocence? The concept of childhood in the punishment of young offenders', *Child and Family Law Quarterly*, vol. 10, no. 1, pp. 77–87.

Fionda, J. (1999) 'New Labour, old hat: youth justice and the Crime and Disorder Act 1998', *Criminal Law Review*, January, pp. 36–47.

Garland, D. (1996) 'The limits of the sovereign state: strategies of crime control in contemporary society', *British Journal of Criminology*, vol. 36, no. 4, pp. 445–71.

Gelsthorpe, L. and Morris, A. (1999) 'Much ado about nothing: a critical comment on key provisions relating to children in the Crime and Disorder Act 1998', *Child and Family Law Quarterly*, vol. 11, no. 3, pp. 209–21.

Goldblatt, P. and Lewis, C. (eds) (1998) *Reducing Offending*, Home Office Research Study 187, London, HMSO.

Goldson, B. (1999) 'Youth (in)justice: contemporary developments in policy and practice' in Goldson, B. (ed.) *Youth Justice: Contemporary Policy and Practice*, Aldershot, Ashgate.

Goldson, B. (2000) 'Whither diversion? Interventionism and the new youth justice' in Goldson, B. (ed.) *The New Youth Justice*, Lyme Regis, Russell House.

Goldson, B. (ed.) (2000) *The New Youth Justice*, Lyme Regis, Russell House.

Goldson, B. and Peters, E. (2000) *Tough Justice*, London, Children's Society.

Graham, J. (1998) 'What works in preventing criminality' in Goldblatt, P. and Lewis, C. (eds) *Reducing Offending*, London, HMSO.

Graham, J. and Bowling, B. (1995) *Young People and Crime*, Home Office Research Study 145, London, Home Office.

Haines, K. (2000) 'Referral orders and youth offender panels' in Goldson, B. (ed.) *The New Youth Justice*, Lyme Regis, Russell House.

Haines, K. and Drakeford, M. (1998) *Young People and Youth Justice*, Basingstoke, Macmillan.

Hester, R. (2000) 'Community safety and the new youth justice' in Goldson, B. (ed.) *The New Youth Justice*, Lyme Regis, Russell House.

HM Government (1999) *Convention on the Rights of the Child: Second Report to the UN Committee on the Rights of the Child by the United Kingdom*, London, HMSO.

Home Office (1997a) *Tackling Youth Crime: A Consultation Paper*, London, HMSO.

Home Office (1997b) *No More Excuses: A New Approach to Tackling Youth Crime in England and Wales*, CM 3809, London, HMSO.

Hope, T. (1998) 'Are we letting social policy off the hook?', *Criminal Justice Matters*, no. 33, pp. 6–7.

Howard League (1999) *Protecting the Rights of Children*, London, Howard League.

Hudson, B. (1987) *Justice through Punishment*, London, Macmillan.

Hudson, J., Morris, A., Maxwell, G. and Galaway, B. (1996) *Family Group Conferences*, Annandale, QLD, Federation Press.

Hughes, G. (1996) 'Communitarianism and law and order', *Critical Social Policy*, vol. 16, no. 4, pp. 17–41.

Hughes, G. (1998) *Understanding Crime Prevention*, Buckingham, Open University Press.

Jordan, B. (1996) *Poverty: A Theory of Social Exclusion*, Cambridge, Polity Press.

King, M. and Piper, C. (1995) *How the Law Thinks about Children*, Aldershot, Ashgate.

Labour Party Study Group (1964) *Crime: A Challenge to Us All* (Longford Report), London, Labour Party.

Levitas, R. (1996) 'The concept of social exclusion and the new Durkheimian hegemony', *Critical Social Policy*, vol. 16, no. 1, pp. 5–20.

Mann, K. (1991) *The Making of an English 'Underclass'?*, Milton Keynes, Open University Press.

McAra, L. and Young, P. (1997) 'Juvenile justice in Scotland', *Criminal Justice*, vol. 15, no. 3, pp. 8–10.

Morris, A. and Gelsthorpe, L. (2000) 'Something old, something borrowed, something blue, but something new? A comment on the prospects for restorative justice under the Crime and Disorder Act 1998', *Criminal Law Review*, January, pp. 18–30.

Morris, A., Giller, H., Geach, H. and Szwed, E. (1980) *Justice for Children*, London, Macmillan.

Muncie, J. (1999a) 'Institutionalized intolerance: youth justice and the 1998 Crime and Disorder Act', *Critical Social Policy*, vol. 19, no. 2, pp. 147–75.

Muncie, J. (1999b) *Youth and Crime: A Critical Introduction*, London, Sage.

Muncie, J., Coventry, G. and Walters, R. (1995) 'The politics of youth crime prevention' in Noaks, L., Maguire, M. and Levi, M. (eds) *Contemporary Issues in Criminology*, Cardiff, University of Wales Press.

Nathan, S. (2000) 'Detention and Training Orders: further experimentation in juvenile incarceration', *Youth Justice Matters*, June, pp. 3–11.

Newburn, T. (1998) 'Tackling youth crime and reforming youth justice: the origins and nature of "New Labour" policy', *Policy Studies*, vol. 19, nos 3–4, pp. 199–211.

Rutherford, A. (1989) 'The mood and temper of penal policy: curious happenings in England during the 1980s', *Youth and Policy*, no. 27, pp. 27–31.

Scraton, P. (1999) 'Threatening Children: Politics of Hate and Policies of Denial in Contemporary Britain', paper presented to the Organization for the Protection of Children's Rights, Quebec, October.

Straw, J. and Michael, A. (1996) *Tackling the Causes of Crime: Labour's Proposals to Prevent Crime and Criminality*, London, Labour Party.

Thorpe, D.H., Smith, D., Green, C.J. and Paley, J.H. (1980) *Out of Care: The Community Support of Juvenile Offenders*, London, Allen & Unwin.

Utting, D. (1996) *Reducing Criminality among Young People: A Sample of Relevant Programmes in the UK*, Home Office Research Study 161, London, HMSO.

White, R. (2000) 'Social justice, community building and restorative strategies', *Contemporary Justice Review*, vol. 3 no. 1, pp. 55–72.

Wonnacott, C. (1999) 'The counterfeit contract: reform, pretence and muddled principles in the new referral order', *Child and Family Law Quarterly*, vol. 11, no. 3, pp. 271–87.

Young, J. (1994) 'Incessant chatter: recent paradigms in criminology' in Maguire, M., Morgan, R. and Reiner, R. (eds) *The Oxford Handbook of Criminology*, Oxford, Clarendon Press.

Young, J. (1999) *The Exclusive Society*, London, Sage.

From voluntary to statutory status

Reflecting on the experience of three partnerships
established under the Crime and Disorder Act 1998

Coretta Phillips

The multi-agency partnership has been the preferred approach for implementing local crime prevention for over fifteen years. Its virtues have been
espoused in Home Office circulars and reports dating from the mid-1980s,
and it has often been a prerequisite of funding for crime prevention
projects and initiatives. The partnership approach is premised on a notion
that crime problems cannot be effectively tackled by the police, nor indeed
by any agency on its own (Home Office, 1991). Instead what is required is
a holistic approach whereby effort, information, resources and expertise
are shared and co-ordinated among key agencies. Moreover, the problem-
solving model of crime prevention has been increasingly promoted as

the vehicle for achieving reductions in crime and disorder, particularly in the police service (HMIC, 1998; Goldblatt and Lewis, 1998; Goldstein, 1990).

In 1990 an independent working group chaired by James Morgan was tasked with monitoring progress in the delivery of crime prevention through the partnership approach in the light of Home Office guidance in this area. The fifth recommendation of the Morgan Report, as it became known, was that local authorities, working with the police, should be given statutory responsibility for the development of *community safety* through the multi-agency partnership approach (Home Office, 1991). This recognized the role of the local authority in providing key services and resources that were necessary for enhancing the safety of communities, as well as ensuring ownership among partners so the burden did not rest solely with the police. This approach also allowed for the more permanent and continuous involvement of elected members, and of the business and voluntary sectors. Although the recommendations were not acted upon by the Conservative government, they did make their way into legal statute under the new Labour government of 1997 as part of the Crime and Disorder Act 1998, although without the additional core funding for partnerships that was recommended in the Morgan Report.

Section 5 of the Act, which was implemented in July 1998, placed a statutory duty on local authorities, the police, health authorities, police authorities and probation committees to work together to tackle problems of crime and disorder in their area. Section 6 of the Act, following the problem-solving framework, stipulated that by 1 April 1999 partnerships had to produce and publish a strategy for reducing these problems, based on evidence drawn from an audit of crime and disorder in the locality. The strategy had to be informed by local consultation on the findings of the audit.

The aim of this chapter is to consider the extent to which Sections 5 and 6 of the Crime and Disorder Act have encouraged the kind of progress on community safety envisaged by the Morgan Report. It will also assess whether some of the well documented pitfalls of partnership working are evident in the new statutory Crime and Disorder Partnerships. The empirical data on which the discussion will be based come from the initial findings of an on-going Home Office research study that is examining the implementation of Sections 5 and 6 in three statutory Crime and Disorder Partnerships.[1] The research, like much of that currently undertaken by the Home Office, aims to provide principles of good practice to assist practitioners in the short term and contribute to evidence-based policy in the medium term. Its focus is on the local infrastructure, which, in many cases, will be the mechanism through which projects funded under the £400 million Crime Reduction Programme are delivered. The project sits alongside the major programme of research that is evaluating this programme.

The project consists of two phases, the first being to document the development of the partnerships in the three case-study sites and to understand how the partnerships compiled their crime and disorder audits, undertook consultation and formulated their crime and disorder strategy/ action plan. The research began in October 1999 and Phase I was thus retrospective, as partnerships' crime and disorder strategies had to be published by 1 April 1999. The second phase of the research study, which is on-going, focuses on the implementation, monitoring and evaluation of partnerships' crime and disorder strategies. It is the findings from Phase I that are used throughout this chapter.

The three research partnerships could not possibly serve as a representative sample of the 376 statutory partnerships that exist in England and Wales. However, they were selected according to a number of criteria, which do reflect some of the variation between partnerships across the country, and thus can give some idea of how the new multi-agency partnerships are developing. The first partnership area, Collingbridge,[2] is a large unitary authority that is predominantly rural but with a number of small towns, and which has a relatively low crime rate. Sandford is in a two-tier authority and covers a semi-industrial town and surrounding rural areas with pockets of affluence and deprivation. The third partnership, Riverton, is in a densely populated, multi-ethnic local authority which has high levels of social and economic deprivation, and which experiences a broad range of crime and disorder problems.

The research methods for studying multi-agency working have included observation of meetings, analysis of partnership documentation (such as minutes of meetings, protocols, monitoring exercises and other management information) and forty-nine in-depth interviews with partnership representatives. This approach has offered the opportunity to study dynamic processes, such as consultation, negotiation and co-operative working in depth, although since the first phase of the research was retrospective it necessarily relied much more on the interview data than the observational data. The majority of the interviews were face-to-face and were tape-recorded and transcribed verbatim. These data along with the field notes have been coded and analysed using NUD*IST, a qualitative data analysis computer package.

The main limitation of this methodological approach has been that, at the time of interviewing in early 2000, there were some memory lapses in interviewees' recollection of events, and these have had to be filled by examining partnership documentation. Observational research also carries with it the potential for atypical behaviour by research participants, including their providing socially desirable responses or engaging in behaviour which would not occur if observers had not been present. While it is impossible to rule out atypical behaviour in the current study, the use of multiple methods of data collection has assisted in minimizing the impact of this methodological problem. Moreover, Phillips and Brown (1997) contend that it is difficult for individuals to conceal 'normal' behaviour for extended periods of time.

Turning now to the research findings, this chapter will include an exploration of the structural dynamics of the three statutory Crime and

Disorder Partnerships and an assessment of the internal and external constraints which bear upon partnership working. It will end with a review of the nature of the relationship between the Home Office and local statutory partnerships, paying particular attention to recent changes in policy rhetoric.

The same old structural dynamics?

Partnership structures

In the three research sites the partnership structures were multi-tiered. In each a partnership group was in existence before the enactment of the Crime and Disorder Act 1998. Although there were variations in the composition of this body in each partnership, this structure had broad representation, including agencies such as the police, local authority service departments, elected members and MPs, local businesses, educational institutions, the media, and representatives of business, voluntary, community and justice organizations. To respond to the statutory requirements of Sections 5 and 6, two of the three partnerships had established a new structure including – again with some variation in each – the police basic command unit commander, the chief executive (or nominated delegate), chief officers of key local authority departments such as housing, education, social services, environmental services and legal services, the Assistant Chief Probation Officer, youth offending team manager, police/local authority liaison officers, community safety officers, and including representation from the voluntary sector. The seniority of representatives in this structure suggests that the partnerships attached great importance to their statutory responsibility, at least at the strategic level (see Liddle and Gelsthorpe, 1994b; HMIC, 2000). The primary function of this group was to co-ordinate the compilation of the crime and disorder audit, undertake consultation, and formulate a strategy and action plan to reduce crime and disorder in the locality. The former group, which antedated the Crime and Disorder Act, was seen by partnership representatives as a vehicle for keeping wider groups informed about progress on statutory responsibilities and for exchanging information about community safety activity more generally.

Representation: statutory and non-statutory partners

It has been nationally acknowledged that health authorities have been difficult to engage in crime and disorder partnerships, and this was reflected in all three partnerships (see Audit Commission, 1999; HMIC, 2000). In part it appeared to be due to the lack of resources which health authorities could commit to the partnership process. However, the following extract from one interviewee in Riverton suggests it may also have been because of more fundamental doubts about the appropriate role of the health authority in *crime and disorder* activity:

> It's been difficult to get people engaged in processes because they don't feel it's a part of their core responsibility . . . For Health Authorities generally one can say there's clearly an engagement around the drugs and alcohol agenda, that's straightforward. But we have got DATs [Drug Action Teams] for that . . . if I was looking for areas outside the direct health agenda which had a big impact on people's health locally, I would look at housing or traffic. Crime and Disorder clearly is there and is significant, but our ability to make changes is probably much more likely and is going to be much more productive if we focus on some of those environmental issues . . .

In contrast, crime and disorder are the core business of the probation service. In the research representatives of the probation service were enthusiastic about crime reduction/community safety work, although their financial contribution to the partnership effort was limited by lack of discretion in deciding how probation service resources can be used.

The police authorities in Collingbridge and Sandford were not active in the day-to-day work of the partnerships, although in the latter partnership the police authority had considered the resource implications of partnerships' crime and disorder strategies across the county.

In the three research partnerships, elected members were kept informed about the work of each partnership through briefings, committees, and via the main partnership groups on which they were represented. 'Community' representatives were not involved at the strategic level of the partnership, except in Sandford, where a local resident was a member. Despite recent governments' attempts to encourage commercial sector involvement in multi-agency partnerships, local businesses had a limited role in the three partnerships, as was also found in the recent HMIC (2000) thematic inspection of partnerships (see also Home Office, 1991; Liddle and Gelsthorpe, 1994b).

Power differentials in partnership relations

The academic literature has highlighted the importance of structural power differentials in multi-agency partnerships (Sampson et al., 1988; Crawford and Jones, 1995). In this research there was little evidence of the con-spiratorial model of multi-agency working referred to by Sampson et al. (1988) as the 'police take-over', in which the police determined the agenda and objectives of the partnership. The perception of those interviewed in the three partnerships was that they did not appear to be overly dominated by any one agency; the police were not 'first among equals'. In fact, at the strategic level of the partnership there was considerable confidence in what the multi-agency approach could achieve whereby 'each [agency] can contribute its own expertise and together they can achieve far more than they can do on their own' (Single Regeneration Budget manager, Sandford). Indeed, some representatives, particularly those working in the statutory sector, tended to idealize the multi-agency approach as 'the way forward' for promoting crime reduction/community safety. Stokes-White (2000) has suggested that this is a characteristic of partnerships in the early stages of development, where the potential for partnership working appears exciting. The key question, of course, is whether the rhetoric of idyllic partnership working was in evidence in reality.

The general view in Sandford and Riverton was that the 'prime movers' of the partnership were the police and the local authority (Liddle and Gelsthorpe, 1994b). Indeed, as Gilling (2000, p. 53) notes, '[I]f the buck stops finally with these two agencies, it is difficult to envisage a scenario where they will not be motivated to take a lead.' Implicit in the notion of lead agencies is some degree of hierarchy (Liddle and Gelsthorpe, 1994a). Yet in the Riverton partnership it was accepted that the legislation required statutory accountability by these two agencies; it was their core business (supported by resources), so it was deemed appropriate that they should have the 'lion's share' of the work load and decision-making powers within the partnership.

On the face of it, then, there appeared to be a clear consensus among the partnerships about the corporate aims of partnership working in the locality. However, feelings of marginalization were still voiced in some quarters. In both the Collingbridge and Riverton partnerships, comments by smaller voluntary and community organizations suggested some resentment regarding statutory dominance within the partnership:

> Either we're there as equal partners or we're not there at all, and I think that you still have some discrepancies . . . I think that we want to be involved, we want to have an equal say in things when there are decisions on bidding for money and decisions on various things. It's a bit like CCTV. There's another round coming up now, isn't there, about money for CCTV? . . . I'm not quite sure at this stage whether it's the [partnership] who make an overarching decision for everybody in the [area] on where the priorities are.

These views contrasted with those of some statutory representatives in all three partnerships who questioned the value of contributions by non-statutory organizations to the partnership effort, for example:

> Although you can see they have a valid role in it, they [the voluntary sector] could be more proactive . . . They come along, but you think: why are they here? They're not having an input in the meeting.

> There is a frustration that there are a lot of partners there whose input is to attend the [partnership group], but they have no input into either the output or the outcomes, nor do they have any input in terms of resources other than their attendance . . .

At the time of the first phase of the research these negative comments did not appear to have affected the willingness of partners to work together. Nor was there any indication that less powerful partners were being excluded from key decision-making by informal networks of powerful agencies, as previous research has documented (Sampson et al., 1988; Crawford, 1994b; Phillips and Sampson, 1998).

Reflecting on the benefits of working in partnership, interviewees noted that multi-agency working had encouraged inter- and intra-agency networking, as well as raising the profile of crime reduction/community safety work within some agencies. This co-operation had facilitated the development of information-sharing protocols, a significant achievement, bearing in mind that previous research has highlighted how information exchange and confidentiality concerns can thwart the implementation of crime reduction initiatives (see, for example, Phillips and Sampson, 1998). The protocols were not, however, without problems. Although they were considered to be operating effectively by some partners, concern was also raised about information exchanged being susceptible to abuse, including refusing particular services to individuals. Bureaucratic delays in accessing information and unresolved issues about the type of personal information that could be provided under data protection legislation had also affected the efficiency of the protocols. Notwithstanding this, the general impression from representatives in all three sites was that the partnership process had facilitated information exchange beyond data exchange for the purposes of conducting the audit, but that this was most common among the statutory agencies:

> the exchange of information has gone further than just an exchange of information on a 'committee' level . . . it's encouraged people actually to pass on information to police intelligence . . . It cuts through a lot of the red tape in a way, because if you want information, you know exactly who to ring and exactly what information they can give you . . . if you wanted information two years ago that would have been considered totally confidential and no way. (Probation service representative, Sandford)

The absence of conflict?

As Crawford (1998) notes, one of the key structural dynamics of multi-agency partnerships is the bringing together of diverse agencies whose ideology, mission and interests differ considerably and, indeed, may be in conflict with each other. Conflict between partners may be most likely at three stages of the problem-solving process: first, where the definition, extent or nature of the crime problem is contested; second, when decisions have to be made about which crime and disorder problems are to be prioritized for action; and third, where the appropriate preventive solutions are proposed.

In the current research, the audit process effectively bypassed potential sticking points at the problem definition stage in two ways (cf. Saulsbury and Bowling, 1991; Sampson and Phillips, 1992; Phillips and Sampson, 1998; see also Crawford, 1994a). First, and most important, the audits were contracted out to external consultants. This limited the impact of any disagreements about how particular crime and disorder problems were to be defined or how the data on them should be interpreted. The only difference of opinion that emerged was in Riverton, where the audit consultant had interpreted crime reduction/community safety as including issues such as the policing of marginalized communities. In fact, while the Crime and Disorder Act 1998 referred specifically to crime and disorder reduction, the Guidance on Statutory Crime and Disorder Partnerships (1998), which was issued by the Home Office, encouraged a community safety focus, as recommended by Morgan in 1991. However, this is still a long way from the wider aim of minimizing *all harm* through an integrated policy and service response which makes public authorities accountable to local communities, as advocated by Wiles and Pease (2000).

A draft of the audit submitted to the partnership had included police data on stop-and-search rates by ethnic origin. This had resulted in a somewhat politically charged discussion about the kinds of topics that were appropriate for inclusion in a crime and disorder audit. This discussion was managed within the sub-group responsible for project-managing the audit. It did not appear to be an issue in which other partners (as members of the larger partnership group) were actively involved, nor did it appear to have any long-lasting effect on partnership relations.

A second way in which the audit process sidestepped potential conflict was in the 'nothing ruled in, nothing ruled out' approach, which permeated the legislation and the Home Office (1998) Guidance. This meant that at the audit stage there did not need to be any prioritization of what crime and disorder issues were included for review. The Guidance advised a two-tier approach, beginning with an examination of the main crime and disorder patterns in the locality before more detailed collection and analysis of major local problems. In practice the audits produced by the three partnerships included data on a wide range of crime and disorder problems. There was heavy reliance on police recorded crime and incident data, but the partnerships also variously used data from local authority departments (such as housing, education, social services, legal services), the probation service, fire service, child witness service, the drug action team and a variety of voluntary and community organizations. Additional data were provided by residents, business, victimization/community safety surveys and various focus group discussions.

Partnerships are also typically faced with the need to prioritize which problems are to be tackled first, which is the second stage at which there is the potential for ideological disagreement between partners. The qualitative data from the three case-study sites indicated that a pragmatic approach was adopted whereby priorities were decided on the basis of the audit findings and consultation with the community, dovetailing with existing strategic priorities identified in other statutory plans, such as the Annual Policing Plan. The sometimes deliberate vagueness of the strategy undoubtedly assisted in ensuring consensus, as suggested in interview by one community safety officer in Riverton: 'With the strategy everybody was OK because it's generic, it's our desires, our aspirations, so everyone said, "Oh yes, we can stand that."' Indeed, a review of the first strategies produced by partnerships in England and Wales also found that many published documents contained very broad, overarching aims for crime and disorder reduction, rather than detailed action plans (Phillips et al., 2000).

The third key stage at which partnership relations may be adversely affected is where there is a conflict about the most appropriate preventive interventions to reduce particular crime and disorder problems (Crawford, 1994b; Sampson and Phillips, 1992; Phillips and Sampson, 1998). The research evidence, for example, has pointed to the chasm between the police service, on the one hand, and social services and the probation service on the other. The former, it is argued, advocates a situational approach, particularly favouring measures focused on increasing detection. The latter are more likely to adopt a client-focused perspective which gives primacy to social crime prevention (Sampson et al., 1988; Sampson and Smith, 1992; Crawford, 1994b). Indeed, Gilling (1994) suggests that the so-called neutral problem-solving process actually privileges the situational preventive discourse. Since problem-solving relies on statistical data on opportunities for crime commission and patterns of victimization, and requires the identification of 'hotspots', crimes against property become a primary focus; it is therefore in this area that situational crime prevention measures have been most commonly applied and shown to be effective. Thus the potential for conflict between partners arises where diverse ideological interests are brought together to decide how crime and disorder can be reduced.

The all-inclusive crime and disorder strategy

In the three research partnerships, the development of the strategy/action plan was not marred by overt or covert conflict about preventive approaches. There are three possibilities as to why this may have been the case. First, the Home Office Guidance (1998) encouraged partnerships to set both short-term objectives – which, using situational methods, would bring 'quick wins' – and longer-term criminality-reducing objectives. Thus partnerships were able to accommodate strategic solutions incorporating both types of approach which might be favoured by different partners (see also Mills and Pearson, 2000). In fact the review of partnerships' strategies by Phillips et al. (2000) showed a fairly even balance between situational and social crime prevention techniques: while 79 per cent of documents included situational measures to reduce crime and disorder, 95 per cent planned educational activities/actions to raise awareness, and 67 per cent sought to rehabilitate offenders or provide drug treatment programmes.

Second, the Crime Reduction Programme has also promoted interventions spanning the spectrum. Whether the changing policy context of local crime reduction has limited the extent to which this two-pronged approach is being promoted by the Home Office is open to question, and I will return to this point later in the chapter.

Finally, a major research finding was that instead of the formulation of the strategy/action plan being an opportunity for partners to brainstorm solutions to particular crime and disorder problems, it was a rather rushed process driven by community safety officers. Moreover, there was clear evidence that some partnership representatives resisted fully engaging in the process, as the following quotation demonstrates:

> [For] the action plan we wanted to do a bottom-up approach, get all the different departments, all the different agencies to say: 'This is what we'd like to do, this is our input into the strategy' . . . but in the process that didn't quite happen, people came back with empty sheets . . . Because I think what the government wants is everybody to say, 'Let's chip in, this is what we would like to do' – put it in. And that's the way we thought it was going to work. But later on we found no one was saying, 'This is what we're going to do.' We had to tell them; we had to look through their plans and say, 'This is what you're doing, this is what you could be doing.' (Community safety officer, Riverton)

In Sandford the strategy-setting process was referred to as a 'nightmare' in that some partners refused to contribute at all or deliberately avoided signing up as lead agency for strategic objectives. Owing to time pressures, in Collingbridge the actions in the strategy had to be drafted by the community safety officer with minimal consultation with other partners. They were deliberately broad, so that the agency nominated as the lead could not later respond that it could not deliver on a particular objective. Thus the strategies which emerged were broad enough to appeal to all constituent partners, particularly as they often included 'easy wins' or activities already being undertaken by agencies to enhance community safety in the local area.

To summarize, there was little indication that conflict – destructive or constructive – was yet part of the landscape of partnership relations. There had been few occasions on which conflictual situations had arisen, and optimism about the partnership approach was still very much in evidence at the time the research was conducted. This seems somewhat surprising, given the concern raised about the participation of the voluntary sector in the partnership and the imbalance in the contributions made by agencies to the development of the strategy. Practice certainly contrasted with the idealization of the multi-agency approach discussed earlier. However, despite Sampson et al.'s (1988, p. 482) warning that 'conflict is, at the very least, always latent even in situations of apparent co-operation and consensus between the state agencies', it had not yet come to the fore in the three partnerships under study. Nonetheless, the unwillingness of some partners to contribute actively to the partnership effort raises concern about what can be realistically achieved, particularly at the implementation stage, where significant effort is required.

Internal and external constraints on partnership working

In addition to the power dynamics of multi-agency partnerships affecting the operation of the partnership, there are other constraints that can bear on partnership activity and these were present in the three research partnerships too. While ensuring immediate implementation of Sections 5 and 6, the 1 April 1999 deadline – by which partnerships had to have conducted the audit, consulted, and published a first crime and disorder strategy – put an inordinate amount of pressure on partnerships. In only the Riverton partnership were community safety officers available throughout the whole process; in Collingbridge the community safety officer was appointed at the same time as the audit consultant, while in Sandford the post was filled after the audit had been compiled.

Pre-audit consultation with the general public had taken place utilizing some form of public opinion, victimization or community safety survey, sometimes supplemented by additional focus group discussions or topic-based surveys such as a business survey. Post-audit consultation to confirm the public's priorities in the local area using summarized audits was carried out through newsletters to households or other media forms, in addition to the use of local authority customer service centres. Public meetings with a broad range of local organizations, including crime prevention panels, residents' panels, parish councils, youth groups and schools, were used only in Collingbridge.

Time pressures particularly hit partnerships' ability to contact and consult those sectors of the community which have traditionally been inaccessible ('hard to reach' groups). Certainly in Riverton opportunities were missed to use existing consultative mechanisms or benefit from the consultation expertise within the partnership. In the main, however, the results from the consultation exercises in all three case studies largely mirrored the audit findings, albeit that these were largely based on a sample of those living in the partnerships' communities which was not necessarily representative.

While time pressures constrained what could be achieved by the three partnerships, there was also an indication that many partnership representatives did not possess the requisite skills to deliver what was necessary in compiling the audit, consulting and formulating the strategy and action plan (see also Stafford and Silverlock, 2000). The expertise required to produce an audit of local crime and disorder problems, for example, includes generic research and analysis skills, but also specific knowledge about crime and disorder patterns and recording systems. As previously noted, the crime and disorder audits were contracted out in all three sites: to a health sector researcher, to Crime Concern and to a university academic. It was felt that the prerequisite skills or resources were unavailable in the three sites. While this was clearly a pragmatic response to a tight deadline, there is a danger that the expertise necessary to interpret local patterns of crime and disorder intelligently for the audit and during ongoing monitoring exercises is not capitalized on.

Moreover, although the problem-solving approach to crime reduction/community safety was the guiding framework in the Home Office Guidance (1998), it was little in evidence in the first strategies and action plans produced in the three research partnerships. A more common approach was for partnerships to list a range of activities which have shown some success in reducing a particular crime problem (often cited in the 'good practice' literature), regardless of its appropriateness to local patterns of crime and disorder. The resultant strategies, therefore, particularly where the input from some partnership representatives had been minimal, included some tasks that were difficult to achieve or monitor, or others which were too easily achievable. Other tasks did not clearly relate to objectives or they omitted agencies which were already involved in such work at a local level. Deficiencies were also apparent in the setting of Specific Measurable Achievable Realistic Time-scaled (SMART) performance targets, which were frequently output- rather than outcome-focused, a common weakness observed in multi-agency strategies (Crawford, 1998; see also Home Office, 1998).

The absence of financial support from central government for the administration of partnerships also undoubtedly played a part in the quality of contributions by partnership representatives in the first round. Although the Labour government acted on the Morgan Report (Home Office, 1991) recommendation to make local authorities statutorily responsible for local crime reduction/community safety, it has not assisted in the financing of this new duty. The difficulties experienced in funding the single community safety officers/co-ordinators in the Collingbridge and Sandford partnerships were testimony to the lack of resources available for the administration of partnerships. This, coupled with complaints about central government 'initiative overload', the difficulties of developing crime reduction/community safety work alongside existing service delivery responsibilities, and the very exacting demands of the bidding process for Crime Reduction Programme funding, were all common complaints, as the following quotations show:

> The difficulties in getting people to commit to the C&D [Crime and Disorder] partnership work also arise because so many new agendas are forthcoming from central government, for example, relating to social services, education. C&D is only one part of already very full work loads. (Senior representative of chief executive's department, Sandford)

> The difficulty with all legislation that comes out of central government is that the actual time scales from consultation to delivery are impossibly short. It's almost we want it, we want it now, do it. And the reality is that to do that it almost means we have to drop everything else, and if we drop other things then we get it in the neck from other people. The services still have to be maintained, and it's difficult. If you had more time I think it would ultimately make the actual strategies themselves in this case, more realistic. (Youth service representative, Sandford)

> Bids have been very rushed, and the work on the bids deflects time and resources for crime and disorder partnership working. Central government does not recognize the time and effort it takes to put bids together. (Community safety officer, Sandford)

Thus the backdrop of partnership working at the local level is one of skill and resource constraints. This has implications for partnerships' ability to implement their crime and disorder strategies fully and to mainstream crime reduction/community safety work while responding to existing responsibilities and new ones imposed by the Government. The final section of the chapter considers the changing relationship between local partnerships and the central state.

Changing central government discourses: from prioritizing the local agenda to prescription and inspection

The foreword to the Home Office *Guidance on Statutory Crime and Disorder Partnerships* (1998) states that 'the people who live and work in an area are best placed to identify the problems facing them and the options available for tackling those problems, and that maxim was kept very much in mind when drafting the legislation.' At the heart of Sections 5 and 6 of the Crime and Disorder Act 1998, then, was the acknowledgement that local practitioners have the expertise to create cogent strategies to reduce crime locally. Gilling (2000) questions whether this governance of 'responsibilization' which 'passes the metaphorical buck' to local agencies to reduce crime without the concomitant resourcing recommended by Morgan (1991) is a deliberate strategy employed by the government. The current policy climate certainly does reflect the centre's directive approach to making local partnerships accountable for reductions in crime and disorder in the short term. In November 1998, for example, the Home Office Minister Paul Boateng wrote to partnerships to draw their attention to the importance of addressing domestic violence in their audits and strategies. Not surprisingly, 86 per cent of partnerships included a strategic priority to reduce domestic violence in their locality (Phillips et al., 2000).

More significantly (as domestic violence is frequently underreported and underrecorded and undoubtedly should be prioritized for reduction by partnerships), in November 1999 the government published its crime reduction strategy. The first chapter begins by highlighting the anomaly whereby partnership areas that are socially and demographically similar can have very different rates of crime. The aim, therefore, it is argued, should be for the police and crime and disorder partnerships to emulate the practice of professionals working in the education and health services to 'commit[s] themselves to reaching the standards of the best', to reduce crime nationally. Performance league tables to encourage 'poor performers to raise their game', clear and challenging targets, the dissemination of good practice and hard work are the prerequisites of success. In the space of months, partnerships previously recognized as those most appropriate to determine locally important crime and disorder problems are instructed to set five-year targets with annual milestones to reduce vehicle crime, domestic burglary and robbery. The reaction from partnerships in the research sites was unsurprising:

> They introduced crime and disorder locally, and then they say you've got to concentrate on burglary, auto crime and robbery, and then we've got drugs . . . it just goes on . . . whereas everything becomes a priority . . . robbery accounts for less than one per cent of all our crime, so it's not a priority . . . the problems locally are more about juvenile nuisance, criminal damage, antisocial behaviour, drugs . . . it lends itself, if people wanted to say: 'There's so much confusion now. I haven't done it because I've got to do this.' (Police service representative, Sandford)

The inspection and auditing of partnerships have also been accelerated, reflecting the public managerialist tendencies now familiar to the police (Crawford, 1994a; Johnston, 2000). Early in 1999 the Audit Commission inspected around 250 partnership infrastructures, examining their audits, the extent and nature of the consultation undertaken, and their resultant community safety strategies (HMIC, 2000). In two of the three partnerships under study, the District Auditors' report highlighting weaknesses, particularly in strategic objectives, was viewed by representatives as very insightful and served as a stimulus to revise the strategy/action plan to include SMARTer objectives. As well as the local inspection process, HM

Inspectorate of Constabulary (HMIC) launched its own inspection in January 2000 working in collaboration with the Home Office, the Audit Commission, the Local Government Association, the Office for Standards in Education and the Social Services Inspectorate. By its own admission, this inspection of twelve police forces and thirty-six partnerships, tasked with establishing the critical success factors for achieving crime reduction and, in particular, providing a template for successful partnership working, was established very soon after the implementation of the Crime and Disorder Act. Further auditing of partnerships is to be expected under the Best Value regime. This rigorous performance management process has put additional pressure on partnerships, particularly police partners:

> We've got force key performance indicators, then we've got Ministerial Objectives, we've got Police Authority involvement in what we should be addressing, we've got local targets to achieve through crime and disorder [partnerships], then we've got Best Value reviews to do in terms of efficiency gains and things of that nature. It just goes on and on. (Police service representative, Sandford)

This process will be further amplified now that recorded crime statistics are available by partnership area, and crime reduction targets will be set centrally for each partnership on the basis of each achieving reductions compared with the top performing quartile of each 'family of partnerships' (Povey et al., 2000; Home Office, 1999; Leigh et al., 2000). In advance of this process, Section 7(1) of the Act has already been used by the Home Office to request an annual progress report from partnerships. They were asked to supply detailed information about short- and long-term outcome targets for crime reduction for all crimes, violent crime, vehicle crime and burglary, and the extent to which these had been achieved a year after the first strategy was developed. This information would be used to 'provide a central perspective on the direction of the partnerships and [to] identify those partnership areas in which further support or assistance may be needed' (Home Office, 1999, p. 12). This exercise was viewed rather cynically in one of the research partnerships:

> whether that is the best use of our time is highly debatable . . . If we don't fill in any of the Home Office questionnaires, if we don't produce any of the PI information generally that's required, nobody will talk to us, we'll be pariahed, we won't get any money . . . I think generally we ought to do less of that [completing questionnaires] and more of what's going to make a difference . . . (Senior representative from Chief Executive's department, Riverton)

What Crawford (1997) has referred to as 'government at a distance' can be seen in the arrangements put in place by the Home Office to provide the support referred to in the last paragraph. The Partnership Support

Programme involves the 'contractualization' of two voluntary organizations, NACRO and Crime Concern (which receive some central government funding). This builds on previous neo-corporatist practices of creating local alliances which, controlled by the centre, are given responsibility for promoting compliance with public policy (Crawford, 1994a; Hughes, 1996). The programme consists of giving partnerships individual consultancy support to meet the strategic and operational challenges they face, mounting a national conference and a series of regional seminars to share and promote good practice and networking, along with a series of briefings which have a practitioner focus and emphasize good working practices. This will be supplemented by the work of the high-level national Crime Reduction Task Force of senior central and local government officials. 'Raising the game' of Crime and Disorder Partnerships will be assisted by the use of a series of toolkits focused on different crime types and a toolkit focused on good practice in partnership working. In essence, then, the governmental crime reduction project encompasses strict adherence to public managerialist tendencies which give primacy to objective performance management and scrutiny of partnership activity coupled with a support programme provided outside government and a funding regime which is still somewhat short-term in nature.

Conclusion

By November 2000 there were 376 statutory Crime and Disorder Partnerships in England and Wales implementing their first three-year strategy to reduce crime and disorder in their local areas. This new statutory infrastructure for crime reduction/community safety represents a significant advance in that there are now locally accountable authorities, rather than the police alone, whose task it is to reduce crime locally.

This chapter has considered the extent to which these new arrangements have been able to leapfrog some of the difficulties associated with multi-agency partnerships documented in the academic and policy literature. The research on the three case-study partnerships revealed a rather mixed picture. On the one hand, there appears to be considerable commitment to partnership working at a strategic level. The domination of partnerships by statutory agencies is an issue but it does not appear to be holding partners back in their day-to-day activities. Nor is there evidence of partners being deliberately disempowered through informal decision-making outside formal partnership forums. Indeed, there is a sense in which partners are in a 'honeymoon phase' where conflict has not surfaced in partnership relations. This may in part be due to the all-inclusive nature of the audit and strategy formulation process in the first year.

On the other hand, multi-agency activity has been limited by the time, resources, skills and expertise available to partnerships. The lack of financial support for administering local partnerships has hindered progress, while the skills deficit within partnerships, particularly in relation to problem-solving, has shown itself in the inadequacies of the strategies/ actions plans produced in the three research areas. The fact that the crime and disorder agenda is, in effect, competing with other national social policy agendas has also been a fundamental difficulty facing local partnerships. In addition, the move towards much greater direction from central government has been problematic for partnerships, not least because it represents a major departure from the original spirit of the legislation and guidance to partnerships. It has increased the administrative work load of partnerships and has often meant adding to existing strategic priorities to accommodate government demands on national targets.

This research has been able to provide only a snapshot of practice in the early history of three statutory partnerships. This is a new and fast-moving area of policy and it is impossible to predict what the future holds for the new structures established to tackle local crime reduction/community safety. It does, however, seem likely that the future will see further prescription, major auditing and inspection of local partnerships through a variety of means, including rigorous performance management. This will be complemented by guidance from the centre with some financial support being provided through the newly established Partnership Development Fund.[3] It is also more than possible that the political drive to reduce crime and disorder in 2001–2 will encourage more partnerships to seek the 'quick wins' associated with situational crime prevention, rather than opt for the longer-term measures which seek to reduce criminality. Undoubtedly these and other issues will form the basis of further research to examine the evolution and development of statutory Crime and Disorder Partnerships.

Notes

1   This research has been undertaken by Matt Carter, Mary Considine, Jessica Jacobson, Rachel Lewis and the author of this chapter. The views expressed in this chapter are those of the author, not necessarily those of the Home Office (nor do they reflect government policy).
2   Pseudonyms have been used to preserve the anonymity of the research sites.
3   Since this chapter was prepared, the Home Office has established the Partnership Development Fund. Providing £60 million for partnerships over three years, it aims to support cross-cutting work on information systems, data analysis, the effective implementation of partnerships' strategies, and to promote good and innovative practice through consultancy, training and development work with partnerships.

References

Audit Commission (1999) *Safety in Numbers: Promoting Community Safety*, London, Audit Commission.

Ballintyne, S., Pease, K. and McLaren, V. (eds) (2000) *Secure Foundations: Key Issues in Crime Prevention, Crime Reduction and Community Safety*, London, Institute for Public Policy Research.

Crawford, A. (1994a) 'The partnership approach: corporatism at the local level?', *Social and Legal Studies*, vol. 3, no. 4, pp. 497–519.

Crawford, A. (1994b) 'Social values and managerial goals: police and probation officers' experiences and views of inter-agency co-operation', *Policing and Society*, vol. 4, pp. 323–339.

Crawford, A. (1997) *The Local Governance of Crime: Appeals to Community and Partnerships*, Oxford, Oxford University Press.

Crawford, A. (1998) 'Delivering multi-agency partnerships in community safety' in Marlow, A. and Pitts, J. (eds) *Planning Safer Communities*, Lyme Regis, Russell House Publishing.

Crawford, A. and Jones, M. (1995) 'Inter-agency co-operation and community-based crime prevention', *British Journal of Criminology*, vol. 35, no. 1, pp. 17–33.

Gilling, D. (1994) 'Multi-agency crime prevention: some barriers to collaboration', *Howard Journal*, vol. 33, no. 3, pp. 246–57.

Gilling, D. (2000) 'Surfing the crime net: UK Home Office guidance on the Crime and Disorder Act 1998', *Crime Prevention and Community Safety*, vol. 2, no. 1, pp. 51–4.

Goldblatt, P. and Lewis, C. (1998) *Reducing Offending: An Assessment of Research Evidence on ways of Dealing with Offending Behaviour*, Home Office Research Study 187, London, Home Office.

Goldstein, H. (1990) *Problem-oriented Policing*, New York, McGraw-Hill.

HM Inspectorate of Constabulary (1998) *Beating Crime: A Thematic Inspection of Crime Prevention*, London, Home Office.

HM Inspectorate of Constabulary (2000) *Calling Time on Crime: A Thematic Inspection of Crime and Disorder conducted by HM Inspectorate of Constabulary in collaboration with the Home Office, Audit Commission, Local Government Association, Office for Standards in Education and the Social Services Inspectorate*, London, Home Office.

Home Office (1991) *Safer Communities: The Local Delivery of Crime Prevention through the Partnership Approach* (Morgan Report), Standing Conference on Crime Prevention, London, Home Office.

Home Office (1998) *Guidance on Statutory Crime and Disorder Partnerships*, London, Home Office.

Home Office (1999) *The Government's Crime Reduction Strategy*, London, Home Office.

Hughes, G. (1996) 'Strategies of multi-agency crime prevention and community safety in contemporary Britain', *Studies on Crime and Crime Prevention*, vol. 5, no. 2, pp. 221–44.

Johnston, L. (2000) *Policing Britain: Risk, Security and Governance*, Harlow, Longman.

Leigh, A., Arnott, J., Clarke, G. and See, L. (2000) *Family Values: Grouping Similar Policing and Crime Reduction Areas for Comparative Purposes*, Home Office Policing and Reducing Crime Unit Briefing Note 3/00, London, Home Office.

Liddle, A.M. and Gelsthorpe, L.R. (1994a) *Inter-agency Crime Prevention: Organizing Local Delivery*, Home Office Crime Prevention Unit Paper 52, London, Home Office.

Liddle, A.M. and Gelsthorpe, L.R. (1994b) *Crime Prevention and Inter-agency Co-operation*, Home Office Crime Prevention Unit Paper 53, London, Home Office.

Mills, A. and Pearson, S. (2000) 'From audit to strategy: a practice view' in Ballintyne, S., Pease, K. and McLaren, V. (eds) *Secure Foundations: Key Issues in Crime Prevention, Crime Reduction and Community Safety*, London, Institute for Public Policy Research.

Phillips, C. and Brown, D. (1997) 'Observational studies in police custody areas: some methodological and ethical issues considered', *Policing and Society*, vol. 7, pp. 191–205.

Phillips, C. and Sampson, A. (1998) 'Preventing repeated racial victimization: an action research project', *British Journal of Criminology*, vol. 38, no. 1, pp. 124–44.

Phillips, C., Considine, M. and Lewis, R. (2000) *A Review of Audits and Strategies produced by Crime and Disorder Partnerships in 1999*, Home Office Policing and Reducing Crime Unit Briefing Note 8/2000, London, Home Office.

Povey, D., Cotton, J. and Sisson, S. (2000) *Recorded Crime Statistics, England and Wales, April 1999 to March 2000*, Home Office Statistical Bulletin issue 12/00, London, Home Office.

Sampson, A. and Phillips, C. (1992) *Multiple Victimization: Racial Attacks on an East London Estate*, Police Research Group Crime Prevention Unit Paper 36, London, Home Office.

Sampson, A. and Phillips, C. (1995) *Reducing Repeat Racial Victimization on an East London Estate*, Police Research Group Crime Prevention Unit Paper 67, London, Home Office.

Sampson, A. and Smith, D. (1992) 'Probation and community crime prevention', *Howard Journal*, vol. 31, pp. 105–19.

Sampson, A., Stubbs, P., Smith, D., Pearson, G. and Blagg, H. (1988) 'Crime localities and the multi-agency approach', *British Journal of Criminology*, vol. 28, no. 4, pp. 478–93.

Saulsbury, W. and Bowling, B. (1991) *The Multi-agency Approach in Practice: The North Plaistow Racial Harassment Project*, Home Office Research and Planning Unit Paper 64, London, Home Office.

Stafford, J. and Silverlock, L. (2000) 'What works and what makes what works work' in Ballintyne, S. et al. (eds) *Secure Foundations*, London, Institute for Public Policy Research.

Stokes-White, S. (2000) 'Partnership: rhetoric or reality?' in Ballintyne, S. et al. (eds) *Secure Foundations*, London, Institute for Public Policy Research.

Wiles, P. and Pease, K. (2000) 'Crime prevention and community safety: Tweedledum and Tweedledee?' in Ballintyne, S. et al. (eds) *Secure Foundations*, London, Institute for Public Policy Research.

10

Conflict, crime control and the 're-'construction of state-community relations in Northern Ireland

Kieran McEvoy, Brian Gormally and Harry Mika

The socially divisive potential for crime and crime control strategies has been well highlighted over the past thirty years in Northern Ireland. The relationship between 'ordinary' and 'political' crime, the contested legitimacy of the police and criminal justice system, paramilitary involvement in 'policing' antisocial crime, and the relationship between these various protagonists and local communities – these have all been hotly contested issues both during and after the conflict. As a result, the Good Friday Agreement included provision for major reviews into both policing and criminal justice. In addition, since 1997 two of the major paramilitary groupings have been engaged in processes designed to supplant punishment attacks with community-based restorative justice projects. Collectively these three initiatives have the potential to constitute a radically altered relationship between the traditional crime control agents and the communities in which they operate.

The next section of this chapter deals with the intersection between 'ordinary' and 'political' crime and the way in which discourses on both became enmeshed with, and intricately linked with, differing state crime control strategies. The section also considers paramilitary crime control strategies and the way in which such activities reflect particular configurations of paramilitary/community relations. The following section then considers whether a *transformation* is occurring in state/community relations as a result of the peace process. The provisions of the Northern Ireland Criminal Justice Review, the Patten Commission on Policing and the developments in community-based restorative justice are examined as three key sites in which the character of any such transformed relations may be decided upon.

Crime control, community and the political conflict

One of the key criminological features of Northern Ireland since 1970 has been two overlapping sets of disputes concerning the relationship between 'crime' and the political conflict. One relates to the 'criminal' nature of political violence, the degree to which the state took cognizance of the politically motivated nature of the paramilitary protagonists who carried out 'terrorist' acts. The second relates more broadly to the relationship between the conflict and 'ordinary' crime.

Northern Ireland experienced a violent struggle between paramilitaries and the state as to whether conflict-related violence could accurately be considered as *political*. That struggle, often fought out in practice in a number of criminal justice battlegrounds, including the courts and the prisons, has seen activists refuse to recognize the courts, engage in 'dirty protest' and hunger strikes to the death, as well as widespread acts of violence (Gormally et al., 1993; Campbell et al., 1994; McEvoy, 2000). Such a struggle regarding the distinction between what constitutes *political* and what are *criminal* acts is not, however, unique to Northern Ireland.[1]

In the Northern Ireland context, the British state and the British courts have had relatively few problems in defining and understanding what is meant by 'terrorism' in a straightforwardly technical or instrumentalist fashion.[2] From 1972 up to the present day, 'terrorism' has been defined in successive pieces of emergency legislation as

> the use of violence for political ends and includes any use of violence for the purpose of putting the public or any section of the public in fear. A terrorist is defined as a person who is or has been concerned in the commission or attempted commission of any act of terrorism or in directing, organizing or training persons for the purpose of terrorism.[3]

Since 1973 in Northern Ireland any person charged with a suspected 'terrorist' offence has their case heard in court before a single judge without a jury and with amended rules of evidence (Jackson and Doran, 1995). The offences are contained in a schedule to the emergency legislation.

Such an instrumentalist view of terrorism has enabled successive British governments to acknowledge that while people may be engaged in acts of violence 'for political ends', such acts remain criminal in nature and should be treated as such, albeit by using a necessarily amended criminal justice process. Thus, despite the fact that the definition of terrorism enshrined in emergency legislation has explicitly recognized 'political ends' as the rationale of terrorist activity, this has had little ideological impact on the state's recognition of the political character of the conflict (McEvoy, 2001).

Ordinary crime, conflict management and crime control

If we accept that acknowledgement of the notion of 'political' crime is by definition problematic for a state engaged in managing a violent conflict, the next logical consideration is to examine the role which discourses on 'ordinary' crime may play. As elsewhere (for example, Ryan, 1999), such discourses are themselves deployed in an explicitly *political* fashion. High or low 'ordinary' crime rates have been explicitly linked with broader conflict management strategies.

During the conflict, two competing theses about 'ordinary' crime and its relationship with the conflict emerged (for more on this, see Morison and Geary, 1989). The first, drawn in particular from psychological studies of the impact of violence, emerged from the mid-1970s onwards. It suggested that political violence and the anti-authoritarian attitudes it engendered 'spilled over' into ordinary crime and were passed on to younger generations similarly affected by the loosening of social controls. An Irish joint Church report referred to 'the catastrophic and terrifying decline' in respect for human life and property and concluded that 'a concomitant of political violence has been a great increase in plain vandalism, theft and crime' (Christian Churches, 1976, p. 4). The Chief Constable's annual report for 1979, looking back at the previous ten years, argued that 'the general lawlessness brought about by a decade of terrorism has lowered community restraint and personal discipline' (RUC, 1979, p. 2). Juvenile justice-related research refers to papers prepared and circulated within government departments in the mid-1970s which express the view that 'at some stage the prolonged period of civil disorders could produce an increasing volume of juvenile delinquency' (Northern Ireland Office circular, 1976, cited in Powell, 1982; Caul, 1983).

Such a 'breakdown in the social fabric thesis' depended upon denying the validity of the official statistics, which generally showed lower rates of crime in Northern Ireland than in the rest of the United Kingdom and Ireland. This was explained by questioning whether hostility to the police, particularly within nationalist/republican communities, and the activities of paramilitaries (for example, in dissuading people from going to the police or in carrying out their own policing activities) combined to produce lower reporting rates. Such an account fitted within a broader perspective, wherein paramilitaries were 'blamed' for the social and political upheaval which had occurred since the outbreak of the Troubles. Indeed, the low levels of 'ordinary' crime in the pre-Troubles Stormont era (Brewer et al., 1997) were used explicitly in official discourse to underpin a somewhat idyllic notion of the past (see, for example, RUC, 1977). Paramilitaries were engaged in crime themselves and could be held responsible for a broader decline in the bonds of social control, particularly among the younger generation.

The other thesis, which emerged during the late 1970s and early 1980s and has gained currency since, suggested that Northern Ireland, given the Troubles, has a 'surprisingly low crime rate'. In spite of high levels of socio-economic deprivation, this view suggested that the fabric of society had 'withstood' the violence wrought by the paramilitaries and that what the security forces have long referred to as 'ordinary decent crime' remained low compared with the United Kingdom and the Irish Republic (Heskin, 1981). This view was backed up by the statistical evidence then available from the Chief Constable's annual reports and the Northern Ireland Office's *Commentaries on Northern Ireland Crime Statistics*. Crime indices were used again to underpin a political framework that Northern Ireland was a decent, churchgoing, family-oriented, low-crime society – a 'paradise on earth' as one former Tory Minister described it – marred only by the onslaught from the 'men of violence'.

Since the emergence of these two conflicting theses the level of available information has changed dramatically. In 1989 Northern Ireland was included in the International Crime Survey, although not in the 1992 version. In 1996 Northern Ireland was included in the British Crime Survey for the first time, although at the time of writing none of the results has yet been published. Northern Ireland was also included in the 1996 International Crime Victims Survey (ICVS) (Mayhew and van Dijk, 1997) and a Northern-Ireland-wide crime survey was conducted in-house by the Northern Ireland Office in 1994/5, only selected extracts from which have been published (Boyle and Haire, 1996). In addition, there are a large number of on-going public opinion surveys carried out on behalf of the Police Authority for Northern Ireland and a local communities crime survey has been published (O'Mahony et al., 2000). All these surveys have confirmed comparatively low rates of victimization, although considerable variances have emerged with regard to attitudes towards the police, particularly among working-class Catholic communities (*ibid.*).[4]

For current purposes, other than the political framework within which crime rates have been presented, perhaps what are of most relevance are the insights which the competing paradigms provide into state/community relations concerning crime and criminal justice.

The 'breakdown in the social fabric' thesis occurred largely in the context of a broader range of security policies which were in essence a military-led response to what was perceived as an armed insurrection (Cunningham, 1991; Kitson, 1991). Such a view necessitated distinctions between 'enemy' and 'friendly' communities, with little significant energies devoted by the state to improving relations with the enemy community, in this instance the 'Catholic/nationalist' community. It also saw the introduction of harsh security measures directed primarily against that community[5] and the subjugation of the policing of ordinary crime by the RUC to the overall needs of the army-led anti-terrorist security effort. Within such a context, the visible signs of criminogenic anti-authoritarianism, such as ritualized rioting and destruction of property by young people, fitted well within a thesis which linked moral decline and a loosening of social control in working-class communities with the violent activities of the paramilitaries.

The 'surprisingly low levels of crime despite the Troubles' thesis took root gradually in the context of a deliberately reconfigured set of conflict management policies. Following the recommendations of the Gardiner Committee, the twin strategies of criminalization and 'Ulsterization' were introduced from 1976 onwards. Arguably, both were to dominate government policy in Northern Ireland until the peace process of the 1990s.

Criminalization was a strategy designed to delegitimize and depoliticize those involved in paramilitary violence by removing the practical and symbolic state recognition of the political nature of terrorist violence. Internment without trial was ended, as was 'Special Category status' (in effect *de facto* prisoner-of-war status) for convicted paramilitary prisoners. In the prisons, all practical and symbolic differences between terrorist and ordinary prisoners were taken away, prisoners were forced to work and to wear prison uniform in a concerted attempt to 'break' the paramilitaries in the prisons (Gormally et al., 1993). In the community, under the policy of *Ulsterization*, the police were given primary responsibility for security policy, their numbers were increased dramatically and army support was to be largely in the shape of the locally recruited Royal Irish Regiment. The government's aim was to portray the conflict as a security rather than a political problem. The position of the British state (at least to an international audience) was that of an umpire trying to defend the rule of law in on-going factional fights between two communities long divided on religious and historical grounds. (See Gormally et al., 1993, and Ellison and Smyth, 2000, for a fuller exposition of this strategy.)

Such a reshaped security strategy required a parallel reformulation of the relationship between the state and the Catholic community in particular. The Gardiner Report had made specific links between such changes and social measures designed to marginalize the 'terrorists' from their own communities.[6] A tough security policy, designed, in the words of the Northern Ireland Secretary of State, to 'squeeze the IRA like toothpaste' (Hamill, 1985, p. 221), was allied on the other hand with 'relatively generous social policies', a stance mirrored by successive Conservative administrations in the 1980s (Gaffiken and Morrissey, 1990, p. 206). From the mid-1970s onwards, considerable resources were deployed in areas such as West Belfast from which the republican movement derives much of its support, albeit channelled through the more conservative elements within those communities such as the Catholic Church (Tomlinson, 1998, p. 98).

These new policies also required a radically different role for the local police force, the Royal Ulster Constabulary. Emergency legislation, the non-jury Diplock courts and extensive police powers remained as part of a necessarily altered criminal justice response to the 'terrorist' threat (Jennings, 1990; Jackson and Doran, 1995). However, the criminalization and Ulsterization policies envisaged that the police and the criminal justice system would no longer be 'fighting a war' against the terrorists on behalf of the state, but rather tackling terrorism as one additional specialism of a broader crime control strategy. Kenneth Newman, a British police officer who took over as RUC Chief Constable in 1976, argued that 'British' policing methods would be central to such a strategy (Newman, 1978, cited in Ellison and Smyth, 2000, p. 85). This 'British' model of policing would emphasize the professionalism of RUC officers, acting impartially and within the law, and be characterized by increased liaison with local communities and what he referred to as a multi-agency initiative between the RUC, government and community groups willing to engage with the police (Hillyard, 1983, pp. 46–7). The sharpest edge of coping with terrorist violence was met through an expansion of the RUC Special Branch and the increased deployment of small specialist army units such as the SAS involved in covert operations (Ryder, 1989).

For the sake of brevity, despite these changes, suffice it to say that the RUC has failed to win large-scale support in the Catholic community as a whole.[7] Its role as a predominantly Unionist force perceived as defending the union with Britain, harassment and intimidation, compelling allegations of collusion with loyalist paramilitaries in the killing of nationalists, involvement in covert shoot-to-kill operations and the lack of any credible accountability structures have all combined to ensure that such a relationship remains problematic (Weitzer, 1995; O'Rawe and Moore, 1997; McGarry and O'Leary, 1999). As Mulcahy has argued, 'As long as these factors undermined any gains that the RUC's professionalization might secure, it was clear that the problems associated with policing in Northern Ireland could not be resolved at a purely organizational level' (2000, p. 70).

Despite manifest difficulties in its relationship with the Catholic community in particular, RUC police/community relations discourses have selectively utilized survey data (Ellison, 2000) to suggest 'hidden levels of community support' which is obscured from view by intimidation by republican paramilitaries. As Mulcahy has argued cogently, such discourses rely upon anecdotal evidence from police officers of 'behind closed doors' support wherein members of the Catholic community offer words of encouragement to RUC officers once inside their homes which they cannot do in public for fear of paramilitary intimidation (2000, pp. 77–9). Such support, from what the police sometimes refer to as 'ordinary decent Catholics' (Brewer and Magee, 1991), has been used by the RUC to criticize those seeking to reform policing in the jurisdiction as 'politically motivated' and to offer an alternative vision of harmonious police/community relations if only the scourge of 'terrorism' could be removed.

Perhaps of equal interest, although it tends to be underrepresented in survey data (Patten, 1999), is the fact that there is some evidence of a problematic relationship between the RUC and working-class urban Protestants (McVeigh, 1994). Such difficulties, particularly concerning the public order policing of Orange marches, have led to sporadic attacks on police officers, their homes and their families by loyalists outraged at what they perceived as 'betrayal' by their police (Bryett, 1997). Allegations of strong-arm police tactics in policing such loyalist demonstrations have led some wags to describe the force now as 'equal opportunity harassers' (McGarry and O'Leary, 1999, p. 35) and others to point to it as evidence of police impartiality. However, as Ellison and Smyth (2000, p. 162) argue, leaving aside whether the highly contestable claim that RUC malpractice is visited equally upon loyalist and nationalist protestors is actually true (see, for example, CAJ, 1997), 'equal bashing of heads' is hardly a solid foundation upon which to construct a legitimate police force.

The community relations work attempted by the RUC during the conflict in both working-class loyalist Unionist and republican nationalist communities has been hampered by the real security dangers on the ground, tension between the force's anti-terrorist and 'ordinary' policing responsibilities, the antipathy of local community networks in some instances regarding engaging with the police and the attitudes and working practices of the police themselves.

Clearly the inability of the RUC to move around republican nationalist areas unless heavily armed, in armoured vehicles, with army support and often a helicopter presence has inhibited traditional 'community policing'. As McWilliams and Spence (1994) suggest regarding the issue of domestic violence, the security demands which led to such policing techniques have been a major inhibitor of women from such communities calling the police for assistance.

A related issue, however, has been the tension between the demands, led by Special Branch, to acquire intelligence on paramilitary activists and the community's needs regarding the policing of 'ordinary crime'. The RUC has long utilized local petty criminals and young offenders as sources of information on such 'players', often in return for small sums of money and reduced or dropped criminal charges (McVeigh, 1994).

It is also true that the RUC has met with organized community and political resistance, particularly in working-class nationalist communities, to 'normal' community policing initiatives such as school visits, traffic controlling measures and the like (Brewer et al., 1997).

Finally, we would argue that the RUC's own organizational culture and working practices have impeded the development of effective working relations within communities and with other organizations. Following Kenneth Newman's urgings, it has relied upon very *British* policing community outreach strategies such as 'blue lamp discos', Crimestoppers, Community/Police Liaison Committees[8] and the like, none of which took particular cognizance of the exigencies of the Northern Ireland context. As argued above, it has tended to adopt a distrustful disposition towards those who were not clearly 'pro-RUC' and constructed typologies of individuals or indeed communities (e.g. 'ordinary decent Catholics') with whom business could be done and it has demonstrated considerable unwillingness to be other than a lead agency even in inter-agency working groups with other professional organizations.

In sum, the predominant state-led crime discourse in Northern Ireland since the mid to late 1970s has been to subsume political or terrorist illegality into one further 'crime' category which then fell within, and arguably dominated, an overall crime control strategy. Low levels of 'ordinary' crime were utilized as a vision of how an alternative society would look if terrorists could be 'gotten off the backs of the people' (PFNI, 1995, p. 2). The changed security policy entailed a systemic attempt to 'prise open and progressively widen the gap between the terrorist and the ordinary people so that they will be increasingly perceived as criminals and not wayward political heroes' (Newman, 1992, cited in Ellison and Smyth, 2000, p. 82). Such efforts required attempts at building bridges with communities who were estranged from the police. For the reasons identified above, such efforts have been less than successful.

Paramilitarism, crime and crime control

The other key protagonists who have been engaged in 'crime control' activities during the Northern Ireland conflict have been republican and loyalist paramilitaries. Before examining such activities, however, and in particular how such crime control activities were interconnected with the relationship between paramilitaries and their respective communities, it is important to reflect upon the extent of the involvement of the paramilitaries themselves in illegal activities. Between the various republican and loyalist factions, paramilitaries have been responsible for almost 90 per cent (that is over 3,200) of conflict-related deaths, including civilian and security force casualties, with the security forces responsible for 360 killings between 1969 and 1999 (McKittrick et al., 1999; Ní Aolainn, 2000). Thousands more have been injured in bombings, shootings and other acts of political violence (Fay et al., 1999). In order to fund their respective campaigns, paramilitaries have been responsible for a range of other offences, including robberies, kidnapping, extortion, smuggling and, in the case of loyalist paramilitaries and republican splinter groups, dealing in and distributing illicit drugs both for organizational funds and for personal gain (Bowyer-Bell 1993; McEvoy et al., 1998; Sluka, 1995). As discussed below, loyalist paramilitaries in particular, as well as republican splinter groups,[9] have had endemic problems with volunteers engaged in 'ordinary' criminal activity, or 'homers', as they are known in Northern Ireland parlance.

In addition to their own unlawful activities, paramilitaries have also engaged in crime control activities in the local communities in which they are active. In such communities paramilitaries have assumed responsibility for 'policing' 'their' areas, with alleged criminal or antisocial offenders being violently punished or banished. Since 1973, police figures suggest, approximately 2,300 people have been the victim of paramilitary punishment shootings (usually in the knees, thighs, elbows, ankles or a combination) and since 1983 approximately 1,700 people have been the victim of paramilitary punishment beatings (involving attacks with baseball bats, hurling sticks studded with nails, iron bars and other heavy implements (RUC website, 2000). While the reliability of punishment statistics is keenly contested, there is little dispute concerning the realities of the extreme violence visited upon the victims of punishment attacks, with a number having died of injuries or been permanently disabled. Such attacks have persisted in the era of the peace process, albeit waxing and waning in the light of political developments and events on the ground. While the issue has been written about in some detail elsewhere (McEvoy and Mika, 2001; Mika and McEvoy, 2001), a number of key points are worth drawing out for current purposes.

With regard to republicans some commentators have suggested that the system represents a mechanism for the IRA to maintain power and control in local communities, facilitating internal repression and allowing a venue for 'warped personalities to indulge themselves in extreme violence' (Kennedy, 1995; O'Doherty, 1998). For current purposes, however, we would place greatest emphasis upon four related themes in understanding punishment violence in republican communities. These are: the notion among the republican movement of their 'responsibility' for dealing with antisocial crime; a parallel culture of reliance and dependence which has developed in working-class republican communities upon the IRA to 'deal with' problems of crime and antisocial activity; the lack of legitimacy or effectiveness of the formal justice system (in particular the RUC) in such communities; and the relationship between punishment attacks and broader political developments, particularly since the 1994 cease-fires.

The IRA's resurgence in the early 1970s was influenced in large part by the perceived need for the organized defence of nationalist communities from loyalist mobs, either supported by or ignored by a belligerent police force (Bowyer-Bell, 1979; Coogan, 1987; Bishop and Mallie, 1987). This notion of 'responsibility' for the defence of their community is a key tenet in modern republican ideology (MacIntyre, 1995; O'Doherty, 1998) and it extends beyond defence from loyalist or state violence to include defence and protection from antisocial crime. Similarly with regard to the reliance of republican communities upon IRA policing, surveys and ethnographic work in such communities have produced candid acknowledgements of the importance of such paramilitary activities in dealing with antisocial crime (Brewer et al., 1997; O'Mahony et al., 2000). The arguments concerning the RUC's lack of legitimacy in working-class republican and nationalist communities have been extensively discussed above. Finally, the relationship between punishment attacks and broader political developments has become increasingly significant since the 1994 cease-fires. In the pre-1994 context of major explosions, killings and so forth, punishment violence was of less obvious political significance. However, once the main republican and loyalist paramilitaries had called cessations of 'military' operations, the political significance of punishment attacks increased significantly.

With regard to loyalist punishment violence and crime control strategies, the picture here is arguably more complicated. Like republicans, the involvement of loyalist paramilitaries in punishment attacks cannot be understood without reference to their ideology and politics, and its impact upon their organizational structure and the quality of recruits.[10] As a pro-state 'terrorist' group (Wilkinson, 1986), loyalists share the political aspirations of the state to maintain the union with Britain (although ever mistrustful of British duplicity) but are frustrated at the inability of the security services to 'take on' the IRA and protect the Protestant community from them. Structurally the loyalist paramilitaries, at least until the period of the cease-fires, tended to be much less formalized and centralized than the IRA, built around strong personalities and control of particular territories rather than particular military or organizational ability (Bowyer-Bell, 1993; Bruce, 1992). Consequently there is a considerable degree of geographical autonomy among loyalist paramilitary groups, particularly in the larger group (the UDA), and problems of internal discipline are endemic.

They, too, lay claim to the policing of antisocial activities, including petty crime and drug dealing, and express frustration at the apparent inability of the police to deal with such problems. The loyalist tariff system is considerably looser and more truncated than its republican counterpart, with less warning given, and no clear pathway between exiling, beatings, shootings and death (Conway, 1997). Bell (1996) and Conway (1997) argue, for example, that while young people who are punished by republican paramilitaries are rarely associated with the republican movement, punishment shootings and beatings on the loyalist side are significantly about loyalist organizations policing their own members. Young people in loyalist areas engaged in 'ordinary' criminal activity may be encouraged to 'join up' or at the very least contribute a percentage of the proceeds obtained through criminal activity (Conway, 1993, p. 8). In addition, as noted above, involvement in ordinary criminal activity has been a systematic problem for loyalist paramilitaries since their inception (Dillon, 1989; Cusack and McDonald, 1997).

The relationship between loyalist working-class communities and loyalist paramilitarism is also arguably more complex than on the republican side. First, the political parties associated with the loyalist paramilitaries have a considerably smaller electoral base than their republican counterpart, Sinn Féin (McAuley, 1996). With a much smaller political infrastructure than Sinn Féin, and arguably less politicized paramilitary activists, these political parties have shown remarkable skill in steering their constituency through the period of the peace process. Second, despite the tensions noted above around harassment and the marching season, many in working-class Protestant communities place greater reliance upon, and appear to have greater confidence in, the RUC than their working-class Catholic counterparts (Brewer et al., 1997; O'Mahony et al., 2000). Third, it has been consistently argued that the infrastructure and levels of community activity within loyalist working-class communities are considerably less developed than in republican areas (Opsahl, 1993; Brewer et al., 1997).

To recap, operating within a different community context, loyalist punishment attacks are therefore best understood as a combination of internal disciplining of members, internecine disputes between factions, and personality disputes, as well as punishments for antisocial crime (as in republican areas).

In sum, therefore, in order to understand crime control discourses in Northern Ireland one must also consider the complex (and distinct) sets of relationships between republican and loyalist paramilitaries and their respective communities. Taken together with the activities of the state, its security forces and the particular styles of interaction with communities which their crime control strategies entailed, these provide the necessary context in which to consider the transformative implications wrought by the peace process and the implementation of the Good Friday Agreement.

Peace, the criminal justice system and transformation

The concept of a peace process implies that no side has gained a military victory.[11] The corollary is that there must be an accommodation or agreement between all sides, including the violent actors and the state. So, whatever the gap between protagonists, they must, in the end, agree, do a deal, make a contract. This fact has profound consequences. One of the most important is that the process must be inclusive: those who have taken up arms against the state must be represented around the negotiating table. The further implication is that room must be found in the future polity for ex-combatant communities to play a positive and peaceful role in all aspects of society.

So the state has to deal, but the state also has to change. In a conflict such as we have described, there is some dysfunction in the polity but the legitimacy of the state itself is also challenged. To remove the causes of violence, political change is required that removes whatever actual barriers exist to the incorporation of all citizens and, as important, wins their allegiance to the state (Galtung, 1996). It is inconceivable that this can happen without the structures and, in all probability, the nature of the state itself changing (Lederach, 1997). So, for a peace process, political change is needed that changes the relationship between the state, other structures in society and the community. We would term this deep process of change a *transformation*.

We believe it is not just legitimate but essential to use this concept as a test, a benchmark against which to measure any particular element in the new social and political arrangements consequent upon the peace process. Up to a point, the transformative character of both the overall political settlement and particular aspects flowing from it has to be judged in terms of their contribution to addressing the actual causes of this particular conflict. In more general terms, however, we should examine the extent to which particular measures or projects create new and dynamic relationships with the community.

The Good Friday Agreement aspires to be the foundation of a new polity – a 'new beginning' in the way social and political relations are articulated. It explicitly creates a new constitutional framework and complex political institutions designed to reflect and implement it (Harvey, 1999). It is, as Brendan O'Leary has argued, a 'consociational agreement' (1999, p. 1630).[12] The intricate system of checks and balances built into the political and constitutional arrangements would not have been enough, however, if the negotiation process had neglected the basic instruments of state rule: army, police and criminal justice system. For the army 'normalization' or 'demilitarization', depending on the choice of terminology, would involve withdrawal to barracks and the progressive dismantling of fortifications and bases as the reduction in violence continued. As noted above, for the police an independent commission was established to conduct a thorough examination of the issue and to recommend a structure that could achieve widespread acceptability (Patten, 1999). For the criminal justice system an internal government review body, with an independent element, was established with a similar brief (CJR, 2000).

It is also important to remember that this whole process was predicated on the assumption that similar transformations were going on among those who had challenged the state in arms. Republicans and loyalists were on cease-fire, decommissioning of their weapons was and is demanded, as is an end to brutal forms of the informal policing discussed above. It would not be surprising if on this terrain of dismantling or, better, transforming the combatant structures both of the state and paramilitary organizations the most severe problems of the peace process arose. Indeed, at the time of writing (May 2001), both decommissioning and policing remain highly controversial and possibly deal-breaking issues. These are areas perhaps particularly prone to inconsistencies and reversion to old ways of thinking.

The question we now wish to ask is, to what extent has the opportunity to implement a real transformation of criminal justice, through a new relationship between its structures and the community, been grasped? We will take three examples: the Criminal Justice Review; the Patten Report on policing; and alternatives to republican and loyalist punishment violence.

The Criminal Justice Review and community involvement in crime control

As was noted above, the Northern Ireland criminal justice system has operated extraordinarily draconian special laws since its inception; jury trial has been dispensed with, the laws of evidence and the right to silence have been modified (Amnesty, 1994; CAJ, 1995). Moreover, two defence solicitors have been assassinated, more intimidated, several judges and members of their families have been murdered and all have lived under extraordinary security measures (Cumaraswamy, 1998; Livingstone, 2001). In such a context, one might have expected that a criminal justice system which had been so fundamentally affected would be viewed as due for the most radical change as part of a peace process. Interestingly, however, and in stark contrast to the explicitly *independent* Patten Commission on policing, the signatories to the Good Friday Agreement agreed to a review of criminal justice (excluding policing and emergency law) 'to be carried out by the British Government through a mechanism with an independent element'. The end result was a Criminal Justice Review led by civil servants with four independent members. The tone of the Review was set by the former Secretary of State, or at least her civil servants, in the introduction to the Criminal Justice Review's original consultation document: 'The criminal justice system has served Northern Ireland well over the past thirty years, often in the face of considerable difficulties' (Northern Ireland Office, 1998, p. i).

The Review is complex and wide-ranging, and it would be well beyond the scope of this chapter to analyse it in detail. For current purposes what interests us most is whether the Review can be adjudged to provide the basis of a transformed relationship between criminal justice structures and the communities which they serve.

One key consideration in making such an assessment is that the criminal justice system should be inclusive through being 'reflective' of the make-up of society as a whole. The Criminal Justice Review takes some steps towards this goal. There is a section on equality monitoring in the report, which is necessary, given that there is a current imbalance in the system, with Catholics being generally underrepresented, especially in 'operational' arms. There are other imbalances, especially with regard to gender. The Review says: 'The attainment of a workforce that is, at all levels, and in its constituent agencies, broadly reflective of the community in Northern Ireland . . . is an objective for the criminal justice system which we strongly endorse' (CJR, 2000, para. 3.35).

Equality monitoring of the work force, compulsory in any case for normal employers in Northern Ireland, is recommended for the criminal justice system as part of a 'concerted and proactive strategy for securing a "reflective" workforce in all parts of the system' (*ibid.*, para. 3.35). One difficulty, however, is that the implementation of such a strategy is not discussed but is left to whatever machinery will operate the system in the future. The report recommends devolution of criminal justice to the local Assembly but whether and when such a development will occur is unknown. Intriguingly, however, the Review does suggest immediate monitoring by community background for the effects of the criminal justice system on those subject to it.

The sections of the Review which deal with the involvement of the community are extremely weak. The Review rejects a lay magistracy, claiming that lay people could not handle being involved in 'high profile' cases (*ibid.*, para. 7.43). It also recommends that the Probation Board, currently independent, should be brought back into the civil service as a Next Steps agency, effectively subservient to the prison service (*ibid.*, para. 12.103). When it comes to the possibility of actual communities engaging with the system, the Review is even more dismissive.

There has been a massive upsurge of interest in the ideas of restorative justice in Northern Ireland over the past three or four years. Communities in both loyalist and republican areas have taken enthusiastically to the principles and practice which we describe below. In explicit reaction to this, a whole chapter of the Review is devoted to the subject.

In relation to community restorative justice, the Review is at first dismissive:

> community-based schemes which have no or only tenuous links with the formal criminal justice system will by definition not lie at the heart of mainstream approaches . . . We do not therefore see these as central . . . but, in view of the interest in them and their existence in parts of Northern Ireland, we address the issues that they raise at the end of this chapter. (CJR, 2000, para. 9.57)

This patronising comment hides the reality that there has been an ideological war raging around these projects, in public and in private, since before the time of the agreement.

The publication of the 'Blue Book' (Auld et al., 1997), an account of dialogue about community restorative justice between republican community activists and a number of people from the voluntary and academic sectors (including two of the present authors), sparked a government response which was fed into the peace negotiations. This basically insisted that any such scheme must work under the supervision of the RUC. A number of policy papers and protocols followed, all demanding police involvement, a condition flatly rejected by projects based in republican areas.

The Review Group followed this position in almost every particular. It appears that schemes which are, apparently, not in the 'mainstream' of justice have to be most closely regulated. In this approach, the Review is again demonstrating that fear of the community that is both a bureaucratic response and a particular hangover of the conflict when working-class communities – loyalist or republican – were entered by criminal justice institutions (with the exception of the probation service) only in armoured columns. The Review Group position is backed up by one of the eighteen research reports it commissioned (Dignan, 2000). In his research report Dignan (2000, p. 18) claims the authors of the 'Blue Book' (Auld et al., 1997) accept an authoritarian, exclusionary form of 'communitarianism'. He contrasts it with a vision of 'inclusionary communitarianism'. In fact a specific section of the discussion document (*ibid.*, pp. 41–4) is taken up with discussing and answering the charge that the authors might be helping to create a 'totalitarian community', a feature that Dignan somehow fails to mention. The devotion to 'inclusionary communitarianism' by Dignan and the Review Group seems purely theoretical, however, although we would argue that the concept fits what the community-based restorative justice projects are trying to do. Dignan and the Review, however, propose a model of restorative justice fully integrated into the state machinery with little or no scope for community representation.

This 'fully integrated' model is one end of a typology spectrum, with community-based schemes, with few links with the formal justice system (the 'stand-alone' model), at the other (Dignan, 2000, p. 45). This arbitrary typology appears designed to establish a structural opposition between the community and formal justice. It cannot 'see' a situation in which autonomous, self-generating community organizations co-operate closely with all statutory agencies in a truly 'three-cornered' system of restorative justice. This tripartite structure – with the involvement of the offender, the victim and the community – is one of the defining characteristics of restorative justice (Braithwaite, 1999). The project of fully integrating restorative justice ideas into the formal justice system is an exciting idea, though not yet fully accomplished in any jurisdiction of which we are aware. If it means anything other than co-option, putting a restorative gloss on a basically retributive system, however, it must mean mainstreaming local community involvement in the criminal justice system.

This prospect – with local community organizations and volunteers involved in crime prevention, mediation, the organization of community service, victim support schemes, developing reparative solutions for the formal courts, liaising with the statutory services in reintegrating ex-offenders – is truly challenging. Unfortunately the Review Group, following Dignan, has no time for this vision. In a startling and radical suggestion, the group proposes that the entire youth justice process should be based on 'youth conferencing', and that research should be done into how restorative justice could come to dominate the adult system. This looks like an amazing conversion, until one looks at the detail. There is no representation for the community in the youth conferences, unless one counts the 'significant others' of the offender as such, thus ignoring one of the three dimensions of the restorative relationship (CJR, 2000, para. 9.76–7). We may also note that retributive and restorative disposals are all proposed to be available and may be mixed in any combination in a suggested jumbo 'youth conference order'.

In the less controversial area of community safety the Review is hardly more radical. Its major proposal is that the old Community Safety Centre, a largely failed attempt to forge links between statutory agencies and communities, should be absorbed into a new government Community Safety Unit. This is another civil service solution to a problem that actually exists out in the neighbourhoods where people live. The Review does support the Patten proposals for District Policing Partnerships discussed below. However, it recommends that they should be renamed 'Community Safety and Policing Partnerships' (CSPPs) (*ibid.*, para. 11.61). It also supports the Patten idea that these bodies, made up half of local councillors (by proportion of party seats on the local council) and half of social partner representatives, should have the right to raise 3p on the rates to fund community safety initiatives.

These proposals, apparently supportive of Patten, may actually, however, be subversive of it. Under the Patten proposals, councillors and community representatives on the District Boards would be sitting across the table from police officers who are members of a still centralized force. Nonetheless, the boards themselves would not be subject to any central government control. The Review Group proposals bring in that control. The central government Community Safety Unit would control much of the budget, and likely much of the ethos, of the local boards. They would be able to lay down central principles and operating procedures and determine the kind of community safety projects that were eligible for support by the boards. In short, in at least the community safety aspect of their work, the local boards, supposed to represent the community, would come under the effective control of a central government unit. Furthermore, unlike Patten, the Review proposes that these CSPPs should have their role and remit 'set out in statute, supplemented by good practice guidelines' (CJR, 2000, para. 11.61). Again in contrast to Patten, the Review has no proposals for the level between the District Council and the community. There is no obvious role for people from the neighbourhoods where crime and antisocial behaviour actually occur.

In short, the recommendations of the Criminal Justice Review are reflective of a mind set which *fears* genuine community involvement and ownership in the process of justice, particularly when the communities may be ones traditionally alienated from the state structures. Drafted primarily by civil servants with long histories within the criminal justice system of the 'conflict era', it has failed to deliver a new vision of state/community partnership more appropriate to a society in post-conflict transformation.

Patten, the policing bill and relations with communities

If the Criminal Justice Review has largely failed (or at least balked at the challenge) of dramatically altered relationships with local communities, it is only fair to acknowledge that the Patten Report was a rather different affair. The independence of its commissioners was clearly key in setting a completely different tone from that of the Criminal Justice Review regarding relations with the community. The tragedy, however, is that the legislative drafting process has arguably permitted much of the report's central thrust to be undermined.

The first chapter of the Patten Report, wherein the commission describes its task, is strewn with concepts and language about the community to be found nowhere in the Criminal Justice Review. In contrast to the Review, Patten recognizes there has been a violent political conflict for the past thirty years: 'three decades of conflict which have inevitably aggravated the divisions within Northern Ireland society' (1999, para. 1.4). The report admits from the beginning that the past was imperfect, that there has been a dysfunction, a crisis of legitimacy (*ibid.*, para. 1.3).

The Patten Commission saw its role, therefore, as establishing the relationship between various communities and the police.[13] Measures were recommended to redress the religious imbalance in which one Catholic would be appointed for every new Protestant recruit (on merit) from a pool of recruits, a measure which it was envisaged would lead to Catholics reaching the 'critical mass' of over 30 per cent in ten years (*ibid.*, para. 15.10). A genuine partnership with the community, it was argued, is at the heart of democratic accountable policing.[14] Such a partnership was also viewed by Patten as central to effective policing.[15] Within this paradigm of police/community relations, policing is not something done to the community but rather is a matter of 'collective responsibility, a partnership for community safety' (*ibid.*, para. 1.7) with the police having certain professional functions within a network of agencies, groups and individuals at local community level. The Patten Report, however, argues that 'partnership between the police and the community goes well beyond formal arrangements of this sort . . .' (*ibid.*, para. 7.4). It recommends that 'policing with the community should be the core function of the police service and the core function of every police station' (*ibid.*, para. 7.9). It argues for devolved and decentralized power and responsibility down to local District Commanders with neighbourhood policing teams, headed by a 'beat manager', and that each such officer 'and his/her team should organize their own community liaison mechanisms' (*ibid.*, para. 7.14). There is a string of recommendations to make this local police service 'community friendly' and more responsive to local needs (*ibid.*, chapter 7).

The Patten Report proposed a new and much more powerful Policing Board to replace the largely discredited RUC Police Authority (long boycotted by the nationalist parties) which would comprise ten political representatives using the same d'Hont system as that used for Ministerial appointments in the Assembly, thus ensuring three SDLP and two Sinn Féin representatives as well as nine independent members. In addition, the report suggested that each of the twenty-six District Councils should establish District Policing Partnership Boards (DPPBs) which would have a bare majority of elected councillors in proportion to their party strength on the local council. The rest would be from business, trade unions and the community at large. The role of the DPPBs would be to 'reflect community concerns to the police' (*ibid.*, para. 6.30). The commission also reported: 'Like the Policing Board, the DPPBs should be encouraged to see policing in its widest sense, involving and consulting non-governmental organizations and community groups concerned with safety issues as well as statutory agencies' (*ibid.*, para. 6.29). The report also recommended that Belfast (which has one city council) should be divided into four District Partnership Boards, including one for West Belfast, an area in which Sinn Féin is the largest political party.

In a particularly controversial recommendation, Patten suggests that local District Councils should have the ability to contribute as much as a rate of 3p in the £ to their DPPB, 'which could enable the DPPB to purchase additional services from the police or other statutory agencies, or from the private sector' (*ibid.*, para. 6.33). Some commentators argued that this proposal opens the door to paramilitary-controlled services being bought in by DPPBs.[16] A more realistic fear would be that some DPPBs might wish to fund local community restorative justice projects. The government deferred its decision on this proposal, awaiting the view of the Criminal Justice Review (2000, para. 11.60). As we have seen, the Review did support the proposal, but only within the context of the presumed controlling function of the central Community Safety Unit. If this unit adopted the current line of government thinking in its 'guidance packs' (*ibid.*, para. 11.65), it would appear likely that the renamed Community Safety and Policing Partnerships would be discouraged from supporting community restorative justice, even if their statutory remit and practice guidelines permitted it.

The process which was ostensibly designed to implement the Patten Report has been dogged by political controversy and persistent allegations that the civil servants drafting the legislation had drastically diluted the report's potential.[17] While some amendments have been made to meet the demands of nationalists, the Irish government and human rights activists, one of the report's authors argued two weeks before the Bill's final passage that Patten had in effect been 'gutted'.[18] The envisaged powers of the Police Board have been dramatically curtailed, the centrality of human rights has been downplayed, the UK police Ombudsperson's powers have been curtailed and much of the detail on training, ethos, restructuring, decentralization and so on are to be left to an 'implementation plan' much of which will be left in hands of the Northern Ireland Office and the Chief Constable of the RUC. Given that much of the thrust of Patten was to find a policing service that was acceptable to the nationalist community in particular, concern at the legislative dilution of the report has left both the main nationalist parties less than enthusiastic. Sinn Féin has rejected the legislation[19] and the SDLP is awaiting 'further clarification' with regard to the implementation plan before deciding its position. It is difficult to see how the transformative solution envisaged in Patten, wherein policing would become a partnership between all shades of communities, will take shape under the legislative arrangement of the Northern Ireland Police Act.

Community restorative justice, the state and local communities

The third key area in which local communities have taken on responsibilities with regard to crime control during the peace process has been in the development of community-based restorative justice projects. As discussed above, over ten such projects have appeared in concerted attempts to permit republican and loyalist paramilitaries to 'disengage responsibly' from punishment violence. We have described above the brutalities of such paramilitary-enforced informal justice during the conflict. We have also noted the Criminal Justice Review's response to such efforts. The purpose of this section is simply to apply the same tests to the developments in community restorative justice as we have applied to the recommendations of the Criminal Justice Review and the Patten Report: to what extent are the projects transformatory in attempting to create new relations between citizens and the state?

The first point to note is that the projects are explicitly designed to replace paramilitary punishments. On the loyalist side an ex-prisoner was commissioned to canvass the community on the possible alternatives to violent punishments (Winston, 1997). His conclusions formed the basis of the sophisticated and intensive Greater Shankill Alternatives project. On the republican side, a few individuals, including two of the current authors, were asked to engage in dialogue with activists about the informal justice system and how it might be reformed. The progress and results of that dialogue were written up as the 'Blue Book' (Auld et al., 1997) which contained a model for establishing peaceful alternatives to punishment shootings and beatings. That document was subsequently endorsed by the republican movement.[20]

Second, the principles of restorative justice themselves are a critique of notions of retribution on which both the formal system and the paramilitary informal system are largely based.[21] Restorative justice's critique of retributive justice is founded upon a number of principles that, together, amount to a transformed understanding about the relationship between the individual, the community, crime and the state. First is the view that crime *is fundamentally a violation of people and interpersonal relations* rather than simply a breach of the criminal code. The focus of intervention is the relationship affected by crime, and restoration involves a continuum of responses to the needs and harm experienced by victims, offenders and the community (McCold, 1996; Mika, 1997). Second, restorative justice maintains that *crime and antisocial behaviour create obligations and liabilities*. Offenders are encouraged to understand the harm committed and obligated to make things right, as far as possible (Braithwaite, 1994). Victims must have every opportunity to participate in defining the obligation (Wright, 1991). Since local communities bear a responsibility for the welfare of all their members, communities are encouraged to support victims but also to integrate offenders into community life and to ensure that they have the opportunity to make amends to their victims (Bernd-Dieter, 1998). Third, *restorative justice seeks to heal and put the wrongs right.* This means meeting the needs of victims for information, validation, restitution, testimony, safety and support (Zehr and Mika, 1998), recognition that offenders themselves may have been harmed (Harris and Burton, 1997) and a need for *monitoring* and *follow-through* in order to maximize healing, recovery, accountability and change.

The third general point we wish to make about the transformatory character of community restorative justice is its attitude towards the neighbourhood community. A publication by the Alternatives project reiterates that its purpose is to restore social relations between victim, offender and community and goes on to argue that:

> This work can only be approached in the context of the community. It makes no sense at all to treat an offender as if he had no family, no friends, never went to school or work, never visited the local shops, never played football in the park, never hung out on a particular street corner, never shouted slogans over the peace wall. Similarly, how can you help a victim if you ignore the fact that the boy who broke the window lives in the next street, that his dad drinks in the local pub, that his mum serves in the baker's, that the street lamps in this particular street are broken, that this old lady is now too scared to go to her pensioners' club around the corner? Who else, other than concerned people from this particular neighbourhood, can participate in mending these relationships, in sorting out the problems that the crime has created? (Alternatives, 2000, p. 5)

This is not a naive belief in a homogeneous community living in some bucolic golden age. Nor is it 'exclusionary communitarianism' (Dignan, 2000, p. 19). The projects themselves have gone to considerable lengths to recognize the plurality of their local communities.[22] Linked with such concerns regarding exclusionary communities is a view that these projects, which have explicitly recruited ex-combatants among their staff and volunteers as part of the process of *transformation*, is the concern that they will be used as vehicles by paramilitaries to 'control' local communities. As we have argued elsewhere (McEvoy and Mika, 2001), such concern is indicative of an overly simplistic view of the relationship between paramilitaries and their communities as being one of coercion and fear. While the capacity for violence will inevitably lead to fear, the relationship between paramilitaries and community is a more complex dialectic of 'responsibility and reliance' in the area of punishment violence. For example, in republican communities, republican activists, Sinn Féin members and former prisoners are highly active throughout civil society. However, they are only part of a diverse, vibrant and heterogeneous community sector of community groups, economic forums, women's groups, Church groups, tenant associations and so forth. The notion that power is maintained by physical coercion or the supine acceptance of republican directives by such groups is conspiratorial fantasy. Provided restorative justice projects can attract recruits from across the disapora within local communities and are professionally managed, their power in such settings can be exercised only as one organic element as part of a broader contested space.

The fourth point is the way in which community restorative justice projects are trying to establish a new relationship between the community and the police. This may seem ironic, given the fact that it is the refusal of projects in republican areas to work with the police that draws so much hostility from the authorities. Their objection is, however, to the unreformed RUC, not necessarily to a new policing service.[23] Projects in loyalist areas have no ideological problems with the RUC and, although there is frequent friction with the police in loyalist working-class areas, they have a degree of legitimacy absent from republican communities. Shankill Alternatives works closely with the police at local level but has so far failed to establish an acknowledged partnership, despite having left available places on its management committee as yet unfilled by the police. Perhaps the problem is their vision of community/police relations.[24]

Given crime's inherent tendency to bifurcate the 'rough' from the 'respectable', Adam Crawford has questioned the role of crime in the development of 'open, tolerant and inclusive communities' (Crawford, 1997, p. 274). Such concern is highly germane to the current discussion. However, as Crawford goes on to argue, the key to ensuring that anxieties concerning crime do not result in defensive or parochial communities is to link community activity with *social justice*.[25] The realities of the brutality of punishment violence have been a moral imperative for the establishment of these projects. Their origins in dialogue with paramilitary groups, the realities of operating in a hostile political environment and the background and skills of the staff and volunteers have meant that the groups have continuously demonstrated their commitment to principles of social justice in their recruitment, training and practice.

Punishment violence has not completely ended in such communities. However, high levels of commitment, energy and enthusiasm in local communities have seen a throughput of over 1,000 cases across Northern Ireland in just over two years, a significant number of which would have previously resulted in either a paramilitary beating or a shooting. Several hundred volunteers have completed training on restorative justice, non-violence, human rights and a range of other key themes relevant to restorative justice theory and practice. Both the projects in republican and loyalist areas have now developed and published sophisticated standards documents and put in place mechanisms to ensure that they are complied with. As John Braithwaite (2001) argued at a conference held in Belfast:

Northern Ireland has a more mature debate on standards and principles of restorative justice than any society I know . . . I suspect this is because Northern Ireland has a more politicized contest between state and civil society models of restorative justice than can be found in other places. Such fraught contexts are where there is the greatest risk of justice system catastrophes. But they are also the contexts with the richest prospects for rising to the political challenges with transformative innovations through restorative justice. In my short time in Northern Ireland I have found the restorative justice programs in both the Unionist and Republican communities inspiring.

Conclusion

Much of the recent criminological discussion of the relationship between state and communities in the area of crime is to be found in the literature of governmentality and crime control (Garland, 1996; O'Malley, 1999; Rose, 1999). Simplifying for the sake of brevity, such literature tends to emphasize a reshaped role for the state as 'no longer the guarantor and ultimate provider of security' but rather as a 'partner, animator, and facilitator', 'steering and regulating rather than rowing and providing' as citizens and communities become 'governed at a distance' (Rose, 2000, pp. 323–4). 'Prudent' citizens are urged to take on ever greater 'responsibility' for their own security through insurance and engagement with 'experts' in self-protection, risk minimization and so forth (O'Malley, 1996). As Garland has argued, this responsibilization strategy applies not only to individual citizens but also to families, neighbourhoods, communities, schools, employers and so forth, all of whom must now recognize that an all-powerful state can no longer meet all their security needs and that they are obliged to work in *active partnership* with the police, private security services and their neighbours (Garland, 1996).

Many of these themes have obvious resonances for our attempt to examine the changes in the nature of the relationship between the state, crime control and local communities during the Northern Ireland conflict and peace process. However, we should share the concern of some other Northern Ireland-based commentators regarding the application of governmentality literature to the Northern Ireland context. As Hillyard and Tomlinson (2000, pp. 404) argue in their analysis of the Patten Report's implications for policing, much of this literature tends to eclipse or jettison the state as an analytical category in understanding modern policing. They argue (*ibid.*, pp. 405–6) that the scale of the state's coercive capacity in Northern Ireland – in terms of expenditure on law and order, high number of personnel involved, interpersonal relations between the Northern Ireland Office, MI5, the RUC and other elements of the 'security state', and the determination of political Unionism to resist change – all these factors combine to frame the problem of policing being defined in traditional security terms rather than being recast as a partnership with the communities. They conclude: 'The problem of transforming policing in Northern Ireland therefore goes beyond dismantling a large, heavily armed, Protestant police force; it goes to the very heart of the state itself' (*ibid.*, p. 406).

Like Hillyard and Tomlinson, we would argue that the Northern Ireland experience brings sharply into focus the need to retain a keen appreciation of the centrality of the notion of the state in examining partnerships concerning crime and its control. The Criminal Justice Review and Northern Ireland Police Act have highlighted that, at least in this context, there remains a state infrastructure that is determined to resist sharing responsibility with local communities unless it is firmly on the state's narrow and restrictive terms. This is not simply about ensuring high standards of service delivery, it is about the retention of political power and ownership over criminal justice matters. On the other hand, the development of the community restorative justice projects has demonstrated willingness by some of the communities in which the conflict was fought to engage in significant transformation regarding crime control strategies. Such developments have not, as yet, been accompanied by a similar willingness to transform on the part of the state. That said, the history of the Irish peace process has been one in which the British state has often been in the position 'catching up' with the other protagonists, and perhaps the Northern Ireland Police Act and Criminal Justice Review are just further resting stages in an evolutionary process yet to gestate into true *transformation*.

Notes

1 For some criminologists the starting point for unpacking such definitional difficulties is acknowledgement that all acts deemed criminal arise as a result of a political process of definition (Quinney, 1970; Chambliss, 1976; Tunnell, 1993). Attempts by criminologists to rescue criminality from positivistic notions concerning determinism and pathology in the 1960s and 1970s led to some reductionist accounts in which crime was seen as 'either the expression, symbol or equivalent of political resistance or the product of the political order of capitalism' (Cohen, 1996, p. 3). Other criminologists have defined *political* crime by reference to the ideology, motive or beliefs of the particular offender (Schafer, 1974; Hagan, 1997). Other disciplines, including international relations, political science, terrorism studies and international law, have also struggled with providing adequate definitions of terms such as 'crime', 'political violence' and 'terrorism' (Van Den Wijngaert, 1980; Teichman, 1989; Greenwood, 1989). The feature common to all such attempts at definition is to have been shaped by the means chosen for distinguishing or indeed disregarding the 'political' or 'politically motivated' element of the offenders' actions.

2 See McKee *v.* Chief Constable of Northern Ireland (1984) 1 WLR 1358 (HL).

3　The original definitions, replicated in later versions of the Emergency Provision Act and the Prevention of Terrorism Act, are taken from the legislation to enact internment (discussed below), the Detention of Terrorists (NI) Order 1972, SI no. 1632 (NI 15), Article 2 (2).

4　For a critique of using traditional survey methodology in Northern Ireland, see Ellison (2000).

5　Such measures included a military curfew on the predominantly Catholic Falls Road in July 1970, the introduction of internment without trial of 'terrorist' suspects in August 1971 and the shooting dead of thirteen Catholic civilians by the Parachute Regiment in Derry, on what has become known as Bloody Sunday, in January 1972. By way of illustration of the partiality of these measures, the number of loyalist internees was never much greater than 10 per cent of the total (Spujt, 1986). As Bowyer-Bell argues, the authorities largely ignored the British Home Secretary Reginald Maudling's 'mild advice to add a few Protestants to the list' (Bowyer-Bell, 1993, p. 216).

6　'A solution to the problems of Northern Ireland should be worked out in political terms, and must include further measures to promote social justice between classes and communities . . . Though these matters, strictly speaking, lie outside our terms of reference, we should like to see a number of developments: the implementation of the recommendations of the Van Straubenzee Report on Discrimination . . . further improvements in housing; and a new and more positive approach to community relations. Consideration should be given to a Bill of Rights' (Gardiner, 1975, pp. 7–8). A version of the Van Straubenzee Report was implemented in 1976 with the Fair Employment Act 1976, outlawing discrimination on the grounds of religion.

7　See O'Mahony et al. (2000) for some differences in attitudes towards the RUC between different types of Catholic communities.

8　Community Police Liaison Committees were almost entirely boycotted by nationalist republicans: see Weitzer (1995) for a detailed analysis.

9　Such groups would include the Official IRA, the Irish National Liberation Army and the Irish People's Liberation Organization.

10　It has been suggested that the lower quality of loyalist recruits, in terms of the sophistication of their 'military' activities, and their past involvement in criminal activities, may be at least in part accounted for by their pro-state position. Bruce (1992, pp. 272–3), the primary researcher on loyalist paramilitarism, argues that those who wish to fight to maintain the union in Northern Ireland can join the 'legitimate' state forces (i.e. the RUC or the Royal Irish Regiment, the locally recruited regiment of the British army) for better pay and a more respectable lifestyle, and therefore generally loyalist paramilitary recruits often include those with ordinary criminal records.

11　See Gilligan and Tonge (1997) for a discussion of 'peace' as the absence of war and as a dynamic process.

12　Drawing upon the political science literature relevant to Ireland, O'Leary defines a consociational agreement as 'one which includes cross-community executive power sharing, proportionality rules applied throughout the relevant government and public sectors, community self-government and public sectors, community self-government or autonomy and equality in cultural life, and veto rights for minorities. A consociation is an association of communities' (1999, p. 1630).

13　'How can professional policing become a genuine partnership for peace on the streets with those who live, work and walk on those streets?' (Patten, 1999, para. 1.5).

14 'Accountability involves creating a real partnership between the police and the community – government agencies, non-governmental organizations, families, citizens; a partnership based on openness and understanding; a partnership in which policing reflects and responds to the community's needs' (Patten, 1999, para. 1.16; see also the whole of chapter 5).

15 'Policing should be a collective community responsibility: a partnership for community safety. This sort of policing is more difficult than policing the community. It requires an end to "us" and "them" concepts of policing' (Patten, 1999, para. 1.16; see also chapter 7).

16 'The prospect of local councils raising funds to engage private security firms for "additional services" is simply inconceivable in Northern Ireland. The money, of course, is totally irrelevant, as paramilitaries have provided their inhuman form of dealing with "antisocial behaviour" free of charge over the last thirty years. The people of Northern Ireland deserve the highest quality service in the field of policing and this can only be delivered by a properly trained and resourced police service, the Royal Ulster Constabulary' (Police Federation of Northern Ireland (2000) Response to Patten, para. 3.17).

17 One senior political commentator and author of a key text on the RUC described the Bill thus: 'The Bill is a fundamental breach of faith, perfidious Britannia in caricature. It represents old Britain; it was drafted by the forces of conservatism, for the forces of conservatism. It keeps or preserves the powers of the Secretary of State, the Northern Ireland Office and the Chief Constable' (O'Leary, 2000).

18 'The core elements of the Patten Commission's Report have been undermined everywhere. The district policing partnership boards that are so vital to the Patten Commission's vision have been diluted. So have its recommendations in the key areas outlined in its terms of reference – composition, recruitment, culture, ethos and symbols. The Patten Report has not been cherry picked, it has been gutted . . . It will not serve the people of Northern Ireland nor will it serve the many, many dedicated persons within the RUC who have been looking for a new vision for policing that will move and inspire them to police in partnership with the community they serve' (Shearing, 2000).

19 'Police Act won't wash', *An Phoblacht*, 30 November 2000.

20 See McEvoy and Mika (2001) for a detailed account of these developments.

21 'Restorative justice appeared to us a useful framework within which to address the various needs of victims, offenders and the community. It has emerged as one of the most important counters to the punishment or retribution orientated formal justice system in criminal justice debates in the past twenty or thirty years, and therefore it seemed logical to us that it might form the basis of an alternative to the even more punitive informal systems of punishment beatings and shootings' (Auld et al., 1997, p. 3).

22 'For us, communities are defined simply by their geography – people who live in a particular area. Within that all people, whatever their background or views, are members of the community with equal rights. We recognize plurality and diversity; we are not about enforcing conformity, we are about healing relationships in the communities in which we work and promoting the ideas of restorative justice. This is not always easy . . . Punitive attitudes within the community mirror those of penal authorities and wide sections of the

media . . . To confront these attitudes and to establish projects that are completely non-violent are no easy tasks (Alternatives, 2000).'

23 'We do want a partnership with a reformed police service in the future. We know that our kind of restorative justice scheme works best with a good relationship with the formal system. We intend to plan for that day. But it is not, unfortunately, here yet' (CJR, 2000).

24 'No police service can deal with all antisocial behaviour and every police service relies on its relationship with the community to catch offenders. But . . . "the community" should not mean hand-picked worthies sitting round a desk looking at coloured flow charts. It should mean autonomous groupings of motivated people, working with the police on a practical level and in genuine partnership, in a common enterprise of community safety and security' (Alternatives, 2000, p. 16).

25 'The challenge for local participatory initiatives is to mediate competing claims through processes and strategies which are open, inclusive, democratic, egalitarian – in the sense that they recognize and appropriately compensate for power differentials – and are grounded in principles of social, rather than local, justice' (Crawford, 1997, p. 291).

References

Alternatives (2000) *Alternatives: Victim, Offender and Community*, Belfast, Greater Shankhill Alternatives.

Amnesty (1994) *Political Killings in Northern Ireland*, London, Amnesty International.

Auld, J., Gormally, B., McEvoy, K. and Ritchie, M. (1997) *Designing a System of Restorative Justice in Northern Ireland*, Belfast, the authors.

Bell, C. (1996) 'Alternative justice in Ireland' in Dawson, N., Greer, D. and Ingram, P. (eds) *One Hundred and Fifty Years of Irish Law*, Belfast, SLS.

Bernd-Dieter, M. (1998) 'Restorative justice: a new paradigm in criminal law?', *European Journal of Crime, Criminal Law and Criminal Justice*, vol. 6, no. 2, pp. 125 39.

Bishop, P. and Mallie, E. (1987) *The Provisional IRA*, London, Corgi.

Bowyer-Bell, J. (1979) *The Secret Army: The IRA*, Dublin, Poolbeg.

Bowyer-Bell, J. (1993) *The Irish Troubles: A Generation of Violence*, Dublin, Gill & Macmillan.

Boyle, M. and Haire, T. (1996) 'Fear of crime and likelihood of victimization in Northern Ireland', Research Findings 2/96, Belfast, Northern Ireland Office.

Braithwaite, J (1994) 'Thinking hard about democratizing social control' in Alder, C. and Wondersitz, J. (eds) *Family, Conferencing and Juvenile Justice*, Canberra, Australian Institute of Criminology.

Braithwaite, J. (1996) 'Restorative Justice and a Better Future', Dorothy J. Killam Memorial Lecture, Halifax, Nova Scotia, Dalhousie University.

Braithwaite, J. (1999) 'Restorative justice: assessing optimistic and pessimistic accounts' in Tonry, M. (ed.) *Crime and Justice: A Review of Research*, vol. 25, Chicago, IL, University of Chicago Press, pp. 1–127.

Braithwaite, J. (2001) 'Reconciling models: balancing regulation, standards and principles of restorative justice practice', *International Perspectives on*

Restorative Justice Conference Report, 26–7 October 2000, Belfast, Queen's University of Belfast.

Brewer, J. and Magee, K. (1991) *Inside the RUC: Routine Policing in a Divided Society*, Oxford, Clarendon Press.

Brewer, J., Lockhart, B. and Rodgers, P. (1997) *Crime in Ireland, 1945–95: 'Here be Dragons'*, Oxford, Oxford University Press.

Bruce, S. (1992) *The Red Hand: Protestant Paramilitaries in Northern Ireland*, Oxford: Oxford University Press.

Bryett, K. (1997) 'Does Drumcree '96 tell us anything about the RUC?', *Critical Criminology*, vol. 8, no. 1, pp. 49–62.

Campbell, B., McKeown, L. and O'Hagan, P. (1994) *Nor Meekly Serve My Time: The H Block Struggle 1976–1981*, Belfast, Beyond the Pale Publications.

Caul, B. (1983) 'Juvenile offending in Northern Ireland – a statistical overview' in Caul, B., Pinkerton, J. and Powell, F. (eds) *The Juvenile Justice System in Northern Ireland*, Jordanstown, Ulster Polytechnic.

Chambliss, W. (1976) *Criminal Law in Action*, Santa Barbara, CA, Hamilton Publishing.

Christian Churches (1976) *Violence in Ireland: A Report of the Churches*, Belfast, Christian Journals.

Cohen, S. (1996) 'Crime and politics: spot the difference', *British Journal of Sociology*, vol. 47, no. 1, pp. 1–21.

Committee on the Administration of Justice (1995) *No Emergency, No Emergency Law: Emergency Legislation Related to Northern Ireland: The Case for Repeal*, Belfast, Committee on the Administration of Justice.

Committee on the Administration of Justice (1997) *The Misrule of Law: A Report on the Policing of Events during the Summer of 1996*, Belfast, Committee on the Administration of Justice.

Community Restorative Justice (2000) *Values and Standards of Practice*, Belfast, CRJ.

Conway, P. (1993) 'The threat of violence' and 'Working with the threatened', *Criminal Justice Matters*, pp. 2–10, London, ISTD.

Conway, P. (1997) 'A response to paramilitary policing in Northern Ireland', *Critical Criminology*, vol. 8, no. 1, pp. 109–22.

Coogan, T.P. (1987) *The IRA*, London, Fontana.

Crawford, A. (1997) *The Local Governance of Crime: Appeals to Community and Partnerships*, Oxford, Oxford University Press.

Criminal Justice Review (2000) *Review of the Criminal Justice System in Northern Ireland*, Belfast, HMSO.

Cumaraswamy, P. (1998) *Report of the Special Rapporteur on the Independence of Judges and Lawyers, Report on the Mission of the Special Rapporteur to the United Kingdom of Great Britain and Northern Ireland*, Geneva, UN Commission on Human Rights.

Cunningham, M. (1991) *British Government Policy in Northern Ireland 1968–1989: Its Nature and Execution*, Manchester, Manchester University Press.

Cusack, J. and McDonald, H. (1997) *UVF*, Dublin, Poolbeg.

Dignan, J. (2000) *Restorative Justice Options from Northern Ireland*, Belfast, HMSO.

Dillon, M. (1989) *The Shankill Butchers: A Case Study in Mass Murder*, London, Hutchinson.

Ellison, G. (2000) 'Reflecting all shades of opinion: public attitudinal surveys and the construction of police legitimacy in Northern Ireland', *British Journal of Criminology*, vol. 40, no. 1, pp. 88–111.

Ellison, G. and Smyth, J. (2000) *The Crowned Harp: Policing Northern Ireland*, London, Pluto.

Fay, M.T., Morrissey, M. and Smyth, M. (1999) *Northern Ireland's Troubles: The Human Costs*, London, Pluto Press.

Gaffiken, F. and Morrissey, M. (1990) *Northern Ireland: The Thatcher Years*, London, Red Books.

Galtung, J. (1996) *Peace by Peaceful Means: Peace and Conflict, Development and Civilization*, London, Sage.

Gardiner, Lord (1975) *The Report of a Committee to Consider, in the Context of Civil Liberties and Human Rights, Measures to Deal with Terrorism in Northern Ireland*, Cmnd 5847, Belfast, HMSO.

Garland, D. (1996) 'The limits of the sovereign state: strategies of crime control in contemporary society', *British Journal of Criminology*, vol. 36, no. 1, pp. 445–71.

Gilligan, C. and Tonge, J. (eds) (1997) *Peace or War? Understanding the Peace Process in Northern Ireland*, Aldershot, Ashgate.

Gormally, B., McEvoy, K. and Wall, D. (1993) 'Criminal justice in a divided society: Northern Ireland prisons' in *Crime and Justice: A Review of Research*, vol. 17, Chicago, IL, University of Chicago Press, pp. 51–135.

Greenwood, C. (1989) 'Terrorism and humanitarian law: the debate over Additional Protocol 1', *Israel Yearbook on Human Rights*, vol. 19, pp. 187–207.

Hagan, F. (1997) *Political Crime: Ideology and Criminality*, Needham Heights, MA, Allyn & Bacon.

Hamill, D. (1985) *Pig in the Middle: The Army in Northern Ireland 1969–1984*, London, Methuen.

Harris, N. and Burton, J. (1997) 'The reliability of observed reintegrative shaming, shame, defiance and other key concepts in diversionary conferences', Canberra, Australian National University.

Harvey, C. (1999) 'Legality, legitimacy and democratic renewal: the new Assembly in context', *Fordham International Law Journal*, vol. 22, no. 4, pp. 1389–415.

Heskin, K. (1981) 'Societal disintegration in Northern Ireland: fact or fiction?', *Economic and Social Review*, vol. 12, pp. 97–113.

Hillyard, P. (1983) 'Law and order' in Darby, J. (ed.) *Northern Ireland: The Background to the Conflict*, Belfast, Appletree Press.

Hillyard, P. and Tomlinson, M. (2000) 'Patterns of policing and policing Patten', *Journal of Law and Society*, vol. 27, no. 3, pp. 394–415.

Jackson, J. and Doran, S. (1995) *Judge without Jury: Diplock Trials in the Adversary System*, Oxford, Clarendon Press.

Jennings, A. (1990) *Justice under Fire: The Abuse of Civil Liberties in Northern Ireland* (updated edn), London, Pluto Press.

Kennedy, L. (1995) 'Nightmares within nightmares: paramilitary repression in working class communities' in Kennedy, L. (ed.) *Crime and Punishment in West Belfast*, Belfast, Summer School.

Kitson, F. (1991) *Directing Operations*, London, Faber.

Lederach, J. (1997) *Building Peace: Sustainable Reconciliation in Divided Societies*, Washington, DC, US Institute of Peace.

Livingstone, S. (2001) 'And justice for all? The judiciary and legal profession in transition' in Harvey, C. (ed.) *Human Rights, Equality and Democratic Renewal in Northern Ireland*, Oxford, Hart.

MacIntyre, A. (1995) 'Modern Irish republicanism: the product of British state strategies', *Irish Political Studies*, vol. 10, pp. 97–122.

Magill, D. (ed.) (1995) *Fair Employment Law in Northern Ireland: Debates and Issues*, Belfast, SACHR.

Mayhew, P. and van Dijk, J. (1997) *Criminal Victimization in Eleven Industrialized Countries*, Wetenschappelijk, Onderzolk-en Documentatiecentrum.

McAuley, J. (1996) '(Re)constructing Ulster loyalism? Political responses to the peace process', *Irish Journal of Sociology*, vol. 6, pp. 127–53.

McCold, P. (1996) 'Restorative justice and the role of community' in Galloway, B. and Hudson, J. (eds) *Restorative Justice*, New York, Criminal Justice Press.

McEvoy, K. (2000) 'Law, struggle and political transformation in Northern Ireland', *Journal of Law and Society*, vol. 27, no. 4, pp. 542–71.

McEvoy, K. (2001) *Paramilitary Imprisonment in Northern Ireland: Resistance, Management and Release*, Oxford, Oxford University Press.

McEvoy, K. and Mika, H. (2001) 'Punishment, policing and praxis: restorative justice and non-violent alternatives to paramilitary punishments in Northern Ireland', *Policing and Society*, vol. 11 (in press).

McEvoy, K., McElrath, K. and Higgins, K. (1998) 'Does Ulster still say no? Drugs, politics and propaganda in Northern Ireland', *Journal of Drug Issues*, vol. 28, no. 1, pp. 127–54.

McGarry, J. and O'Leary, B. (1999) *Policing Northern Ireland: Proposals for a New Start*, Belfast, Blackstaff.

McKittrick, D., Kelters, S., Feeney, B., and Thornton, C. (1999) *Lost Lives: The Stories of the Men, Women and Children who Died as a Result of the Northern Ireland Troubles*, Edinburgh, Mainstream Publishing.

McVeigh, R. (1994) *It's Part of Life Here . . . The Security Forces and Harassment in Northern Ireland*, Belfast, Committee on the Administration of Justice.

McWilliams, M. and Spence, L. (1994) *Taking Domestic Violence Seriously: Issues for the Civil and Criminal Justice System, A Report to the Northern Ireland Office*, Belfast, HMSO.

Mika, H. (1997) 'Mediating neighbourhood conflict: conceptual and strategic considerations', *Negotiation Journal*, October, pp. 397–410.

Mika, H. and McEvoy, K. (2001) 'Restorative justice in conflict: paramilitarism, community and the construction of legitimacy in Northern Ireland', *Contemporary Justice Review*, vol. 4 (in press).

Morison, J. and Geary, R. (1989) 'Crime, conflict and counting', *Howard Journal*, vol. 28, pp. 9–26.

Mulcahy, A. (2000) 'Policing history: the official discourse and organizational memory of the RUC', *British Journal of Criminology*, vol. 40, no. 1, pp. 68–88.

Newman, K. (1978) 'Prevention *in extremis*: the preventative role of the police in Northern Ireland', *The Cranfield Papers*, London, Peel Press.

Ní Aolainn, F. (2000) *The Politics of Force: Conflict Management and State Violence in Northern Ireland*, Belfast, Blackstaff.

Northern Ireland Office (1998) *Introduction to the Criminal Justice Review Consultative Process*, Belfast, HMSO.

O'Doherty, M. (1998) *The Trouble with Guns: Republican Strategy and the Provisional IRA*, Belfast, Blackstaff.

O'Leary, B. (1999) 'The nature of the agreement', *Fordham International Law Review*, vol. 22, no. 4, pp. 1628–68.

O'Leary, B. (2000) 'Perfidious Britannia', *Guardian*, 15 June.

O'Mahony, D., Geary, R., McEvoy K. and Morison, J. (2000) *Crime, Community and Locale: The Northern Ireland Communities Crime Survey*, Aldershot, Ashgate.

O'Malley, P. (1996) 'Risk and responsibility' in Barry, A., Osborne, T. and Rose, D. (eds) *Foucault and Political Reason*, London, UCL Press.

O'Malley, P. (1999) 'Volatile punishments, contemporary penality and neo-liberal government', *Theoretical Criminology*, vol. 3, no. 2, pp. 175–96.

Opsahl (1993) *A Citizens' Inquiry: The Opsahl Report on Northern Ireland*, Dublin, Lilliput Press/Initiative 92.

O'Rawe, M. and Moore, L. (1997) *Human Rights on Duty: Principles for Better Policing, International Lessons for Northern Ireland*, Belfast, Committee on the Administration of Justice.

Patten, C. (1999) *A New Beginning: Policing in Northern Ireland, Report of the Independent Commission on Policing for Northern Ireland*, Belfast, HMSO (http://www.belfast.org.uk/report.htm).

Police Federation of Northern Ireland (1995) 'Terrorism continues', *Police Beat*, February.

Police Federation of Northern Ireland (2000) Response to Patten on the Police Federation for Northern Ireland (http://www.policefed-ni.org.uk).

Powell, F. (1982) 'Justice and the young offender in Northern Ireland', *British Journal of Social Work*, vol. 12, pp. 565–86.

Quinney, R. (1970) *The Social Reality of Crime*, Boston, MA, Little Brown.

Rose, S. (1999) *Powers of Freedom: Reframing Political Thought*, Cambridge, Cambridge University Press.

Rose, D. (2000) 'Government and control', *British Journal of Criminology*, vol. 40, pp. 321–39.

Royal Ulster Constabulary (1977) *Annual Report of the Chief Constable*, Belfast, HMSO.

Royal Ulster Constabulary (1979) *Annual Report of the Chief Constable*, Belfast, HMSO.

Royal Ulster Constabulary (2000) Official website of the Royal Ulster Constabulary (http://www.ruc.police.uk).

Ryan, M. (1999) 'Penal policy making towards the millennium: elites and populists, New Labour and the new criminology', *International Journal of the Sociology of Law*, vol. 27, no. 1, pp. 1–22.

Ryder, C. (1989) *The RUC: A Force under Fire*, London, Methuen.

Schafer, S. (1974) *The Political Criminal: The Problem of Morality and Crime*, New York, Free Press.

Shearing, C. (2000) 'Patten has been gutted', *Guardian*, 14 November.

Silke, A. (1999) 'Ragged justice: loyalist vigilantism in Northern Ireland', *Terrorism and Political Violence*, vol. 11, no. 3, pp. 1–31.

Sluka, J.A. (1995) 'Domination, resistance and political culture in Northern Ireland Catholic-Nationalist ghettos', *Critique of Anthropology*, vol. 1, pp. 71–102.

Spujt, R. (1986) 'Internment and detention without trial in Northern Ireland (1971–1975)', *Modern Law Review*, vol. 49, pp. 712–39.

Teichman, J. (1989) 'How to define terrorism', *Philosophy*, vol. 64, pp. 505–17.

Tomlinson, M. (1998) 'Walking backwards into the sunset: British policy and the insecurity of Northern Ireland' in Miller, D. (ed.) *Rethinking Northern Ireland: Culture, Ideology and Colonialism*, London, Longman.

Tunnell, K. (ed.) (1993) *Political Crime in Contemporary America: A Critical Approach*, New York, Garland Publishing.

Van Den Wijngaert, C. (1980) *The Political Offence Exception to Extradition: The Delicate Problem of Balancing the Rights of the Individual and the International Public Order*, Boston, MA, Kluwer.

Van Dijk, J. and Mayhew, P. (1992) *Criminal Victimization in the Industrialized World*, The Hague, Ministry of Justice.

Weitzer, R. (1995) *Policing Under Fire: Ethnic Conflict and Police Community Relations in Northern Ireland*, Albany, NY, State University of New York Press.

Wilkinson, P. (1986) *Terrorism and the Liberal State* (2nd edn), Basingstoke, Macmillan.

Winston, T. (1997) 'Alternatives to punishment beatings and shootings in a loyalist community in Belfast', *Critical Criminology*, vol. 8, no. 1, pp. 122–8.

Wright, M. (1991) *Justice for Victims and Offenders*, Buckingham, Open University Press.

Zehr, H. and Mika, H. (1998) 'Fundamental concepts of restorative justice', *Contemporary Justice Review*, vol. 1, no. 1.

Part III

Comparative Trends and Futures

The growth of crime prevention in France as contrasted with the English experience

Some thoughts on the politics of insecurity

Adam Crawford

Our contemporary condition has been variously described as one of 'high' or 'late' modernity in which the apparent juggernaut of 'globalization' has challenged and uprooted many of the previously taken-for-granted certainties of social relations. In the process, many traditional forms of place-based authority and social control have been torn up. Global flows of capital and culture have significantly affected and recast territorial communities. Moreover, globalization and recent economic restructuring have not had uniform or homogenizing effects. Rather, they have encouraged segmentation, social differentiation and dislocation. Structural changes in the economy have seen the importance of social class supplemented by other indicators of difference. And yet a person's social position and where they live remain fundamentally important with regard to that person's 'life chances'. Economic polarization takes on a positively social and spatial form. This produces a distinct unevenness in local economic development between, and within, cities in late modernity. At a cultural level, social diversity, which is reproduced locally, collides and fuses with a global culture. Globalization, as Bauman suggests, 'divides as much as it unites; it divides as it unites' (1998, p. 2).

This has heralded both a process of *delocalization* – or 'disembedding' of social relations – in which social systems are stretched across time and space, as well as an apparently contradictory process of *relocalization* – or 're-embedding' of social relations (Giddens, 1990, p. 79) – in which forms of control are increasingly inscribed into the fabric of local territorial and spatial interactions (Robert, 2000). Here disembedded social relations are recast within local conditions of time and place. This relocalization produces the conditions under which time and space are organized within given locales so as to connect presence and absence. In consequence, global pressures are increasingly refracted through local meanings, identities and sensibilities. Hence spatial relations have become saturated with, rather than emptied of, meaning (Lash and Urry, 1994).

At the same time the modern state is being restructured and its powers are being re-articulated (Crawford, 2001). As a result, we are witnessing the fragmentation, dispersal and pluralization of modes of regulation and control. Under these conditions a politics of insecurity has come to play a prominent role. This politics of insecurity combines a preoccupation with personal safety and future risks with the importance of 'local structures of feeling'. In this new politics, there is a particular salience to a sense of locality within an increasingly globalizing economy and culture. Responses to (in)security and (un)safety appear increasingly to inform decisions made by governments, organizations and ordinary people in their social inter-actions. Increasingly, towns and cities vie for new positions of influence and wealth in the reorganized national and international economy. The ability of cities to reposition themselves in a global economy increasingly depends upon their capacity to attract investors, both capital and people, which is determined, in part, by the attractiveness of a city as a 'safe place', particularly inner-city business districts. At the level of the individual, insecurity can encourage withdrawal into the 'safe havens of territoriality', producing a market in security which places increasing emphasis upon creating and offering 'environments of trust' where symbols of security and safety, as well as strategies of control, are inscribed into the architecture and surroundings. Concerns with 'safety' have become saturated with anxieties informed by wider uncertainties and the apparent uncontroll-ability of the modern era.

In Britain, as in many other English-speaking countries, this new politics of insecurity has become bound up with discourses of 'community safety' and 'crime prevention partnerships' (Crawford and Matassa, 2000). In non-English-speaking mainland Europe this preoccupation with local safety has taken on slightly different referents. Nevertheless, it shares a common orientation and genesis. This new politics is simultaneously 'beyond the state' and reflects the limited capacity for state action as well as a dramatic narrowing of the horizons of state sovereignty (Robert, 1999). Its orientation focuses upon low-level incivilities and sub-criminal categories of 'disorder' and antisocial behaviour. The extensive breadth of this new politics was no more apparent than in the seemingly international spread of 'zero tolerance' policing, which saw both globalizing and localizing tendencies collide and infuse strategies of crime control and regulation.

Hence this new politics of 'community safety', in so far as it is concerned with 'quality of life' issues, is saturated with wider concerns about social change, personal identity and safety. It constitutes a realm of governance which connects with locality and people's everyday experiences of it under globalizing pressures. At a psychic level, it allows people to delve into the nostalgic 'imagined communities' of tradition. The rhetorical force of the language of community (in English at least) lies in the fact that it echoes and seeks to appease our fears and anxieties at the same time as it evokes and appeals to our fantasies. It holds out the ideal of genuine human identity and reciprocity precisely at a time in which they appear most absent. 'Community safety' signifies that 'something is being done': something achievable in an uncertain world. Symbolically, it reaffirms control of a given territory, which is visible and tangible. In this sense, community safety both reflects a field of policy that is saturated with wider concerns about contemporary social change and is a referent for an unfolding form of governance. In sum, the anxieties produced by the endemic insecurity and uncertainty of late modernity tend to be conflated and compressed into a distinct and overwhelming concern about personal safety, law and order.

In this chapter I want to consider these broader issues through a comparative lens, by seeking to draw out similarities within, and contrasts between, the recent experiences of France and England. First, I begin by outlining key contours in the growth and development of crime prevention and the politics of urban safety and insecurity in France over the last two decades. Next, I analyse some of the ambiguities and tensions expressed within the French experiences. I do so, not only because I believe it is within these sites of conflict that we find some of the key determinants of contemporary and future French law-and-order policy and practice, but also because the dominant perceived wisdom among British criminologists about French developments all too often has been viewed through rose-tinted glasses (see Crawford, 2000a). Finally, I explore some of the issues raised by comparing the experiences of France and England.

The growth of crime prevention in France

In essence, the recent growth of crime prevention in France can be viewed as having passed through four broad phases, which I shall explore in turn in this section.

The Bonnemaison report and prevention as social solidarity, 1981–88

The modern French approach to crime prevention is rooted in the Bonne-maison Committee report, *Face à la délinquance, prévention, répression, solidarité* (1982), which has come to assume a pervasive hold over ensuing policy discourse and practice. In response to the urban disorders in many French cities in the summer of 1981, the new Socialist government estab-lished a national commission to review crime control policies. The subse-quent report was the product of a commission of 800 mayors chaired by Gilbert Bonnemaison, then Mayor of Epinay. The report embodied a number of key themes around a number of concepts: 'solidarity', 'integra-tion', 'prevention' and 'locality'.

First, it suggested that the causes of crime are rooted in deep and complex social factors. It argued the state should promote strategies of 'integration', by which those groups and individuals perceived to be at the margins of the bonds of social *solidarité* are deemed to require (re)incor-poration. Social isolation and exclusion of certain groups, notably dis-affected youths, immigrants and the unemployed, were seen as the central problem affecting French society.

Second, the report emphasized *prévention* as distinct from *répression*. Although repression and punishment through the criminal justice system were identified as essential elements in crime control, they were not seen as capable of addressing the fundamental causes of crime. Therefore, it was contended, prevention required a separate and new administrative structure outside the criminal justice system, without the repressive and authoritarian aspects associated with the police and courts. Moreover, in relation to prevention, the Bonnemaison Report stressed that the key decision-making should not be assigned to traditional criminal justice institutions.

Third, the Bonnemaison Report emphasized the local dimension of new administrative structures. To be effective, it argued, policy should be flexible and capable of adapting to local circumstances. To this end, it stressed the need for 'horizontal' solutions to make communities safer from crime, bringing people with different expertise together in local partner-ships. These structures should be inclusive, linking all the relevant local partners, including locally elected representatives, trade union officials, social services and non-profit organizations as well as the police and other criminal justice institutions. The aim was to break down bureaucratic barriers through local inter-agency co-operation.

The report advocated a distinctly 'social' approach to crime preven-tion. It stressed the need for a strategy of *intégration* and *solidarité*, as well as recommending the delivery of prevention through partnerships between various criminal justice and social agencies. Emphasis was to be given to the (re)integration of deprived neighbourhoods, notably the *banlieues*, suffering from high crime and a concentration of other indicators of social malaise and alienation.

The local sphere was to become the new terrain of political action. It expressed the will to devolve power and authority and connected with wider decentralization reforms. As a consequence of the Bonnemaison recommendations a three-tier structure was established: steered from the centre by a National Council for the Prevention of Crime – Conseil National de Prévention de la Délinquance (CNPD); with regional or county-wide councils – *conseils départmentaux de prévention de la délinquance* (CDPDs); and local crime prevention councils, which act as the key operational element in the delivery of the crime prevention strategy – *conseils communaux de prévention de la délinquance* (CCPDs).

This institutional framework embodies a certain degree of overlap of personnel in order to mitigate conflict between the different tiers. Initially, the National Council was chaired by the Prime Minister and attended by the majority of town mayors and representatives of relevant government Ministries. The broad intention of this political initiative was to revive a sense of 'citizenship' within the institutions of the Fifth Republic. At each level the councils draw upon representatives from three principal sectors of society: elected officials, the judicial administration and citizen groups.

The CCPDs are chaired by the elected mayor. They set local policies on crime prevention and co-ordinate fund-raising and resource allocation to various local agencies and projects. Elected officials have traditionally occupied an important role within the CCPDs, which has given the CCPDs significant legitimacy.

By 1985 some 400 CCPDs had been established. The figure rose to 850 by the end of the millennium. The CCPDs have provided a structure out of which local concerns and initiatives have successfully been developed, against the background of a traditionally highly centralized state. As such, they are part of a much wider decentralization and restructuring of the French state (Donzelot and Estèbe, 1994).

The Bonnemaison Report set the agenda for a specifically social approach to crime prevention which remains largely intact today, despite the various subsequent changes in political leadership. A notable early example of this approach was the so-called *anti été chaud* (anti-hot summer) programme, also referred to as the *étés jeunes* (youth summers) programme. Interestingly, the *étés jeunes* projects were the first initiatives put in place by the new Socialist government. Their inception was dramatic in its urgency. There was perceived to be a pressing need to get something in place before the summer of 1982 to avoid a repetition of the urban disorders in Lyon and any spreading of unrest to other cities. In line with the integrationist approach the programme was targeted at groups perceived to be 'at risk' because of their social marginalization. It took underprivileged youths from deprived areas out of cities to structured holiday camps and provided those who remained with a variety of activities over the summer months. In its first full year of operation 10,000 young people were given holidays, while a further 100,000 participated in some form of organized summer activity (King, 1988, pp. 9–10).

One of the successes of the *étés jeunes* was that they established the foundations for more permanent and enduring local projects. For example, it gave rise to a new breed of professional youth organizers, known as *animateurs*. These youth workers who helped to organize and run the local *étés jeunes* projects were drawn from young people of North African origin selected initially for their leadership qualities, and the fact that they commanded the esteem of other youngsters. This was the result of a deliberate strategy aimed at 'penetrating' North African communities by eliciting the support and co-operation of the young, while at the same time providing paid employment for the most capable, and co-operative, of these young people. This had two important social implications: it gave employment and self-respect to those recruited; and these early recruits drew in other youths from among their family and friends.

Continuing this theme of 'penetrating' and 'incorporating' marginal youths, a number of areas have established special reading programmes for children of North African origin and schemes to develop employment skills. Whilst in Britain this would be regarded as a 'welfare' programme, in France it is viewed as long-term crime prevention in the battle against social exclusion, albeit the activities are concerned more with improving social and racial integration than crime prevention.

It was also out of the experience and development of the *étés jeunes* projects that a new breed of social worker specializing in crime prevention emerged during the 1980s. These specialists have no direct British equivalent and are distinct from other types of French social workers, in that they operate outside the criminal justice system. They aim to (re)integrate disaffected young people into mainstream social institutions. They work with the consent of the young people rather than under a court order. As a consequence, the workers often act as advocates of the young people in their dealings with other agencies, as well as acting as mediators among youths and between them and their families or community.

The approach adopted in France during the 1980s departed significantly from that unfolding across the Channel, notably through the Safer Cities programme. In many senses, the experiences in the two countries represented contrasting models and became seen as almost polar opposites. Whilst the French model emphasized a broad social approach to crime and social exclusion, the English model stressed a narrow, police-led and technicist approach to situational crime prevention. Where the English model established short-term funding structures and institutional arrangements with a resultant 'project orientation', the French developed structures with a long-term and more strategic commitment to crime prevention. While the English model emphasized competitive sources of funding, the French model offered more co-operative contracts between locality and nation-state. Where the English model circumvented structures of local democratic representation, the French model was tied firmly into traditional channels of local representation, notably through the role of locally elected mayors. While the English model encouraged private sector involvement in partnership structures, the French model looked to traditional representatives of the 'public sphere' including representation from trade unions. Finally, while the English approach placed a heavy emphasis upon output measurements and performance monitoring to satisfy efficiency criteria, the French approach saw an absence of such concerns.

The contrast between the two approaches reflected the very different political programmes with which they were aligned and out of which they each grew. Whereas the developments in France were the product of a left-wing administration, in England they reflected the New Right ideology of the then Conservative government. In England the Thatcher government's antipathy to local authorities, trade unions and social explanations of crime, combined with its desire to unleash the 'entrepreneurial spirit' of the free market, to roll back the state, responsibilize individuals, families and communities and inject a new competitive culture into aspects of public policy, resonated throughout its crime control policies. The French approach, by contrast, echoed the socialist politics of the Mitterrand government, for which the state remained a central vehicle in ensuring social cohesion.

As a package the Bonnemaison initiatives managed to halt and reverse the steady increase in recorded crime. Moreover, comparisons between areas with a CCPD and those without suggested that, for a range of common crimes, there were larger reductions (by about 10 per cent) where a CCPD existed, even though the latter tended to have higher rates of crime. However, lack of sufficient evaluation research makes it difficult to conclude that the reductions in crime were caused by the various Bonnemaison initiatives. During the 1980s, whilst crime rates soared in Britain, most notably in the poorest neighbourhoods, they actually declined in France and, more important, the fall was most marked in deprived areas. Nevertheless, crime rates rose rapidly in the late 1980s and early 1990s. Moreover the crime prevention efforts did not stop rioting in some French cities in the 1990s.

The rise of urban policy, 1988–94

Despite the initial enthusiasm and activity, by the late 1980s the CCPDs had begun to drift. One of the few pieces of early research into their work, by Gérard Chevalier, showed many of the initiatives to be stillborn or paper exercises (cited in Roché, 1999, p. 402). Moreover, the CCPDs increasingly became entangled within the development of 'urban policy' – *la politique de la ville* – both nationally and locally. Under the influence of locally elected officials, the programmes became increasingly focused on 'community outreach activities which were both easier to implement and more image-enhancing in the eyes of public opinion' (Wyvekens, 1997, p. 27).

Crime prevention became increasingly supplanted by urban policy and specifically by concern about the fragmentation of French cities, focused on particular sensitive urban areas. The Délégation Interministérielle à la Ville

(DIV) was created in 1988 to establish a clear administrative structure for urban policy. Crime prevention was combined with urban policy and social action more generally. The DIV became the operational structure for implementing governmental action plans through contracts with local government representatives.

Following the urban disorders in Vaulx-en-Velin (a *banlieue* of Lyon), this shift was reinforced in 1990 when responsibility for crime prevention was handed to the new Minister of State for Cities, Michel Delebarre. His work was supported by the Comité Interministériel des Villes, a commission of Ministers presided over by the Prime Minister (Lazerges, 1995, pp. 213–16). The establishment of interdepartmental and cross-cutting Ministries has helped to ensure that concern about social exclusion and insecurity has begun to affect the mainstream services and policies of a number of agencies. The financial contributions of different Ministries were consolidated in a single block budget for urban issues. However, as Sophie Body-Gendrot (2000) notes, the loss of control over their budgets merely meant that the Ministries concerned lost interest in urban policy itself, which served to isolate the DIV. Moreover, the Ministries concerned sought to regain at the local level – via the *préfet* and elected officials – the control they had lost at the national level. The will, in the 1980s, to devolve power confronted the ambiguity of central concern over losing too much control. Prompted by the pluralization and fragmentation spawned by the Bonnemaison reforms, central government sought to intervene and co-ordinate developments through an increasingly 'hands on' approach to the partnerships it had helped generate.

The politics of insecurity, 1994–97

Since the mid-1990s there has been greater emphasis upon two themes: public or 'semi-public' job creation schemes and concern over minor incivility and disorder. These two themes became linked in the belief that the employment of young people would reduce the level of hooliganism (Roché, 1999, p. 397). The election of a centre-right government in 1993 produced a period of stagnation. However, in 1994 *la politique de la ville* was relaunched. This new politics saw a greater territorialization through the identification of priority areas constituting a tiered hierarchy: 700 *zones urbaines sensibles* (ZUs) of which there were 350 *zones de revitalization urbaine* (ZRUs) within which were located fifty *zones franches urbaines* (ZFUs), perceived to be the most disadvantaged and problematic areas. The extent of financial assistance was to be dependent upon where in this hierarchy a particular area was located. Together, these developments added an economic component to the traditionally social approach to urban issues. One further innovation, in part inspired by the British experience, was the introduction of a process of selective tendering for the ascription of a particular zone. Yet, in contrast to the competitive urban policies in Britain, priority areas in France were selected and the central state and local officials then negotiated the nature and content of interventions. The role of the *préfet* (the formal departmental representative of the state) was crucial in these negotiations. One problem was that in order to avoid criticism from local mayors and elected officials the *préfet* often distributed the funding across the board rather than targeting it at particularly deprived areas, as the policy was meant to.

More recently the French have developed a contractual model of 'local security contracts' (*contrats locaux de sécurité*). These new local security contracts require the completion of a formal analysis of local crime and security issues as the first stage towards a contract (a weak version of the crime audits required in England and Wales by the Crime and Disorder Act 1998).

Under a discourse of *sécurité*, this new policy sought to reinvigorate crime prevention and simultaneously to relate it more directly to the operation of the traditional criminal justice system. This entailed a closer focus on the identification of other 'indicators of risk', including 'at risk' groups, notably the young, and high 'risk zones'. The shift towards a policy of 'security', as represented by the installation of the recent 'local security contracts', to some extent calls into question the future role and place of the CCPDs which for the past fifteen years have focused upon the elaboration of social crime prevention. However, it also potentially allows the CCPDs to return to their original concern with crime prevention, which had become somewhat lost sight of within the broader policy of urban regeneration. The signing of the *contrats locaux de sécurité* since 1997 has signalled the return of the national police – under the guise of community-based policing (*'la police de proximité'*) – as major actors in contemporary crime prevention. Some French commentators see this as risking a major shift away from the traditional social approach to crime prevention towards a more situational approach (Body-Gendrot and Duprez, 2001).

Uncertainty and drift, 1997–2000

The left was returned to power in 1997 but has done little to reinvigorate an issue which had become associated with Socialist governments of the past. In November 1998, according to opinion polls, fear of urban disorder was the second highest preoccupation of French people (Body-Gendrot, 2000, p. 66). Mayors of large towns and cities ranked public safety as their second most important priority, only unemployment taking precedence. Meanwhile the rate of officially recorded juvenile crime rose by 50 per cent over the figure for 1990. As a consequence, urban disorder and unrest in the 'anxious city' has become the leitmotif driving much new policy. As such, concern about the growth of 'balkanized urban areas' is at the forefront of political consciousness (Bailleau, 1998, p. 101).

The emphasis upon 'security' has continued. To reflect this, in March 1999 the CCPDs were renamed CCPSs (*conseils communaux de prévention et sécurité*). The youth employment theme has continued with the government's announced *plan emploi jeunes* to employ hundreds of thousands of young people between the ages of eighteen and twenty-six at the level of the minimum wage. In response, the *gendarmerie* hope to create 10,000 new jobs as local mediators or 'city wardens' while the national police propose to recruit 20,000 security deputies (to assist in police stations) and local mediators or wardens without firearms or uniforms (Roché, 1999, p. 399). The wardens are intended to resolve conflicts and encourage good behaviour by their presence near schools, on public transport and in public places.

Ambiguities in implementation

At the turn of the millennium crime prevention policy in France had become a pale shadow of that offered by the bold urgings of the Bonnemaison Report and lauded by British commentators (King, 1991; Pitts, 1995; Pitts and Hope, 1997). Nevertheless, despite the apparent lack of direction, the politics of insecurity remains a pressing concern. Let us explore a few reasons why the high ideals and initial frenetic activity of the post-Bonnemaison era have faded during the ensuing years of implementation.

The dissonance between discourse and practice

The first point to note relates more to the way in which commentators have misinterpreted developments rather than the developments themselves. There has been a failure on the part of criminologists, especially British ones, to look beyond the discourse of policy at the more complex manner in which policies have (or have not) been implemented in practice. This is not helped by the lack of a domestic tradition of empirical research in France.

The pervasive dissonance between the imaginary and the real – between rhetoric and reality – in criminal justice is itself a notable feature of French criminal justice and legal culture (Garapon, 1995). The symbolism and idealism of legal rules and state institutions occupy a central place. In France one of the essential functions of legal rules is that they act as a 'promise' (Garapon, 1996). They are aspirational: what they aspire to is almost as important as what they actually achieve in practice. It often seems as if the legal rules and certain social institutions are concerned less with the co-ordination and regulation of social behaviour than with symbolizing collective ideals and public values.

British criminologists, too often, have been seduced by the language of *integration* and *solidarité* which peppers French official discourse. This stems from a simplistic interpretation of 'social inclusion' which juxtaposes it conceptually with 'social exclusion' – the former being positive, and the latter negative, strategies. And yet this fails to pose the question: inclusion into what and, more fundamentally, inclusion upon what terms? In addition, such an approach neglects to acknowledge the fact that forms of inclusion and exclusion can operate alongside each other and at different social, economic, political and cultural levels. This suggests a more nuanced understanding of the way in which groups of people are simultaneously incorporated into, and ejected from, the mainstream and dominant society. In France the idea of the 'citizen' is itself dismissive of divergent ethnic identities. The reality in many of the *banlieues* of France's major cities, with their rich ethnic mix, is far removed from the idealizations of French political and legal discourse with its emphasis upon 'social inclusion'. French strategies of 'social integration' – aimed particularly at marginal youths of North African origin – are often experienced by those at whom they are targeted as culturally stifling. Disaffected youths are called (back) into the republican fold rather than having their difference affirmed, and yet remain economically and politically marginal. As Roché notes, the recent experience of strategies of social inclusion – often in the name of crime prevention – has exposed the 'frailty of the republican model of integration' (1994, p. 173).

The eclipse of crime prevention by urban policy

Since 1981 urban disorders have been at the forefront of public debate in France. This has seen the 'social question' gradually replaced by the 'urban question', with the emphasis upon problem areas rather than the failings of institutions: on places rather than on disenfranchised subjects. As a consequence of this 'territorialization', urban disorders have been seen as the product of structural inequalities requiring government action. This discourse of solidarity was embedded in the *politique de la ville* and has captured the political agenda.

After the urban disorders in Vaulx-en-Velin in October 1990, President Mitterrand (of the Socialist left) called for an urgent redistribution of resources within cities to address the problem that 'where disorder reigns, solidarity is missing'. Prime Minister Rocard (from the political right) added that 'urgency lies with solidarity . . . To combat social segregation, we need to construct and organize that solidarity.' Whether governments have been of the right, left or 'cohabiting', the discourse of solidarity and social integration has remained largely unchanged.

However, the shift to a preoccupation with territories has seen the decline of the social crime prevention strategy articulated by Bonnemaison. With the administrative focus firmly located at the city level, the prevention of delinquency as a specific target of enquiry has become somewhat blurred. Whilst, on the one hand, this has emphasized the separateness of crime prevention from penal policy, on the other it has diluted its distinctness from social and economic policy.

The failure to engage the criminal justice system

This separation from the repressive criminal justice system has tended to limit the dominance of criminal justice agencies – notably the courts and the police – over the policy-making process within the CCPDs, but at the same time it has allowed the traditional institutions of justice to remain largely untouched by the discourse of crime prevention. The police and public prosecutors have largely evaded engagement with local crime prevention structures. Frequently the participation of the police in local partnerships has amounted to little more than the provision of statistical information on crime rates.

This lack of involvement on the part of the police derives largely from an institutional anomaly. Whilst the Bonnemaison reforms sought to decentralize authority and decision-making, the police remained primarily a highly centralized national force. Approximately 230,000 police officers are under the authority of central government and, as such, did not connect with the new administrative structure created by the Bonnemaison-inspired reforms. The number of locally accountable police officers is relatively small (Roché, 1998), leaving local mayors and CCPD partnerships unable to engage with policing concerns. This led to a situation in which, at local levels, crime prevention partnerships worked to try to (re)integrate disaffected young people, who simultaneously were caught up in a spiralling relationship of animosity and alienation with the police who stood outside and unaccountable to the local partnerships (Wieviorka, 1999).

The tension between national and local control was exacerbated by ideological differences. The dilemma was 'to find a way to resolve this conflict of ideologies and practices (between the police and local authorities) without the mayor becoming chief of police or the commissioner of police assuming ultimate responsibility for crime prevention' (Dourlens and Vidal-Naquet, 1994, p. 15). More recently, particularly since the return of the left to government in 1998, under the leadership of Jospin, there have been important moves to decentralize more aspects of policing under a policy of *police de proximité*. If effective, this would allow greater police involvement in local partnerships.

Judicial institutions, on the other hand, have had problems entering into the partnership logic of urban policy and the local crime prevention structures. They have preferred to stay at arm's length from the priorities of the *politique de la ville* for fear of compromising their autonomy and losing their identity. Given their traditionally dominant role in judicial and legal affairs, public prosecutors have not made very good partners, preferring vertical relations of authority to horizontal relations of co-operation. Despite this, governments have continued to encourage judicial institutions into city-level arrangements.

One of the implications of this failure to involve key criminal justice institutions in any significant way in the politics of crime prevention has been the development by judicial institutions and the Ministry of Justice of a distinct and separate politics of *justice de proximité* – local justice. Since the mid-1990s this politics of proximity has embodied many of the same referents as the earlier crime prevention policy – decentralization, a partnership logic and a preoccupation with crime and 'incivility' in localities where these are deemed problematic. However, it reflects an internal judicial logic rather than one imposed upon it by other public institutions (Faget and Wyvekens, 1996; Crawford, 2000b). As such, it is a specifically judicial response to local crime prevention agendas. It is out of this policy that the *maisons de la justice et du droit* (MJDs) and the *groupes locaux de traitement de la délinquance* (GLTDs) have been established in recent years.

The MJDs are multi-agency 'houses of justice' which bring together a variety of local services – probation, social services, juvenile justice workers, legal assistance, victim support, prosecutors and, in some instances, judges – under one roof. They aim to provide access to the law through free legal advice and victim support services, mediation in disputes involving both parties and the promotion of alternatives to prosecution, and the 'reinsertion of law into problem areas' through local initiatives. They tend to be located in what are referred to as *les quartiers sensibles* or *les quartiers hors droit* – literally, 'lawless areas' – with high levels of petty crime. MJDs are assumed to represent a comforting reassurance that the state has not abandoned the area and that the issue of people's insecurity is taken seriously by the public authorities. The horizontal linkages they offer potentially allow a more problem-oriented and holistic approach to local issues and draw judicial institutions firmly into the process.

Like the MJDs, the GLTDs or 'local crime prevention groups' are a new initiative led by public prosecutors. They are designed to intervene in targeted neighbourhoods where it is perceived that there is a growing problem of juvenile delinquency, incivilities or more serious crime. These groups are set up and directed by prosecutors but draw together various 'figures of authority' within a specific area, notably the police (Donzelot and Wyvekens, 1998). They also include elected officials, representatives of the education and social services as well as a variety of local associations. Like the MJDs they entail the decentralization of the public prosecutor's office. The GLTDs seek to saturate a specific area with targeted day-to-day activity, particularly focused on local schools. The idea is to 'nip in the bud' any perceived heightening of tension within specific localities and to recreate the conditions enabling the revitalization of a 'lost public sphere'. They are reactive, intended only to have a short-term duration and offer a concentrated symbolic presence.

In both the MJDs and the GLTDs we see reflected the overriding concern with the territorialization of judicial intervention in particular urban areas deemed 'beyond the law', where incivility and antisocial behaviour are perceived to be rife. In some senses, the new structures of the *justice de proximité* have supplanted those of the earlier Bonnemaison-inspired crime prevention reforms.

Universalist discourse and differentialist practice: strategies of integration

Throughout the 1980s the French held on to the republican ideal of social integration – namely individual integration on the basis of equal opportunity – particularly with regard to immigrant populations. The responsibility for such integration fell largely upon an educational system which is highly centralized, offering a universal education in citizenship. Such strategies collided with the increasingly unequal opportunities available to urban youth from disadvantaged areas and (in response) the growing presence on peripheral housing estates of a growing subculture of youth alienation (Bailleau, 1996). As some French commentators have noted (Roché, 1994), the fear of the far right in France – in the form of the National Front – encouraged a detrimental stifling of any critical debate about strategies of integration, particularly of marginalized North African youths.

Recent experience in practice has also involved targeting initiatives at particular neighbourhoods. This has left a tension between the continued universalist discourse of French legal and political culture and the increasing preoccupation with the zoning of specific problematic peripheral housing estates and the subsequent development of differentialist strategies of integration. Partnerships with local security contracts have not only diffused responsibility at the local level, but have also admitted a differentiating logic into the heart of the politics of insecurity. Crime control, unlike the ideal of schooling, for instance, is no longer recognized as universal: the nature and priorities of policing in one locality are very different from those in another. Furthermore, specific initiatives such as the MJDs and GLTDs have added to this differentialist logic. France has moved from a situation in 1982 in which there were twenty-seven zones of urban social regeneration to one in which by 1998 there were 1,300 sites of *la politique de la ville* (Roché, 1999, p. 391). This sits awkwardly with the often reiterated commitment to the undifferentiated republican pact between state and citizen.

The path of recent French politics has been concerned with attempting to reassert, at every critical turn, republican integration and 'universalism' at the level of rhetoric at least, despite the reality of considerable social *différence*. The existence of powerful social identities and group interests outside, and sometimes in conflict with, that expressed by the universal notion of French *citoyenneté* is something that the law and politics refuse to recognize. Witness, for example, the public neurosis engendered by the furore over the wearing of the veil by Muslim girls in school. Here the national principle of *laïcité* (secularism) collided headlong with the desire to affirm cultural difference on the part of a segment of the population (Bell, 1995; Poulter, 1997).

A further example of the state-centred and universalist strategies of social inclusion occurred in 1996 when an adolescent was stabbed in Marseille by a youth of Algerian origin. The Education Minister F. Bayrou required all high-school pupils to stage a debate on violence on a specific day, at a specified hour, renewing and reasserting the Third Republic's 'regalian' and 'virtuous' approach (Body-Gendrot, 2000, p. 72).

Increasingly, some French commentators have become more willing to recognize that the model of integration is in crisis (Wieviorka, 1997). And yet, at the level of politics, there remains ambivalence. On the one hand, universalist strategies fail to accommodate the diverse cultural and plural social make-up of modern France. On the other, the politics of targeting particular areas is criticized for turning its back on the republican ideal and simultaneously encouraging a process of ghettoization. In consequence, there is a hesitant movement between universalist discourse and differentialist practice, in which the politics of insecurity has become increasingly racialized.

Comparing and contrasting

At this juncture it is worth considering some of the salient divergences and continuities between the experiences of France and England.

The role of the state

The state plays a prominent role in constructing the meaning and practices of social identity in France (Garapon, 1997). As a political ideal the state is identified as a 'moral unifier', a role which requires it to be strong and prominent so as to transcend particular interests. This role of the state is expressed through law and reflected in the legal culture. As Garapon notes 'It is not exaggerated to say that, for the French, law is the purveyor of identity' (1995, p. 499). Traditionally the French derive their identity and autonomy from, rather than in contrast to, the state and the law.

In England, by contrast, the state traditionally occupies a more malignant role: it is seen as 'a vaguely threatening monolith' (Prosser, 1995, p. 510). As such, it is viewed as the antithesis of individual freedom. Liberty, in the tradition of Locke and Mill, exists beyond the reach of the state. Hence community safety, in an Anglo-American context, feeds upon an anti-statist tradition, the counterpart of which is largely absent in French discourse. Recently this has been nourished by neo-liberal ideas, which impute the modern welfare state to be the harbinger of contemporary social ills, such as high crime rates, which simultaneously destroys enterprise and voluntarism (Murray, 1990).

Against this background it is interesting to note some significant ambiguities in the role of the state in the elaboration and development of a politics of insecurity in the two countries. First, whilst the past two decades in France have seen a considerable decentralization of a traditionally centrist state, there has been something of a counter-process of centralization under way in England and Wales, often conducted in the name of managerial efficiency. Whilst this process of recentring in England and Wales has been not unambiguous in itself, accompanied both by a decentring impulse to communities and consumers and a restructuring through 'partnerships', nevertheless it has had significant effects. For example, it is difficult to explain (particularly to the French) why the development of community safety in England and Wales should have required central government legislation – the traditional instrument of the state – in the form of the Crime and Disorder Act 1998 imposing a statutory duty on the police and local authorities to establish and maintain crime and disorder partnerships and strategies (without even any additional resources being earmarked). Moreover, it is not entirely comprehensible to many French commentators that in England and Wales local authorities themselves lobbied for the introduction of such legislation. The statutory duty, under the Crime and Disorder Act 1998, appears a strangely centrist and normative approach to the politics of insecurity.

Divergent traditions of voluntarism

The differing role of the state in England and France also has implications for the nature and development of the institutions of civil society. As Nelken notes:

> Despite the many similarities at the level of practice brought by the homogenizing and converging influences of the European Union, the debate about solidarity versus exclusion takes rather different forms depending on whether it is the representatives of the state or the members of civil society who are allocated the main role in creating an integrated sense of identity and community. (Nelken, 2000, p. 3)

In France this role has traditionally fallen upon, and been celebrated by, the state. The national culture does not encourage people to resort to self-help (Body-Gendrot, 2000, p. 66). People turn to the state for solutions. State intervention remains the primary means of resolving social problems. Hence institutions such as mediation schemes designed to encourage people to solve their disputes outside the state and encourage greater dispute resolution within civil society (Faget, 1997; Crawford, 2000b), perversely, have often ended up reproducing state involvement as well as increasing the demand for crime control and judicial intervention (Dourlens and Vidal-Naquet, 1994; Garapon and Salas, 1996).

Moreover, partnerships have tended to remain within the public sector. The use of the *contrat de ville* has tended to reinforce this rather than disrupt it, primarily because the implementation of contracts is so complex that the voluntary and private sectors have had difficulty in participating. As a consequence, the CCPDs have not incorporated or addressed in any significant way the role of the growing private security industry (Ocqueteau, 1998).

The appeal to community and the absence of community

Whilst there is a clear decentralizing impulse and localizing element in the politics of insecurity it is very different from the appeals to community in Anglo-American policies. The meaning of appeals to community – central to the politics of community safety in England – has not only a very different sense in France but is also largely absent in the equivalent politics of insecurity.

The word 'community' does not translate easily into French. The term *communauté* tends not to be used in relation to communities of place but is reserved to ethnic, religious and cultural collectivities. French law and politics are marked by the absence of a public discourse acknowledging the existence of ethnic and cultural identities. There is even explicit unease about using the term *communauté*, in part owing to its association with recent Anglo-American political, cultural and social experience. Hence the term *communautés*, unlike the rural idylls which English communities conjure up, is directly connected with a more recent process of social disintegration and polarization. Talk of 'community' is often associated with 'ghettoization', particularly the racialized ghettos of the contemporary United States.

Rather like 'race' and 'ethnicity', French politics evades direct debate about 'community' – in part owing to the connections between group identity and difference, which challenge universalist ideals of equality. To recognize and embrace a politics of 'community' is to celebrate a politics of difference and group identity, inimical to egalitarian ideals of nationhood. This has resulted in what Wieviorka (1997) describes as a 'damaging silence' surrounding different cultural and ethnic identities, their place in French society and their claims to recognition. The emphasis upon social inclusion is a reminder that the structure and experience of social, particularly urban, exclusion are very different from those of the United States (Wacquant, 1996; Body-Gendrot, 2000). Nevertheless, the phantom of the US ghetto is an ever-present image in political debate, against which the French perceive their distinct political culture standing in bold contrast.

Universalist and differentialist strategies of social inclusion

In both France and England the new politics of insecurity has become intrinsically tied up with the notion of locality and a process of territorialization. In consequence there are a number of interesting lessons to be learnt from the French experience with regard to strategies of social inclusion in England, which has traditionally been marked by a *laissez-faire* approach. Whilst the English state has never had the same preoccupation with republican ideals, the recent emphasis upon strategies to address social exclusion – as promoted by New Labour – and the central place given to community safety and social order therein, represent a belated recognition of the social polarization that has characterized the economic restructuring of the last two decades. The establishment of the interdepartmental Social Exclusion Unit and the tone of its most influential reports (SEU, 1998, 2000a), echo the work of the DIV in France, which has set community safety within an urban policy framework. Moreover the recent emphasis upon a plethora of health, employment and education action zones exhibits strong parallels with recent French developments. The extent to which France and England can reincorporate the socially dislocated 'islands of neglect' which mark the urban landscape through targeted intervention without fragmenting the 'social' or 'solidarity project' is a major challenge.

The reality in both England and France is that recent restructuring of the economy, state and public sector has had differential consequences for different groups of people. These condition – in terms of social practices and cultural sensibilities – their experience of crime and disorder. Crudely put, there are both winners and losers from the social and economic changes of recent years.

The losers – the supposed underclass – are those often trapped in places of disadvantage, increasingly disconnected from the wider consumer society, and socially and politically marginalized. Crime is often endemic both as a function of an alternative economy and in terms of the impact of victimization. The language of the underclass is itself problematic, in part because such debates reinforce and lend credibility to the notion of the 'pathological community'. This can allow a shift from poverty as 'our' problem to poverty as 'their' problem. The question of social inclusion is the extent to which poverty is a social or public rather than an asocial or private issue.

The winners, by contrast, move between two responses to restructuring (Robert, 1999, pp. 231–2). The first is acceptance that 'islands of neglect' and pockets of high crime and disaffection – which sometimes erupt into violent disorder – are a price worth paying. The second is a desire to be insulated from the fallout of restructuring, such that crime and disorder, are 'elsewhere', something to be avoided, 'out of sight' if not always 'out of mind'. There is a danger of what Lasch (1995), in the US context, describes as a 'revolt of the elites', whereby the privileged 'winners' increasingly exclude themselves from the public services and provision (and from funding them through taxes) which have connected them, however tenuously, with their fellow citizens. 'Security enclaves' and 'gated communities' are the most obvious expression of this trend (Blakely and Snyder, 1997): they represent the winners' claim to opt out of society *de facto*, in the process rupturing the bonds of social solidarity.

Between the winners and the losers lie a more ambiguous category who are uncertain of their position: 'these are the people who exhibit hypersensitivity to insecurity' (Robert, 1999, p. 232). The quest for security becomes an aspect of self-identity. The political questions are how to address such anxieties in an inclusionary public polity and how to mitigate the consequences of economic restructuring in ways which insure against creating 'no go' areas for some and 'no exit' areas for others.

Social versus situational crime prevention

The French have pioneered a social approach to crime prevention, not only in terms of policies which address the social and economic causes of crime, but also in terms of the use of people as key agents of social control, as witnessed by the expanding number of 'local agents of social mediation' (Roché, 1998). The French approach has targeted specific urban zones with a saturation of interventions in order to try to avoid social dislocation. This concern has led the French model to place significant emphasis upon the symbolic presence of public authorities within targeted neighbourhoods – notably public spaces – operating in a socio-educative and conflict-resolving capacity. From the *animateurs* through the MJDs to the GLTDs and city wardens, these new 'local agents of social mediation' have emerged from a perceived need for an effective public presence in certain localities but at the same time demonstrate the difficulty of the state redeploying its own traditional agents of social control in such areas. Robert describes these policy developments as a recourse to a 'security sub-proletariat' which costs less, is more accessible and is closer to the local population (1999, p. 230). He suggests the demand for security is being bounced back on to those it came from, under the guidance and monitoring of the police. In sum, these are responsibilization strategies, the burden of security being transferred to the shoulders of those who live in 'high-crime' areas (Crawford, 1997).

This approach stands in contrast to the often short-term, situational and technologically driven developments in England. The two approaches have often been seen almost as polar opposites (King, 1991). Certainly the English experience (particularly during the 1980s) has seen the proliferation of technological interventions and 'opportunity reduction' – based on modifications of the built environment, notably the use of CCTV cameras – which have largely neglected any 'people dynamic' in crime prevention. However, the more recent experience of both countries exhibits elements of conversion, with France appropriating more situational developments and England experimenting with social crime prevention. Hence in England there has been more emphasis on issues of social exclusion (SEU, 1998, 2000a), 'at risk' youth and the introduction of city guards and community wardens (SEU, 2000b).

The criminalization of social policy or the socialization of criminal policy?

The subject matter of community safety and the essence of interorganizational partnerships inherently blur the boundaries of traditional distinctions between the work of criminal justice and other public agencies. We are also witnessing a blurring of the fields of intervention notably with reference to notions of 'safety', 'disorder' and 'quality of life' issues. In consequence the ultimate purpose of policies can be unclear. The French experience, at first glance, appears to offer an illustration of the possible socialization of criminal justice policy through its emphasis upon social crime prevention. However, the failure to transform workings of the key criminal justice institutions, and the fact that they have embarked upon their own policies of reform within the framework of the politics of insecurity, raise the spectre of social and economic policy becoming increasingly defined by crime and disorder issues. As a result of the politics of *justice de proximité* – and institutions like the MJDs and GLTDs – local prosecutors and the police have extended their role and significantly increased their authority. Locally elected representatives have been keen to embrace the establishment of MJDs, where they have been set up, often because they offer direct lines of communication with local prosecutors (who have much more authority within the criminal justice system than their English counterparts) and through them to the Ministry of Justice.

As in England, there is genuine anxiety that the high degree of influence given to *crime* prevention – as opposed to poverty prevention, for example – in the politics of insecurity may result in social policy, its direction and funding being redefined in terms of its implications for crime and disorder. In the rush to promote crime prevention there is a need to be wary of requiring mainstream public services, local initiatives and community groups to address social issues through the lens of crime and disorder – particularly in securing limited funding – and in the process transforming and redefining their activity. The fear is that public issues may become marginalized except in so far as they are defined in terms of their crimogenic qualities. Consequently, the dominant role of crime and insecurity in public policy-making needs to be held in a deliberately precarious balance.

Conclusion

David Garland (2000) has sketched out an important framework for comparative criminological analysis of the emergence of new strategies of crime control in late modern, high-crime societies. His thesis locates the development of an 'adaptive strategy', stressing rationalistic and administrative partnerships and crime prevention alongside a 'sovereign state strategy' which emphasizes the morally toned and expressive 'punitive populism'. These almost 'twinned, antithetical phenomena' (Garland, 1997, p. 203) in which one provokes the other, and both differ from the penal welfare policies that preceded them, arose in response to the problem of high crime rates as a normal social fact of late modern societies. One of the reasons that Garland gives for why 'penal welfare solutions fell into disrepute' lies in the 'adaptation to the experience of high rates of crime' by the professional middle classes and liberal elites (2000, pp. 348–9). This group, he argues, was previously attached to penal welfarism because its political and economic interests were tied to welfare state polices and institutions. In addition 'the social distance that, until quite recently, separated the professional middle class from crime and insecurity' allowed it to adopt a 'civilized' attitude towards crime and criminals (*ibid.*, p. 357). According to Garland, the declining influence of social expertise combined with the novel experience of crime for the liberal elite, as it became a 'prominent fact of life not only for the urban middle classes but for many middle-class suburbanites as well' (*ibid.*, p. 357). Crudely put, whereas the middle classes in the 1950s and 1960s typically 'lived at a distance from criminal events' (*ibid.*, p. 357) and, hence, were able to 'adopt a civilized attitude', now, thanks to the shared experience of crime, they no longer can.

This analysis offers important and valuable insights into the relationship between changing cultural sensibilities and the politics of crime control. Nevertheless, it fails to differentiate a number of issues that are important in explaining the rise of crime prevention and community safety, particularly when looked at through the comparative experiences of France and England. First, it conflates the 'experience of high rates of crime' with, on the one hand, experiences of urban dislocation and social polarization and, on the other, anxieties about 'signs of crime' or what Wilson and Kelling (1982) refer to as 'incivilities' and 'signs of disorder'. Rather than reducing the 'social distance' between the professional middle classes and crime, the process of counter-urbanization and mass migration to the suburbs has increased the social distance between them and areas in which 'high crime rates are a normal fact of life'. The flight from Britain's metropolitan areas over the past fifteen years has been marked, as Champion et al. (1996) have shown. More to the point, the flight from cities to suburban and rural areas is in large measure driven by concern and anxiety about crime. The tentative and always unstable search for the rural idyll conjured up by the image of 'community' in England, free of crime and the fear of crime, appears a compelling reason to travel long distances to and from work. The investment in this 'imagined community' – crime-free and stable – leaves occupants anxious and uncertain.

As the various British Crime Surveys remind us, crime is highly concentrated both socially and spatially. Moreover this is more and more rather than less and less the case (Trickett et al., 1995). It is less the 'experience of high rates of crime' that the liberal elite are responding to than the experience of anxiety driven by low-level incivilities and concern about 'disorder': what I have referred to as the politics of insecurity. Such anxiety is fuelled by social distance from the places where crime is most concentrated – the inner city and its 'badlands'. The liberal elites who travel across the city are reminded of the 'experience of high rates of crime' for others but generally flee to low-crime areas, taking their anxieties with them. Rather than the distance between the elite and crime narrowing, there is a growing social and spatial distance between the elite and the places where crime is increasingly concentrated. Crime may well have a new salience in everyday life but it is not a shared collective experience. What is more problematic is that de-urbanization means that the spaces vacated by any intimate knowledge of areas in and around cities are likely to be filled by distorted media representations and occasional panic stories. Areas that are unknown can more easily acquire a reputation for danger, which may be unwarranted. Greater, rather than less, knowledge of our cities is more likely to breed tolerance. Urban fragmentation, social polarization and the changing relationship between the middle classes and the city may adversely impact upon their sensibilities, their cultural beliefs about safety and danger, and the appropriateness of place.

Second, the experience of France seriously questions the applicability of Garland's thesis beyond the cases of the United States and United Kingdom. In France the professional middle classes and liberal elite have not flown from the inner cities like their American and, to a lesser extent, British counterparts. On the contrary, they maintain a deep cultural attachment to their metropolitan centres. The city is often seen as the expression of liberal culture and the arts and, therefore, the natural home of the middle-class elite. For the French, their social link with the city's dangerous places remains preserved. They are more likely to *experience* 'high levels of crime as a normal social fact'. Yet the crime control policies of the last two decades, at least, have remained very much within a penal welfare model. Apart from the National Front, all political parties remain committed to a discourse on crime which is couched in the language of social solidarity, inclusion and *la politique de la ville*. This is due not only to their continued relationship with the modern state as a power-containing institution but also to their on-going relation to the city as a place of loosely connected (but connected nevertheless) strangers.

The contrasts between the experiences of many mainland European countries, notably France, and those of the United States and the United Kingdom raise the question of the extent to which the latter represent atypical rather than typical political responses. It would seem that Garland's analysis has less relevance to some continental European societies where the state and the law have come to assume a fundamentally different cultural place and play a different social role from those in Anglo-American jurisdictions. Moreover, even in a global age, it reminds us that, as Girling et al. note, there exist 'some obdurate cultural sensibilities that shape the kinds of things people are willing to countenance in the name of crime control' (2000, p. 169).

The experience of France and England suggests points of convergence and departure. Moreover, it highlights the interconnectedness of cultural difference and strategies of crime control, but reminds us that we should not exaggerate either the differences between cultures or their separateness from global trends. What is clear from the study of the recent French experience is that we cannot merely extrapolate from Anglo-American trends in crime control policy. Influential as they are, in an increasingly global economy and culture, the English-speaking experience diverges significantly from that of France and other countries of mainland Europe. The limits to the transferability of crime control policies and practices, as well as criminological accounts of them, which commentators often claim to be universal, derive from the cultural connections and political programmes out of which they arise.

One common theme is the rise of the 'anxious city' (*la ville inquiète*), or as Hope (1995) calls it 'the frightened city', in which public safety and fear of crime have become central political issues and an important influence on where people go, live and shop, on the nature of their leisure activities, and so on. In this context, insecurity has not only become politicized but also commodified. The acquisition of ever greater 'security as commodity' may serve, perversely, to undermine genuine feelings of 'security' by institutionalizing anxiety. Moreover the individualistic quest for personal security may adversely affect the public sphere, and people's experience of it, as people withdraw from 'unsafe areas'. The question remains, how far the rise of crime prevention and community safety in England and France, with their converging and contrasting contours and emphases, amounts to the advent of a new 'security state' (Robert, 1999, p. 232)? The particular extent to which the strategies developed in England and France will be able to hold together 'anxious cities' ravaged by social dislocation and incorporate the 'islands of neglect' into an inclusive urban frame will depend on political choices. Patterns of criminal activity and responses to crime are not immutable but are the outcome of conscious and unconscious decisions by the public, politicians and agencies of regulatory power. Governments and publics are presented with choices as to the unfolding direction of the rearticulation of powers in the governance of crime, and the experience of France and that of England offer, in their own ways, important lessons and insights as to ways of responding to the politics of insecurity. It remains questionable how far there is a political will to address these issues and to learn the lessons of the two countries' experience.

Note

This chapter has benefited greatly from comments by, and discussions with, Sophie Body-Gendrot, Philippe Robert, Sebastian Roché and Anne Wyvekens. It has also been informed by comparative empirical research supported by ESRC grant R000221717.

References

Bailleau, F. (1996) *Les Jeunes face à la justice pénale*, Paris, Syros.
Bailleau, F. (1998) 'A crisis of youth or of juridical response?' in Ruggiero, V., South, N. and Taylor, I. (eds) *The New European Criminology*, London, Routledge.

Bauman, Z. (1998) *Globalization: The Human Consequences*, Cambridge, Polity Press.

Bell, J. (1995) 'English law and French law – not so different?', *Current Legal Problems*, vol. 48, pp. 63–101.

Blakely, E.J. and Snyder, M.G. (1997) *Fortress America: Gated Communities in the United States*, Washington, DC, Brookings Institution Press.

Body-Gendrot, S. (2000) *The Social Control of Cities? A Comparative Perspective*, Oxford, Blackwell.

Body-Gendrot, S. and Duprez, D. (2001) 'Les politiques de sécurité et de prévention dans les années 1990s en France' in Duprez, D. and Hebberecht, P. (eds) *Les Politiques de sécurité et de prévention dans les années 1990s en Europe*, Paris, L'Harmattan.

Bonnemaison, G. (1982) *Face à la délinquance, prévention, répression, solidarité*, Paris, Documentation Française.

Champion, T., Wong, C., Rooke, A., Dorling, D., Coombes, M. and Brundson, C. (1996) *The Population of Britain in the 1990s*, Oxford, Clarendon Press.

Crawford, A. (1997) *The Local Governance of Crime: Appeals to Community and Partnerships*, Oxford, Clarendon Press.

Crawford, A. (1998) *Crime Prevention and Community Safety: Politics, Policies and Practices*, Harlow, Longman.

Crawford, A. (2000a) 'Why British criminologists lose their critical faculties upon crossing the Channel: some thoughts on comparative criminology from an empirical investigation in France and England', *Social Work in Europe*, vol. 7, no. 1, pp. 22–30.

Crawford, A. (2000b) '*Justice de proximité* – the growth of "houses of justice" and victim/offender mediation in France: a very unFrench legal response?', *Social and Legal Studies*, vol. 9, pp. 29–53.

Crawford, A. (2000c) 'Contrasts in victim-offender mediation and appeals to community in France and England' in Nelken, D. (ed.) *Contrasting Criminal Justice*, Aldershot, Ashgate.

Crawford, A. (2001) 'Vers une reconfiguration des pouvoirs? Le niveau local et les perspectives de la gouvernance', *Déviance et Société*, vol. 25, no. 1, pp. 3–32.

Crawford, A. and Matassa, M. (2000) *Community Safety Structures: An International Literature Review*, Belfast, HMSO.

Donzelot, J. and Estèbe, P. (1994) *L'État animateur: essai sur la politique de la ville*, Paris, Éditions Esprit.

Donzelot, J. and Wyvekens, A. (1998) 'Magistrature sociale et souci du territoire', *Les Cahiers de la sécurité intérieure*, vol. 33, pp. 149–74.

Dourlens, C. and Vidal-Naquet, P.A. (1994) *L'Autorité comme prestation: la justice et la police dans la politique de la ville*, Paris, CERPE.

Faget, J. (1997) *La Médiation: essai de politique pénale*, Ramonville Saint-Ange, Editions Erès.

Faget, J. and Wyvekens, A. (1996) 'Urban policy and proximity justice in France', *European Journal on Criminal Policy and Research*, vol. 4, pp. 64–73.

Garapon, A. (1995) 'French legal culture and the shock of globalization', *Social and Legal Studies*, vol. 4, pp. 493–506.

Garapon, A. (1996) *Le Gardien des promesses: le juge et la démocratie*, Paris, Odile Jacob.

Garapon, A. (1997) *Bien juger: essai sur le rituel judiciaire*, Paris, Odile Jacob.

Garapon, A. and Salas, D. (1996) *La République pénalisée*, Baume-les-Dames, Hachette.

Garland, D. (1997) '"Governmentality" and the problem of crime: Foucault, criminology, sociology', *Theoretical Criminology*, vol. 1, no. 2, pp. 173–214.

Garland, D. (2000) 'The culture of high crime societies: some preconditions of recent "law and order policies"', *British Journal of Criminology*, vol. 40, no. 3, pp. 347–75.

Giddens, A. (1990) *The Consequences of Modernity*, Cambridge, Polity Press.

Girling, E., Loader, I. and Sparks, R. (2000) *Crime and Social Change in Middle England: Questions of Order in an English Town*, London, Routledge.

Hope, T. (1995) 'Community crime prevention' in Tonry, M. and Farrington, D. (eds) *Building a Safer Society: Strategic Approaches to Crime Prevention*, Crime and Justice, vol. 19, Chicago, IL, University of Chicago Press.

King, M. (1988) *How to Make Social Crime Prevention Work: The French Experience*, London, NACRO.

King, M. (1991) 'The political construction of crime prevention: a contrast between the French and British experiences' in Stenson, K. and Cowell, D. (eds) *The Politics of Crime Control*, London, Sage.

Lasch, C. (1995) *The Revolt of the Elites and the Betrayal of Democracy*, New York, Norton.

Lash, S. and Urry, J. (1994) *Economies of Signs and Space*, London, Sage.

Lazerges, C. (1995) 'De la politique de prévention de la délinquance à la politique de la ville' in Fijnaut, C., Goethals, J., Peters, T. and Walgrave, L. (eds) *Changes in Society, Crime and Criminal Justice*, vol. 1, *Crime and Insecurity in the City*, The Hague, Kluwer.

Murray, C. (1990) *The Emerging British Underclass*, London, Institute of Economic Affairs.

Nelken, D. (2000) 'Just comparing' in Nelken, D. (ed.) *Contrasting Criminal Justice*, Aldershot, Ashgate.

Ocqueteau, F. (1998) 'La sécurité privée en France: état des lieux et questions pour l'avenir', *Les Cahiers de la sécurité intérieure*, vol. 33, pp. 105–28.

Pitts, J. (1995) 'Public issues and private troubles: a tale of two cities', *Social Work in Europe*, vol. 2, no. 1, pp. 3–11.

Pitts, J. (1997) 'Youth crime, social change and crime control in Britain and France in the 1980s and 1990s' in Jones, H. (ed.) *Towards a Classless Society*, London, Routledge.

Pitts, J. and Hope, T. (1997) 'The local politics of inclusion: the state and community safety', *Social Policy and Administration*, vol. 31, no. 5, pp. 37–58.

Poulter, S.M. (1997) 'Muslim headscarves in school: contrasting legal approaches in England and France', *Oxford Journal of Legal Studies*, vol. 17, pp. 43–74.

Prosser, T. (1995) 'The state, constitutions and implementing economic policy: privatization and regulation in the UK, France and the USA', *Social and Legal Studies*, vol. 4, pp. 507–16.

Robert, P. (1999) *Le Citoyen, le crime et l'État*, Geneva, Librairie Droz.

Robert, P. (2000) 'Les territoires du contrôle social, quels changements?', *Déviance et Société*, vol. 24, no. 3, pp. 15–35.

Roché, S. (1994) *Insécurité et Liberté*, Paris, Seuil.

Roché, S. (1998) *Sociologie politique de l'insécurité*, Paris, Presses Universitaires de France.

Roché, S. (1999) 'Prévention et répression en France: transformations de l'action publique dans les villes (1975–1999)', *Revue Internationale de criminologie et de police technique et scientifique*, vol. 4, pp. 387–413.

Social Exclusion Unit (1998) *Bringing Britain Together: A National Strategy for Neighbourhood Renewal*, London, Cabinet Office.

Social Exclusion Unit (2000a) *A National Strategy for Neighbourhood Renewal: A Framework for Consultation*, London, Cabinet Office.

Social Exclusion Unit (2000b) *Neighbourhood Wardens*, Report of Policy Action Team 6, National Strategy for Neighbourhood Renewal, London, Cabinet Office.

Trickett, A., Ellingworth, D., Farrell, G. and Pease, K. (1995) 'Crime victimization in the eighties: changes in area and regional inequality', *British Journal of Criminology*, vol. 35, no. 3, pp. 343–59.

Vignoble, G. (1995) 'Les Maisons de justice et du droit', presented to the Garde des Sceaux.

Wacquant, L. (1996) 'The comparative structure and experience of urban exclusion: "race", class and space in Chicago and Paris' in McFate, K., Lawson, R. and Wilson, W.J. (eds) *Poverty, Inequality and the Future of Social Policy*, New York, Russell Sage Foundation.

Wieviorka, M. (1997) *Commenter la France*, Marseille, Éditions de l'Aube.

Wieviorka, M. (1999) *La Violence en France*, Paris, Seuil.

Wilson, J.Q. and Kelling, G. (1982) 'Broken windows: the police and neighborhood safety', *Atlantic Monthly*, March, pp. 29–37.

Wyvekens, A. (1996) 'Justice de proximité et proximité de la justice: les maisons de justice et du droit', *Droit et société*, vol. 33, pp. 363–88.

Wyvekens, A. (1997) 'Mediation and proximity', *European Journal of Criminal Policy and Research*, vol. 5, no. 4, pp. 27–42.

The managerialization of crime prevention and community safety

The New Zealand experience

Trevor Bradley and Reece Walters

> The change here has been so extreme that New Zealand could be con-
> sidered a freak among nations, the Kampuchea of the free market, and
> 1984 could be considered year zero. (Jesson, 1999, p. 19)

Since the mid-1980s much academic and political debate has focused
on neo-liberalism and economic reform in Western democratic societies.
The increasing body of literature on 'neo-corporatism', 'neo-liberalism',
'advanced liberalism', 'new managerialism' and so on examines new modes
of governance in late modernity and the influence that such economically
driven policies have had on contemporary social life. Influenced by the
works of Foucault (1977, 1978), researchers across a variety of disciplines

have examined new methods of rule in what is broadly defined as discourses of governmentality (Smandych, 1999). Within these discourses we have witnessed flourishing debates about government accountability and the risk society (Simon, 1987; Beck, 1992; Douglas, 1992) and the concomitant nexus with policies of crime control and prevention (O'Malley, 1998).

These debates have argued that new technologies of rule in late modernity are characterized by actuarial forms of governance (Simon, 1987), prudentialism (O'Malley, 1992) and territories of security (Rose, 2000). Such mentalities of rule or governance aim to manage risks within society. The efficient management of risk populations (those 'at risk' of ill health, unemployment, criminal victimization, benefit dependence and so on) as well as risk industries ('at risk' of profit loss, share devaluation, reduced productivity) becomes a key objective of the regulatory authorities. The identification of risk groups, and the implementation of risk management strategies, have become wedded to processes of prediction and measurement.

The management of risks has occurred simultaneously with the 'hollowing out of the state' (Rhodes, 1994, 1997), where the enhancement of personal security and safety, a traditional function of state legitimacy, has required the recruitment of the 'community' within a politics of responsibilization and economic reform. Individuals within communities or 'territories of security' (Rose, 2000) become responsible for the protection and safety of their local environment within modes of governance that promote technologies of prudentialism. Community crime prevention has become an avant-garde crime control policy in neo-liberal Western societies, yet its popularity and widespread acceptance cannot be reconciled, at least empirically, with its mandate to prevent crime and build resources within local communities (Willemse, 1994; Presdee and Walters, 1997; Crawford, 1998; Hughes, 1998). The spread of community-based crime prevention initiatives has become commonplace in neo liberal, post Keynesian societies and must be examined within broader political frameworks (O'Malley, 1997).

As the opening quotation to this chapter suggests, New Zealand leads the world in economic reform. In the 1993 *World Competitive Report* it was ranked first for its 'quality of government' (World Economic Forum, 1993); in 1984 it embarked upon widespread policies of deregulation and it is now recognized as the most deregulated economy in the world (Henderson, 1999). This chapter aims to explore how the policies of the New Right have influenced the development and implementation of crime prevention and community safety in the world's most economically reformed and restructured public sector.

The New Zealand crime prevention strategy is a centrally developed and driven crime policy and as a result it has been essential to interview and thereby capture the internal working dynamics of central government officials. In doing so, this chapter draws upon original material (Bradley, unpublished) from Cabinet minutes and Ministerial papers, interviews with senior politicians and government officials and discussions with the co-ordinators 'at the coalface' who are responsible for implementing crime prevention and community safety in their local areas.

The rise of community crime prevention

Background and development

General histories of New Zealand's contemporary crime prevention usually begin with the Ministerial Committee of Inquiry into Violence (Roper, 1987; Oughton, 1994). The Ministerial inquiry, more commonly referred to as the Roper Report, is posited as both the catalyst, and the inspiration, for the adoption of an alternative community-based or 'upstream' approach to preventing crime. In contrast to this simplistic and apolitical account, this chapter argues for a more convoluted, contentious and complex genesis, and in so doing uncovers some of its hidden political aspects. New Zealand's promotion of an alternative crime prevention programme must be contextualized within the country's emerging political rationality (neo-liberalism) as well as pre-election party politics. In a similar fashion to the political machinations that shaped Australia's earliest community crime prevention policies (see Presdee and Walters, 1994), New Zealand also exhibits political opportunism and 'crime prevention electioneering'.

During the run-up to the 1990 general election the Labour government avoided the 'get tough' law-and-order rhetoric that characterized the 1987 election (Pratt and Treacher, 1988). Instead the Minister of Justice – and soon to be Prime Minister – Geoffrey Palmer sought an alternative crime policy: one that would develop and evolve over a longer period than the three-year parliamentary term and would be appealing to the voting public. It is clear that Minister Palmer was responding to public opinion polls and wanting to 'capture the public's imagination'. Minutes of a meeting with the Justice Minister and his senior staff stated:

> The Minister produced the findings of a recent public opinion poll (28 November 1987) which placed Law and Order as the number one concern in the public's opinion . . . Officials have one month to report back to the Minister with a policy initiative that . . . offers a fresh approach that engages the interest of young people, potential offenders and captures the public's imagination.[1]

At an international level, Minister Palmer was influenced by overseas initiatives, notably that in France. He subsequently requested his policy staff to prepare a briefing paper about the French experience. In the opening paragraph of this document the political importance of a French-style approach being adopted in New Zealand was emphasized – notably its ability to secure bipartisan political support. It states:

In light of Mr. East's [Opposition justice spokesman] statements on the need for a bipartisan approach to criminal justice issues, there is some prospect of attaining for a crime prevention initiative in New Zealand, the bipartisan support that is such an important feature in the French system.[2]

The Minister of Justice was clearly using the upcoming election to present an innovative and fresh law-and-order campaign to a concerned public. In doing so he was aware of the support that such a policy would secure if he could establish bipartisan political support. As was stated in an interview with the Minister: 'We wanted some new initiatives, with some fresh approaches and with some innovative thinking that did not depend on the same old repetitive pattern that happened at every election.'[3]

The alternative crime prevention model based on the success of France was not in response to an increase in crime in New Zealand; it was an opportunity to reach the voting public, 'to capture their imagination'. The political opportunity presented by crime prevention is clearly articulated by Palmer's successor as Minister of Justice, Bill Jeffries. Minister Jeffries was given the portfolio of Justice when Geoffrey Palmer became Prime Minister in 1990. Minister Jeffries identified the political roots of the unfolding crime prevention strategy:

We aimed at running again projects that unquestionably had a political end in it. I find it immature and silly to say that's a discounted factor because you know it's silly to exclude it but it doesn't mean because it exists that it makes it improper . . . From a political dimension on it I thought that if we assembled our resources and get solidity into this, it would also be politically advantageous to us and we were responding to public demand and meeting the requirement for governments to take a lead in these things.[4]

The party politics that characterized the development of a crime prevention model were complemented by the prevailing political rationality – a neo-liberal ideology that has become increasingly popular in the United Kingdom, the United States and Australia. As discussed below, the reinvention and reconfiguration of the state contributed to the creation of a new mode of governance. In this new mode of governance the 'myth of the sovereign state' (Garland, 1997) is exposed and it results in individuals, families and communities taking greater responsibility for the search for solutions to social and economic ailments. In appealing for a more active responsibility in the 'government' of one's own life and that of the family and the community, this emergent mode of governance represents a profound recasting of the relationship between state and citizen (cf Hughes, 1998) and is central to understanding the development of community crime prevention in New Zealand.

The emergence and development of New Zealand's crime prevention 'model', therefore, requires a more detailed examination of the political, governmental and public policy contexts that provided the necessary conditions for its development and cultivation.

The political and economic transformation

While the first concrete manifestation of community crime prevention came in the form of the 1990 Safer Communities Council Pilot Scheme (SCCPS), it was the election of the fourth Labour government (1984–90), and its agenda of radical economic and governmental reform, that provided the conditions for a devolved, locally based and flexible crime prevention initiative with its attendant appeals to community and individual responsibility. Guided by a schematic offered by an emerging neo-liberalism, between 1984 and their electoral defeat in 1990 the fourth Labour government implemented a programme of systematic reform that called into question, and ultimately redesigned, the very foundations of 'the public' and 'governmental'. While the fourth Labour government initiated the reform process and essentially laid the foundations of the 'new' state, the process of reform was taken further by the incoming conservative National government of 1990–99. Some of the events that shaped economic reform are worth noting, as they provide an important context for understanding the evolution and subsequent development of the country's crime prevention strategy.

Since the 1980s the reform of public (government) management has become a 'global movement' in two primary senses. The first relates to its literal spread around the world, from Mongolia to the United States, while the second relates to the sweeping nature of the reforms. New Zealand proved to be the flagship of this global movement; as Kettle (2000, p. 8) argues, 'modern public management reform had its true start in New Zealand'. The transformation of state and government was effected by a carefully orchestrated plan from a party traditionally on the left of the political spectrum.

In 1984 the fourth Labour government embarked upon a quest for a 'smaller and smarter' government, which Kettle argues, resulted in 'the world's most aggressive and ambitious' reforms (2000, p. 10; see also Henderson, 1999). Prominent among the architects of this programme of reform was the Treasury, particularly the two Ministerial briefing papers it presented to the incoming government in 1984, *Economic Management*, and to the re-elected Labour government in 1987, *Government Management*. Of course, a number of individuals have been instrumental in the transformation of the state. In particular, Roger Douglas, Minister of Finance (1984–88), shared a very similar vision to that of the Treasury and his particular version of a free market and neo-liberal economics became known as 'Rogernomics' (Easton, 1989).

The 1984 briefing paper set out a programme for the full liberalization of the economy and the steps needed to reduce government expenditure. In the space of just six years the economy was transformed from one of the most regulated and 'cocooned' (Schick, 1996, p. 12) to one of the most open and deregulated in the Western world (Jesson, 1999, pp. 39–61). The briefing paper emphasized the poor performance of the government sector, the lack of clear management plans, and the lack of effective control mechanisms to review the performance of departments in meeting 'output' requirements. The above reflected the Treasury's, and subsequently the government's, desire for more effective management of the public sector and was to eventually become a significant feature of the 'management' of crime prevention.

The second phase of the reform programme (1987–90) involved the reinvention of the apparatus and machinery of the state. The second Treasury briefing paper, *Government Management* – described by the English public policy expert Christopher Hood as 'the manifesto of the New Public Management' (1990, p. 210) – provided both the philosophical and the intellectual framework.

Managerialism has significantly influenced public administration/management and policy in Britain, Canada, Australia and New Zealand. The essential assumption of managerialism is that management is a generic activity that can be applied to public as well as private business. This assumption is not a new one and can be traced as far back as Taylor's pioneering work on 'scientific management' (1916). However, in coinciding with public choice theory and the new institutional economics, a convergent model emerged referred to as the 'New Public Management' (Hood, 1990). In relation to the 'management' of crime prevention in New Zealand the more important features of the New Public Management include: emphasis on the management of policy; reliance on quantifiable output measures and performance targets; and the devolution of management underpinned by new reporting, monitoring and accountability mechanisms (see O'Malley, 1996).

These successive reforms produced a distinct 'model' of government and governance and, as Kettle argues, they were as much about politics as about an administrative and managerial quest for efficiency and effectiveness. In other words, political considerations shape modes of governance that in turn shape management options. This New Zealand 'experiment', as Boston et al. (1996) note, has been internationally acclaimed and celebrated.

Emerging in tandem with policies to limit the range and scope of the state and its attendant interventionist mode of government, the adoption of 'anticipatory', future-oriented crime prevention, the responsibility for which is devolved closer to the problem, can be seen as a product of this political and governmental milieu. Thus it is against a backdrop of the 'reinvention' and restructuring of the public sector that the adoption, development and eventual institutionalization of 'upstream' community-based approaches to preventing crime should be seen and understood.

The Safer Communities Council Pilot Scheme

In 1989 the development of a crime prevention initiative progressed further with the establishment of an Officials' Committee on Crime Prevention. It was to investigate with particular reference to the French initiatives, what form a crime prevention initiative might take in New Zealand. The subsequent report, presented to the Cabinet Social Equity Committee in July 1989, laid the foundations for the construction of a model of crime prevention. The report identified five major objectives for a crime prevention initiative (OCCP, 1989, p. 1). These included:

1   The recognition that crime and its prevention concern the whole community and are not therefore the sole responsibility of the agencies of social control and law enforcement.
2   The inititative would provide a forum at the local level to identify crime problems affecting the community and to co-ordinate the resources and expertise of local government, government departments, lwi authorities (i.e. traditionally based Maori tribal groupings), private organizations and, where appropriate, relevant cultural authorities to address the problems.
3   To facilitate and promote local initiatives focusing on crime, its prevention, and the context in which it occurs.
4   To promote the development of effective crime prevention initiatives suited to New Zealand, in particular taking account of the status of the Maori people as Tangata Whenua.
5   To promote and support worthwhile crime prevention projects.

In endorsing a community crime prevention initiative the 1989 report proposed a structure consisting of two main bodies. The first, and most important, was community committees or councils at the local level, comprising representatives of local government, in particular local authority mayors, and central government departments. The aims and objectives of these local bodies included: responsibility for fostering the recognition that crime and its prevention concern the whole community and cannot be left to the traditional agencies of social control and law enforcement; the facilitation and co-ordination of local crime prevention projects and the resources and expertise of their members; promoting interest in and awareness of crime prevention at the local level (Grey, 1993). Second, a small crime prevention unit at the central level would facilitate the establishment of the local crime prevention committees, provide information and expert advice on crime prevention, and act as a liaison and a co-ordination mechanism between government departments, local committees and central government.

Between the presentation of the Officials' Committee report in July 1989 and the launch of the pilot scheme in July 1990, a Prime Ministerial Safer Communities Council (PMSCC) was established, based largely upon the example of the Conseil National de Prévention de la Délinquance (CNPD) but with a notable difference in its lack of bipartisan membership. The PMSCC would serve two 'political' purposes. First, it would be chaired by the Prime Minister and therefore symbolize the importance the government attached to crime prevention. Second, its membership, including the Ministers of relevant departments (Police, Justice, Local Government, Employment, Education, Housing, Recreation and Sport, Social Welfare and Maori Affairs, and the Crime Prevention Adminis-tration Unit) would aim to minimize the rivalries between government departments.

This 'patch protection' mentality, and the departmental rivalries it reflected, which have been demonstrated elsewhere with international multi-agency crime prevention endeavours (Walters, 1996; Hughes, 1998) was to become an on-going feature of the pilot scheme and the national strategy (and is discussed later in this chapter). In spite of the attempts of the Crime Prevention Administration Unit and other bodies to manage these rivalries and co-ordinate the efforts of a wide range of government departments, the lack of co-ordination and co-operation proved to be a frustrating experience, particularly for local crime prevention efforts (Bradley, unpublished).

The rhetoric that accompanied the launch of the pilot scheme, including the Prime Minister's comment that it was 'a major policy initiative to make New Zealand a safer place',[5] was not matched by the level of funding allocated to it. In total the pilot scheme was to cost the government NZ$290,000 per year (£78,300 sterling) with the pilot expected to run for two years.

With structure, funding, objectives and the location of the admin-istration unit decided, the next step involved identifying the community sites in which the initiative was to be piloted. The attempt to convince local government of the merits of the proposed scheme met with some resistance and cynicism. The Local Government Association regarded crime prevention as a core function of central government and felt that the scheme represented yet another attempt to 'dump' unwanted and under-funded responsibilities on local government and communities.[6]

In spite of the suspicions and concern of local government officials, the Safer Communities Council Pilot Scheme (SCCPS) was launched in July 1990 in four local authority areas: Ashburton, Christchurch, Manukau and Wairoa. In launching this pilot scheme the Prime Minister outlined the major principles underpinning the approach to crime prevention that the pilot scheme represented. Among them were the notions of partnership, co-ordination, co-operation and an inter-agency approach, community empowerment and local solutions to local problems.[7]

The 1990 pilot scheme represented an important phase in the evolu-tion of community crime prevention. The four Safer Community Councils (SCCs) that made up the pilots, by comparison with the later 'institu-tionalized' SCCs, were given much freedom to pursue their own crime prevention agendas. The combined result was that the pilot SCCs were allowed a remarkable amount of discretion and autonomy in creating and implementing their own 'homespun' versions of crime prevention.

Implementing and managing a nationwide crime prevention strategy

The Labour government that launched the pilot Safer Community Council crime prevention programme was voted out of office in 1990 and the new conservative government, headed by the Prime Minister, Jim Bolger, expressed reservations about a crime policy that was conceived by a previous administration. In a confidential minute sheet prepared by the manager of the Crime Prevention Administration Unit, Colin Hicks, to the Secretary of Justice, he states:

> It is clear that there is nervousness about seeming to adopt a programme that was essentially the initiative of the previous government, and does not find favour with at least one member of the Cabinet . . . Fiscal restraints will tend to relegate the programme to the 'barely existing' category . . . The Prime Minister does not intend to mention the Safer Communities programme at the Crime Prevention week launch on Monday 8 April next. If asked any questions he will tend to be evasive.[8]

The review of the pilot programme produced several criticisms. It reported that few programmes emerging from the pilot scheme were focused on crime prevention: instead the emphasis had shifted to 'community safety'; that the pilot lacked political commitment, noting that the Prime Ministerial Council had met only once; that departmental input across government was lacking (notably from the police); that government resources were clearly inadequate, that local councils found raising funds for crime prevention very difficult and that the pilot scheme had not successfully involved local Maori (Grey, 1993). Whilst these criticisms were noted, the senior policy advisers to the Minister of Justice highlighted the pilot scheme's economical way of promoting crime prevention.

Following the review, Prime Minister Bolger began to refer to a 'new approach' to crime prevention.[9] Not wishing to attribute the innovations of community crime prevention to the previous government, Bolger implemented his own processes of strategic policy management that would provide his government with true 'ownership' of the local crime prevention concept. In doing so he formed the Crime Prevention Action Group (CPAG), a diverse group of civil servants charged with formulating a national crime prevention strategy. The Action Group recommended that a Crime Prevention Unit (CPU) should be established in the Department of the Prime Minister and Cabinet – thus giving it 'clout' and independence from criminal justice agencies. Moreover, using a 'desktop methodology'

(O'Neill, 1993), the CPAG articulated a number of key objectives that would form the cornerstone of the strategy. As a result, a nationwide crime prevention strategy was officially launched in 1994, its mission to 'enhance community safety and security through crime prevention'. The strategy's (DPMC, 1994, p. 5) seven key crime prevention areas were:

1 Supporting families at risk.
2 Reducing family violence.
3 Targeting young people at risk of offending.
4 Minimizing the formal involvement of casual offenders in the criminal justice system.
5 Developing an approach to the management of programmes that addresses the misuse and abuse of both alcohol and drugs.
6 Addressing the incidence of white-collar crime.
7 Addressing the concerns of victims and potential victims.

These objectives are operationalized through the increasing number of Safer Community Councils. In September 2000 there were sixty-five, each accountable to a sponsor (local government) and each having a crime plan approved and monitored by the central government's Crime Prevention Unit.

Duncan (unpublished) argues that the councils have had difficulty devising and implementing plans that address all the above objectives (notably white-collar crime); instead the crime prevention strategy has overwhelmingly focused on problems associated with young people. Indeed, the Labour Prime Minister, Helen Clark, has reiterated the crime prevention strategy's philosophy of 'local solutions to local problems' and that the 'burden' of crime is the responsibility of local people. Moreover she emphasizes that young people have been the targets of crime prevention strategies. She states:

> The main challenge for communities burdened with crime lies not in punishing the criminals, but in preventing casual offenders – especially young people – from becoming further involved in crime. That is where SCCs have focused their efforts and proved their value. (DPMC, 2000, p. 3)

Intergovernment partnerships

In New Zealand, in common with its European and North American counterparts, the effective co-ordination of the crime prevention activities of government constitutes one of two key components informing the implementation of the national crime prevention strategy. However, as Boston et al. (1996, pp. 134–5) point out, 'ensuring good policy co-ordination is one of the hardest tasks of public management'. This is especially true of New Zealand, given the 'departmentalism' (Martin, 1991, pp. 123–36) and the 'silo mentality' that resulted from the reinvention of the state and the public sector in the mid to late 1980s. Specifically the State Sector and Public Finance Acts 1988 emphasized the 'vertical' relationship between the departmental chief executives and government Ministers at the expense of the 'horizontal' or lateral relations between departments and the collective interests of government as a whole. Logan (1991) has argued that this shift in bureaucratic culture and management proved deleterious to interdepartmental collaboration and co-ordination of resources. The government responded to the apparent lack of strategic planning and intragovernmental collaboration by introducing departmental contracts, which introduced the concepts of 'strategic result areas' and 'key result areas'. These concepts provide a legal mandate by which chief executives of the different departments are expected to attain specific objectives through strategic outputs.

To facilitate greater departmental co-ordination and to improve the strategic nature of the Crime Prevention Strategy, Prime Minister Jim Bolger established two significant bodies in 1994: the Chief Executive's Crime Prevention Group (CECPG) and the Strategic Crime Prevention Co-ordinating Group (SCPCG). The former comprised a group of senior civil servants with the purpose of facilitating intersectoral collaboration. The latter body (SCPCG) consisted of about twenty-five senior policy managers from across the public sector and provided a forum for crime prevention policy development. In spite of these two senior bodies, co-ordination, and the more difficult task of collaboration, remained problematic. A 1995 organizational review prepared by a consultant and former Justice Ministry official described the operations of CECPG as 'key agencies where a protection of boundary mentality still exists' (Smith, 1995, p. 8).

The 'silo' and 'patch protection' mentality continues to cause difficulties in the co-ordination and collaboration of government crime prevention policy and service delivery. During a round of interviews with members of the CECPG a common theme that emerged involved the importance and overriding priority given to the 'core business' of the department or Ministry. The representative of the Department of Social Welfare suggested that cross-government co-ordination is inherently problematic, with the comment that 'boundary issues are inevitable with organizational arrangements as they are, that is, government departments with specific areas of responsibility that can involve attempts at cost shifting as well as patch protection'. Moreover this senior group of executives struggled to come to terms with what was meant by co-ordination. As one member stated, 'this [co-ordination] is not well understood or known. Defining effective co-ordination requires a focus on results rather than on process alone and is yet to develop.'

In a similar fashion to crime prevention experience in Australia (see Presdee and Walters, 1997), this group of senior executives was arguably one of the most powerful, in an organizational sense, to come together in

New Zealand, yet the influence that such a group could exert was never harnessed by the CPU. Its meetings were regularly convened but lacked substance, its mandate was ill defined and its function ambiguous. As a result its purpose has become less significant (downsized and attached to the Justice Ministry) and in its place the bureaucrats of crime prevention have focused on the 'community' as the most effective way to implement the national strategy.

Local and community partnerships

The attempt to co-ordinate the activities of government agencies at the local/community level has been similarly problematic. A *Results-centred Evaluation of Safer Community Councils* (Hamilton, 1999) identified a number of problems and inconsistencies in the role, active participation and collaboration of government agencies. For example, the report pointed out that 'police representatives vary in their reaction to a multi-agency environment. While some appreciate the breadth and additional perspective it can bring to their work, others can be frustrated and feel that the SCC adds little value' (*ibid.*, p. 19). Furthermore the report concludes that, while some social welfare agencies in some instances had taken a lead in identifying a crime problem or played an active part in an inter-agency initiative, 'this more active involvement of social service agencies was unusual' (*ibid.*, p. 20). Other explanations for the unrealized co-ordination potential were that while an agency might have crime prevention objectives 'few could actually articulate them and fewer had sought to align them with the SCC or to achieve them in this context' (*ibid.*, p. 20). Overall, Hamilton concludes:

> On the basis of this research, this co-ordination does not emerge strongly at the local level. On balance, there is little clarity as to the sole agency and multi-agency roles of SCC members. This applies in particular to social service agencies . . . while there are successful joint projects and the development of new channels of communication, the achievements of SCC as regards co-ordination fall short of sustained collaboration. (*Ibid.*, p. 24)

Moreover, local crime prevention co-coordinators express widespread frustration with the lack of multi-agency participation, and the inadequacies of financial and administrative support for the delivery of local crime prevention initiatives. There is increasing cynicism about the role of Safer Community Councils and the commitment of central government. As one local crime prevention co-ordinator stated:

> The Government just wants to be able to say that Safer Community Councils are out there doing this and that, so the more they are

advertised, it's a bit like the more the Safer Community Councils exist, the more the model is succeeding. So it doesn't matter that you're not doing crime prevention work as long as you're in the local rag, as long as you get your photo in the paper, then you're doing well. When I read that *Crime Prevention News* [CPU official publication] I just think it's rubbish, it's just crap.

Whilst Safer Community Councils have been instrumental in funding or supporting dozens of local programmes or agencies, many of these 'initiatives' are existing programmes recycled as 'crime prevention' or community safety to receive top-up funding. Furthermore, local people are not aware of the existence of Safer Community Councils. A 1997 survey conducted in Wellington reported that 87 per cent of respondents were unaware of the existence of the Wellington Safer Community Council, which emphasizes the lack of profile and publicity afforded to the local crime prevention model and lack of citizen participation (Wellington City Council, 1997).

Funding and evaluation

Funding for the community crime prevention strategy in the 1999/2000 budget rose to NZ$5.9 million (or £1.7 million sterling) (DPMC, 1999); however, this amount is small when compared with the NZ$867 million (£251 million) allocated to the police. Coupled with a paucity of funding has been the lack of evaluation research. During 1996 the English criminologist, Adam Crawford, was flown to New Zealand by the Ministry of Justice to write a consultancy paper on the development of the crime prevention strategy. During his closely monitored 'tour', which was prepared by the government, Crawford noted the lack of evaluation and recommended that the entire strategy should be reviewed for future developments. He drew up a list of searching questions that should be included in such an exercise. The extensive review he proposed has not materialized. Instead there have been a number of piecemeal research projects focused on evaluating strategic results and not reductions in crime or increases in community safety (see Hamilton, 1999) or government-funded research that has focused on 'selected' projects (Hungerford et al., 1999; Shepherd and Maxwell, 1999).

General discussion

The institutionalization of community crime prevention

What we have described above is an example of a 'state'-managed crime prevention strategy where the community comprises the regulatory object of governance. Its origins are a haphazard and politically naive policy. Its manifestation was a response not to a growing crime problem or the failures of the criminal justice system, or to grassroots/community demand for input into crime prevention decision-making, but to an emerging neo-liberal ideology and political opportunism. However, its fluid origins became unsatisfactory for a government driven by the New Right and, as a result, crime prevention was reinvented in 1993 as a 'new approach': one that emphasized the strategic nature of crime prevention and community safety and focused on the management of mission statements, strategic result areas and outputs, where the reduction of crime was hoped for as a by-product.

We argue that the crime prevention strategy has become institutionalized within national crime control policy. It remains cost-effective, it appeals to all political parties, it devolves responsibility away from politicians and government officials and, because of its low profile within criminal justice, little is expected of it in terms of reducing crime and enhancing public safety. Provided that the Crime Prevention Unit and the national strategy maintain an image of efficient and accountable management and are able to demonstrate the fulfilment of strategic objectives, the strategy is seen as an effective crime policy. As Pollitt (1993, p. 1) has argued, managerialism is driven by 'the seldom tested assumption that better management will prove an effective solvent for a wide range of economic and social ills'. This definition is relevant to crime prevention. It is a technology of governance that attempts to empower local actors whilst at the same time being monitored and regulated at a distance. As Pavlich cogently argues when describing the New Zealand model,

> It is chiefly through management techniques in the context of a neo-liberal (corporate) vision of government (such as devolution, accountability, central control of funding, co-ordination and centralized strategic planning) that the crime prevention measures are deployed in local 'community' contexts. (1999, p. 116)

Partnerships and policy management

Performance indicators or outputs are frequently the criteria for determining or measuring success. The distinction between 'output' and 'outcome' becomes important when understanding the nature and content of accountability mechanisms as well as the managerialization of community crime prevention. As Crawford (1998, p. 182), notes:

> 'Outputs' often refer to internally defined organisational goals over which organisations have considerable control. These may depart significantly from 'outcomes', the effect of an output, or set of outputs, on the wider community. There is a danger that 'outputs' may take precedence

over 'outcomes' and that the gulf between the two may grow larger, so those social goals are eclipsed by organisational goals.

The crime prevention strategy is clearly output-driven. Indeed, the most impressive aspect of the New Zealand crime prevention model is its administration of policy. It has become a template for criminal justice administrators in other jurisdictions wishing to embark upon a community crime prevention model premised on New Public Management principles of efficiency, effectiveness, devolution and contracting for delivery. The managerial culture that has developed under neo-liberal conditions is one of risk management (O'Malley, 1996). The efficient management of the crime prevention strategy (contractual agreements, community crime profiles, standardized reporting requirements and so on) ensures that risk, in a policy failure sense and not in a crime sense, is efficiently managed. This is a central feature of the 'new regulatory state' (Braithwaite, 2000), where the 'steering process' of policy development is clearly demarcated from the 'rowing process' of implementation in what is now recognized as a fundamental aspect of 'governing at a distance' (Miller and Rose, 1990). Or, as Rose has suggested, the advanced liberal government is characterized by the state as 'partner, animator and facilitator for a variety of independent agents and powers, and should exercise only limited powers of its own, steering and regulating rather than rowing and providing' (2000, pp. 323–4).

We argue that in New Zealand preventing crime is a subsidiary goal to effective policy management. If crime is prevented, and if communities are made safer, all well and good, but first and foremost the crime prevention strategy must be an efficient and inexpensively devolved crime policy. In doing so, it relies heavily on individual participation, whether by public sector officials, or private citizens, to mobilize resources in local areas to implement crime prevention plans (Bradley, unpublished). The Department of the Prime Minister and Cabinet contracts community groups to act as 'providers' of crime prevention. Consistent with the new order of public management, all governments become partners in crime prevention through strategic arrangements that require the delivery of specific crime prevention outputs. The Crime Prevention Unit has spent much time over the past six years convincing departments such as Education, Health, Housing, and Maori Affairs that crime prevention should become one of their 'strategic result areas'. Having managed to 'sign up' these departments, effective crime prevention co-ordination and collaboration have not been achieved. Instead these departments 'use' crime prevention as an opportunity to seek extra funds for their own organizational ends.

Moreover the rhetoric of 'partnerships' at the local level has been a central feature of the neo-liberal crime prevention strategy. Discourses on multi-agency crime prevention have yielded a substantial body of critical scholarship (Gilling, 1994; Crawford and Jones, 1995; Hughes, 1996; Walters, 1996). All the problems of multi-agency crime prevention, whether at the governmental or the local level, have been experienced in New Zealand. Indeed the reported pitfalls of multi-agency models – including agency protection, inadequate resources, dominant agencies and groups, and the 'lolly scramble' for funds – have been exacerbated by a neo-liberal crime policy that is so strategically sophisticated on paper with corporate-speak that it has failed to provide the necessary direction in commonsense language for the local agencies which are expected to form partnerships and implement crime prevention.

This overly strategic approach has paralysed the ability of local agencies to deliver crime prevention. The outputs are so specific that local agencies, in many instances, can offer only verbal support to the corporate accountabilities required by central government. Therefore notions of capacity-building through government sponsorship remain political rhetoric. This, coupled with inadequate funding, has meant that any achievements thus far are arguably attributable to widespread 'voluntarization'. In other words, we would argue, the positive spin-offs of community crime prevention endeavours are the result of unpaid personnel or those working beyond their employment expectations to see things change and not of the highly acclaimed strategic approach to crime prevention. Herein lies a fundamental problem with neo-liberal community crime prevention models of devolved responsibility – the human element (see Tilley, 1993; Presdee and Walters, 1997). It includes those people at the grass roots who work tirelessly without the support they require and eventually withdraw or are burnt out by the burdens that come with implementing local plans without the necessary infrastructure.

Hence the 'technologies of prudentialism' (O'Malley, 1992) that devolve responsibility for safety and security to individuals and local organizations are ultimately counterproductive. They have the potential to alienate and divide local groups through models that promote competitiveness and not collaboration. However, the not-for-profit or community agencies find themselves contractually bound by central government to develop and deliver. Multi-agency crime partnership under neo-liberal conditions inculcates voluntary participation under the guise of empowerment and partnership, yet displaces responsibility via contractual arrangements in what is now referred to as 'contracting for community responsibility' (McMillan, 1998). Community and voluntary groups are legally obliged to act as 'service providers' to a central government which becomes the fee-paying client.

Conclusion

Community crime prevention has become institutionalized within political rhetoric and criminal justice policy. To critique it at a political level is to challenge the underlying neo-liberal rationalities that comprise the cornerstone of contemporary public policy. Whilst it remains fiscally inexpensive, strategically sophisticated, focused on objectives and not outcomes, and devolved to local agencies and groups, it will remain appealing to all political parties. Should community crime prevention experience a tenfold increase in government monies, we argue that it may receive increased and irrefutable political scrutiny and criticism. In a political sense, it currently remains an innocuous, low-risk and low-priority policy, yet important for demonstrating the strategic achievements of a neo-liberal enterprise. The well-coined 'amorphous' nature of crime prevention has become its greatest strength in a political sense. Its diverse and ambiguous manifestations have compromised the challenges that may come its way. Unlike the policies on health, housing and employment, crime prevention offers a unique example of 'window dressing' – of a government seeming to be doing something about issues of public concern but simply providing an exercise in devolved state management with isolated examples of crime reduction and enhanced community safety.

Notes

1 Minutes of meeting with Minister of Justice, 5 February 1988.
2 David Oughton, Secretary of Justice, 'Initiatives in Crime Prevention', Department of Justice briefing paper to the Minister of Justice, 4 April 1988.
3 Interview with former Prime Minister Geoffrey Palmer, Wellington, 10 July 1996.
4 Interview with former Minister of Justice Bill Jeffries, Wellington, 13 May 1997.
5 Geoffrey Palmer, speech to launch the Prime Ministerial Safer Communities Council, Manukau City Chambers, 12 July 1990, p. 1.
6 Interview with G. Geering, ex-mayor of Ashburton and former president of the Local Government Commission, Ashburton, 26 March 1998.
7 Interview with Geoffrey Palmer, n. 3 above.
8 C. Hicks, 'Prime Ministerial Safer Communities Council', Confidential Minute Sheet, Crime Prevention and Administration unit, Department of Justice, Wellington, 5 April 1991.
9 J. Bolger, 'Crime Prevention: a new approach', written correspondence from the Rt. Hon. J.B. Bolger, Prime Minister of New Zealand, to the manager of the Crime Prevention and Administration Unit, Department of the Prime Minister and Cabinet, dated 30 March (1993).

References

Beck, U. (1992) *Risk Society: Towards a New Modernity*, London, Sage.
Boston, J., Martin, J., Pallot, J. and Walsh, P. (1991) *Reshaping the State: New Zealand's Bureaucratic Revolution*, Auckland, Auckland University Press.
Boston, J., Martin, J., Pallot, J. and Walsh, P. (1996) *Public Management: The New Zealand Model*, Auckland, Oxford University Press.

Bradley, T. (unpublished) 'The Politics of Crime Prevention and Community Safety in New Zealand', PhD Dissertation, Victoria University of Wellington.

Braithwaite, J. (2000) 'The new regulatory state and the transformation of criminology', *British Journal of Criminology*, vol. 40, no. 2.

Castles, F., Gerritsen, R. and Vowles, J. (1996) *The Great Experiment: Labour Parties and Public Policy Transformation in Australia and New Zealand*, Auckland, Auckland University Press.

Crawford, A. (1997) *A Report on the New Zealand Safer Community Councils. Prepared for the Strategic Responses to Crime Group of the Ministry of Justice*, Wellington, Ministry of Justice.

Crawford, A. (1998) *Crime Prevention and Community Safety: Politics, Policies and Practices*, London, Longman.

Crawford, A. and Jones, M. (1995) 'Inter-agency co-operation and community-based crime prevention: some reflections on the work of Pearson and colleagues', *British Journal of Criminology*, vol. 35, no. 1, pp. 17–33.

Department of the Prime Minister and Cabinet (1994) *The New Zealand Crime Prevention Strategy*, Wellington, Crime Prevention Unit.

Department of the Prime Minister and Cabinet (1999) *Crime Prevention News*, Magazine of the Crime Prevention Unit, Wellington, Department of the Prime Minister and Cabinet.

Department of the Prime Minister and Cabinet (2000) 'Message from the Prime Minister, Rt Hon Clark, H.', *Crime Prevention News*, Wellington.

Douglas, M. (1992) *Risk and Blame*, London, Routledge.

Duncan, A. (unpublished) 'Youth Crime and its Prevention in New Zealand', PhD Dissertation, Victoria University of Wellington.

Easton, B. (ed.) (1989) *The Making of Rogernomics*, Auckland, Auckland University Press.

Feeley, M. and Simon, J. (1992) 'The new penology: notes on the emerging strategy of corrections and its implications,' *Criminology*, vol. 30, no. 4, pp. 449–74.

Foucault, M. (1977) 'Nietzsche, genealogy, history' in Bouchard, D. (ed.) *Language, Counter-memory, and Practice*, Ithaca, NY, Cornell University Press.

Foucault, M. (1978) 'Governmentality' in Burchell, G. and Gordon, C. (eds) *The Foucault Effect: Studies in Government Rationality*, Hemel Hempstead, Harvester Wheatsheaf.

Garland, D. (1997) '"Governmentality" and the problem of crime: Foucault, criminology, sociology', *Theoretical Criminology*, vol. 1, no. 2, pp. 173–214.

Gilling, D. (1994) 'Multi-agency crime prevention in Britain: the problem of combining situational and social strategies' in Clarke, R. (ed.) *Crime Prevention Studies*, vol. 3, New York, Criminal Justice Press.

Grey, A. (1993) *An Evaluation of the Safer Communities Council Pilot Scheme*, Wellington, Grey Matter Research.

Hamilton, J. (1999) *Results-centred Evaluation of Safer Community Councils*, Wellington, Hamilton Miller Partnership.

Henderson, D. (1999) *The Changing Fortunes of Economic Liberalism: Yesterday, Today and Tomorrow*, Wellington, Institute of Public Affairs.

Hood, C. (1990) 'De-Sir Humphreyfying the Westminster model of bureaucracy: a new style of governance?', *Governance*, vol. 3, pp. 205–14.

Hughes, G. (1996) 'Strategies of crime prevention and community safety in contemporary Britain', *Studies on Crime and Crime Prevention*, vol. 5, no. 2, pp. 221–44.

Hughes, G. (1998) *Understanding Crime Prevention: Social Control, Risk and Late Modernity*, Buckingham, Open University Press.

Hungerford, R., Hutchings, L., Robertson, N., Evans, I. Hamilton, H. and Moeke-Pickering, T. (1999) *'Safer Streets': Neighbourhood-based Demonstration Project*, Department of Psychology, University of Waikato.

Jesson, B. (1999) *Only their Purpose is Mad: The Money Men Take Over New Zealand*, Palmerston North, Dunmore Press.

Kelsey, J. (1995) *The New Zealand Experiment: A World Model for Structural Adjustment?*, Auckland, Auckland University Press.

Kettle, D. (2000) *The Global Public Management Revolution: A Report on the Transformation of Governance*, Washington, DC, Brookings Institution.

Logan, B. (1991) *Review of State Sector Reforms*, Wellington State Services Commission.

Martin, J. (1991) 'Remaking the state services' in Holland, M. and Boston, J. (eds) *The Fourth Labour Government: Politics and Policy in New Zealand*, Auckland, Oxford University Press.

McMillan, K. (1998) 'Contracting for Community Responsibility: Purchase of Service-contracting and the Delivery of Ethnic Social Services in New Zealand', Australian Conference of Political Science, 27–30 September.

Miller, P. and Rose, N. (1990) 'Governing economic life', *Economy and Society*, vol. 19, no. 1, pp. 1–30.

New Zealand Treasury (1984) *Economic Management*, Wellington, Government Printer.

New Zealand Treasury (1987) *Government Management*, vols I and II, Wellington, Government Printer.

Officials' Committee on Crime Prevention (1989) *The Report of the Officials' Committee on Crime Prevention*, Cabinet Social Equity Committee, SEQ 89 M3/5, Wellington.

O'Malley, P. (1992) 'Risk, power and crime prevention', *Economy and Society*, vol. 21, no. 3, pp. 252–75.

O'Malley, P. (1996) 'Risk and responsibility' in Barry, A., Osborne, T. and Rose, N. (eds) *Foucault and Political Reason*, Chicago, IL, University of Chicago Press.

O'Malley, P. (1997) 'The politics of crime prevention' in O'Malley, P. and Sutton, A. (eds) *Crime Prevention in Australia: Issues in Policy and Practice*, Sydney, Federation Press.

O'Malley, P. (ed.) (1998) *Crime and the Risk Society*, Aldershot, Ashgate.

O'Neill, R. (1993) 'Crime prevention strategies: the New Zealand model', *Social Policy Journal of New Zealand*, no. 1, pp. 17–30.

Oughton, D. (1994) 'Background notes on the New Zealand crime prevention strategy', presented at the 'Round Table on Violence Prevention', Asia-Pacific issues for the ninth United Nations Crime Congress, Adelaide, Australia.

Pavlich, G. (1999) 'Preventing crime: social versus community governance in Aetearoa/New Zealand' in Smandych, R. (ed.) *Governable Places: Readings on Governmentality and Crime Control*, Aldershot, Ashgate.

Pollitt, C. (1993) *Managerialism and the Public Services*, Oxford, Blackwell.

Pratt, J. and Treacher, P. (1988) 'Law and order and the 1987 New Zealand election', *Australian and New Zealand Journal of Criminology*, vol. 21, pp. 253–68.

Presdee, M. and Walters, R. (1994) *Policies and Practices of Preventing Crime: A*

Review of the South Australian Crime Prevention Strategy, Melbourne, National Centre for Socio-legal Studies.

Presdee, M. and Walters, R. (1997) 'Policies, politics and practices: crime prevention in South Australia' in O'Malley, P. and Sutton, A. (eds) *Crime Prevention in Australia: Issues in Policy and Practice*, Sydney, Federation Press.

Rhodes, R. (1994) 'The hollowing out of the state: the changing nature of the public service in Britain', *Political Quarterly Review*, no. 65, pp. 137–41.

Rhodes, R. (1997) *Understanding Governance: Policy Networks, Governance, Reflexivity and Accountability*, Milton Keynes, Open University Press.

Roper, C. (1987) *Report of the Ministerial Inquiry into Violence* (Roper Report), Wellington, Government Printer.

Rose, N. (1996) 'Governing advanced liberal democracies' in Bary, A., Osborne, T. and Rose, N. (eds) *Foucault and Political Reason*, London, UCL Press.

Rose, N. (2000) 'Government and control', *British Journal of Criminology*, vol. 40, pp. 321–39.

Schick, A. (1996) *Spirit of Reform: Managing the New Zealand State Sector in a Time of Change*, Wellington, State Services Commission.

Shepherd, P. and Maxwell, G. (1999) *Evaluation of the Child and Young Person's Support Worker Demonstration Project*. Institute of Criminology, Victoria University of Wellington.

Simon, J. (1987) 'The emergence of a risk society: insurance, law, and the state', *Socialist Review*, vol. 95, pp. 61–89.

Smandych, R. (ed.) (1999) *Governable Places: Readings on Governmentality and Crime Control*, Aldershot, Ashgate.

Smith, M. (1995) *Review of the Role, Functions and Location of the Crime Prevention Unit: Report to Chief Executive Department of Prime Minister and Cabinet*, consultant's report, August.

Taylor, F.W. (1916) 'The principles of scientific management' in Shafritz, J. and Ott, S. (eds) (1992) *Classics of Organization Theory*, Belmont, CA, Brooks Cole.

Tilley, N. (1993) 'Crime prevention and the safer cities story', *Howard Journal*, vol. 32, pp. 40–57.

Walters, R. (1996) 'The "dream" of multi-agency crime prevention: pitfalls in policy and practice' in Homel, R. (ed.) *The Politics and Practice of Situational Crime Prevention*, New York, Criminal Justice Press.

Wellington City Council (1997) *1997–1999 Strategic Plan Community Safety Survey*, 8 September, Wellington, Wellington City Council.

Willemse, H. (1994) 'Developments in Dutch crime prevention' in Clarke, R. (ed.) *Crime Prevention Studies*, vol. 2, New York, Criminal Justice Press.

World Economic Forum (1993) *World Competitiveness Report*, Lausanne, International Institute for Management Development.

Towards a replacement discourse on community safety

Lessons from the Netherlands

René van Swaaningen

There is no subject criminologists currently publish so much about as crime prevention and community safety. There is, however, also no criminological field where we can find so many tedious, uncritical and empiricist studies. In the Dutch case there are hundreds of very similar reports that share an administrative orientation or evaluate something on extremely vague criteria (van Swaaningen and Blad, 1999). Discontent with this situation has been the primary impulse for trying to approach this field of research in a different way. Let us start with a rather obvious question. What is 'wrong' with the current development of community safety politics and how can it be 'improved'? The answer to the first part of the question is a critique of community safety. The second part is answered with an alternative discourse.

Such an approach is called a 'replacement discourse'. It fulfils a similar function to 'sensitizing concepts' in sociology, used to raise awareness about an issue which is neglected in research, but about which we are as yet unable to develop a full-fledged theory. Abolitionist criminologists have used a replacement discourse in their claims for a 'criminal' justice system based on redress rather than retribution. They avoid the penal law glossary because it pre-structures penal reactions. Speaking in other terms about criminalized problems opens our eyes to other solutions (Hughes, 1998, p. 123). A replacement discourse carries both empirical and normative elements. It follows empirical developments, but does not consider these as 'facts' that cannot be changed.

The concepts of 'crime prevention' and 'community safety' are seldom defined very clearly. Definitions are either tautological or they just describe the kind of measures they relate to (Crawford, 1998, pp. 6–11; Hughes, 1998, p. 18). Here we refer to all measures and policies that seek to increase public safety and are oriented at the social context in which crime emerges rather than at the punishment of offenders. These measures and policies can be of an individual, situational or structural kind, and are carried out by a multitude of different social, administrative and criminal justice agencies. The difference between 'crime prevention' and 'community safety' is that the first aims to bring crime rates down, and the second is oriented at increasing public (feelings of) safety.

The replacement discourse starts with an analysis of the Dutch politics of community safety. The critique of this development focuses around the question: has the politics of community safety made criminal justice more social or has it rather made social policy more punitive? Let me give the answer straight away: it has done both. The really interesting point is to see how and why this has happened and how the situation could be changed. For this purpose we distinguish two Weberian ideal types, two orientations in community safety that can be witnessed at the same time: an actuarial and a structural approach. The first embodies a pragmatic, administrative and instrumentalist way of thinking about crime prevention in terms of risk management, the latter a more structural, social orientation on community safety in relation to wider social policies on housing, education, the labour market, welfare and suchlike. The former often implies an exclusive vision of social control, the latter an inclusive one.

The alternative vision of community safety takes social justice as a normative touchstone. This implies a plea for a fair distribution of social provision and care for the quality of life over all segments of society. Though it certainly carries utopian components, the replacement discourse is not purely idealistic in the sense that it would recommend things that have no link with the material practice of community safety. We will realistically investigate how those elements of this policy that have a potential to make criminal justice more social can be stressed, and how those elements that make general social work derail into yet another agent of punitive social control which excludes deviants from society can be minimized. The chapter concludes with a checklist of pitfalls and potentials in this respect.

A new perspective in crime control?

The discourse and politics of community safety may have taken a different form in different countries, but they respond to similar political arguments, public sentiments and social developments. They have also emerged around more or less the same time: from the mid-1970s to the mid-1980s. Their rapid growth cannot be understood without paying attention to the growing importance, in the media and in politics, of the victim, the 'fear of crime' debate and the notion of 'protection of the public'. The paradoxical relation between, on the one hand, concern about high levels of street crime and decreasing confidence that the problem can be tackled by punitive measures, on the other, also plays a significant role. Is crime prevention and (the obsession with) safety thus a very specific feature of the late modern era? Since the emergence of the modern school in the penal sciences of 1880s Europe – in which positivist criminological ideas were applied to the classical legal doctrine – criminal law has always connected its fate to a large extent with the prevention of crime (van Swaaningen, 1997, pp. 29–49; Hughes, 1998, pp. 25–57). Punishing an offender means that not only s/he but other potential criminals are deterred. Criminal law and social policy now develop in close connection. David Garland (1985) has called this a penal welfare complex, in which the threat of penal sanctions and preventive social policy are combined into one strategy of care and control. The emergence of the penal welfare complex in the 1880s was also based on widespread concern about the increase in crime and the impotence of the penal system to do anything about it. So neither the idea of prevention, nor the multi-agency approach, nor the primary motives to introduce these, are all that new.

In the modern penal system, welfare programmes were oriented to care for and control of the individual offender. This development culminated in the 1970s, when welfare approaches made a major mark on the penal field. With respect to its orientation and its objects of control, crime prevention *does* imply something new. In the new preventive setting of the twenty-first century the penal welfare system is no longer primarily oriented at individual offenders, but at profiling and monitoring suspect situations and 'risk groups'. Nowadays social intervention takes place *before* a specific criminal act has happened. Here it breaks with the tradition of classical criminal law, which is by definition an after-the-fact approach, based on the establishment of individual guilt.

In the mid-1980s criminal justice bifurcated into a punitive and exclusive system on the one hand and a more social and inclusive one on the other. Today we can hardly speak of 'the' criminal justice system any more. In fact we have two very different systems of crime control. The first continues along the same line of thought as the classical criminal justice system, albeit that both its rule of law and its welfare rationale are given a less prominent place and the punitive, retributive aspects are stressed more than before. In the second system the penal welfare model is continued, though it functions in a new pragmatic rationale of risk management, rather than in a model of moral condemnation and punishment. Today's hyper-incarceration of economically superfluous people is the strongest metaphor of the first system. Community safety symbolizes the rationale of the second system. This 'new' penal welfare system is a pragmatic response to the predicament that crime rates could not be brought down by the traditional penal means. The 'old' penal system's obsession with long and tough prison sentences involves, on a symbolic level, a denial of the predicament that 'prison does not work'. On an instrumental level it provides a place where people who cannot be fitted into a 'free country' of consumer choice can be warehoused (Garland, 2000).

Most welfare elements have been removed from the penal system because the misplaced 'pampering' of criminals, it would imply, was seen to lower the deterrent function of punishment. An argument against the penal welfare model in the modern, twentieth-century criminal law setting coming from the progressive side was that it would widen the net of social control (Cohen, 1985). Can we also apply this net-widening critique to the new penal welfare model of crime prevention and community safety? To some extent, it can be done with even more justice than before. The new penal welfare provisions are installed even deeper in society than the community sanctions that Stan Cohen aimed his shafts at. In this sense, his idea of a 'punitive city' is closer than ever. For this reason, quite a number of scholars are rather sceptical about community safety politics as well (Crawford, 1998; Goris, 2000). Mike Davis's (1998) analyses of the current 'punitive city' and the destruction of public space in Los Angeles lend substantial support to such pessimistic thinking.

In Davis's scenario the rich have entrenched themselves in 'gated communities' for protection against an increasing group of severely policed new 'dangerous classes' of (mainly) African-Americans and Hispanics who live in the 'urban third worlds' of the city. These are useful warnings – roads we should not take if we strive for social justice. But they do not necessarily lead us to reject community safety altogether. First, it is debatable whether the 'preventive' form of self-defence of white, rich and often elderly people against young, poor, black people that Davis describes is actually widening the *penal* net. This form of technology-driven social segregation is, furthermore, not *all* there is to community safety, and Los Angeles is a different place from the average European city. Moreover, we have to admit that the prioritization of social policy over penal intervention, and of prevention over repression, follows from many, not least 'critical', criminological studies. Abolitionists have always stressed the potential of community solutions to crime, and left realists have vigorously pushed a multi-agency approach (Hughes, 1998, pp. 118–26). To some extent, both elements are put into practice in the politics of crime prevention and community safety. Next to some undesirable developments in the current politics, there are, moreover, also some elements in the community safety discourse that are worth supporting from a perspective of social justice. The paradox is that the current politics is both an expression of the sheer pragmatic logic of risk management and of a more structural approach to crime.

Crime prevention politics in the Netherlands

The term 'crime prevention', as we currently understand it, figured for the first time in Dutch criminal justice policy plans in 1976. Some years earlier, the process of what we came to call 'the scientific foundation of policy' started. It implies that in a modern, rational society, government policy should also be as rational and transparent as possible. Next to political choices, it should therefore be grounded in (social) scientific research. In this way, criminological research set quite a strong mark on the development of criminal justice politics. The gradual adaptation to the predicament that punishment 'does not work' (as we would like) and the subsequent pragmatic strategies of crime prevention are supported with criminological studies of the shortcomings and counter-effects of penality. In 1976 the Ministry of Justice established a Department of Crime Prevention that collected all the knowledge in this field and made it available to local police forces. Crime prevention advisers at police stations advised the public about better locks and more advanced technological means of protection, and security-marked the public's belongings. This is a first phase in the politics of crime prevention.

A second phase was announced with the 1977 Green Paper *Politie in verandering* (*Changing Police*). This policy plan pointed to the need for a more proactive and a more community-oriented style of policing, based on a decentralized and problem-oriented approach. In the light of this report, a Bill on police crime prevention was adopted in 1979, and a national co-ordinator of crime prevention politics was established. Crime prevention was considered a task that could no longer be performed by the police alone, but warranted co-operation with various services. The first step towards community policing was also taken at the end of the 1970s. But when in the 1980s neo-liberal managerialism became the dominant political rationale the police were thought to be in need of reorganization according to the principles of business management, and many of these 'good intentions' were not implemented for some time.

In a third phase, social work, above all youth work, came to play a more significant role. In 1981 the Rotterdam Halt bureau was established. Halt consists of reparative and pedagogical sanctions for twelve- to eighteen-year-olds who have committed a 'real' offence or some 'incivility'. Its main characteristics are: (1) the sanction should follow as soon as possible after the rule-breaking behaviour; (2) the content of the sanction should relate to the nature of the act; and (3) it should be made clear that it is the act that is being condemned, not the actor. Herewith, elements of 'reintegrative shaming' are said to have been implemented (Hauber, 1999, pp. 263–4). At the same time, Halt represented a merely pragmatic vision of social control, realizing that a consensual 'It's for your own good' approach was more effective than the threat of punishment. Evaluation research – based on relapse rates – shows that Halt is very successful. Its high success rate may, however, also be due to the fact that Halt mainly deals with the ordinary mischief every 'normal' child commits once in a while and not (yet) with violent crimes. In 2000 there were sixty-four Halt bureaux. However, court delays mean that the shorter and simpler Halt procedure is increasingly used in more serious cases that it was not intended for.

Crime prevention really gained momentum in the early 1980s. In 1983 the Roethof Committee on petty crime was set up, after complaints from Parliament that, because of the scale on which they were happening, everyday, petty crimes were considered to be an important element in the deteriorating quality of life. This 'protection of the public' ideology, oriented to increasing social control rather than to punishing offenders, marked a fourth phase in the debate about crime prevention. The 1984 Green Paper on petty crime in the public domain offers some interesting perspectives. It begins by unravelling the idea of petty crime as such. Instead of leaving it as an abstract notion, the committee concentrated on the concrete social context in which problems emerge and differentiated between petty violence and threats, shoplifting, burglary without serious damage, theft of bicycles, vandalism, soccer-related vandalism, illicit use of public transport and minor traffic violations. An important premise of the Roethof Committee was that the waning attachments to institutions like school, Church or family were not being replaced by other forms of social control. People's feelings of communality and solidarity had eroded, whilst the accent on individual autonomy and individual needs became stronger. The committee also noted that the opportunity to commit petty crimes had increased, because of this same atomization and anonymization of social relations, and because in a situation of growing affluence there are simply more goods to steal. The committee accepted that everyday crime was probably also caused by more structural problems – such as unemployment – but declared these beyond its competence, as its terms of reference were about criminal justice and not about socio-economic policy. The Roethof Committee raised awareness of the relation between crime rates and wider social developments, and the idea that petty crime is to be countered primarily by social policy and by a responsibilization of the general public is common currency in the political and public arena.

The Roethof Committee's 1984 Green Paper included a deconstruction of the container-concept of 'crime' into more concrete problems and incivilities and a 'community approach' to crime control that resembles the abolitionist perspective in criminology. Concrete measures were, however, primarily based on notions from attachment and opportunity theory. The committee wanted to stimulate forms of social prevention that revitalize social control in neighbourhoods, at schools and soccer clubs and so on. Social control should come from persons whose normal occupational duties cover a wider field than policing – such as social workers, teachers and sports coaches. Control should not be a separate task but an implicit part of other main activities. The Green Paper also advocated a reorganization of the urban environment in order to create a situation in which people felt safer in public places.

The bifurcation of criminal justice was marked by the 1985 White Paper *Samenleving en Criminaliteit* (*Society and Crime*). The substantial part devoted to community-building and crime prevention served to 'sell' this policy plan to the left. The debate on 'organized crime' – and later on the influx of foreigners – paved the way for the 'tougher' and more punitive measures that the right wanted. *Society and Crime* marks a fifth phase in crime prevention. The 1985 policy plan gave a more administrative and a more moral spin to the Roethof Committee's non-moralizing and slightly more structural recommendations. It focused more on situational prevention and less on informal social control. Whereas the Green Paper 'responsibilized' social agencies (neighbourhoods, schools, sports clubs, etc.), the White Paper stressed the responsibility of the burgomaster (equivalent to a British mayor), the chief of police and the public prosecutor and so transformed crime prevention into a mere question of public order. The community was now portrayed as having once played an important role in informal social control, but as having regrettably been broken down by the 'loony left' in the 1960s. In this way, nostalgic pandering to the traditional pillars of Dutch society in the 1950s was fused with a conservative politics of law and order and a neo-liberal orientation to risk management (van Swaaningen, 1997, pp. 170–90).

The further development of an integral safety policy

The politics of community safety in the 1990s built further on the policy of administrative prevention of the 1980s, to which some more structural *and* some actuarial elements were added. It is remarkable that most of these new initiatives were not taken by the Ministry of Justice but followed from quite separate developments in social policy, child protection and urban planning and fused into the politics of community safety at a later stage. This process was accompanied by the following three factors. First, the idea of 'socialization' (*vermaatschappelijking*) of justice is foregrounded. This means that criminal justice agencies need to be more responsive to public needs and public opinion, and that the community orientation of various criminal justice agencies and the responsibilization of citizens should be intensified. It is the goal of the new initiatives to see to it that, with the scientifically supported rationalization of policy, the criminal justice system does not lose touch with social reality and public opinion. Second, there is increasing concern about a growing number of juveniles who drop out of school and get into trouble with the police. Third, the term 'integral safety policy' (*integraal veiligheidsbeleid*) is launched. Its main implication is that the broader social context of the (petty) crime and safety problem, not yet included in the 1980s crime prevention politics, should now be taken up in a new policy of community safety.

In 1990 the social democrat Minister of the Interior announced a policy of social renewal (*sociale vernieuwing*). It aimed to prevent a further socio-economic split in society by counteracting social deprivation. The fact that the split in society was increasingly marked along ethnic and gender lines led to some specific initiatives, but the overall emphasis is on deprivation. Job creation is thought of as an important means of giving a sense of meaning to people's lives, and also of strengthening their 'crime-preventive' attachment to society. So-called 'job pools' (*banenpools*) and 'youth employment guarantee schemes' (*jeugdwerkgarantieplan*) offer a (small) extra payment above the normal welfare entitlement to those who accept a specific job in the non-profit sector. Most people accept these jobs to break their social isolation or to improve their chances of obtaining a 'real' job, but as such they have a low social status and the financial incentive is also quite marginal. In the security sector, non-profit functions have been specially created for this purpose: for example, ticket inspectors on public transport, 'economized away' in the cost-cutting of the 1970s, have been reintroduced using social renewal money. In the current discourse they are no longer called ticket inspectors, but *VIC-ers* – that is, functionaries for Safety, Information and Control. Their uniformed presence is thought to heighten feelings of safety on public transport.

The system of civic wardens (*stadswacht*) was also introduced on this basis. A civic warden provides assistance and information to people on the street and to the police. Apart from the job creation aspect, it is aimed at increasing community safety and the quality of life – and not solely at protecting the belongings of individuals or shops. Crime prevention may be one of the consequences of increasing surveillance, but it is not included as an explicit evaluation criterion of the city warden system (Hauber, 1999, p. 267). Civic wardens are recruited from the long-term unemployed and receive training in social skills and conflict management. They are uniformed and they are employed and supervised by the city council. Evaluation research shows that people feel safer in areas patrolled by city wardens. Having started with two initiatives in 1989, ten years later more than 100 municipalities have civic wardens (Hauber, 1999, p. 268).

It can be argued that the politics of social renewal incorporated notions from sociological 'strain theory', with an emphasis on relative deprivation as a major cause of crime. For this reason it can be called the sixth phase in the politics of community safety. The politics of social renewal has encountered much ideological and organizational resistance. Christian democrats and liberal conservatives criticized its social democratic ideology. Bureaucratic structures again turned out to be too rigid to be able actually to co-operate with other departments in one policy. Therefore the politics of social renewal was accompanied by an administrative overhaul, which was aimed at breaking the tendency of (local) government services to overregulate, as well as their compartmentalized style of working and the inflexible bureaucratic culture. All the talk now was of 'products', 'trajectories' and 'markets'.

In 1993 the politics of social renewal and of administrative crime prevention were linked together in the Integrated Safety Policy (*integraal veiligheidsbeleid*). A distinction is drawn between primary, secondary and tertiary prevention. In this seventh phase, five departments co-operated in the politics of community safety: the co-ordinating Ministry of the Interior and the Ministries of Justice, Welfare and Employment, Transport and Public Works, and Housing and Environmental Planning. Every year they publish a joint safety report, which contains quantitative surveys of feelings of unsafety and fear of crime. The politics of community safety since then has been oriented less to crime than to public safety. It is supported with victim surveys rather than crime rates – which are now declining. Remarkably absent from this integrated approach to community safety were the Ministries of Social Work and Public Health and of Education, Culture and Science. At the local level, the city council was supposed to ensure that all public services with a role to play in community safety also collaborated. At the local level, welfare organizations and schools were notably included in the safety policy.

Their involvement mainly followed from policy recommendations on juvenile delinquency. By the end of the 1980s youth welfare organizations were being confronted with an increasing number of vagrants and drop-outs from school. Though juvenile delinquency did not increase in absolute terms, police figures indicated that offences committed by juveniles were tending to be of a more serious, more violent nature. In 1994 the van Montfrans Committee on juvenile delinquency presented its report, *Met de neus op de feiten* (*Facing the Facts*). In line with the Integrated Safety Policy, the committee argued that a joint initiative by the police, the public prosecutor's office, the probation service, social work *and* the school system was the only way to counter the problem. Next to this, the van Montfrans Report has also had a major influence on the politics of community safety, because of its focus on risk profiling. Through a new database, the so-called 'client follow' system (*boefjesbank*) – an early warning and early intervention system – was established in potentially criminogenic situations. This system, in which schools played an important role, also served to single out a so-called hard core of serious juvenile delinquents who would receive extra attention of a mixed preventive and repressive nature. Next to this data system, a clear example of actuarial justice is the establishment of special police units to observe Moroccan youths (who are said to be the most notorious troublemakers) hanging around shopping centres and squares. In 2000 the coercive measures the van Montfrans Report proposed seem to prevail. So-called 'systematic offenders' now receive an intensive programme of training, geared to their individual situation. The van Montfrans Report offers a good illustration of the new development in community safety politics, on the one hand more oriented to notions of strain, 'relative deprivation' and 'attachments', but on the other focusing more strongly on risk profiling and singling out risk groups.

In the second half of the 1990s an eighth phase can be distinguished in the politics of community safety, when the idea of 'community' as such became the key focus. After being put on ice for quite some years, community policing was brought back into the limelight. In order to make it clear that within an integral, multi-agency community safety policy, community policing means something different from what it did in the late 1970s, a new name has been invented for the good old local bobby: he or she is now called a neighbourhood director (*buurtregiseur*). Another new policy line on the community is oriented at urban planning and the integration of ethnic minorities. A last policy line in this respect is oriented at mediation in a neighbourhood setting and at so-called 'community justice centres' where, under the supervision of a public prosecutor, various agencies of the criminal justice system work together. In terms of criminological theory, these initiatives are inspired by respectively neo-Chicago school ecology theory and the more recent, subcultural theories, and – next to sheer efficiency arguments – by ideas of restorative justice.

In 1995 the so-called 'Major Cities policy' started. In many ways it is a successor to the social renewal policy. It is based on the acknowledgement that problems of relative deprivation are worst in the major cities. Safety risks with respect to nuisance caused by the presence of a drug scene, or the emergence of deprived neighbourhoods with a majority of ethnic minorities, or of 'black' schools with bigger problems and poorer educational results, are typical of big cities. It is therefore argued that the major cities should receive extra money to tackle these problems. Every city has to draw up an inventory of the kinds of problems it is confronted with and must develop a concrete plan to tackle them if it is to be offered a 'safety covenant' and the extra money that goes with it. There is even a new Ministry of major cities and integration policy whose primary task it is to co-ordinate interministerial activities with respect to deprivation and ethnic relations. An explicit aim of the Major Cities policy is to reclaim the public domain. The coercive elements included in a 1998 Green Paper that specifically deals with Crime in Relation to the Integration of Ethnic Minorities (*CRIEM-nota*) demonstrate, however, that the policy is not 'just' oriented at fighting deprivation. Again, it is a mixed package of structural and actuarial measures.

The present politics of integrated safety looks quite different from the 1980s politics of crime prevention. Nonetheless, no element of that initial policy has been explicitly abandoned. Criminological theories have been drawn upon eclectically to give new policy orientations some scientific credibility. Thus we cannot speak of an actual 'policy theory'. New plans are constantly implemented, or comparable initiatives are suddenly given new names, making the practice of community safety quite untransparent. The competences and responsibilities of the different partners in the safety policy are still not defined clearly. The result is internal conflicts, in which criminal justice-related agencies such as the police or the probation service seem better able to push their priorities through than the social agencies. This 'muddle through' approach leads to incoherent outcomes and lack of direction.

The structural additions to the 1980s prevention politics were introduced to fight deprivation. But once they were fitted into a policy in which situational and individual prevention and risk management are the dominant orientations, they also had to obey a control ideology. An important question in the establishment of a social justice perspective on community safety is thus how happy we should be with the new, integrated orientation of the policy. Would it not be better to reiterate Stan Cohen's (1985) motto about new forms of social control: let us focus on doing less harm rather than on doing more 'good'?

Conditions for a just politics of community safety

If only because in the 1980s the critique of net widening led to 'Nothing works' defeatism and put an end to any restructuring potential that critical criminology may have had, I prefer to continue 'doing more good'. The actuarial rationale of risk management itself, which I see as a major problem with respect to social justice, is also informed by the nihilistic idea that we cannot do any 'good' and should therefore limit ourselves to preventing 'evil'. A utopian, yet realistic, position seems preferable. Without possible utopias our society becomes, in Jürgen Habermas's words, a desert of banality and meaninglessness. Adam Crawford (1998, pp. 260–1) argues, moreover, that with the 'eclipse of the prevention paradigm' the 'penaholic intolerance' will have even less ideological competition and the punishment industry will probably grow even stronger. The idea of replacement discourse is that we need an alternative vision in order to visualize a possible alternative practice.

Crime, risk, nuisance, unsafety, 'broken windows', deprivation, conflicts . . .

The value of 'community safety' is generally taken for granted and rarely questioned. But do we actually know what it is meant to respond to? When in the early 1980s the administrative crime prevention policy was launched as the spearhead of Dutch criminal justice politics the conceptual vagueness of the new policy became immediately clear. To Labour, crime prevention meant a fight against deprivation; to Christian Democrats it implied a new appeal for communitarianism; and for Liberal-conservatives it was to result in technological and situational measures (van Swaaningen, 1995, p. 66). In the case of Belgium, Jean-Marc Piret

(2000, p. 32) has shown how this conceptual vagueness has even allowed the extreme right to hi-jack the term 'community safety' in a plea for zero-tolerance policing. Instead of making a clear political choice, it very much remains a pragmatic 'anything goes' policy.

It is not clear, either, to which kinds of conduct or problems community safety measures are to respond (de Haan, 1999, p. 253). In practice, they deal mainly with different forms of petty street crime and mere incivilities, but it is not clear why this choice is made. There is simply no mention of large-scale disturbances of public order (such as terrorism or riots), organized or political crime or problems in the domestic sphere. Nor is it clear why general issues of livability that do not imply an objective safety risk (e.g. parking on the pavement, graffiti, noise) are included.

Let us assume that improving the quality of life rather than crime prevention or minimizing objective safety risks is the key object of community safety politics. Certainly, in that case, there are good reasons to avoid the term 'crime'. People often use the word as a label for quite general feelings of anxiety, dissatisfaction and irritation. Crime in the legal sense of the word is undeniably part of the problem, but because tackling the crime problem has such a high place on the political agenda, *all* misery tends to be translated in terms of crime. This raises unwarranted expectations of criminal justice. If crime is the problem, the police are one of the responsible agencies to intervene, but if garbage, run-down blocks of flats or violence in schools is the problem, there are other agencies responsible. Such problems should lead to investment in sanitation, maintenance and education rather than in the police.

Feelings of unsafety and the erosion of public space

Community safety politics is supported by surveys of feelings of 'unsafety'. In the context of this chapter I can do little more than point at the problem of the limited reliability of such surveys in general and for more invisible crimes – for example, in the domestic or the economic sphere – in particular. We also know that national figures say very little about the safety problems in a specific (deprived) neighbourhood. The problem starts, however, at the conceptual level: what are feelings of unsafety actually based on? Willem de Haan (1989) has distinguished objective and subjective factors. Objective unsafety consists of things like low levels of employment and welfare, relative deprivation, a high prevalence of violent subcultures and low social cohesion. Subjective unsafety is determined by moral panics, previous victimization, perceived social vulnerability and deteriorating living conditions. This first distinction already indicates how wide-ranging the safety problem is. The question is what does it mean for a just community safety politics? Too limited an approach may miss the point. Too wide-ranging an approach may on the other hand result in a policy built on quicksand.

The first step in the development of an alternative vision of safety consists of deconstruction of the dominant safety discourse. Macrosociological analyses of the 'death of the social', the 'risk society' and the 'erosion of public space' may be of help in this respect. Maybe these analyses can even help us to identify some basic causes of our (current obsession with) fear, risk and safety. Koen Raes (1997) has argued that, in order to feel safe, we must perceive the street as our natural territory. The current social structure, in which we leave our house or office only for a concrete purpose, means that we lock ourselves out of social life. In the information era there are fewer and fewer things we really need to go out into the street for. Consequently, we seldom meet people in an anonymous setting any more and 'the other' becomes a stranger and the city an eerie place.

The reconstruction of the safety debate can well be based on attempts to counter such tendencies. It seems, however, advisable to be as concrete as possible. There are quite simple ways to show that the deeper social developments, or policy decisions in other areas, have consequences for community safety. Let us quote Amsterdam's chief of police, Jelle Kuiper, in this respect:

> In this country we have economized away virtually all informal means of social control. Now we are replacing these with camera surveillance: the worst solution! There is nothing more preventive than the presence of people in the streets. And what do we do? We put a policeman behind a monitor. (*de Groene Amsterdammer*, 26 January 2000, p. 16)

The Major Cities policy is indeed aimed at reclaiming public space. This mainly implies that streets and squares should become so safe that everybody will dare to use them again. But it should also mean that some places have to be reclaimed from the private sector. We need places where we can just freely walk, sit and talk to other people without being 'forced' to buy a drink and without being treated with suspicion if a private security officer thinks we have nothing to spend.

This is just one example. The next step in our reconstruction of the safety debate consists of making a concrete inventory of the different kinds of fears and problems. It is unavoidable that normative judgements are made here. At some point it must be determined what are 'real' problems that should be dealt with and what is mere petty-bourgeois intolerance that people should simply learn to cope with. The questions of who should do so, on what basis, and which agency should intervene, are still open. But, next to formulating concrete responses to concrete problems, a replacement discourse primarily serves to offer an alternative vision of safety that prepares the ground for a different approach.

A boundless system of crime control?

It could be argued that the abolitionists have finally got what they always wanted. In the politics of community safety the crime discourse is finally decriminalized. It is, however, a somewhat ambivalent gain. There are indeed analytical and practical advantages in talking about concrete problems rather than about a globalizing social construction such as crime. But the fact that it is not made crystal-clear which practices and problems community safety politics is to respond to has also led to a certain boundlessness of crime control. Even when it is by no means obvious that young lads who meet up in a shopping centre represent a threat to community safety they are chased away under the banner of crime prevention. Various nondescript forms of behaviour are now in fact criminalized. And in the process we open the door to arbitrary control without any clearly defined limits. Exactly because of these dangers, classical criminal law, with its strict definitions of criminal acts, individual suspicion and legal means of intervention, was established some 200 years ago. The reach of community safety policy needs to be more strictly defined and controlled. The punitive measures that are included in community safety should be subjected to the classical rule of law; the preventive elements should be judged on their merits. These mainly lie in a fair distribution of the care for safety in all segments of society and in a redistribution of victimization risks (de Haan and van Swaaningen, 1995).

The decline of the welfare state and the criminalization of social policy

Let us for once not mince words. It is simply a disgrace that in an era in which many citizens are richer than ever and the private sector is booming, nearly the whole public sector – health care, education, welfare, the arts – is as poor as a church mouse. Criminal justice is one of the few public services that is actually growing. It is no coincidence that social misery is translated into crime terms and that social policy can be carried out only under the banner of crime prevention. It is, however, a retrograde move in the civilization process that social policy can no longer be judged on its own merits – such as emancipation or welfare for all. The association with the stigmatizing notion of crime is also counterproductive for the realization of the separate goals of social policy. The primacy of economic interests has pushed concern for collective responsibility and social cohesion into the background. The concern with crime is strongly moralized, whereas the care for welfare is demoralized. You can insure yourself against everything, and those who do not have only themselves to blame. The current development in which literally everything and everybody is judged on its utility value is the major threat to social justice.

It is a real ideological success of twenty years of neo-liberal politics that answers to the public anxiety about street crime have been formulated in such a way that causes related to neo-liberal hobbyhorses such as individualization, income differentiation and efficiency have remained out of focus. But the 'calculating citizen', the 'calculating and indifferent state' and the decline of social control, so often pointed out as causes of crime, do have their roots in these factors. There is also a relation between the exclusion of vulnerable groups from the labour market and welfare provision, the emergence of urban marginality and stigmatized 'outcasts' and street crime (Engbersen, 1998). Jock Young (1999) has caught the current neo-liberal care and control model in the metaphor of social bulimia – a process by which the new underclasses are first 'swallowed' (integrated into the hegemonic order) and then 'puked up' (excluded from society). This process will sharpen the split in society between the contented classes and the new underclasses of the mainly homeless, the long-term unemployed, ethnic minority youth, asylum seekers and drug users. Crime control will follow these lines, and Mike Davis's (1998) disaster scenario from Los Angeles may become reality in Europe as well. The current community safety politics is ambivalent: it carries elements that will sharpen the social contrasts and elements that mitigate them. Realistic warnings against our 'bulimic' society seem the only means we have to create the moral ground for a replacement discourse on this aspect of community safety. We need to make normative choices rather than mere economic calculations.

Risk profiling and the risks of stereotypes, stigmatization and secondary deviance

It is impossible to imagine today's police practice without risk profiling. It follows from the rationale that the police should do their work as efficiently as possible. The police often use the following metaphor. In the old days a fisherman just went out with his boat and caught the fish he encountered on the way. Nowadays he maps out the areas where the chance of catching a certain kind of fish is greatest, then goes there. There are many crimes that will never be detected without risk profiling and proactive intervention – think of international drug trafficking or corporate crime. There is, however, a problem if this method is (predominantly) used to profile already vulnerable groups like the above-mentioned new underclasses. The stereotypical association of such people with crime will be amplified, and all the knowledge we have on the labelling process, the following, systematic secondary deviance and on the selectivity of the criminal justice system can be applied to community safety measures. Even more problematic is the fact that in this case people do not even come into contact with the police only if they are suspected of a crime, but because they are said to create 'nuisance'.

Profiling a certain district as a 'bad neighbourhood' can easily make the problem worse. Because no one wants to live in a bad neighbourhood, those who can afford it leave and only 'the truly disadvantaged', as Julius

Wilson has called them, stay. And so the ghetto is born. It should, how-ever, be clear that this danger lies not in the safety programmes as such but in the actuarial logic of social control in which they are embedded. Mapping out the areas in which problems are concentrated can be a means to a solution. Using the knowledge in a stigmatizing way is not. This is yet another argument for prioritizing social intervention and judging it on its own merits, rather than in the context of crime control.

'The social': community, local government and state

On a practical level, working together still remains the weak spot of the Dutch politics of community safety. This is partly due to inflexible bureaucratic structures and the unclear demarcation of tasks, responsibilities and competences, but there are more fundamental problems. On a national level the community safety policy has had a more structural character since fighting relative deprivation was put on the agenda. This aim cannot, however, be realized so easily at the local level. There are many arguments in favour of choosing to give local authorities a co-ordinating role in community safety. Creating a more decisive and responsive system is an important point in this respect. At the same time, however, local authorities are impotent when it comes to the most structural determinants of unsafety. The danger exists that utterly insoluble problems are pushed downwards. Local authorities are in fact invited to do more with less money. The Major Cities policy offers a solution to only part of this problem. Also, in other areas than deprivation and integration, co-operation comes down ultimately to financial means and personnel. Take schools, which have a key role in crime prevention, as an example. They already have too small a budget actually to run all the classes they should and sometimes they have to send children home, for example if a teacher is off sick. There are simply no staff available to pay attention to the personal and development problems that children may have. Other agencies that in the past took care of children in trouble have also become too small – i.e. have been 'economized away' – to do something about it. Consequently everything is left to the police.

It is thus not at all strange that the police basically determine the agenda of community safety initiatives at a local level. They are setting their own priorities in the first place, and move the other agencies into a dependent position (Goris, 2000, pp. 91–9). They could become the 'information brokers of the risk society', as Ericson and Haggerty (1997) put it, because their capacity has been growing while many social partners in the community safety policy have been cut back. Again we can bring forward the same argument from a different angle. In order to make community safety politics work, we first need to invest more in youth work, community work, street-corner work and schools. In the long run, implicit social control works better than a direct short-term orientation to crime and relapse rates.

Privatization

It is paradoxical that pleas for greater community spirit are launched in an era when one public service after another is being privatized. Stimulating community spirit would need to start with the establishment of public services that are not oriented first and foremost to maximizing profits. This may have some mitigating effect, but the privatization of collective provision has already gone far. We already have quite a different state than before, now 'governance at a distance' and 'network society' have become established political slogans. Not all the consequences for crime control can be addressed here (Crawford, 1998, pp. 252–5), but we can consider one. An example immediately suggests itself. There is an apparent safety problem at railway stations. In striving to make the 'company' more cost-effective, the privatized Dutch Rail replaced personnel at smaller stations with ticket machines. In the process an important form of informal social control is economized away. The extra safety problems that are the result of this measure are answered with more cameras and extra security staff. It is clear that such steps do not improve the social 'caring' dimension of community safety.

Next to this, there is the privatization of criminal justice agencies themselves. We have already argued that in the Netherlands control of public space is kept more in the collective sphere than in Britain. Not only the civic warden, but also the so-called 'police assistant' – a less educated and lower-paid member of the force with fewer competences than a 'normal' officer – has been introduced to counter the tendency for well-to-do citizens to hire private security firms because they feel police surveillance is falling short. There is no need to argue against the private security industry *per se*. We should not, however, become dependent on it in the public domain, where the care for safety should be a collective responsibility. It should be of such a quality that not merely those who are able to pay for protection feel safe. The point is to find a balance between those areas which need a public care for safety and those where private control can be allowed. The visible presence of the police is now too much concentrated in the commercial city centres, whereas the most deprived areas are also deprived in respect of (police and other) care for social safety. If choices have to be made in the public sphere, the authorities should concentrate on the problems of those who cannot adequately protect themselves (de Haan, 1999).

Responsibilization and 'ownership'

There is nothing wrong with pointing out to people their responsibilities with respect to community safety. This responsibilization, however, does not work if people have to operate within a given structure, are not provided with sufficient means and have to obey a control rationale.

Successful civic initiatives should not be taken over by professionals as soon as they can be institutionalized in a project, which mainly serves to expand the safety market. Authorities who offer too little support and authorities who take over civic initiatives are not involving people in, and getting their commitment to, community safety, but are in fact putting them off (Zoomer, 1993). Active civic participation and trust in responsive authorities are both preconditions for social justice. Responsibilization can contribute to real community safety, but it should not be an excuse for withdrawing state care.

References

Cohen, S. (1985) *Visions of Social Control: Crime, Punishment and Classification*, Cambridge, Polity Press.

Crawford, A. (1998) *Crime Prevention and Community Safety; Politics, Policies and Practices*, London, Longman.

Davis, M. (1998) 'Beyond *Blade Runner*' in *The Ecology of Fear: Los Angeles and the Imagination of Disaster*, New York, Holt.

de Haan, W.J.M. de (1989) *Structurele Determinanten van Onveiligheid*, The Hague, Sdu.

de Haan, W.J.M. de (1999) 'Sociaal beleid als structurele criminaliteitspreventie' in Lissenberg, E., van Ruller, S. and van Swaaningen, R. (eds) *Tegen de Regels*, Nijmegen, Ars Aequi Libri.

de Haan, W.J.M. de and van Swaaningen, R. (1995) 'Integrale veiligheid en justitiële moralisering: een reactie', in *Justitiële Verkenningen*, vol. 21, no. 8, pp. 89–92.

Engbersen, G. (1998) 'Stedelijke marginaliteit en criminaliteit' in van den Heuve, G. and van Swaaningen, R. (eds) *Criminaliteit en Sociale Rechtvaardigheid*, Nijmegen, Ars Aequi Libri.

Ericson, R.V. and Haggerty, K.D. (1997) *Policing the Risk Society*, Oxford, Clarendon Press.

Garland, D. (1985) *Punishment and Welfare: A History of Penal Strategies*, Aldershot, Gower.

Garland, D. (2000) 'The culture of high crime societies: some preconditions of "law and order policies"', *British Journal of Criminology*, vol. 40, no. 3, pp. 347–75.

Goris, P. (2000) 'Analyse van Relaties Tussen Professionele Actoren in Het Kader van een Geïntegreerde Preventieve Aanpak van Veiligheidsproblemen in Achtergestelde Woonbuurten: op Zoek naar de Krijtlijnen van een Sociaal Rechtvaardige Veiligheidszorg', PhD thesis, Katholieke Universiteit, Leuven.

Hauber, A. (1999) 'Situationele en individuele preventie' in Lissenberg, E., van Ruller, S. and van Swaaningen, R. (eds) *Tegen de Regels*, Nijmegen, Ars Aequi Libri.

Hughes, G. (1998) *Understanding Crime Prevention: Social Control, Risk and Late Modernity*, Buckingham, Open University Press.

Lissenberg, E., van Ruller, S. and van Swaaningen, R. (eds) (1999) *Tegen de Regels: een Inleiding in de Criminologie*, Nijmegen, Ars Aequi Libri.

Piret, J.-M. (2000) 'Veiligheid en rechtsstatelijkheid, rechtsfilosofische en ideën: historische beschouwingen', in *Delikt unt Delinkwent*, vol. 30, no. 1, pp. 31–49.

Raes, K. (1997) *Het Moeilijke Ontmoeten:Vverhalen van Alledaagse Zedelijkheid*, Brussels, VUB Press.

van Swaaningen, R. (1995) 'Sociale controle met een structureel tekort: pleidooi voor een sociaal rechtvaardig veilgheidsbeleid', *Justitiële Verkenningen*, vol. 21, no. 3, pp. 63–87.

van Swaaningen, R. (1997) *Critical Criminology: Visions from Europe*, London, Sage.

van Swaaningen, R. and Blad, J. (1999) 'Criminological Research in the Netherlands in the 1990s'. (This report is published in French and in Spanish: in Philippe Robert and Lode Van Outrive (eds), *Crime et justice en Europe* II, Paris, L'Harmattan, pp. 193-246; and in *Revista catalana de seguretat pública*, no. 5, pp. 191–244. The English version can be obtained from the authors.)

Young, J. (1999) *The Exclusive Society: Social Exclusion, Crime and Difference in Late Modernity*, London, Sage.

Zoomer, O. (1993) *Zelf Doen en Overlaten: acties van Burgers, Politie en Lokale Overheid Tegen Overlast en Kleine Criminaliteit*, Lelystad, Vermande.

Drugs, risks and freedoms

Illicit drug 'use' and 'misuse' under neo-liberal governance

Pat O'Malley

The drug addict suffers from a peculiarly liberal affliction, liberal in the
sense that it is a pathology of the subject's individual freedom – what
Mariana Valverde (1998) has referred to as a 'disease of the will'. It is also
liberal in that the emergence of concern about the impact of drugs on free
will – beginning with alcohol – coincides historically with the ascendancy
of liberal governance. As Levine demonstrates, addiction was invented at a
time when the value of inner discipline and self-control was becoming
paramount:

> Given the structural requirements of daily life for self-reliant, self-making
> entrepreneurs and their families, and the assumptions of the individualistic

middle class world view, it seemed completely reasonable that liquor, a substance believed to weaken inhibitions when consumed (intoxication), could also deprive people of the ability to control their behaviour over the long run (addiction). (1978, p. 168)

Indeed, such liberal concern with self-control and individual freedom is reflected in 'epidemics of the will' that sweep modern societies, in which any substance or any activity – even the desire for individual freedom itself – may be interpreted as excessive and thus addictive (Sedgwick, 1993). Of course, this is not to suggest that the effects of drugs are imaginary in the sense of fallacious. Rather the point is that at other times and in other contexts the effects are understood in other ways altogether, for example as mystical or euphoric states that alter consciousness but do not render the subject *unfree*. In this chapter I wish to examine shifts in the ways in which consumers of drugs, and drugs themselves, are 'imagined' in this sense – that is, the ways in which drug consumption is understood or constituted for the purposes of government. In turn, these shifts, I will argue, are related to the emergence of a specifically neo-liberal form of political rationality.

In discourses of addiction the addict is imagined as experiencing the attrition of free will, which in turn is a symptom of what the International Narcotics Control Board describes as a 'chronic disease' characterized by frequent relapse. Yet this medical imagery has never been very secure, for addiction is something of a hybrid that awkwardly melds the moral, philosophical and political entity of 'free will' with biochemical processes and organic pathology (Valverde, 1998). Resulting ambiguities and paradoxes create dilemmas for government, especially about whether coercion is justified because rationality and freedom are already compromised or whether coercion only weakens free will further rather than restores it. Furthermore, treatment comes into tension with punishment, for, whilst the addict may be suffering from a disease or pathology, it was contracted voluntarily through an illegal act and thus is subject to penalty and deterrence. For such reasons the history of governing addictions is one of ambivalence, ambiguities and dispute, in which medical and judicial regimes have struggled, each with an uneasy grasp.

In this respect, drug addiction is not altogether distinct from other species of problematic behaviour. The 'birth of the welfare sanction' in the later nineteenth century brought together scientific reason and liberal morality in a similar uneasy amalgam across the spectrum of criminal justice (Garland, 1981). The positive criminological sciences interpreted crime as the effect of social or psychological pathology – an interpretation that reduced the individual's moral responsibility for offending and implied that punishment should be displaced by scientific treatment. This view created sufficient opposition among the moral disciplinarians of nine-teenth-century liberalism that treatment could gain a foothold only in hybrid form. The compromise 'welfare sanction' embedded therapeutic correction within a framework of moral culpability and punishment. As with addiction, the welfare sanction compromise has never been stable: 'conservatives' have ever pressed for punishment and coercion, while welfare 'progressives' call for emphasis on treatment.

Perhaps not surprisingly, the assault on the welfare state since the 1970s has seen both the 'welfare sanction' and the category of the 'drug addict' come under pressure. Neo-liberal hostility to 'welfare dependence', for example, sits uncomfortably with regimes that diminish individual responsibility. This is reinforced by suspicion of the social sciences and criminology, on both ideological and cost-benefit grounds (Rose, 1996). Accordingly, the most striking development in criminal justice in the 1970s and 1980s – in Britain, the United States and Australasia – was a trend toward rational choice models of the offender and punitive/deterrence approaches that emphasized the moral and rational foundations of criminal responsibility (O'Malley, 1992). In this sense, offenders' free will was restored to them so that they could be punished.

The response by such regimes to the 'drug problem', however, was far more diverse, but still reflects these foci on restoring rationality and responsibility. In the United States, where the War on Drugs had been declared during the late 1970s, the category of *drug abuse* was extensively mobilized in order to restore to centre-stage the free-willed nature of the criminal offence and the moral turpitude of offenders. The drug *abuser* appeared merely as a normal, voluntaristic and culpable juridical subject, akin to the spouse abuser or 'trust abuser'. Addiction survived, but rather than a medical condition it increasingly became a morally degraded condition consequent upon an immoral act (Matza and Morgan, 1995). Treatment and medically oriented programmes for drug-taking accordingly gave way to punitive responses.

In Britain and Australia, however, the model of addiction came under pressure of an altogether different nature during the mid-1980s. The change involved a form of strategic moralization, registered in law in an increasingly marked distinction between traffickers and users (Dorn and South, 1994, p. 294). More draconian punitive responses were to be directed at 'traffickers', who were understood not as users/dealers but as rationally calculating and exploitative, as creating the harms and miseries of users, and who were thus fully deserving of punishment. New sanctions appeared, including reverse-onus penalties designed to strip traffickers of profits 'made at the expense of others' (Blewitt, 1987; Freiberg, 1992; HM Government 1998, pp. 5–18). However, 'addicts' were to be reimagined as 'problem drug takers' or even 'drug users'. With respect to Britain (and the same will be seen to apply to Australasia), the

> disease-based notion of addiction gave way to the notion of 'problem drug taking' . . . [involving] a broader perspective, moving away from a substance focus and recognizing the personal, social and medical (including dependence) difficulties which may be associated with the use of a range of drugs. (Glanz, 1994, p. 157)

This language of 'problems' and 'difficulties' not only shifted attention from the chemical substance – like the earlier change in America, it re-envisaged drug-takers in ways that do not automatically assume their rationality and freedom to be impaired. However, rather than increasing the load of moral culpability, the effect of this de-moralization of drug consumption was markedly to lessen it – to constitute drug users and drug consumption more in the direction of normal subjects confronting risks, harms, problems, difficulties and so on.

Conservative and neo-liberal technologies of freedom

How can we understand these two contemporaneous but divergent governmental assaults on the 'drug addict'? I would suggest that each strategy was strongly marked by a different element of the 'New Right' politics of the 1980s. The New Right is an alliance of neo-liberal economic rationalism and neo-conservative moral authoritarianism (O'Malley, 1999). Both Margaret Thatcher and Ronald Reagan, for example, not only introduced the extended market principles and generalized economic entrepreneurialism identified with neo-liberalism, but also linked them with what Thatcher extolled as the 'Victorian virtues' (Thatcher, 1993). These virtues highlight self-control, moral responsibility and self-denial. They resonate strongly with the Victorian imagination of the free, liberal subject in terms of 'character' and 'independence': self-discipline and self-denial organized in terms of a common moral code backed up by a disciplinary state. Such virtues formed a kind of conservative (or 'classical liberal') *technology of the self* that distinguished the free, liberal subject from lesser beings weakened by indiscipline and mere subjection to pleasure and desire (Bell, 1976).

This rationality of classical liberal freedom had considerable currency from the early nineteenth century to the middle of the twentieth. Whether or not it had actually declined by the 1970s, neo-conservatives believed that it had been assaulted not just by the rise of welfare liberalism, which corroded independence, but equally by the emergence of moral relativism and consumerism. In Daniel Bell's words, we:

> . . . have witnessed an effort by anti-bourgeois culture to achieve autonomy from the social structure . . .

> In both doctrine and lifestyle, the anti-bourgeois won out. This triumph meant that in the culture antinomianism and anti-institutionalism ruled . . . in the realm of art on the level of aesthetic doctrine . . . few opposed the idea of boundless experiment, of unfettered freedom, of unconstrained sensibility, of impulse being superior to order, of the imagination being immune to merely rational criticism . . .

The traditional bourgeois organization of life – its rationalism and sobriety – now has few defenders in the culture . . . (1976, p. 53)

The War on Drugs, and its valorization of 'drug abuse', may be associated with this *neo-conservative* project to defend and restore essentially nineteenth-century classical liberal visions of rational yet morally disciplined freedom against the 'culture of narcissism' (Lasch, 1985). While this resonates well with some neo-liberal themes – especially those associated with individual responsibility and rationality – tensions were clearly set up with what Rose (1996) has referred to as neo-liberalism's 'revised autonomy of the self'. The idealized, neo-liberal self of switched-on capitalism is much more shaped by self-fulfilment and 'activity', and the assemblage of a 'lifestyle' through the commodity market:

> Rather than being tied rigidly into publicly espoused forms of conduct imposed through legislation or coercive intervention into personal conduct, forms of life, types of 'lifestyle' are on offer, bounded by law only at the margins. Forms of conduct are governed through personal labour to assemble a way of life within the sphere of consumption and to incorporate a set of values from among the alternative moral codes disseminated from the world of signs and images . . . These new technologies of citizenship formation were to gain their power through the subjective commitments to values and ways of life that were generated by the technique of choice and consumption . . . (Rose, 1990, pp. 226–7)

Such subjects may be freed to undertake an 'enterprise of the self', assembling from the available alternatives a freely chosen lifestyle (Rose, 1990). Such a revised technology of the liberal self does not sit easily with 'Victorian virtues' and sobriety, and there is no essential place for the coercive and morally monolithic discipline of conservatism. Increasingly, as neo-liberalism developed apace during the 1980s, an array of governing techniques emerged which cater for, and promote, such revised individual freedom. They include: new forms of voluntarism and contractualism (given form in imageries of 'partnerships' and 'charters') that enhance the 'activity' and participation of individuals in their own government; new programmes to 'empower', 'skill' and 'inform' subjects to 'take command of their own future'; new applications of the model of the market and associated techniques of entrepreneurship and innovation; and new means of fostering 'communities' as governmental categories through which diverse moral, social or regional interests are mobilized (Rose, 1996; O'Malley, 1992).

Thus two forms of liberal freedom can be contrasted, each associated with different technologies of government and techniques of the self: a neo-conservative, classical liberal freedom of independence, sobriety and moral responsibility; and a morally more relative neo-liberal freedom of choice, involving enhanced autonomy, activity and self-fulfilment. While they share much in common, notably faith in markets and competition, and dislike of state-based 'interventionism' associated with the welfare state, the differences and tensions encompassed in the New Right alliance were a fertile soil for divergence – especially in more morally valorized fields. Accounts vary as to why the United States has taken the more neo-conservative road in the War on Drugs, ranging from the impact of the failed Vietnam War and the racial dimensions of drug use to the political strength of the religious right. Perhaps the early emergence of a large drug problem in the United States meant that its course was directed by the readily available neo-conservative forms of punitivism, rather than the more slowly emerging and innovative forms of neo-liberal intervention. But, whatever the reason, in Britain and Australasia a different – and specifically neo-liberal – route was taken, beginning in the mid-1980s. It is this I wish now to explore.

Risk, enterprise and indeterminism

During the 1980s, and gathering pace in the 1990s, observers in Britain and Australia began to note the appearance of some surprising innovations in correctional practice. For example, developments aimed at creating 'enterprising prisoners' began to take shape. Such schemes, as Garland suggests, partake of a positive and 'active' framework in which prisoners are 'trained for freedom'. They:

> enlist the prisoner as an agent in his own rehabilitation, and as an entrepreneur of his own personal development . . . [prisoners] take part in the government of their own confinement. They are permitted to choose their preferred options from within the available range of developmental activities. (1996, p. 462)

At the same time – although too much can be made of terminological shifts – prisoners sometimes shed the welfare label of 'clients' and re-emerged as 'customers' (Lacey, 1994, p. 544). This shift re-envisaged the correctional system in terms of neo-liberal technologies of the market (often accompanied by extensive privatization of prisons, competitive tendering and outsourcing of prison services), and reconstituted offenders in terms of idealized forms of neo-liberal citizenship – the entrepreneur and the sovereign consumer. In this governmental framework, prisoners are 'empowered' rather than 'corrected'. Not simply subjected to the authoritative command of experts, they enter a form of partnership with them, in which freedom is restored through the exercise of choice and responsibility. They are to be transformed by neo-liberal techniques of the active self into the subjects of a specifically neo-liberal freedom. About the same time – somewhat earlier in Australia – parallel shifts emerged in the field of drug regulation.

In 1992 the Australian commonwealth (federal) government launched the National Drug Strategy (Task Force on Evaluation, 1992), cementing in place a 1980s harm minimization framework for the government of licit and illicit drugs. One of the striking things about this document, and its substantial accompanying programme, was that the terms 'addict', 'addiction' and 'abuse' scarcely appeared. A year later, when the state of Victoria launched the *Victorian Drug Strategy, 1993–1998* (HCS, 1993), a state-based programme formally operating within this federal rubric of harm minimization, 'addiction' and 'drug abuse' had entirely given way to discourses of 'drug use'. A few years later, much the same stance was adopted by the New Zealand *National Drug Strategy* (New Zealand government, 1998) and by the Major and later Blair governments in Britain with *Tackling Drugs Together* and *Tackling Drugs to Build a Better Britain* (HM Government, 1995, 1998). Here, too, abuse and addiction were marginalized in favour of discourses of the 'drug user' (New Zealand) or 'drug misuser' (Britain). This shift was associated with a reimagining of drug use in terms of choice. It restored free will to new categories of 'dependent' or 'problem' drug mis/users, and understood the process of becoming a drug consumer as involving rationality. Rather than progressing from this foundation to the punitive-deterrent or heavily moralized response, as in the United States, it seeks to 'enable' or even 'empower' its subjects, by inculcating 'skills' and providing 'information', and to create treatment resources through which these neo-liberal subjects may 'make informed choices' and reorient their lives in the direction of 'healthy and crime-free lives' (HM Government, 1998).

In these regimes, instead of a blanket imagery of addictions and abuses, there emerges a spectrum of qualified conditions and forms of 'use' or 'misuse': in the Australian context it ranges from 'dependent' ('problem misuse' in Britain) to 'informed' and 'responsible drug use' (CDHSH, 1993). Even in some of its strongest warnings Blair's *Tackling Drugs* displaces the traditional narrative of pathological addiction and inexorable decline with the much more conditional observation that 'drug-taking *can be harmful*' (HM Government, 1998, p. 7; emphasis added), while the New Zealand government (1998) policy refers to a 'continuum of harm associated with drug use'. Drug 'use' and 'misuse' in this discourse, it appears, are linked with risks and possibilities of harm – drug-taking has nothing inevitable or absolute attached to it. While these 'harm mini-mization' approaches all seek to deflect or reduce the acceptability of drug use on grounds of risk and harm, only rarely is drug consumption (as opposed to trafficking) defined explicitly as morally or criminally culpable. In this there is a strong contrast with strategies formerly in place. In Britain in the 1980s, for example, campaigns such as 'Heroin screws you up' and 'Smack isn't worth it' depicted users as morally corrupt, unhealthy and helpless, and suggested a typical career of use, addiction and despair (Davies and Coggans, 1994, p. 311). The key factor underlying this quite dramatic shift away from abuse and addiction, it seems clear, is to be found in the development of forms of harm-minimizing, risk-based approaches that are inflected with neo-liberal technologies of freedom and self government.

The National Drug Strategy, endorsed by all federal, state and territory governments in Australia, defines harm minimization as aiming to 'reduce the adverse health, social and economic consequences of alcohol and other drugs by minimizing or limiting the harms and hazards of drug use' (CDHSH, 1993). More explicitly, the *Victorian Drug Strategy* (HCS, 1993) describes itself thus:

> The specific objectives of the Drug Strategy focus on changing behaviours and reducing other risk factors which have been shown to increase the potential for drug related harm . . . There is a strengthened commitment to the principle of harm minimization in its broadest sense. All objectives are defined in terms of risk factors linked to specific harms, with emphasis on prevention wherever possible and on minimizing the negative impact of drug use problems where they occur.

Likewise, the British *Tackling Drugs* strategy is saturated with risk talk, stressing that 'action will be concentrated in areas of greatest need and risk', that it seeks 'big reductions in crime and health risks', that 'significant health risks are associated with drugs' and so on. Such risk management strategies place an analytical and governmental grid across the social terrain they seek to govern that does not necessarily correspond to the grid laid down by prohibitive laws or medical regimes of addiction. For example, some harm minimization programmes stress that 'it is important to recognize that illicit drugs are, in functional terms, the same as legal drugs' (PDAC, 1996). While they recognize 'the devastating effects that illicit drug use can have', they do so in the context of observations that align them in terms of harm with licit drugs (HCS, 1993). Similarly, as part of its 'Vision', *Tackling Drugs* states baldly that 'all drugs are harmful', while the New Zealand policy states that 'of all drugs tobacco and alcohol result in the most harm in New Zealand'.

As other commentators have noted, the past twenty years have witnessed the rise of such risk-based approaches to dealing with crime and social problems, seeing them as displacing regimes that identify and reform or punish offenders through individually focused clinical or judicial techniques (Simon, 1987; Feeley and Simon, 1992, 1994; O'Malley, 1998). However, one of the shortcomings of much of this new criminology of risk and actuarial control is that it reflects the ways in which such technologies were introduced into criminal justice in environments of conservative liberalism and are being mobilized in relation to dangerous offenders. Accordingly, emphasis has been placed on such negative programmes of risk-based incapacitation and surveillance as mass warehousing of prisoners, 'Three strikes and you're out', Megan's Law in the United States and, in the United Kingdom, sexual offender orders under the Crime and Disorder Act 1998 (Simon, 1998; Hebenton and Thomas, 1996; O'Malley, 2000). These use risk techniques to identify, incapacitate and punish rather than to reform offenders and potential offenders. However, as suggested, more recent risk programmes that incorporate neo-liberal approaches to governance may take a very different character: approaches that are inclusive rather than exclusionary, and that enlist actual and potential drug-users in the process of their own government.

Harm minimization and normalization

One of the major concerns of harm minimization policies is the capacity of prohibition's exclusionary categories and procedures to 'demonize' illicit drug users. Harm minimization, legal exclusion and the demonization of drug use create problems of 'deviance amplification' and resistance to effective intervention – for compulsion and coercion create resistance among the very drug-using subjects upon whom the programme is intended to have its effects (see, for example, PDAC, 1996). The strategy of harm minimization, therefore, is to 'emphasize voluntary treatment rather than punishment of users and minimize the stigma of criminalization of drug users' on pragmatic grounds (Task Force on Evaluation, 1992). Thus, in contrast to the Foucauldian sense of normalization as bringing deviant subjects into conformity with a constructed norm (licit drug use or no drug use), 'normalization' in the lexicon of harm minimization takes on the meaning of rendering illicit drug-taking subjects into normal subjects of government (Glanz, 1994, p. 158). As Strang (1984) argued '[a]s notorious drugs (such as the use of heroin) become more widespread in a population, the people using them are likely to be more normal (statistically and in other senses) than the abnormal population who presented originally'. In consequence, 'if some of the drug-takers are becoming more normal then perhaps some of the drug services should do likewise' (Strang, 1989). This was to be achieved through 'the gradual shift from disease and criminal models', precisely because of awareness 'that "drug addicts" and "alcoholics" can bear the brunt of problems in our community and can be the scapegoats of more severe social ills' (Task Force on Evaluation, 1992). Instead of coercive, long-term residential models, voluntary and short-term 'out-patient' models became preferred options, and 'the view that drug misusers need to be dealt with by specialists was undermined' (Glanz, 1994).

As part of this normalization strategy, even in a harm minimization document as opposed to illicit drug consumption as is *Tackling Drugs to Build a Better Britain*, a distance is created between criminality and drug misusers by stressing that 'all drug users do not commit crime' and that the aims of the programme include to 'concentrate our . . . law enforcement effort on those who produce, process and sell [drugs]' (HM Government, 1998, p. 8). With respect to misusers, the strategy is one that 'enables' and 'helps' and with respect to potential users is not so much to prohibit as to provide guidance. The stress in *Tackling Drugs* is not on dependence-creating subordination to expertise, but on assistance and enablement: '[h]elping drug-misusing offenders to tackle their problems and become better integrated into society' and intervention to 'enable people with drug problems to overcome them'. Such normalization, we shall see, is under-taken precisely in order to govern drug users more effectively, to align the wills of such subjects with the project of harm minimization, and to align the distribution of risks and harms with the objectives of government programmes. In a sense, these 'users' and 'misusers' – unlike 'addicts' and 'abusers' – are to be governed through the exercise of their enhanced freedom.

We have seen that discourses of addiction and abuse focus on the presence (abuse) or absence/attenuation (addiction) of 'free will'. In these essentially binary models the subject is or is not a wilful law-breaker, is or is not diseased, and thus is or is not a subject of governmental intervention. However, by regarding drugs as part of the general issue of risk manage-ment, harm minimization operates within a statistical and irreducibly *probabilistic* model that erodes the binary of free will and determinism or, more precisely, creates a form of freedom that is 'shaped' by probabilities (Hacking, 1991). Whether with reference to alcohol, tobacco, pharma-ceuticals or 'illicit drugs', harm reduction involves 'a recognition that drug use involves varying degrees of risk for the user' (DSEV, 1995). Thus *Tackling Drugs* (1998) stresses that 'almost half of young people are likely to take drugs at some time in their lives, but only one-fifth will become regular misusers (i.e. at least once a month), with a tiny minority of that group taking drugs on a daily basis'. In place of the 'narrative of inexorable decline and fall' (Sedgwick, 1993) the drug-user is understood to be free, but in an environment of varying risk. In this way of thinking, this conditioning of freedom and constraint emerges in the form of a subject who must make choices from among a range of risk-bearing alternatives. The drug user as informed *choice-maker* becomes the key form of subject through which the government of drugs proceeds.

Drug use, empowerment and informed choices

Regimes of drug addiction and drug abuse both assume that drug-taking begins with a rational decision to consume. However, the consequences – moral and medical – are so constituted that this decision is not represented as one that should be simply a matter of free choice. In both cases the assumption is that the decision to take drugs should be constrained by moral condemnation and/or the threats of punishment and addiction. 'Just say no!', as the most salient manifestation of such approaches, is an instruction: it does not suggest that the potential users should consult the spectrum of choices and select that which suits them, weighing up the probabilities and making a lifestyle choice. Thus, in the shadow of the War on Drugs, the view of *Tackling Drugs* (1998) that 'we need to ensure that young people have all the information they need to make informed decisions about drugs' signals a distinct shift. Consider also the following view from the Victorian state drug education programme for schools:

> A harm minimization approach acknowledges that many young people will use drugs at some stage in their life, making it critical that students acquire knowledge and skills that will assist them in making informed decisions about their drug use and so minimize any harmful effects associated with that use. (DSEV, 1995)

Here potential users have been rendered choice-makers whose consumption choices cannot be governed by coercive regimes of legal or medical prohibition. The Victorian Drug Education Program makes no bones about 'accepting that drug use by young people is a personal choice that is not within the control of teachers or schools', while the New Zealand policy specifically notes that 'people are often highly resistant to "Just say no" messages about drug use, even when they are aware of the health, legal and other risks associated with such use. Innovative strategies are needed to communicate to them the value of staying drug free' (New Zealand Government, 1998, p. 10).

In these instances the shift towards government through choice is clearly founded on pragmatism: on the recognition that governing through risk-informed freedom may be a more effective mode of aligning the wills of the governed than the threat or practice of constraint. But both Australasian programmes go beyond this to suggest that the discourse of rights genuinely applies to the decision to use drugs. In the New Zealand case (New Zealand Government, 1998, p. 37) 'choices – which may be harmful to the individual – are legal and acceptable if the user does not unreasonably impinge on others. That is, individual choices are respected where the costs of the choices are not borne by others.' The Australian programme for secondary schools not only 'respects others' right to make their own decisions' but, more important, deploys such freedom of choice as the key element in the self-government of 'responsible' users and potential users. For this reason they 'should have access to accurate information and education programs relating to drugs and drug use, on the basis that informed, skilled individuals are able to make better choices which help prevent drug problems' (HCS, 1993).

Buried in these models is a series of key assumptions. The first is that the freedom of the individual as a choice-maker is established and facilitated. The second is that these choice-makers can best be assumed to make rational decisions that accord with the aims of government if they are given 'accurate' information and the skills required to make choices. The third is that the role of government is to provide access to the necessary skills and information. In this sense, there is an enhanced autonomy of the self when compared with models of all previous liberalisms (Rose, 1996). But, as might be anticipated, the skills and the information to be presented are understood as aimed to minimize risks. Thus *Tackling Drugs* (1998) aims to 'increase levels of knowledge of 5–16-year-olds about the risks and consequences of drug misuse', and urges that '[i]nformation, skills and support need to be provided in ways which are sensitive to age and circumstances, and particular efforts need to be made to reach and help those groups at high risk of developing very serious problems'. The Australian *Get Real* drug education package describes itself as providing:

> accurate and meaningful information. It provides a framework for understanding the forces that shape choice. It develops an awareness of risk situations. It develops skills to avoid situations of risk and to manage them when they arise. It encourages open discussion about drug use. It is open to young people's views and experiences. It does not encourage, condone or condemn the use of drugs by young people. It develops skills that enable young people to influence and change their environments. It helps students understand that drugs perform many useful functions in our society. (DSEV, 1995)

Built into this array is a series of carefully developed tactics for governing at a distance, through shaping the choice-making freedom of potential and current users. The emphasis on providing accurate and meaningful information follows from the assumption that government is intended to work through the actions of choice-makers. But examination of the texts of harm minimization policy indicates another layer to this strategy of self-government. It is noted frequently in the literature that the provision of biased or incomplete information aimed at deflecting people from drug use has been found to be counterproductive (for instance, PDAC, 1996). Information that distinguishes between illicit and licit drugs on the basis of the harmfulness of the former, for example, is found to limit the credibility of drug education, particularly among young people. Information that provides distorted and alarmist accounts of illicit drug use, such as tales of the inevitable slide from marijuana use into opiate addiction, is likewise found to discredit the programme because it can be refuted by the experience of users. Thus *Tackling Drugs* (1998, p. 8) goes to some pains to dismiss 'misconceptions' by asserting that 'all drug takers are *not* addicts; all drug takers do *not* commit crime' (emphasis in original). The provision of 'accurate information' is preferred partly because it is understood to govern more effectively. However, it is also clear that provision of accurate information alone is not regarded as sufficient, for evidence is produced to show that by itself it does not reliably reduce risk-taking behaviour (for example, PDAC, 1996; New Zealand Government, 1998).

It is at this point that 'responsible' choice-making users are to be *created* by government for, as noted, such programmes are to provide 'skills' as an essential adjunct to information. The *Get Real* education package, for example, provides potential users with 'a framework for understanding the forces that shape choice. It develops an awareness of risk situations. It develops skills to avoid situations of risk and to manage them when they arise' (DSEV, 1995). Likewise, *Tackling Drugs* (1998) seeks to 'teach young people from the age of five and upwards – both in and out of formal education settings – the skills needed to resist pressure to misuse drugs'. In particular these risk management skills include building self-esteem, recognition of the importance of peer group influence on choice-making and skills for managing such pressures. These skills are specified and given shape on the basis of evidence indicating their role in reducing risky behaviour. Put another way, the choice-makers are being given skills to render them more autonomous, but this autonomy renders the subjects more able to isolate themselves from pressures other than those preferred by harm minimization. Such is the nature of government at a distance.

These strategies and tactics are also shaped in such a way that another effect becomes possible. The tolerance associated with freedom of choice is founded in evidence that the information about drug risks, appearing as objective and accurate, will present itself as no more than mapping out a *quasi-natural order of risks*. It does not take the form of an imposed order formed and policed by moral and political governance, for the risks appear as probabilistic events triggered by the failure of the user to take the necessary avoiding steps. The governmental presentation of information appears as a service provided to enable individuals to chart their own course through the risk-laden domain of drug use.

Drug dependence: 'responsible addiction'

Most of what we have examined thus far enlists potential users/misusers and seeks to govern through their freedom of choice. Yet what of those who – in the words of *Tackling Drugs* – are 'problem misusers' or, in the Australian discourses, 'dependent drug users'? At first blush, drug depen-dence appears to be merely a synonym for addiction. However, the gov-ernment of dependent users operates primarily through methadone or other drug maintenance programmes. Surprisingly, these do not take the dependence itself as the target of governance. While methadone, for example, is regarded as ultimately delivering a way out of dependence, this is regarded neither as a necessary outcome nor as the primary benefit to the user delivered by the programme. Indeed, it is emphasized in the infor-mation provided to potential participants that methadone maintenance involves not only continued dependence on opiates, with the associated biochemical risks, but a dependence that often proves significantly more difficult to break (HCS, 1995). Methadone maintenance programmes under harm minimization regimes have as their primary target the govern-ance of risks and harms generated by drug dependence. These risks, and the ways in which methadone programmes manage them, are identified quite clearly in literature made available to dependent users, and include the following:

1 Methadone is administered orally (usually in solution with a fruit juice) thereby reducing the health risks associated with injection.
2 Standard quality control by the administering agency prevents harms associated with drug adulteration.
3 Because methadone does not give the user a 'high', it may be used to stabilize the dosage required by users, thus breaking the spiral of demand for larger dosages at greater cost.
4 Because its effects are longer-lasting than are those of other opiates (between twenty-four and thirty-six hours) methadone allows increased calculability of lifestyle, and normal patterns of work and life become possible – which in turn produces economic harm reduction and associated risk reduction with respect to the need to commit crimes to finance drug use.
5 Because it is legally available at low cost, participation in a methadone programme reduces the risks associated with violation of the criminal law.
(Source: HCS, 1995.)

Such 'benefits of the methadone scheme' are presented to the user alongside a series of other issues to be considered by a potential participant. These include the fact not only that the user remains opiate-dependent, but also that there are requirements of the programme demanding a regularizing of the user's lifestyle: for example, '[Y]ou are committed to attending daily for your dose [and] travel or holidays can be difficult and must be organized well in advance' (HCS, 1995). There is not, as is sometimes implied by critics, a *secret* agenda of surveillance. As with the transmission of 'accurate' information to responsible users, the effects of the programme, and their associations with the governance of risk, are presented openly to the dependent user as a matter of choice rather than as matters to be concealed: 'Your treatment team can support, advise and listen to you but basically you have to decide whether methadone is right for you' (HCS, 1995).

Again, such voluntarization and responsibilization emerge out of the recognition that compulsory programmes 'failed' to deliver results because of the fear, stigmatization and hostility that compulsory treatment created among users. Voluntary programmes, that work through users' preferences in a rational way, and are therefore based on the users' recognition of the risk reductions associated with enlistment in such programmes, are held to deliver better results. Governing through freedom of choice thus displaces government through coercion, not simply on the basis of 'humanity' (although such ideas are certainly present) but primarily on the basis of optimizing effective rule. Through their participation in the programme methadone consumers are normalized and, as rational choice-makers and calculating risk takers, they enter the sphere of responsible drug use.

Conclusion: neo-liberalism and the volatility of drug policies

The critical point that emerges is that while both neo-conservative and neo-liberal regimes 'restore' to drug takers their rationality, freedom and responsibility, each makes very different governmental strategies follow from the reconstitution of the addict. For neo-liberalism, drug users and misusers come to resemble any other subject who is, or is to be enabled to become, an active and enterprising subject of freedom of choice. It would be a simple matter to extend this analysis, and point to many other techniques of neo-liberal governance appearing in these strategies for governing drug use and misuse: the definition of users, police and others as 'stakeholders' to be included in 'partnerships' for governing drugs; the evocation of 'communities' as the locus of government and at the same time as participants in partnerships; the *conditional* regard given to expertise and the increased emphasis on programme evaluation and cost–benefit maximization – all are prominent in these governmental strategies, and all can be explicitly linked with neo-liberalism (see Rose, 1996).

Yet it is crucial to recognize that such neo-liberal strategies for governing illicit drugs through freedom of choice do not necessarily represent the future, nor is this harm minimization model the only possible one that can be associated with neo-liberalism. We have seen already that the continued strength of the War on Drugs in the United States indicates clearly that neo-liberal rationalities can coexist with punitive responses and discourses of addiction and abuse. The future may well see a reassertion of this situation, for it must be noted that the same British and Australian regimes that are fostering 'tolerant' blueprints and programmes for drug users are at the same time introducing increasingly oppressive risk-based regimes bearing on 'sexual' and 'violent' offenders – with whom until quite recently drug users shared the mantle of 'dangerousness' (O'Malley, 2000).

Equally, new alternatives are possible. The 'third way', for example, can be interpreted as an amalgam of neo-liberal and revised welfare responses, the latter being recast in ways more consistent with models of 'active citizenry' but nevertheless creating significant changes in the form of neo-liberal policies (Rose, 1999; O'Malley, 2000). One of the generally unnoticed features of the Australian programmes is that, while emphasizing freedom of choice and 'tolerance' to a noticeably greater extent than *Tackling Drugs Together* (1995) and *Tackling Drugs to Build a Better Britain* (1998), they have been almost totally silent about the array of such 'welfare state' concerns as poverty, accommodation and unemployment. The governmental focus on providing the skills and information to 'enable' choice-making in Australia assumes almost disembodied rational subjects, divorced from problems of the material world that are closely associated with drug use. *Tackling Drugs* (1998) differs significantly here – and is markedly critical of its 1995 precursor on the grounds that the former is regarded as having 'treated drug misuse largely in isolation from other social and environmental factors' (1998, p. 11). Indeed, the Conservative government's *Tackling Drugs* (1995) was rather dismissive of such sociological arguments, claiming that 'it is a matter for conjecture what causes an individual to misuse drugs. The social environment may be relevant in one case, personal inclination in another' (p. 54). Accordingly one of *Tackling Drugs* (1998)'s critical principles – 'Integration' – explicitly links the drug strategy with more welfare-oriented responses:

> Drug problems do not occur in isolation. They are often tied in with other social problems. The government is tackling inequalities through the largest ever programme to get people off benefit and into work and a series of reforms in the welfare state, education, health, criminal justice and the economy. And a new Social Exclusion Unit is looking at many of the problems often associated with drug taking such as school exclusions, truancy, rough sleeping and poor housing. (HM Government, 1998, p. 13)

At first blush this is a major advance. Yet is this move towards recognizing agendas of social welfare at the same time an invitation to remoralize drug use and misuse? Certainly the British programme is more explicitly intolerant of drug consumption than its Australian counterpart. And is it also to invite back the paternalistic and intrusive dominance of welfare expertise that the political left and right both rejected in the 1980s? Elsewhere – for example, with respect to developmental psychologists and their power to identify and 'treat' crime risk factors among very young children – this expert–authoritarian shift is already noticeable (O'Malley, 2000). Is the 'third way' advance in recognizing social constraints worth the risk of increased moral governance by expertise? On the other hand, is the 'neo-liberal' advance in freedom of choice worth the cost – even discounting the implied obliteration of issues of social inequality – if that cost is that we will be more effectively governed through our freedom? Ironically, then, the dilemmas of freedom and constraint that for so long haunted the governance of drugs have not gone away with the marginalization of addiction and abuse. Rather, they have assumed new guises. Perhaps, as Rose (2000) argues, these dilemmas of freedom will disappear only when government itself is abolished.

References

Bell, D. (1976) *The Cultural Contradictions of Capitalism*, London, Heinemann.
Blewitt, D. (1987) *National Campaign against Drug Abuse: Assumptions, Arguments and Aspirations*, Canberra, Australian Government Publishing Service.
Commonwealth Department of Human Services and Health (1993) *Drug Education Programs in Australia*, Canberra, Australian Government.
Davies, J. and Coggans, N. (1994) 'Media and school based approaches to drug education' in Strang, J. and Gossop, M. (eds) *Heroin Addiction and Drug Policy*, Oxford, Oxford University Press.
Directorate of School Education, Victoria (1995) *Get Real: A Harm Minimization*

Approach to Drug Education, Melbourne, Victorian Government Directorate of School Education.

Dorn, N. and South, N. (1994) 'The power behind practice: drug control and harm minimization in inter-agency and criminal law contexts' in Strang, J. and Gossop, M. (eds) *Heroin Addiction and Drug Policy*, Oxford, Oxford University Press.

Feeley, M. and Simon, J. (1992) 'The new penology: notes on the emerging strategy of corrections and its implications', *Criminology*, vol. 30, no. 4, pp. 449–74.

Feeley, M. and Simon, J. (1994) 'Actuarial justice: the emerging new criminal law', in Nelken, D. (ed.) *The Futures of Criminology*, Thousand Oaks, CA, Sage.

Freiberg, A. (1992) 'Criminal confiscation, profit and liberty', *Australian and New Zealand Journal of Criminology*, vol. 25, pp. 44–81.

Garland, D. (1981) 'The birth of the welfare sanction', *British Journal of Law and Society*, vol. 8, pp. 17–35.

Garland, D. (1996) 'The limits of the sovereign state', *British Journal of Criminology*, vol. 36, pp. 445–71.

Glanz, A. (1994) 'The fall and rise of the general practitioner' in Strang, J. and Gossop, M. (eds) *Heroin Addiction and Drug Policy*, Oxford, Oxford University Press.

Hacking, I. (1991) 'How should we do the history of statistics?' in Burchell, G., Gordon, C. and Miller, P. (eds) *The Foucault Effect: Studies in Governmentality*, London, Harvester/Wheatsheaf.

Health and Community Services (1993) *Victorian Drug Strategy, 1993–1998*, Melbourne, Victorian Government Department of Health and Community Services.

Health and Community Services (1995) *Methadone Treatment in Victoria. User Information Booklet*, Melbourne, Victorian Government Department of Health and Community Services.

Hebenton, B. and Thomas, T. (1996) 'Sexual offenders in the community: reflections of problems of law, community and risk management in the USA, England and Wales', *International Journal of the Sociology of Law*, vol. 24, pp. 427–43.

HM Government (1995) *Tackling Drugs Together*, London, HMSO.

HM Government (1998) *Tackling Drugs to Build a Better Britain*, London, Stationery Office.

Lacey (1994) 'Government as manager, citizen as consumer: the case of the Criminal Justice Act 1991', *Modern Law Review*, vol. 54, no. 4, pp. 534–54.

Lasch, C. (1985) *The Culture of Narcissism*, New York, Scribner.

Levine, H. (1978) 'The discovery of addiction: changing conceptions of habitual drunkenness in America', *Journal of Studies on Alcohol*, vol. 39, pp. 143–74.

Matza, D. and Morgan, P. (1995) 'Controlling drug use: the great prohibition' in Blomberg, T. and Cohen, S. (eds) *Punishment and Social Control*, Chicago, IL, Aldine de Gruyter.

New Zealand Government (1998) *National Drug Strategy*, Wellington, Government Printer.

O'Malley, P. (1992) 'Risk, power and crime prevention', *Economy and Society*, vol. 21, no. 3, pp. 252–75.

O'Malley, P. (1998) *Crime and the Risk Society*, Aldershot, Ashgate.

O'Malley, P. (1999) 'Volatile and contradictory punishment', *Theoretical Criminology*, vol. 3, pp. 175–96.

O'Malley, P. (2000) 'Risk, crime and prudentialism revisited' in Stenson, K. and Sullivan, R. (eds) *Crime, Risk and Justice: The Politics of Crime Control in Neo-liberal Societies*, Cullompton, Willan Publishing.

Premier's Drug Advisory Council (1996) *Drugs and our Community: Report of the Premier's Drug Advisory Council*, Melbourne, Victorian Government.

Rose, N. (1990) *Governing the Soul*, London, Routledge.

Rose, N. (1996) 'Governing "advanced liberal democracies"' in Barry, A., Osborne, T. and Rose, N. (eds) *Foucault and Political Reason*, London, UCL Press.

Rose, N. (1999) 'Inventiveness in politics', *Economy and Society*, vol. 28, no. 3, pp. 467–93. (Review article on Anthony Giddens's *The Third Way: The Review of Social Democracy*.)

Rose, N. (2000) *Powers of Freedom*, Cambridge, Cambridge University Press.

Sedgwick, E. (1993) 'Epidemics of the will', *Tendencies*, vol. 4, pp. 130–42.

Simon, J. (1987) 'The emergence of risk society: insurance, law, and the state', *Socialist Review*, vol. 95, pp. 61–89.

Simon, J. (1998) 'Managing the monstrous: sex offenders and the new penology', *Psychology, Public Policy and Law*, vol. 4, pp. 452–67.

Strang, J. (1984) 'Changing the image of the drug taker', *Health and Social Service Journal*, vol. 11, pp. 1202–4.

Strang, J. (1989) 'A model service: turning the generalist on to drugs', in MacGregor, S. (ed.) *Drugs and British Society*, London, Routledge.

Strang, J. and Gossop, M. (eds) (1994) *Heroin Addiction and Drug Policy: The British System*, Oxford, Oxford University Press.

Task Force on Evaluation (1992) *No Quick Fix: An Evaluation of the National Campaign against Drug Abuse*, Melbourne, Ministerial Council on Drug Strategy.

Thatcher, M. (1993) *The Downing Street Years*, Basingstoke, Macmillan.

Valverde, M. (1998) *Diseases of the Will: Alcohol and the Dilemmas of Freedom*, Cambridge, Cambridge University Press.

Boundary harms

From community protection to a politics of value: the case of the Jewish eruv

Davina Cooper

Today, in Britain, public policy discourse recognizes that racism is harmful. Nevertheless, considerable disagreement exists about how to safeguard communities from its threat. Does protection, for instance, require extra (or fewer) police, greater (or less) surveillance, extending the criminal law to encompass racially motivated crimes, or the introduction of more effective anti-poverty strategies? The broad consensus that racism causes injury contrasts with the public policy response confronting religious and ethnic forms of difference.[1] Before turning to the question of safety, policy-makers must tackle two prior concerns, namely is there a risk of harm? And if so, for whom? Diverging opinion can be seen in relation to a series of conflicts over Muslim headscarves and veils (Galeotti, 1993), Sikh daggers (Wayland, 1997), turbans (Bennett, 1999) and the subject of this chapter: symbolic religious structures in shared outdoor space. In relation to this last, conflicts have arisen over whether such structures pose a form of cultural security for believers, a provocative incitement to violence by others, or a 'weapon' which, without intending to, threatens the peace and well-being of non-believers.

This chapter focuses on one particular conflict involving a Jewish symbolic structure: the eruv. In particular, it explores the place of such structures within the wider context of community protection. 'Community protection' is a term that has been variously used, within different jurisdictions, to identify practices, policies and structures that seek to secure, protect and enhance local communities. Although used frequently in relation to anti-crime initiatives, particularly in relation to child sex offenders, I am using community protection more broadly as a hybrid of two discourses: community safety and cultural protection. On the surface these discourses may seem to have little in common, functioning in the contrasting environments of crime prevention (see, for example, Hughes, 1998, 2000; Pease and Wiles, 2000), and minority cultural rights (see Kymlicka, 1995; Margalit and Halbertal, 1994; Prott, 1999; Taylor, 1994), respectively. Yet, despite some of the tensions between their different normative assumptions, they do converge into a dominant liberal project that both straddles and knits together: (1) the measures necessary to secure the bodily integrity and existing life chances of individuals within a particular locality; (2) the policies and processes required to assist and safeguard communities, whether identified as geographical, ethnic, religious or otherwise; (3) the protection of those artefacts and practices through which communities are defined, both on the grounds of inherent value and as a means of protecting the community's identity and existence.

The aim of this chapter is to evaluate the response to ethnic and religious conflicts offered by liberal community protection paradigm in comparison with a more explicitly normative, public policy approach. I thus draw on writers who have adopted more critical perspectives on multiculturalism and cultural protection (for example, Anthias, 1998; Légaré, 1995; Segal and Handler, 1995; Vasta, 1993; Vertovec, 1996). Yet, rather than simply arguing against minority rights or for a more celebratory, empowering response to questions of difference (see also Cooper, 2000b), the approach I am adopting focuses instead on the social values that underpin competing versions of the 'good' heterogenous society. Although I emphasize the general need for a more explicitly normative engagement with social practice, underlying my argument are two less ideologically 'neutral' objectives: that a normative approach should recognize and respond to prevailing power imbalances; and that it should seek to dismantle rather than entrench community boundaries.

The chapter opens with a brief account of the conflict that flared up over the proposal to establish a London eruv. It then turns to explore the theme of community protection. In particular, it considers the form which community protection has taken in relation to the Jewish community, and the problems raised for a more critical analysis. Because contrasting norms and values underlie most political engagements with cultural practices, the final section of the chapter examines the relationship between value and discourses of harm. While harm is interpreted in diverse ways, the approach I am adopting treats harm as injury to social value. Thus contests over harm function as surrogates for conflicts over value. In this chapter I focus on how value-based conflicts are played out through the eruv; however, in the conclusion I return to the question of what this approach might mean for injurious mainstream practices as well.

Installing an eruv: encircling neighbourhoods with a symbolic perimeter

On the Sabbath, Jewish law permits carrying only within an enclosed, private area. This generally means that people can push and carry objects needed during the Sabbath only within their home. The eruv is a halakhic (Jewish law) device for easing this restriction. By turning the area it encloses into a single private domain, it enables observant Jews to push objects such as pushchairs and wheelchairs, or to carry keys and glasses, beyond the perimeter of the home (see Metzger, 1989). Eruvs have existed for centuries; however, they became particularly visible in the latter half of the 20th century as many communities, especially in the United States, sought to establish new eruvs or redesign those already in existence. To be effective an eruv needs to enclose the entirety of an observant community. Thus new eruvs are created as the community they encompass changes. At the same time, eruvs may also generate or reinforce demographic shifts as orthodox Jews move to live within an eruv boundary: this was a central concern of opponents of London's eruv.

The halakhic rules governing the area and population that can be enclosed by an eruv as well as the nature of its boundaries are incredibly complex.[2] While these rules are subject to rabbinical disagreement, and in many instances creatively reinterpreted in response to the problems raised by modern spaces, such as a golf course or motorway,[3] they are not completely flexible. This became only too apparent in the proposal to build a London eruv.[4] While a large part of the boundary encompassing the six and a half square miles would be formed by existing structures, it nevertheless required the installation of additional poles and wire to complete the perimeter.[5]

It was this application to install approximately eighty poles connected by a thin high wire to complete the boundary that became the focal point of a highly fraught local struggle. Ranged against the eruv was a loosely assembled group consisting mainly of non-orthodox Jewish, Christian and anti-religious objectors. While the opposition remained diverse in terms of class, age and political affiliation, the leadership and momentum appeared, from interviews and coverage, to emanate from older, middle-class residents with a particular antipathy to state-supported, religious-inflected multiculturalism.

In February 1993 Barnet Council turned down the planning application for additional poles and wire, citing environmental reasons; the applicants, United Synagogue Eruv Committee, appealed. In November 1993 an inquiry was held,[6] at the end of which the planning inspector recommended that permission should be granted. This was accepted by the Minister for the Environment, and subsequently the council agreed to an amended version of the original application. However, that did not stop protesters, who, having unsuccessfully sought judicial review, continued to oppose the eruv's installation.[7]

Cultural protection or the politics of accommodation

The subject of cultural protection has received considerable interest globally in recent decades, particularly in relation to indigenous peoples whose cultures and identity have been seen as jeopardized by the aggressive – whether exclusionary, assimiliationist or appropriating – practices of their colonizers (see generally Kymlicka, 1995). Cultural protection or survival has also been mobilized in relation to minority national communities in bi- or multinational states, such as the French Québécois of Canada (for example, Taylor, 1994, p. 58). Because my focus in this chapter is on Britain, where cultural protection does not have the same official status or popular currency as in some other countries, I am using the term, as one strand of the wider notion of community protection, to identify policies, initiatives or arguments that seek, at least ostensibly, to: (1) enable the survival of collective identities or communities that seem at risk; (2) look after the material and psychological well-being of peoples whose emotional health is contingent on the viability of a currently vulnerable culture; and (3) ensure the practices, traditions and artefacts associated with a fragile or assaulted culture are not lost or forgotten.

While cultural protection does not form an official stance in relation to Jewish practices and identity in Britain, the state does have policies and legislation which offer some form of limited accommodation (see Montgomery, 1992). This has tended to be grounded in a politics of recognition, by which I mean a limited measure of acceptance, entitlement and responsiveness towards what is perceived as a well-organized religious constituency with a long history in Britain. While as individual initiatives many of these policies and laws may be applauded, combined into a project or strategy of accommodation they are open to the accusation that such liberal forms of minimal recognition maintain an unequal society in which Jewish cultural traditions and practices are sustained and reproduced as marginal. At the same time, accommodation offers an inadequate response to anxious insiders who perceive the Jewish community as declining in both numbers and significance. While the latter tend to look to Jewish bodies rather than the state for solutions, a more proactive governmental strategy is seen by some as a constructive response to the inability of certain cultural forms and identifications to compete in the cultural market place (cf Waldron, 1995, p. 109). Yet what would a more proactive, cultural protection strategy entail? The practices and culture of the Jewish diaspora inevitably lack the spatial connections and intimate geographies of Aboriginal and First Nation communities, recognition of which forms a major plank of many cultural protection policies. While there is no locality in Britain officially organized according to a historically continuous 'Jewish way of life', a conventional cultural protection policy applied to Britain's Jews might look five ways: (1) to safeguarding individual Jews from antisemitic forms of expression; (2) to protecting and expanding the autonomy of Jewish community governance and legal provisions both within and beyond particular localities; (3) to facilitating the discrete practices associated with Jewish observance, such as the Sabbath, religious festivals, circumcision and ritual slaughter; (4) to protecting the Jewish identity and customs of 'vulnerable' community members, such as those in non-Jewish residential care; and (5) to funding and encouraging Jewish cultural and intellectual events, while protecting significant Jewish sites, such as synagogues and cemeteries, from vandalism and decay.

In exploring the political implications and relative merits of cultural protection strategies, writers have drawn attention to several key issues. These are also relevant to any attempt to extend cultural protection policies in relation to a Jewish 'community'. First, cultural protection, with its imagined mosaic of adjacent difference, tends to downplay the impact on identity formation of racializing processes: the (re)production of categories, exclusions, power differences and other injustices based on historically contingent understandings of geographically determining 'origins' (see generally Anthias, 1998; Segal and Handler, 1995; Vasta, 1993; Vertovec, 1996).[8] If racial processes remain bracketed, cultural protection not only disregards the interconstitutive relations between different identities, but can also sustain and fortify majority cultures as well as those traditionally defined as vulnerable.

Second, how can polities prevent cultural protection policies from further embedding the subordinate status of minority constituencies as a result of state reliance and patronage (e.g. see Brown, 1995)? This also raises a more general issue: to what extent are cultures perceived as shaped and structured by government action? Cultural protection discourse encounters a paradox at this point. On the one hand, it is premised on the belief that government policies and legal protection can make a difference; on the other, it tends to assume that cultures are relatively autonomous of governments. In other words, while prior governmental action may have injured minority communities, it did not shape their culture in any significant way. Thus an authentic, continuous culture can be identified – indeed, often must be identified – before cultural protection policies will be activated: a requirement criticized by several writers (e.g. Kline, 1994).[9]

Protection is thus largely backward-looking: oriented towards what was and is. It cannot protect that which does not exist; it cannot deal with cultural omissions other than to help sustain them. The best it can do in terms of being forward-looking is to grant rights and exemptions to a community so that it can decide the course of its own development. But this, whilst in some ways beneficial, also causes difficulties. If communities are to receive different treatment, then how group membership is defined becomes an important, and provocative, issue: for instance, in this context what are the conditions of Jewish membership and who gets to decide the criteria and whether they have been met (see also Cooper and Herman, 1999)? Many commentators have argued that when decision-making authority is given to a 'community', it is frequently given explicitly or in effect to the most traditional, powerful, male or conservative voices within it (see also Montgomery 1992, pp. 200-1; Mukta, 2000; Vertovec, 1996, p. 57). This also affects which cultural forms receive 'protection'. In the main, cultural protection targets those aspects of a culture identified by the (minority or majority) establishment as integral to a community's existence. Thus, in relation to Judaism, emphasis centres on rituals of religious significance or the reproduction of a religious heritage between generations. It is unlikely that cultural protection would be used, for instance, to safeguard the 'special relationship' between Jews and Chinese food, despite the fact 'Jews who went to Chinese restaurants together were helping to define Chinese food as an essential element in the lifestyle of modernized . . . Jews' (Tuchman and Levine, 1993, p. 394).[10] While this relationship would tend to be seen as a contingent and incidental development, far from the core of Jewish identity and cultural life, for non-religious Jews, spatially and temporally specific food, manners, forms of interaction, attitudes and relationships to politics, sex and work may seem far more significant than religious law in the construction and identification of a Jewish life.

But if cultural protection fails to target less mainstream practices, artefacts, relations or physical structures as sites for shielding or safeguarding, is the solution a more extensive response to the question who or what should count as Jewish? Should a polity protect, for instance, the special relationship between Ashkenazi Jews and Chinese food? The problem with seeing the solution in an expansionist strategy is that it sidesteps the question: why protect? Despite a tendency of cultural protection to collapse peoples into cultures,[11] the strands outlined earlier should be seen as sometimes pulling in different directions. For instance, protecting all existing practices may not be the best way of sustaining a community over time. Indeed, communities that develop in diasporic or colonized environments are used to adapting and responding to the conditions – both negative and positive – that they face (see, for example, Buckser, 2000, p. 727).

This suggests that communities can change without it affecting their ability to maintain an enduring identity. But this, in turn, raises a further dilemma: if cultural protection is concerned with community survival, what does survival mean in the context of a constantly evolving community? Is it dependent on an inner perception, an unchanging core or essence, the integration of change, or simply the retention of a group name? Again, how continuity is identified will depend on the justification for community protection. In other words, is survival valued because it maintains diversity, because its prospect is important to the well-being of *existing* communities, or because the existence of traditions and enduring practices is vital to a community's quality of life?

Having raised some critical concerns regarding cultural protection as a model of politically engineered change, I want now to turn to an alternative approach which shifts the starting point from safeguarding difference to engagement with social norms. While protecting cultures emerges out of normative debate, as a policy stance it can overwhelm the reasons for its initial advocacy. In the following discussion I want to recentre the question of values by exploring the way in which protagonists fought over the London eruv (see also Cooper, 1998b; for eruv conflicts elsewhere, Metzger, 1989; Valins, 2000). Both sides emphasized the various harms they saw their opponents as causing. My argument is thus twofold: first, that these harms are tied to particular social values; second, that processes which enable competing values to come to the fore facilitate a more satisfying and richer public debate. In the discussion that follows, I focus on the first part of the argument; I return to the second part in the conclusion.

Contesting harm, negotiating value

Beyond the thwarting of interests

Within traditional liberalism, the harm principle provides a core tenet around which social regulation takes place. In other words, individual liberty is permitted as long as, and as far as, it does not harm others. Yet the deeply embedded character of this premise does not eliminate ambiguity and contestation: one person's perception of injury can be another person's reasonable conduct. Here I am not referring to a brawl where several participants, and even onlookers, suffer physical hurt, but the more complex social scenario where harm identifies less directly corporeal forms of pain. For instance, in Britain and elsewhere, at the turn of the twenty-first century, conservative Christian organizations are vociferously claiming that their inability lawfully to discriminate against lesbians and gay men in their hiring practices injures their religious autonomy as well as potentially their business. At the same time, permitting employment discrimination undeniably hurts the economic, social and psychological well-being of those encountering rejection.

Identification of harm, then, is clearly non-exclusive: all sides can identify its presence or possibility. Does this render harm unusable as a criterion of public policy? Should other principles be found by which to identify the legitimate boundaries of social activity? The trouble is that, despite its rhetorical and often strategic manipulation (see, for example, Mukta, 2000, pp. 446–7), bracketing harm ends up erasing a principle of profound social significance. In other words, sensitivity to harm and injury – whether caused to or by ourselves – is a core plank of current inter-personal relations. That being the case, we need to consider more closely than often takes place how best harm may be conceptualized (see also Howe, 1987; Feinberg, 1984; Kernohan, 1998). The question of harm is central to both criminology and criminal/civil law. While criminology tends to focus on exploring, critically or otherwise, the structures, culture and procedures established to discourage criminality or harm (e.g. see Hughes, 1998, 2000; Hope and Sparks, 2000), criminal law concerns the relationship between harm and the location of responsibility (Hirsch, 1996) in the light of such issues as remoteness, culpability, probability and social consequences.

We can see these issues at play in relation to the contested legal arenas of corporate crime and racially aggravated assault. Here, in contrast to so-called 'victimless crimes', the left project has often tended towards extending the contours of what constitutes harm and injury (Muncie, 2000, pp. 222–3), compressing complex chains of causation and the accumulations of history in order to locate responsibility. This does not mean a legal remedy is always demanded. Public policy responses to harms such as the misrecognition or marginalization of a culture (see Taylor, 1994, p. 64; Wolf, 1994, p. 823; Fraser, 1997), while they may entail new legislation, centre social and economic strategies rather than prohibition and punishment. Calls to develop a more socially nuanced, less individualist approach to harm both within and outside the criminal law have also come from feminist quarters (see Howe, 1987). Equating harm with social forms of oppression and dominance, feminist activism has sought to extend the law to encompass specifically gendered practices (see also Conaghan, 1996).[12]

In the discussion that follows I want to approach harm as 'injury to that which has social value'. This contrasts with the more formal, but potentially subjective, definition of harm used by many legal scholars; the 'thwarting, setting back, or defeating of an interest' (Feinberg, 1984, p. 33; see also Archard, 1998, p. 70), that is, undermining 'those things in which one has a stake' (Feinberg, 1984, p. 34). While views of what has worth will clearly differ, in the approach adopted here harm is not restricted to individuals' own perception of what they value about themselves and their life. For instance, if individuals wish to be subordinated, humiliated or physically injured, they may feel any restriction constitutes a form of harm. Instead of getting entangled in questions of interests and their relation to preferences, we can ask instead: what of value has been injured? At first glance, this may appear to resemble a standard harm analysis in which judgement about whether a wrong has occurred emerges from balancing the injury to the subject – here humiliation – against the value of the conduct, and the degree to which a prohibition will curtail freedom (see generally Feinberg, 1984, p. 216; Hirsch, 1996). Yet, while theorists tend to relate value to the secondary question of wrong, thereby treating the designation of harm as a prior issue, the approach I am adopting treats questions of value as constitutive of harm itself.

The second distinctive aspect of this approach is to avoid restricting harm to the 'cutting back' or injuring of an existing state. This means incorporating an analysis of omissions, such as a government's refusal to extend welfare benefits. It also means expanding harm to encompass continuous acts, such as the subordination of women, where no state prior to injury can be confidently identified. The reason I want to conceptualize harm in this way is that I am interested in a wider range of policy responses than simply the criminal law, to consider appropriate policy responses in contexts where no criminal action or even negligent conduct has taken place. Social, economic and cultural policies need a way of being able to evaluate and tackle harm in situations where there is no offender, of being able to recognize harm when they cannot point to a state prior to its commencement. This means they require a thicker conception of harm than simply impeding another's interests.

My final general point concerns the way in which a value-based approach focuses attention on the recipient of harm. While often seemingly self-evident, our easy identifying of the 'victim' is actually a product of the subconscious internalization of social norms and rules. This is evident if we consider an example of 'victim' identification which now clashes with current values. For instance, in an earlier era, when a woman was raped the person recognized as harmed was the husband, since his property in her person was given far greater value than her entitlement not to experience non-consensual, intimate physical contact (see also Conaghan, 1998, pp. 137–8). A similar ambiguity over who or what has been harmed is still apparent in relation to children (see Butler and Williamson, 1994). While smacking by a parent is not ubiquitously defined as harmful, frequent physical attacks, assault by a stranger or sexual touching are. Although in a state of flux, the distinction between the two is, at least in part, based on the notion that the subject of harm is not the 'autonomous child' but the 'healthy future adult'. Thus what constitutes harm is defined by the subject positions that different societies value.

Battling over the eruv's harms

In the conflict over the proposed North London eruv, notions of harm were verbalized by both sides in multiple ways. Opponents identified the risks of installation as the aesthetic, cultural, religious and physical injury to community and environment. Their objections ranged from the claim that the poles required to complete the perimeter would prove an eyesore, and constitute unnecessary additional street furniture to arguing that the eruv would convert the neighbourhood into a religious enclave, generating unwelcome demographic shifts and the cultural dispossession of non-believers who found themselves living in orthodox Jewish space. In addition, opponents argued, building an eruv would provoke antisemitic acts of vandalism and possible violence, while reminding concentration camp victims of the Holocaust every time they passed under its gateways. In response, supporters claimed that establishing an eruv would not harm anyone, while refusing planning permission would cause the parents of young children (predominantly mothers) and disabled people to face restricted mobility on the Sabbath. In addition, denial would make religious observance harder to sustain, and thus contribute to the 'decline' in Jewish orthodoxy.

While all these conflicting issues were framed largely within the language of harm, I do not want to suggest this rendered harm superfluous. Instead, I want to suggest that harm's relationship to value offers a way through the dispute. Let me unpack some of these claims to show what I mean, starting with the most unequivocal conception of harm: physical violence, here by strangers provoked into action through their hostility to the eruv. Leaving aside questions of causation, likelihood or directness of injury, does the possibility of violence – to the eruv structure or to local Jews – render the eruv harmful? Eruv objectors' arguments suggested that harm emanated from the provocative spatial expression of (orthodox) Jewish visibility, thus implying that what had been undermined was minority invisibility, particularly in terms of its relationship to space. But is this invisibility something to be preserved? If not, we might avoid imputing responsibility for physical violence in the eruv's installation, locating it instead in those actors who decide to vandalize Jewish structures or to attack Jewish residents. Adopting this approach means that responsibility is not a simple, linear effect of causation – for, on one reading, the installation of the eruv might precipitate violence – but is rather a political decision based on determining the nature of the 'contribution' in relation to bodies, practices, norms or artefacts of social value.[13]

A similar approach can be adopted to unpacking the values underlying other accusations of eruv harm. If the neighbourhood is harmed through an influx of orthodox Jews, this suggests a value in demographic limitation, raising the (usually neglected) counterpoint: is there a similar optimum level of Anglican concentration? Equally, if opponents claim that the identification of the territory as 'Jewish' is harmful, this can only be because the identification and sense of belonging of others is undermined (since nothing is practically expected of non-believers as a result of this symbolic interpellation). But what was this, now seemingly injured, sense of belonging of others based upon? While some objectors I interviewed depicted neighbourhood space as previously neutral, others acknowledged the generally embedded character of the Anglican Church, and of Christianity (see Cooper, 1996). Yet, given the status of Anglican Christianity in Britain, it seems doubtful that an eruv would realistically challenge the prevailing cultural skewing even within the locale in which it was installed. It therefore seems plausible that what objectors really perceived as harmed was a certain cultural monopoly which kept at a distance the ties and non-exclusive claims to space of cultural minorities. Again we might ask: is this worth preserving?

While the objections raised so far may seem to fail uncontrovertibly when discussed according to the language of value, the two potentially strongest claims in this respect, I would suggest, relate to the question of landscape and memory triggers. Yet, whilst environmental aesthetics may be a legitimate concern, the level of physical unsightliness that eighty more poles would cause to a borough with thousands seems insignificant. Indeed, the question of spatial 'good looks' seems to have functioned largely as a surrogate for more racially infused aesthetic fears. Similarly, while the mental health of Holocaust survivors may generally be regarded as important, arguably more evidence was needed of the hurt the eruv would cause than was proffered by objectors. It is probably not sufficient simply to declare that survivors entering beneath the eruv perimeter will be reminded of a camp or ghetto. Indeed, the planning inspector declared on this point, '[T]he objectors' assertions that the mere existence of the poles would be an offensive and upsetting reminder of the Holocaust to Jews . . . are difficult to substantiate.' Here, then, is an instance where causation and its empirical demonstration are relevant. At the same time, showing the emotional suffering caused to Holocaust survivors may not negate the value of the eruv. This is not because, as eruv advocates suggested, such views or feelings are mistaken: the eruv is *not* a camp, for survivors obviously knew this. Identifying harm in this context cannot be premised on a single, authentic response; and eruv proponents cannot demand that outsiders interpret the eruv only in terms of its meaning within halakhic law. Rather, it is because even if the eruv was identified as causing psychological suffering to survivors, that would need to be considered in the light of the harms generated by planning refusal.

Before turning to the question of how such conflicts of harms might be addressed, I want to sketch some of the injuries rejecting an eruv might engender: the most immediate and direct being the restricted movement of parents and wheelchair-mobile people. Freedom of movement may be of generally recognized value, but objectors counter-claimed that since the constraint was self-imposed it did not count. In other words, through choosing not to push or carry, observant Jews had restricted their own freedom, bringing harm upon themselves. Given this, it was not the job of the state, opponents argued, to remedy such a self-imposed injury. The notion of self-imposed constraint raises interesting and difficult issues; does consent or willingness eliminate any responsibility upon the state or wider community to (mitigate) harm? And when should public policy recognize choice or consent as existing? For instance, what does it mean to say orthodox Jews have a choice whether or not to comply with religious law? There is not the space to discuss the issues this raises about religious identification, agency and the social constitution of belonging. However, one way of approaching the question from a public policy perspective is to ask whether there is a social value in recognizing people's commitment to religious law in a context where recognition would mean enabling people to carry in halakhically recognized ways rather than requiring them to contravene religious law.

Finally, I want to refer to two other potential harms of planning rejection: declining religious observance and injury to a Jewish sense of belonging. Both raise questions of causation; however, my interest here is in what they suggest about social value. Is religious observance something of value worth protecting? Should people's relationship and commitment to their 'own' culture be sustained, a position espoused by Margalit and Halbertal (1994, p. 506)? And is it important that orthodox Jewish residents feel they belong to, and are part of, a neighbourhood? This second issue is less concerned with the reproduction of Jewish faith, and with sustaining religious diversity, than with the experiences of individuals who happen to identify, encounter and shape their neighbourhood, at least in part, as orthodox Jews. My own view is that equal belonging is more important than sustaining religious orthodoxy. Indeed, I have argued elsewhere (Cooper, 1998b, 2000a) that facilitating the symbols and practices of different communities can help to create heterogeneous spaces, in which people identify more equally as both belonging and positively as strangers.

Highlighting the centrality of value to claims of harm is a plea for a more explicitly normative politics. Admittedly, this might sometimes end up with one harm or social good being balanced against another in ways familiar to those who have watched rights discourse similarly used: 'a woman's right to choose' versus 'the rights of the unborn child', for example. But rights are often formalistic, particularly where the focus is on rights already granted legal recognition. In contrast, centring value means engaging with the kind of society we want. This is rarely, if ever, a clear-cut, uncontested process. Its merit, however, is in the way it centres different, competing 'strings' of interconnecting norms, beliefs and values. In this context, a political process which highlights the fact that both building and refusing permission for an eruv may cause recognized forms of harm demands something more than simply a balancing act between two sets of injury. This may be flexibility and compromise on the part of participants; however, it may also call for a more structural form of adjustment or resolution that both exceeds and reconfigures the options, authority and cleavages drawn in battle.

Conclusion: towards a cultural politics of value

My aim in this study of the eruv has been twofold. First, I have sought to explore the benefits and limitations of community protection as a policy response towards ethnic and religious differences; second, I have suggested ways in which a paradigm of harm linked to social value may help in clarifying the normative issues at stake. In relation to the eruv, my own view is that the harm of denying permission is greater and more serious than the reverse. Most concretely, permitting an eruv enables a wider traversing of common, outdoor space and eases the Sabbath. Symbolically, it helps to make common spaces more public to the extent that it extends their heterogeneous character and thus disrupts the link between any single constituency and the locale. Elsewhere I have argued for public space as a process rather than a physical entity, defining it as the spatial dimension of the on-going, contested process of building a sense of collective identification and belonging between strangers sharing equal regard (Cooper, 1998b).

Clearly, the eruv may not achieve this; indeed, opponents claimed the reverse would occur: that the space 'enclosed' by the eruv would become more homogeneous, converting into an orthodox Jewish neighbourhood, inimical to others (see generally Margalit and Halbertal, 1994, p. 507). To some extent, the impact of London's eruv remains an open question, dependent in part on the response of 'outsiders' who find themselves living within it. Nevertheless, despite this, and despite the fact that some orthodox communities may prove relatively inward-looking (e.g. see Van Praagh, 1996, p. 195), with thick, well defined boundaries,[14] governmental and community support for structures based on minority ethnic claims goes some way to rupturing a unitary public, defined by hegemonic exclusions and inequalities. In other words, even if the eruv neighbourhood itself becomes less heterogeneous, less internally oriented towards equal regard between cultural strangers, its articulation of minority ethnicities to physical community spaces may contribute to wider, external processes of public creation.

The development of an egalitarian public – in a context of competing shifts towards the privatizing of social responsibility and relationships, and in a historical context intimate, differentiated relationships are valorized (Cooper, 2000a) – is one value-based development I would like policy responses to ethnic and religious difference to pursue. In this final section of this chapter, then, I want to leave the specific case study of the eruv to one side to consider more generally the 'turn' to values. To suggest that we reorient cultural conflicts explicitly around differences of value is far from risk-free, given the contribution of value-laden discourses, including freedom, equality and culture, to the rationalization of racism and colonialism. Indeed, it is against this background of normative imperialism that multiculturalism has ostensibly sought to bracket the judging of 'our ends': the different values given to contrasting ways of life (see discussion in Kymlicka, 1995, p. 81; Raz, 1994, pp. 159–64; Taylor, 1994, p. 56). But this does not render multiculturalism value-free.

Leaving to one side the tangled debate over which values and 'ends' actually get bracketed, given the normative premises, implications and explicit claims of multiculturalism, I want also to suggest that there is a heavy political cost to a refusal to consider questions of value. As Jeffrey Weeks (1995, p. 64) argues, drawing on the work of Agnes Heller, Ernesto Laclau and Charles Taylor, justice requires the possibility of evaluating and even 'ranking' different ways of life. For Weeks, in the context of sexual intimacy, the key criteria are whether actions enhance life choices and freedom, recognizing that both are located within, and given meaning, by particular social contexts. Although I am unhappy with the concept of 'ranking', since, in the different context of ethnicity, it suggests that cultures are coherent, individual units which can be ordered according to merit or worth, Weeks's attempt to find a way of juggling questions of value in the light of their potential risks is an important one. In particular, it has implications for any process of cross-cultural communication in pursuit of progressive or radical change (see also Segal and Handler, 1995, p. 395), a process, I want to suggest, that is stymied by a liberal conception of community protection.

Let me take an example from the field of sexual politics to make my argument clearer. Lesbian and gay communities and cultures, particularly since the 1970s, have generated important, critical insights about desire, gender and heterosexuality on the one hand, as well as ways of living that emphasize friendship-based kinship structures, egalitarian domestic relationships, and counter-cultural forms of creativity, social interaction and humour. In saying this I am not suggesting there exists a unified, coherent gay culture or that these developments are exclusive to lesbian and gay communities; I accept Solomos's (1998, p. 62) useful reminder that human values should not be conflated, identified and celebrated as the characteristics of particular communities. At the same time, practices and perspectives emerge out of particular social conditions and experiences. The problem with liberal community protection paradigms is that they recognize this but identify the solution as one of walls between communities. In this example, the likely effect is to reproduce the bordered, minority status of lesbian and gay community critiques and social practices, causing any wider meaning or implications, except at a superficial level – the mainstream commodification of camp, for example – to become lost.[15] Yet, in other contexts, where community protection has been a less prominent paradigm, crossing-over has been more apparent. Feminism, for instance, has had some success in revising the discourses – if not the practices – of a normative masculinity according to values conventionally associated with women. Likewise, in the area of environmental politics, the values, traditions and practices of certain indigenous cultures have been drawn upon to challenge the West's pursuit of growth and naturalized hierarchy of life forms.

As with all broad normative agenda, a value-based approach can become a trite intellectual stance. Although there is not the space here to flesh it out in depth, I want to raise some of the issues that a value-based approach needs to consider (cf Mouffe, 1999). Let me start with an issue raised at different points throughout the chapter: who are the collectivities likely to emerge as subjects of any normative critique? One advantage of an approach which begins and ends with respect is that it seems to protect more vulnerable constituencies from criticism, condemnation and pathologizing. In the main, cultural and discursive conflicts do not revolve around the practices of dominant groupings, which tend to remain taken for granted and unmarked. Consequently, if conflict frames the terms and subject matter of evaluation,[16] it will steer interrogation towards the practices and values of minorities: the eruv rather than the parish system, for example; the veil rather than the conventions of Western, liberal democracies in which – except on the beach – only men go topless.[17]

At the same time I do not want to overstate the discursive invisibility of dominant practices and identities. Paralleling work on heterosexuality and masculinity, scholars and activists have begun to make visible the character and production of whiteness and hegemonic Anglo ethnicities (see, for example, Frankenberg, 1993; Roediger, 1994). In addition, from a less progressive perspective, others have leaped into the breach to name and protect traditional ethnicities from the perceived encroachment of other faiths and cultures (Smith, 1994; see also Feinberg, 1988, pp. 71–9). Blauner (1994, p. 27), for instance, describes the emergence of 'European-American' clubs among students at Californian colleges. In the British context, Christian hegemony became explicitly defended as the normatively valuable 'we' through the introduction and enforcement of the Education Reform Act 1988 (Cooper, 1998a). While these conservative moves were clearly not intended to challenge dominant norms, their efforts at engendering visibility have paradoxically also offered a foothold for those attempting to problematize and critically evaluate the *status quo*.

But do the activities of right-wing nationalist forces also highlight the irrelevance of a value-based approach, even one which seeks to argue against the norms underlying dominant practices and identities? Are inequalities of power, here most particularly racism, far more important? And is a shift in values dangerous to the extent that it obscures such fundamental issues? These are important concerns. However, to the extent that they dichotomize power and values they are also problematic. While equalizing power is important, as a single normative principle, it cannot do all the work. For instance, it does not tell us which way equality should go: levelling up or down; nor does it tell us which kinds of power should be encouraged or eliminated.

Yet, even if we accept that a value-based approach can both draw attention to and go beyond prevailing power inequalities, a further concern arises, namely: is there a risk that focusing on normative differences simply encourages counterproductive confrontation? Jeffers et al. (1996, p. 122) usefully raise this issue in a discussion of practice-based community relations. Their findings, based on a series of local cross-community initiatives, led them to suggest that any move which required participants to voice all their views and beliefs could prove destructive, and that many organizations worked better where people were encouraged to keep certain attitudes and feelings to themselves. However, a value-based approach does not mean that all opinions are voiced. Values can also be used to generate ground rules covering those topics or views which may most profitably remain unspoken within community fora, for instance, homophobic or racist opinions which explicitly identify some participants as of lesser value.

The flexible, plastic and open-ended character of value-based politics leads me to a final concern: if everything is of value, albeit at different levels of abstraction, adopting a value-based approach encompasses everything, and therefore tells us nothing. On the one hand this is true. Liberal forms of community protection are also based on values: that, in the good society, defined ways of life are entities worth preserving. At the same time, my example of lesbian and gay politics demonstrates the productively disruptive potential of a value-based approach: that it has a kind of universalism which asks, 'How might this way of living apply to others?' In other words – reversing cultural relativist debates – there is no assumption that values should be restricted to particular constituencies. A value-based approach can thus centre a wider, heterogeneous community or 'public' rather than individual constituencies within it. In this way it differentiates itself from two processes: the imposition of moral judgement upon the 'you' and, second, the production of a narrow identity politics which treats groups as discrete entities with the exclusive right and requirement to represent and speak only for themselves.[18] To the extent that it rejects the retreat to a mosaic of defined, immutable differences, a value-based approach can complement, and assist, the move towards hybrid, ambivalent identities, rejecting the communalization of responsibility on the grounds that the affairs of others are 'none of my responsibility'.

Value – the good society – is a messy, murky, highly risky space for political engagement. However, it has never been evacuated by liberals, conservatives or, for that matter, by progressives either. What has happened, though, in recent decades, particularly following the downfall of the Soviet Union, and the rising influence of anti-utopian poststructuralism, has been reluctance on the part of many of the pluralist left to engage with it fully and openly. Freedom, rights, privacy, equality, democracy, even efficiency – the stuff of modern political discourse – are clearly normative concepts, despite having a successful existence passing as technocratic, obvious and natural. While there are clear strategic incentives to engage in such 'passing' if it carries legitimacy and silences opponents, there is also a down side. The political emphasis on efficiency, effectiveness and formal rights has caused a stunting within British politics in its development of a rich, complex engagement with values. The problems this generates are perhaps at their most vivid in the contested space of ethnic, sexual and cultural difference.

Notes

My thanks to Joanne Conagham and Richard Sparks for their help and to Didi Herman and Gordon Hughes for their suggestions on this chapter. The field research on which the chapter is based – approximately fifteen interviews with leading figures in the eruv conflict, as well as examination of documents and media coverage – was carried out in Barnet, north London, in 1995–96.

1 A similar ambivalence is apparent in British public policy responses, in the late 1990s, to the influx of refugees. More generally, I do not want to create a boundary between issues to do with racism and those concerning ethnic/ religious difference, as they are clearly entwined in complex, inextricable ways. However, within public policy and academic discourse, one or other is usually centred, with discussion and policy proposals developing in different ways. Thus my focus in this chapter is on issues *identified* as predominantly matters of ethnic and religious difference rather than of 'race'. For a useful discussion of the intersection of ethnicity and race, see Anthias, 1998, where questions of protection and harm are frequently contested at an earlier stage.

2 See, for example, Rabbi Jachter, 'The laws of creating an eruv' http:// www.tabc.org/ koltorah/ jachter/ 57/ eruv.htm (accessed November 2000).

3 For instance, in Miami Beach, Florida, halakhic issues arose regarding how to treat the golf course and waterways; see *The Record*, 20 September 1994.

4 See *Barnet LBC* and *United Synagogue Eruv Committee* (1995) 10 PAD (Planning Appeal Decisions) 209.

5 United Synagogue Eruv Committee, Barnet Council Briefing, 3 June 1992.

6 See *Barnet LBC* and *United Synagogue Eruv Committee*, op. cit.

7 See 'Eruv objection thrown out', *Hampstead and Highgate Express*, 20 June 1997; 'Eruv survives legal challenge', *Jewish Chronicle*, 20 June 1997.

8 The power of different origins to 'determine' 'race' is historically and culturally specific and frequently uneven. For instance, the US 'one-drop' laws meant people could be legally defined as black even though most of their ancestry was legally white: see Zack (1995).

9 See also, for example, *R. v. Van Der Peet* [1996] 2 SCR 507; 137 DLR (4th) 289; 2 CIIRLD 69, where a majority of the Canadian Supreme Court held that protection required identifying a continuity of commercial fishing practice with pre-European times.

10 Tuchman and Levine's (1993) article focuses on New York, but their arguments have a wider salience. The article explores some of the reasons why eating in Chinese restaurants held a special, long-standing attraction for Jewish immigrants to New York from Eastern Europe and to their descendants. Their argument suggests that East European Jews saw Chinese food as cosmopolitan, urbane and sophisticated; Chinese restaurants (unlike Italian ones) did not display Christian icons; Chinese food while unkosher was, and still is, prepared in ways that render it less threatening to Jews used to Kosher cuisine; and the communal, discursive aspects of ordering and eating appealed.

11 While the character of a 'people' may be radically different without a particular form of cultural expression and identification, peoples are more than their particular cultures. This is partly because our lives are shaped by the intersection of a range of cultural, social and economic systems – class, gender, ethnicity, sexuality – but also because the experience of being human cannot

be reduced to the combinations, however complex, of such locations or memberships. The danger of ignoring this, of overstating the mutual con-stitutiveness between people and culture, is that whilst the link is intended as a facilitative one – mobilized to anchor aid and protection – it is always at risk of flipping over, so that the despisement of a culture promotes the elimination of a people.

12   Attempts by left and feminist forces to extend the remit of harm have not been without their critics. Liberals fear that expanding the category of injury erases the divide between harm and offence. Even if the criminal law does not intervene, extending the remit of responsibility for collective and historical wrongs, and for acts that mirror – even if they do not reinforce – current inequalities of power assumes, while simultaneously undermining, personal agency. Thus the libertarian and poststructuralist left have also been ambi-valent about widening harm, in terms of what constitutes harm as well as in locating responsibility.

13   Locating responsibility and identification of harm at the point of physical violence is premised on identifying value in two things. The first is relatively uncontroversial: freedom from unwanted, painful, physical contact. The second only slightly more: that symbols of minority ethnic and religious communities should not be subject to attack. This does not necessarily imply that the symbols themselves are of value, but that criticism should be expressed in ways that recognize and respect the identification constituencies have with particular symbolic structures.

14   Eruv organizers also stress the importance of staying within the eruv's boundaries on the Sabbath and that local congregants should check, before carrying, to ensure that the eruv is properly up and running each week – that no parts of the structure have been vandalized or breached by bad weather.

15   But if values emerge out of particular social experiences, can they be gener-alized beyond those experiences? If, for example, lesbian and gay men created 'families of choice' in part as a response to rejection by 'families of birth', can the value of non-biological, friendship-based kinship structures be transferred to communities where the need to create alternative families does not apply? This question raises several issues: can people be convinced that a particular structure is of wider value and should be supported or facilitated through public policy? Is recognizing the value of something sufficient to generate its adoption? Can the normative meaning of particular structures be effectively communicated and implemented across differences of experience and social location? These questions highlight the need for a value-based approach to steer away from becoming an idealist stance in which 'successful' normative claims are located at the start of a linear chain that ends with their replication in wider practices and public policy.

16   This is a point unfortunately neglected by Waldron (1995) in his critique of cultural preservation. Waldron adopts a 'survival of the fittest' approach to cultural exchanges and evolution, ignoring the fact that the cultures which prevail tend to be the most powerful rather than the most environmentally suited or beneficial.

17   While many current motivations for these two forms of covering up diverge, in other respects similarities exist. For instance, both are represented in public discourse and by many women as necessary techniques for shielding them-selves from the public sexualization, disrespect and physical vulnerability that

male visual access to the body is feared to generate. In other words, it is not only in the Muslim context (see Read and Bartkowski, 2000), that women take responsibility for and manage, by covering up, the constant threat posed by 'excessive' male sexuality.

18 This does not mean a relegitimization of 'imperialist' forms of representation where white middle-class men speak for everyone. But it also means going beyond the current practice where less powerful constituencies speak for themselves and can be marginalized as 'special interests' while constituencies identified as the majority, in particular contexts, speak on behalf of us all.

References

Anthias, F. (1998) 'The limits of ethnic "diversity"', *Patterns of Prejudice*, vol. 32, no. 4, pp. 5–19.

Archard, D. (1998) *Sexual Consent*, Oxford, Westview Press.

Bennett, F. (1999) 'The face of the state', *Political Studies*, vol. 47, no. 4, pp. 677–90.

Blauner, B. (1994) 'Talking past each other: black and white languages of race' in Pincus, F. and Ehrlich, H. (eds) *Race and Ethnic Conflict: Contending Views on Prejudice, Discrimination and Ethnoviolence*, Boulder, CO, Westview Press.

Brown, W. (1995) *States of Injury*, Princeton, NJ, Princeton University Press.

Buckser, A. (2000) 'Jewish identity and the meaning of community in Denmark', *Ethnic and Racial Studies*, vol. 23, no. 4, pp. 712–34.

Butler, I. and Williamson, H. (1994) *Children Speak: Children, Trauma and Social Work*, Harlow, Longman.

Conaghan, J. (1996) 'Gendered harms and the law of tort: remedying (sexual) harassment', *Oxford Journal of Legal Studies*, vol. 16, pp. 407–31.

Conaghan, J. (1998) 'Tort litigation in the context of intra-familial abuse', *Modern Law Review*, vol. 61, no. 2, pp. 132–61.

Cooper, D. (1996) 'Talmudic territory? Space, law and modernist discourse', *Journal of Law and Society*, vol. 23, no. 4, pp. 529–48.

Cooper, D. (1998a) *Governing out of Order: Space, Law and the Politics of Belonging*, London, Rivers Oram.

Cooper, D. (1998b) 'Regard between strangers: diversity, equality and the reconstruction of public space', *Critical Social Policy*, vol. 18, no. 4, pp. 465–92.

Cooper, D. (2000a) 'And you can't find me nowhere: relocating identity and structure within equality jurisprudence', *Journal of Law and Society*, vol. 27, no. 2, pp. 249–72.

Cooper, D. (2000b) 'Promoting injury or freedom: radical pluralism and orthodox Jewish symbolism', *Ethnic and Racial Studies*, vol. 23, no. 6, pp. 1062–85.

Cooper, D. and Herman, D. (1999) 'Jews and other uncertainties: race, faith and English law', *Legal Studies*, vol. 19, no. 3, pp. 339–66.

Etzioni, A. (1997) 'The end of cross-cultural relativism', *Alternatives*, vol. 22, pp. 177–89.

Feinberg, J. (1984) *The Moral Limits of the Criminal Law*, vol. 1, *Harm to Others*, New York, Oxford University Press.

Feinberg, J. (1988) *The Moral Limits of the Criminal Law*, vol. 4, *Harmless Wrongdoing*, New York, Oxford University Press.

Frankenberg, R. (1993) *White Women, Race Matters: The Social Construction of Whiteness*, Minneapolis, MN, University of Minnesota Press.

Fraser, N. (1997) *Justice Interruptus*, New York, Routledge.

Galeotti, A.E. (1993) 'Citizenship and equality: the place for toleration', *Political Theory*, vol. 21, no. 4, pp. 585–605.

Gutmann, A. (ed.) (1994) *Multiculturalism: Examining the Politics of Recognition*, Princeton, NJ, Princeton University Press.

Hirsch, A. von (1996) 'Extending the harm principle: "remote" harms and fair imputation' in Simester, A.P. and Smith, A.T.H. (eds) *Harm and Culpability*, Oxford, Clarendon Press.

Hope, T. and Sparks, R. (2000) 'For a sociological theory of situations (or how useful is pragmatic criminology?)' in Garland, D., von Hirsch, A. and Wakefield, A. (eds) *Situational Crime Prevention: Ethics and Social Context*, Oxford, Hart Publishing.

Howe, A. (1987) 'Social injury revisited: towards a feminist theory of social justice', *International Journal of the Sociology of Law*, vol. 15, pp. 423–38.

Hughes, G. (1998) *Understanding Crime Prevention: Social Control, Risk and Late Modernity*, Buckingham, Open University Press.

Hughes, G. (2000) 'In the shadow of crime and disorder: the contested politics of community safety in Britain', *Crime Prevention and Community Safety*, vol. 2, no. 3. pp. 47–60.

Jeffers, S., Hoggett, P. and Harrison, L. (1996) 'Race, ethnicity and community in three localities', *New Community*, vol. 22, no. 1, pp. 111–26.

Kernohan, A. (1998) *Liberalism, Equality, and Cultural Oppression*, Cambridge, Cambridge University Press.

Kline, M. (1994) 'The colour of law: ideological representations of First Nations in legal discourse', *Social and Legal Studies*, vol. 3, pp. 451–76.

Kymlicka, W. (1995) *Multicultural Citizenship: A Liberal Theory of Minority Rights*, Oxford, Clarendon Press.

Légaré, E. (1995) 'Canadian multiculturalism and Aboriginal people: negotiating a place in the nation', *Identities*, vol. 1, no. 4, pp. 347–66.

Margalit, A. and Halbertal, M. (1994) 'Liberalism and the right to culture', *Social Research*, vol. 61, no. 3, pp. 491–510.

Metzger, J. (1989) 'The eruv: can government constitutionally permit Jews to build a fictional wall without breaking the wall between church and state?', *National Jewish Law Review*, vol. 4, no. 1, pp. 67–92.

Montgomery, J. (1992) 'Legislating for a multi-faith society: some problems of special treatment' in Hepple, B. and Szyszczak, E. (eds) *Discrimination: The Limits of Law*, London, Mansell.

Mouffe, C. (1999) 'Deliberative democracy or agonistic pluralism?' *Social Research*, vol. 66, no. 3, pp. 745–58.

Mukta, P. (2000) 'The public face of Hindu nationalism', *Ethnic and Racial Studies*, vol. 23, no. 3, pp. 442–66.

Muncie, J. (2000) 'Decriminalizing criminology' in Lewis, G., Gewirtz, S. and Clarke, J. (eds) *Rethinking Social Policy*, London, Sage.

Pease, K. and Wiles, P. (2000) 'Crime prevention and community safety: Tweedledum or Tweedledee?' in Ballintyne, S., Pease, K. and McLaren, V. (eds) *Secure Foundations: Key Issues in Crime Prevention, Crime Reduction and Community Safety*, London, Institute for Public Policy Research.

Prott, L. (1999) 'Understanding one another on cultural rights', *Art, Antiquity and the Law*, vol. 4, no. 3, pp. 229–41.

Qadeer, M. (1997) 'Pluralistic planning for multicultural cities', *Journal of the American Planning Association*, vol. 63, no. 4, pp. 481–94.

Raz, J. (1994) *Ethics in the Public Domain*, Oxford, Clarendon.

Read, J.G. and Bartkowski, J. (2000) 'To veil or not to veil? A case study of identity negotiation among Muslim women in Austin, Texas', *Gender and Society*, vol. 14, no. 3, pp. 395–417.

Roediger, D. (1994) *Towards the Abolition of Whiteness*, London, Verso.

Segal, D. and Handler, R. (1995) 'US multiculturalism and the concept of culture', *Identities*, vol. 1, no. 4. pp. 391–407.

Smith, A.M. (1994) *New Right Discourse on Race and Sexuality: Britain, 1968–1990*, Cambridge, Cambridge University Press.

Solomos, J. (1998) 'Beyond racism *and* multiculturalism', *Patterns of Prejudice*, vol. 32, no. 4, pp. 45–62.

Taylor, C. (1994) 'The politics of recognition' in Gutmann, A. (ed.) *Multiculturalism*, Princeton, NJ, Princeton University Press.

Tuchman, G. and Levine, H. (1993) 'New York Jews and Chinese food', *Journal of Contemporary Ethnography*, vol. 22, no. 3, pp. 382–407.

Valins, O. (2000) 'Institutionalized religion: sacred texts and Jewish spatial practice', *Geoforum*, vol. 31, no. 4, pp. 575–86.

Van Praagh, S. (1996) 'The chutzpah of chasidism', *Canadian Journal of Law and Society*, vol. 11, no. 2, pp. 193–215.

Vasta, E. (1993) 'Multiculturalism and ethnic identity: the relationship between racism and resistance', *Australian and New Zealand Journal of Sociology*, vol. 29, no. 2, pp. 209–25.

Vertovec, S. (1996) 'Multiculturalism, culturalism and public incorporation', *Ethnic and Racial Studies*, vol. 19, no. 1, pp. 49–69.

Waldron, J. (1995) 'Minority cultures and the cosmopolitan alternative' in Kymlicka, W. (ed.) *The Rights of Minority Cultures*, Oxford, Oxford University Press.

Wayland, S. (1997) 'Religious expressions in public schools: Kirpans in Canada, hijab in France', *Ethnic and Racial Studies*, vol. 20, no. 3, pp. 545–61.

Weeks, J. (1995) *Invented Moralities: Sexual Values in an Age of Uncertainty*, Cambridge, Polity Press.

Wolf, S. (1994) 'Comment' in Gutmann, A. (ed.) *Multiculturalism*, Princeton, NJ, Princeton University Press.

Zack, N. (1995) 'Mixed black and white race and public policy', *Hypatia*, vol. 10, no. 1, pp. 120–32.

Teetering on the edge

The futures of crime control and community safety

Gordon Hughes, Eugene McLaughlin and John Muncie

This chapter discusses possible futures and visions of crime control and the new politics of safety and security in the twenty-first century. We begin by attending to the broad debates about the new 'post-social' society and related cultural understandings of our present 'condition' and competing scenarios of the future. The chapter then examines where mainstream, 'policy-relevant' criminological thinking and research may be heading. In particular, we take up the debate about the shifting boundaries of the subject and what appears to be a potentially new paradigm of what constitutes 'the criminological' and the new technologies of crime reduction, surveillance and control. In the conclusion we focus on the parallel development of what may be termed the 'new moralism' around the problems of crime and disorder. It is argued that both these features are crucially implicated in, and associated with, the emergent crime control complex at the beginning of the twenty-first century.

The coming of the new 'post-social' society?

In the countdown to the new millennium a multitude of books, official reports, managerial manuals, documentaries and films appeared, offering a bewildering number of future scenarios. Studying the future is said to enhance our ability to understand wider historical contexts, provide us with greater awareness and enable us to participate in policy formulation and decision-making:

> Either we take hold of the future or the future will take hold of us. We need to be futurewise. That means planning to change tomorrow, future thinking at every level, taking a broad view to out-plot the opposition. Being futurewise is about more than mere predictors, its about shaping the future, making history, having contingencies, staying one step ahead and in control. (Dixon, 1998, p. xi)

A word of caution is needed from the outset. There is a long and tarnished tradition of futurological prediction in social sciences, ever since Auguste Comte and the cult of sociological positivism in the early nineteenth century. It could be plausibly argued that what we are seeing in the most recent wave of future-focused narratives, which posit a decisive break with the past and the birth of a new society, is in many respects a replay of previous 'new technology equals new world' theses with all the inbuilt potential for technological determinism. There are common deficiencies to futurology and both utopian and dystopian visions of order and control, past and present. Such claims tend to fall 'off the edge' in terms of positing extreme and untenable contrasts between 'past', 'present' and 'future'. Visualizations of the future, very often gleaned from the canon of science fiction, also run the risk of presenting totalizing accounts which fail to recognize the sources of human diversity and the uneven, contradictory, highly contingent processes of social change, adaptation and resistance. If predictors are framed too closely in relation to prevailing socio-economic and political structures, limitations are being built in that exclude or marginalize other imaginaries. Finally, Esping-Anderson (1990, p. 223) offers an important cautionary note about the nature of the current transformations and the grand claims made about them which nonetheless takes cognizance of the possibility of a radical break with the past. He warns that the utilization of labels, such as 'postmodern', 'post-materialist', 'post-Fordist' or 'post-industrial', often substitutes for rigorous analysis. For him it is more sensible to declare that 'we are leaving behind us a social order that was pretty much understood, and entering another the contours of which can be only dimly recognized'. Such a guarded, open-ended verdict on contemporary social transformations accords well with the systematic scepticism which lies at the heart of Wright Mills's (1959) notion of 'the sociological imagination' and is a fitting reminder of the dangers of over-predicting and over-reading trends and of closing down alternative futures, not least in the contested field of crime reduction and crime control.

Nevertheless, there is a major debate about the nature of the 'new world order' and its future trajectory. Across the ideological spectrum, commentators are united by a common belief that we are in the midst of a multi-faceted global transition that is transforming the organizing principles of the 'social' in an unprecedented manner. The main intertwined themes implanted in the current futurology and the nascent 'post-social' society thesis, across theories of postmodernity, late modernity, the risk society and the information society, can be most commonly identified as follows. First, the key drivers of the networked global economy will be technology, information and knowledge. Second, globalization will intensify the movement of capital, goods, services, cultural values and people. Third, the fragmentation of bonds of family, community, locality and nation and the appearance of hyper-individualism and the new 'inner worlds' of cyberspace will result in increased cultural diversity and social complexity. Finally, traditional structures and institutional patterns of local, national and international governance will undergo radical transformation.

On the positive side, some commentators point to the greater choice, diversity, individualism and rapid progress that result from technological and scientific innovation and the potential it opens up for a more densely 'connected' world. Mulgan (1997), Beck (1998) and Leadbetter (1999) focus on the 'runaway qualities' of knowledge and information societies, the rise of mutual understanding and capacities to communicate and the emergence of a global public space in which to debate questions of morality and citizenship. In a similar fashion, Giddens's (1998) 'runaway world' thesis acknowledges that the increasingly frenetic pace of global change is producing novel risks and hazards. However, he insists that, for all the uncertainties, globalization is a progressive force and has the potential to generate a new detradi-tionalized cosmopolitanism defined by economic interdependence, a tolerant morality, the deepening of democratic principles and extension of the rule of law. We should also learn to embrace rather than fear the new risks, according to Giddens (1998, p. 35), because 'active risk taking is a core element of a dynamic economy and an innovative society'.

However, according to the pessimists, there are many grounds for believing that all that is solid is in the process of disintegrating into 'post-social' chaos. Nightmare scenarios, or what O'Malley (2000, p. 153) describes as 'semiologies of catastrophe', are to the fore both in commentaries on the future of the heartlands of the 'West', with the imagery of the underclass and urban 'badlands', and in analyses of the anarchic nature of swathes of the 'developing' world. It is now common currency in some academic circles to assert that we are witnessing the rise of the exclusionary society with growing socio-economic divisions and the catastrophic rise of a dualist system of 'haves' and 'have-nots' (Young, 1999; Hobsbawm, 1995). According to the pessimists, the new world order is often viewed as the 'new barbarism', marked by a form of neo-feudalism, with global criminal overlords fusing with a voracious multinational corporate 'informational' capitalism. Manuel Castells's work is particularly representative of pessimistic 'Welcome to the neo-liberal jungle' diagnoses put forward by many left-wing thinkers. According to Castells, the new informational capitalism is indifferent to the concerns of humanity and is creating an ever sharper and deeper divide between valuable and non-valuable people and locales. Indeed, he argues that we are now witnessing the rise of a 'Fourth World' across many parts of the world, including the ghettos of the richest countries. Castells (1998, pp. 161–2) terms these areas and locales the 'black holes of informational capitalism' which 'concentrate in their density all the destructive energy that affects humanity from various sources'.

Bauman also has increased scepticism about the effects of hyper-globalization:

> An integrated part of the globalizing process is progressive spatial segregation, separation and exclusion. Neo-tribal and fundamentalist tendencies, which reflect and articulate the experience of people on the receiving end of globalization, are as much legitimate offspring of globalization as the widely acclaimed 'hybridization' of top culture . . . A particular cause of worry is the progressive breakdown in communication between the increasingly global and extraterritorial elites and the ever more localized rest. (1998, p. 3)

From the right of the ideological spectrum Robert D. Kaplan (2000) presents a chilling vision of the post-Cold War twenty-first century, detailing the threat to the West posed by the resurgence of savage racial and ethnic violence, the social pressures of unchecked disease, environmental scarcity and overpopulation, the withering away of national governments, the setting up of criminal regimes and the postmodern blurring of the boundaries between 'crime' and 'war'. Much of his prognosis is reminiscent of the work of Samuel P. Huntington (1998), whose 'clash of civilizations' thesis identifies an emerging trend toward global conflict taking place along cultural, rather than economic or ideological, lines and forecasts internal conflict between groups from different civilizations within a nation-state. For Huntington the new global order will witness governments rallying around the 'core states' of their civilizations, for example, China for Sinic civilization, Russia for Orthodox civilization, and the United States for Western civilization. The possibility of global conflict can be reduced only if core states adhere to a doctrine of non-intervention in conflicts taking place within other civilizations.

The CIA's National Intelligence Council report *Global Trends 2015* identifies the major drives and trends that will shape US foreign policy in the post-Cold War future. Although the report, which is informed by a range of sources, recognizes that globalization can contribute to a political stability and economic progress, it also narrates a future marked by the distinct possibility of increased instability and volatility. Three potential 'underside of globalization' scenarios are identified as centrally significant and deserving of close attention. First, regions, states or groups left outside the globalization loop will face increasing socio-economic and political instability and could 'foster political, ethnic, ideological and religious extremism, along with the violence that often accompanies it' (CIA, 2000, p. 7). Second, internal conflicts resulting from state repression, religious and/or ethnic grievances, migration flows and the emergence of new protest movements could result in civil wars, interstate conflict and regional destabilization. And, finally, states with inadequate governance, weak economies, ethnic heterogeneity and porous borders provide 'breeding grounds' for terrorists and insurgents who have the organizational and technological ability to strike hard at Western interests.

A few criminologists have attempted to address the crime implications of the broader socio-economic and political trends discussed above. In the United Kingdom, Reiner (2000), for example, commenting on the future of the discipline, has written of a 'social earthquake', with a bleak picture of deepening exclusion alongside a culture of the survival of the fittest. In less dystopian terms Garland and Sparks (2000, p. 189) note that the 'restructuring of social and economic relations, the fluidity of social process, the speed of technological change, and the remarkable cultural heterogeneity that constitute "late modernity" pose intellectual challenges for criminology that are difficult and sometimes discomforting but ultimately are too insistent to ignore'. However, as Cohen (1996) noted, the real hard-headed discussion about the future of crime is taking place increasingly outside the confines of conventional criminological discourse.

In the CIA's *Global Trends* report, for example, it is anticipated that transnational criminal organizations will pose a serious challenge to national and international governance because they will acquire the skills necessary to exploit the global diffusion of information, financial and transport networks:

> Criminal organizations and networks . . . will expand the scale and scope of their activities. They will form loose alliances with one another, with smaller criminal entrepreneurs, and with insurgent movements for specific operations. They will corrupt leaders of unstable, economically fragile or failing states, insinuate themselves into troubled banks and businesses, and co-operate with insurgent political movements to control substantial geographic areas. Their incomes will come from narcotics trafficking, alien smuggling; trafficking in women and children; smuggling toxic materials, hazardous wastes, illicit arms, military technologies, and other contraband; financial fraud and racketeering . . . The risk will increase that organized criminal groups will traffic in nuclear, biological or chemical weapons. (CIA, 2000, p. 27)

The real worry for the CIA is that in certain parts of Latin America, Africa and Eastern Europe we will see the emergence of fully functioning state/criminal complexes. In this doomsday scenario, organized crime will be in a strategic position to shift from peripheral activities to infiltrating the state, corrupting the economy, disabling the criminal justice system and neutralizing the intelligence agencies. CIA thinking on how crime is 'folding' into core areas of government and the economy has also inflected the conclusions of future-scanning police and intelligence reports produced for the European Union (Castells, 1998).

To date, in the United Kingdom, perhaps the most significant attempt to address the future of crime is the deliberations of the Department of Trade and Industry Foresight Programme which was established in 1993. Panels of experts, operating on a five-year cycle, have been attempting to anticipate future challenges and opportunities across a variety of policy areas. In 1999 a Crime Prevention Panel was established and funded from the government's Crime Reduction Programme to consider how developments in science, technology and society will impact upon crime and crime control. *Just around the Corner*, the consultation document (DTI, 2000), and the final report, *Turning the Corner* (DTI, 2001), provide fascinating insights into how key opinion formers are conceptualizing crime and crime control in the first decades of the twenty-first century. The Crime Prevention Panel employed the Foresight document, *Britain towards 2010* (Scase, 2000), and various environmental future scenarios to argue that the following social characteristics will play a central role in influencing near-future forms and levels of crime and criminality. First, increased individualism and independence will lead to the erosion of familial and communal controls and the consolidation of anti-social group ideologies. Second, augmented use of information and communications technology (ICT) will produce new forms of techno-crime marked by increasing speed, scale, sophistication and complexity. In turn the retreat from the public to the private associated with new information technologies will transform the public into a threatening hostile environment.

Increased non-human interaction sets in motion a process of dehumanization where we become more tolerant of extreme reactions and interactions, and an unwillingness to intervene also alters the relationship between the offender and the victim. Finally, globalization, in conjunction with consumerism, fuels new forms of crime without boundaries, facilitates new criminal connections and networks and exposes the limitations of local and national law enforcement strategies.

The trends will also produce new categories of criminals. 'Empowered small agents' and new social groups will be capable of creating crime and havoc on a level previously limited to organized or career criminals. A generation of techno-sophisticates will possess the skills and ability to pursue their virtual criminal tendencies across cyber-borders. Meanwhile frustrated members of a technologically disenfranchised 'underclass' are likely to engage in nihilistic violence and disorder. An increasingly elderly population, as well as producing many more potential victims, could also spawn a new class of criminals with the time and money to familiarize themselves with new technologies and engage in crime. Organized crime will also adapt so that it can operate more effectively in the new technological environment. The report concludes that, if all the trends and shifts are put together, 'there is the potential that, left unchecked, the future will see violence and disorder rise; fraud, personation and extortion increase; more crime committed by those outside national jurisdiction; and theft targeting electronic devices' (DTI, 2000, p. 9).

To reinforce its thinking, the DTI futurologists also provide us with two scenarios of what the United Kingdom will look like in 2020.

The first future scenario – 'Brightlands' – scripts an anarchic, post-social world where those who can, buy protection in tightly regulated, claustrophobic gated communities protected by alarmed perimeter fences, private security guards, and personal security devices. Public aspects of social life are run-down and there is widespread insecurity as a result of high levels of violence and crime. Those living outside gated communities live under the surveillance of fortified watch towers and an empowered police force. Half the male population has a criminal record and the prison population has reached record levels. The risks of criminal victimization remain high because of the decreased deterrent impact of tough law enforcement and imprisonment and because even those who can buy private security have to use the black market to access desirable goods. Thus, despite technological advances, the fortified enclaves are not self-sufficient.

In the second future scenario – 'TECHies' – the United Kingdom is a considerably more integrated and secure society. New technologies associated with the information society have impacted upon every aspect of life and inaugurated much more flexible working and living arrangements. Most products and services have been 'crime-proofed' and the latest technologies are utilized by both the private security sector and the public police. The criminal attacks that do occur are high-risk, no-reward events. The integrated nature of the anti-crime technologies means that there is very little chance of criminals escaping undetected and profiting from their criminal activities.

Making the future of crime control work: the new anti-social criminologies of everyday life

As we have noted, these are important qualifications to any grand narrative which posits a radical break with the past. Nonetheless, there are tendencies which suggest that radical 'stories of change' (Cohen, 1985) are in play in criminological theory and crime control practice at the beginning of the twenty-first century. In particular, there has been a profound unsettling of the old social or causal criminologies, both mainstream positivist and critical, together with the arrival of seemingly new and often refurbished 'older' ways of thinking. Nor are these intellectual developments of merely academic interest. Foucault (1977) famously noted that 'knowledge is power', and changing ways of thinking in the academy about crimes and related harms are closely bound up with changing visions of social order and the governing rationalities of social control. In what follows, we focus on the recent rise to prominence of the most influential 'policy-relevant' approaches to a policy field that is increasingly reconstituted as 'crime reduction' and security-based 'risk management' rather than 'crime prevention' and 'community safety'. It is striking that, despite widespread public alarm about broad societal changes and developments in crime and control, there is an ascendant optimism in much contemporary mainstream policy thinking on crime reduction programmes in countries such as the United Kingdom and the United States, particularly when compared with the 'Nothing works' pessimism of the 1970s and 1980s. How may this seeming paradox be explained? To answer this question, the rise of the 'new anti-social criminologies of everyday life' needs to be briefly plotted.[1]

The new anti-social criminologies of everyday life are most closely associated with such cognate approaches as opportunity theory, situational crime prevention (SCP), routine activity, rational choice, problem-solving and neo-ecological theories (see Felson and Clarke, 1998). As Garland notes:

> The striking thing about these criminologies is that they begin from the premise that crime is a normal, commonplace, aspect of modern society. It is an event – or rather a mass of events – which requires no special motivation or disposition, no pathology or abnormality, and which is written into the routines of contemporary social and economic life. In contrast to earlier criminologies, which began with the premise that crime was a deviation from normal civilized conduct, and was explicable in terms of individual pathology or else faulty socialization, the new criminologies of everyday life see crime as continuous with normal social interaction and explicable by reference to standard motivational patterns. Crime becomes a risk to be calculated (by the offender and the potential victim) or as an accident to be avoided, rather than a moral aberration which needs to be specially explained. (1996, pp. 450–1)

These new anti-social criminologies challenge the four core assumptions of the old causal criminology and its attachment to 'the social':

1 The causes of crime lie deep in the institutional arrangements of the social structure.
2 Crime needs to be tackled by addressing the underlying psychological and social conditions which generate both individual and communal pathologies.

3   Policy needs to be 'long-termist' in its orientation to solving criminality.
4   The sovereign state and its specialist bureau-professional criminal justice agencies represent the most appropriate body to deal with the practical resolution and collective management of crime prevention.

In place of this aetiological fixation with ultimate causes and reliance on statist interventions, the new anti-social criminologies promote at best a vision of 'the social' as pre-sociological, with crime 'events' of the here and now being viewed as tractable by means of pragmatic, targeted, specific measures, often delivered by private bodies beyond the orbit of the state and the formal criminal justice system. In this emergent paradigm, 'the social' and the attendant conditions which generate crime events are thus reconstituted as a simpler and more tractable terrain.

Of these new anti-social criminologies of everyday life, situational crime prevention appears to be the most influential organizing component.[2] Recent decades have seen the growing global influence of SCP, with the offender largely desocialized in its 'purist' versions. Situational crime prevention has been viewed as destroying the discipline's 'biographical individual as a category of criminological knowledge', replacing it with its polar opposite, the 'abstract and universal "abiographical" individual' (O'Malley, 1992, p. 264). Situational crime prevention sits close to the discourse of actuarialism and the world of insurance, 'the home base of risk management discourses, and an industry closely connected to the promotion of SCP' (*ibid.*). According to its proponents, SCP avoids blame allocation, unlike the rationale of the rest of criminal justice system (Wilkins, 1997). In Cusson's words, the rallying call is to 'change situations rather than souls' (quoted in Sève, 1997, p. 190), thereby depersonalizing and de-psychologizing the study of crime and robbing 'delinquency' of its special status. However, some critics take up an opposite line of argument with regard to SCP's relationship to the attribution of blame. According to the latter, the 1980s and 1990s witnessed a period of extraordinary success for SCP which could not be attributed to the evidence of its superiority over both correctionalism and social and causal criminologies. According to its critics, the answer to SCP's success instead lies in its links and affinities with economic rationalist, neo-conservative and New Right political programmes, particularly the increasing punitiveness with respect to 'calculating' offenders and, with respect to victims, the displacement of socialized risk management by 'privatized prudentialism'. In turn, it is argued that the elimination of cause restores individual responsibility, arising out of 'rational choice', to the centre of the crime debate. Accordingly, SCP may be viewed as the handmaiden of the strong state and the free market (O'Malley, 1992).

Despite the misgivings of its critics, it is common to find a triumphalist attack on both positivist criminology, particularly its sociological variants, and criminal justice system 'solutions' among proponents of SCP. Russo, for example, has argued:

Criminology seems weighted down, for the most part, by its tradition of overlooking personal responsibility on the part of the offender, and its deterministic heritage. Criminological literature appears completely unrelated to the new forms of criminality and society's perceptions of the same. Criminology is thus placed in the position of having to take up new strategies and develop new models of victim-oriented crime prevention. SCP falls within these new models of prevention. It is capable of providing answers to society's demands for safety through immediate and testable solutions which can function independently of the criminal justice system. (1997, p. 180)

Much of the 'success' of SCP appears to be linked with the key role played by its leading proponents as 'policy entrepreneurs', 'that is, social scientifically informed "experts" who are nevertheless in positions of political influence and thus able to shape practice' (Hope, 2000, p. xxii). In the case of SCP it was originally key administrative criminologists in the Home Office, particularly Ron Clarke, supported by and aligned with policy-makers who promoted and 'marketed' the project. Despite its origins in the government department of the Home Office in Britain in the 1970s and 1980s, SCP in fact has closer links with business and the private sector than with the criminal justice system and the old public sector. The subsequent departure of Clarke to the United States and his close collaboration with Marcus Felson throughout the 1990s consolidated the increasingly anti-statist logic of SCP as well as its challenge to mainstream criminology's status as the 'handmaiden' of the social democratic state. According to Felson and Clarke (1997, p. 5), 'the fact that business has a practical bent puts it at the core of crime prevention'. In turn, SCP researchers/experts promote more 'prudential', problem-focused policies which, rather than being 'owned' by the police, involve a shift in the location of responsibility for security away from the police to situations where problem-solving can take place (Shearing, 1997, p. 226). According to Felson and Clarke:

Central to this enterprise is not the criminal justice system, but a host of public and private organizations and agencies – schools, hospitals, transport systems, shops and malls, manufacturing business and phone companies, banks and insurance companies, local parks and entertainment facilities, pubs and parking lots – whose services, products and modes of operation spawn opportunities for a vast range of different crimes. (1997, p. 197)

The above statement of intent may be read as a key element of the 'mission statement' of the new anti-social criminologies of everyday life.

There has been a shift of late from SCP being 'ghettoized' from mainstream criminology in the United Kingdom to being a key component of a new crime reduction 'settlement',[3] characterized by an eclectic and pragmatic mix of techniques/theories based on a 'what works' and 'evidence-led' paradigm. Much of the impetus behind this new paradigm has arisen from a 'trade in ideas' among an increasingly global network of influential 'policy entrepreneurs'. Such developments have also resulted in significant policy and technology transfers between the United States and the United Kingdom as well as other states (Chan, 2000). With the rise of the new eclecticism, we have even witnessed a call for the integration of SCP with offender-oriented criminology, the previous *bête noire* of SCP practitioners. According to Ekblom and Tilley (2000, p. 394), 'as a broad research programme SCP is healthy but it remains largely quarantined from the rest of criminology'. It is argued by the latter that it is time at the start of the twenty-first century to breach the ghetto walls and bring the offender into the picture more fully.

More broadly there is a new optimism in policy-oriented research circles about 'what can be done about' reducing crime. At the very centre of the new paradigm is the powerful appeal to rational, systematic research evaluation of policy and practice as the tool which can tell us in scientifically objective terms what does and what does not 'work' in crime reduction (Sherman et al., 1998; Felson and Clarke, 1998; Goldblatt and Lewis, 1998). Writing about the role of 'preventers', the Home Office-based researcher Paul Ekblom suggests:

> We are developing a better understanding of the causes of crime and the principles of intervening in the causes systematically, with the aid of research and evaluation. In this, to borrow a vision from engineering science, adaptability comes from being equipped with principles capable of being applied to many problems rather than a fixed expertise in any one field of technology that could sooner or later be bypassed. (1999, p. 48)

In turn the focus in the new 'what works' paradigm is on immediate or 'proximal' factors of direct relevance to 'those who have to deal with offenders *in the real world*' (Felson and Clarke, 1998, p. 1; emphasis added) as against 'old 'criminology's focus on (largely irrelevant) distant factors. Tellingly, this is believed to be attainable 'without the major social reforms implied by sociological analyses of the "root causes" of crime' (Reiner, 2000, p. 72).

Pragmatism and the appeal to simplicity and common sense – key elements in the new anti-social criminologies – are also evident in Farrington's celebration of the 'global' spread of the risk factor paradigm around 'criminality prevention' in his 1999 presidential address to the American Society of Criminology:

> A key advantage of the risk factor prevention paradigm is that it links explanation and prevention, fundamental and applied research, and scholars and practitioners. Importantly, the paradigm is easy to understand and to communicate, and it is readily accepted by policy makers, practitioners, and the general public. Both risk factors and interventions

are based on empirical research rather than theories. The paradigm avoids difficult theoretical questions about which risk factors have causal effects. (2000, p. 7)

This resurgence of concern with the prediction of risk in the new paradigm is also shared by proselytes of the budding, evidence-led and inter-disciplinary 'crime science'(see DTI, 2000). Ken Pease makes the case for a predictive crime science and for the proper job of the criminologist in the future as follows: 'Put bluntly, until they fully engage with the future, criminologists are doomed to track trends in crime, rather than head them off. Science is taken seriously when it predicts. We owe it to ourselves to predict' (1997, p. 243). According to this project, it is vital to try to manipulate the world to produce a more desirable future (Rogerson et al., 2000, p. 265).[4]

In some ways the claims of SCP and related approaches of rational choice, routine activities, ecological/environmental theories, risk factor prevention approaches and crime science are surprisingly close to the Foucauldian notion of 'capillary power' (see Rose, 1999). Accordingly, reductive and preventive initiatives are viewed as not being restricted to the 'sovereign state' and its criminal justice agencies. Instead the new paradigm would promote micro networks and processes throughout society, and in communities, for the realization of its crime control aims. The new discipline of 'preventers' as an expert system is in turn made up of a hybrid coalition of psychologists, evolutionary and ecological theorists, geneticists, engineers, designers, architects, planners and geographers, with sociologists and criminal justice experts conspicuous by their absence. In this new crime reduction/prevention paradigm, lessons from other evolutionary struggles for survival and against predation have been drawn. In Paul Ekblom's messianic words, 'Crime prevention faces a perpetual struggle to keep up with changing opportunities for crime and adaptable offenders. To avoid obsolescence, it has to become adaptive itself' (1999, p. 27). Nor is the struggle a mere academic game. Instead the 'evolutionary perspective is one that we need to adopt in crime prevention to keep up with our opponents just as the military, medical and agricultural scientists, predators, prey, or bacteria must with theirs' (*ibid.*, p. 47).

Nick Tilley (see Chapter 2 in this book) has written of the idea of 'infection and mutation of institutions and disciplines' in his history of crime prevention in Britain; proponents of the 'what works' paradigm appear to be making the case for evolutionary hybridization for themselves, with their work going beyond criminology as we have known it and also going back to the pre-sociological 'social'. In turn it is claimed that the more generalized crime production and prevention consciousness which is currently in play in contemporary societies takes developments in crime reduction away from their traditional roots in criminology and social sciences. In particular, there is a renewed interest in all things 'natural', epitomized by the overarching idea of 'natural crime prevention'. According to Marcus Felson (1994, p. 129), 'Natural crime prevention may be described as the chunking and channelling of human activities, in imitation of nature, to reduce crime temptations and increase controls.' In this discourse, appeals to the 'natural' come to the fore while appeals to the 'social' (as complex) take a back-stage role.

Important aspects of this break with 'old' dispositional, causal criminology were already foreseen by Stanley Cohen in 1985:

> For some time now, the few criminologists who have looked into the future have argued that 'the game is up' for all policies directed at the criminal as an individual, either in terms of detection (blaming and punishing) or causation (finding motivational or causal chains). The technological paraphernalia previously directed at the individual will now be invested in cybernetics, management, systems analysis, surveillance, information gathering and opportunity reduction. This might turn out to be the most radical form of behaviourism imaginable – prevention of the act of crime by the direct control of whole populations, categories and spaces. (Page 147)

Many of Cohen's prescient words are clearly evident in the new paradigm of – and mixed bag of tools for – crime reduction. Members of this 'invisible college' in turn are 'upbeat' about what can be done about reducing crime. For example, Bennett's (1997, p. 397) claim that the future of criminology is that of 'theoretical integration' – albeit with significant absences – is typical of the new 'what works' eclecticism and optimism. In similar fashion, Farrington (2000) notes that the 'new criminology' will be a mix of new biological, genetic and psychological approaches alongside and superseding social ones. Viewed more sceptically, such developments are part of an intellectual struggle for power and influence over 'governmental *savoir*' (Stenson, 1998). The pragmatic 'what works' evaluation-, research- and evidence-led paradigm may be best viewed as a transnational, intellectual and policy project. Whilst wishing to avoid crude conspiracy theory, we do seem to have witnessed the rise of a closed network of researchers and policy experts and a trade in ideas, policies and practices across the world but located largely in the 'export' centres of the United States and United Kingdom.

In the 'what works' crime reduction paradigm it would appear that 'nothing is ruled in and nothing is ruled out', spanning such factors and techniques as genetic and psychological risk factors, environmental design, target hardening, rational choices, everyday routines, natural surveillance, evolutionary defence strategies and so on. But for all its seeming pragmatic inclusiveness, some things are marginalized, not least the macro-sociological 'social' approach concerned with underlying structural causes of crimes and related harms in communities. It would seem that causes are thus too difficult to deal with and are, in the words of James Q. Wilson, irrelevant to policy, since 'ultimate causes cannot be the object of policy efforts, precisely because being ultimate they cannot be changed' (Wilson, 1974, p. 49). Social reforms are thus low in the mix. In Cohen's words once more:

> The talk now is about the 'spatial' and 'temporal' aspects of crime, about systems, behaviour sequences, ecology, defensible space, environmental psychology, situations, opportunity structures, feedbacks, target hardening, spatial distribution of offenders. Crime is something that can be 'designed out' by changing the planning and management of the physical environment. (1985, p. 148)

In the context of this challenge to traditional criminological thinking, some leading criminologists appear to be holding on to the modernist 'raft' in stormy seas, relying on the safe haven of the social democratic, sociological discourse of crime causation and social prevention (see, for example, Reiner, 2000). However, other leading commentators from mainstream criminology such as Garland and Sparks (2000, p. 191) appear to be calling for a *rapprochement* between the two criminologies of 'theory' (the old) and of 'practice and policy' (the new).[5] In particular, the latter admit there were 'blind spots' in the 'old' criminology and in turn accept the important insights of the 'new' present-day criminology of practice and policy. Such insights are especially associated with the latter's interest in crime events, criminogenic situations, victim behaviour, and the everyday, mundane social and economic routines that produce criminal opportunities (Garland and Sparks, 2000, p. 195). If not interpreted as a surrender to the assault of the new anti-social criminologies of everyday life with regard to the *raison d'être* of criminology, then such a call for integration is clearly indicative of the growing influence of the new, pragmatic, policy-oriented 'anti-social' paradigm on the body of the old-established discipline.

And it must be acknowledged that aspects of the crime reduction paradigm are difficult to argue with, such as the thesis that new products and technologies generate new 'desires' and 'needs' which may take criminal forms. Furthermore, much of the logic of the discourse may also be read as 'normalizing' both the criminal and the crime event in some ways similar to that advocated by new deviance theory in the early 1970s. There is also much that is compelling, for abolitionists and communitarians alike, in the appeal of moving beyond traditional criminal justice solutions to crimes and harms. In Marcus Felson's words, 'Any society that has to rely on these slow and uncertain public agencies as the main sources of prevention has already lost the battle against crime' (1994, p. xi). Instead it is recommended that we look to informal control as offering simple, benign, unobtrusive and inexpensive contributions to crime prevention. There is also much truth in the recognition of the process of greater diversification away from government and public services to individuals and private companies in crime control and managing risks in the context of late modern or postmodern conditions.

Whatever stance is taken with regard to the emergent new anti-social criminologies of everyday life, it is difficult to ignore their contemporary importance in the new governance of crime. The 'what works' paradigm of policy and practice appears to hold out the promise for criminologists and allied policy experts that they may become practical technicians of social order, particularly by means of their involvement in the ascendant governmental rationalities of crime reduction and the new architecture of crime control.

Watching the future of crime control work: the new technologies of surveillance

Much of the 'success' of this new crime reduction paradigm lies not so much in its theoretical sophistication as in its 'policy and practice' pay-off for the governance of crime and disorder. In particular, its suggestions for the development of policies and techniques, especially associated with SCP, have entered into the programmes and everyday, institutional 'architecture' of crime control of contemporary societies.

The development of ever more sophisticated and pervasive forms of surveillance technologies has generated equal degrees of fear and fascination in much of the public debate on the issue. It appears that there are in our current times insistent and powerful demands for the production of ordered space, largely due to a culture of fear of the stranger. One technocratic solution to this fear of strangers is to resort to enclosure and electronic surveillance. Across many countries closed-circuit television (CCTV) is now viewed as a key element in the reconstitution of the 'public' as spaces and spheres of activity, and in the new architecture of crime control, urban security and community safety. In the United Kingdom and United States CCTV appears to have attained the status of icon of the emergent post-social zeitgeist or structure of feeling. This structure of feeling lives off and in turn generates a widespread fear of contact with strangers in public places and a felt need and desire to extinguish the possibility of insecurity and lack of safety for the 'sovereign' consumer. It has been claimed by supporters of CCTV that such technology helps build and sustain communities; however, it may do so by criminalizing those who live on the fringes, as well as amplifying the sense of risk and fear for those under its protective gaze (Norris and Armstrong, 1999). As Palmer notes, 'To be good citizens in this intersecting mesh of glances is to be measurable and predictable consumers' (2000, p. 93). The technology of CCTV thus offers the possibility of a 'soft', generally imperceptible ordering of people's movements, but it also acts to exclude disadvantaged groups from certain places and spaces (McLaughlin and Muncie, 2000).

Most commentary on these developments conjures up a dystopian vision of social control, segmentation and social polarization alongside total corporate power and absolute surveillance (for a fuller discussion see

Hughes, 1998). A question that is less often asked is, what are the spaces for resistance strategies in the context of this new architecture of control and security? As Graham (forthcoming) notes, important qualifications need to be made regarding the apparent deterministic consequences of technological innovation. The reality of technological innovation is much messier, contingent and open to contested interpretations than is implied in much of the literature to date. The recognition of the new powers of technological surveillance in the contemporary social control complex thus needs to be tempered by some scepticism regarding its seemingly all-pervasive reach and capacity for control over potentially resistant forces.

However, new surveillance technologies do not end with CCTV networks. There are major developments in electronic surveillance, defined as devices and systems which can monitor, track and access the movements of individuals, their property and other assets. Perhaps the most exciting developments in this new 'security field' which cuts across the traditional boundaries between the work of the police and security forces (Bigo, 2000) are the blending of surveillance techniques with those of simulation, the merging of information and communications technologies and developments in biotechnology, genetic screening and biometric surveillance. These shifts may result in the emergence of socio-technical systems which attempt to monitor, control and guide social processes with unprecedented precision and power as well as being virtually invisible and unregulated (Graham, forthcoming). Indicative of such shifts in the technology of social control and security are the widespread fears of surveillance subverting human rights, for example the potential for 'electronic eavesdropping', not least from the increasingly powerful and unconstrained global corporations. The latter are, for example, employing 'web investigation agencies' to monitor online critics such as non-governmental organizations.[6]

Producing 'anti-crime' communities of the future

This chapter does not claim to be a comprehensive and tidy account of the possible futures of crime control. To limit our discussion several questions have structured our brief survey of present and future trends in preventive, reductive and safety and security discourses. Why are these crime control developments occurring at this socio-historical juncture? This question was answered in terms of the transformations associated with the seemingly 'post-social' condition of our times. What are the main developments at play in contemporary criminological thinking on crime and crime control? Put simply, it was argued that a new paradigm was emerging around a cluster of approaches which we may term 'post-social' and pragmatic criminologies. In turn a new crime control complex is being constructed with a broader range of 'players' involved than previously and also crucially informed by 'policy-relevant' criminology and other intellectual disciplines.

There is a danger, of course, in exaggerating the ascendancy of a purely technicist and amoral, actuarialist logic in contemporary discourses of crime reduction despite the ever-growing presence of such techniques as CCTV and ICT-based surveillance as part of the new urban architecture of crime control and security management. Older, pre-sociological notions of the social as 'moral' and 'natural' are also being resuscitated and played out in influential ways in contemporary debates on crime control. Consequently, it would be premature and unwise to discount the continued and revitalized appeal to moralizing and responsibilizing discourses alongside, and possibly in partnership with, technocratic-cum-managerialist solutions. Looking at criminal justice on the verge of the new millennium, O'Malley (2000) rightly alerts us both to the danger of exaggerating the 'newness' of the present and its departure from past tendencies, and to the likelihood of contemporary criminal justice regimes amalgamating and combining often rather contradictory governing rationalities. Note, for example, the calls for a new moral 'rearmament' of the community, family and individual in the 'zero tolerance' fight against crime and disorder (see Wilson and Kelling, 1982; Kelling and Coles, 1997; Etzioni, 1994). Under this guise, community safety is being imagined and realized as a majoritarian strategy, guided by an exclusivist and moralizing communitarian impulse.

Such developments are arguably part of wider transformations in contemporary politics in which we see the rise of what Rose (1999) terms a 'new ethico politics' organized around the valorization of the community rather than the state. In this context it should be noted that the subtitle of Kelling and Coles's (1997) influential text, *Fixing Broken Windows*, is 'restoring order and reducing crime in our communities'. Donning the breastplate of righteousness, commentators and 'policy entrepreneurs' such as James Wilson and George Kelling claim to be part of a 'community safety' movement guided by an explicitly moral agenda about the standards of civic life, with a rallying call of the community reclaiming its public places. Such an influential and morally infused communitarian project is not necessarily in contradiction with the more technical solutions of SCP and the 'what works' reduction paradigm. Rather it may be viewed as coexisting alongside these in claiming to protect the victimized members of the moral community and in calling for community responses to crime and disorder and the punitive exclusion of the 'calculating' wrongdoer-cum-'predator'.

We would argue that the connections between the new moralism and the seemingly 'amoral' risk management technologies of surveillance, security and crime reduction are quite crucial to the contemporary crime control complex. Such developments in the new architecture of crime control and security have been linked with the break with the social democratic tradition and its solidarity project (Garland and Sparks, 2000; Garland, 2001). The eclipse of this project sees the death of the ideal that order is guaranteed ultimately by the inclusion of citizens within a framework of welfare and justice over and above sectional and parochial interests. Shorn of this foundation, it is feared that much crime prevention and community safety is likely to become part of the general process of exclusion, complementing rather than forestalling the ever greater expansion of the penal field (Hope, 2000, p. xxiii). What, then, are the main features of this new emergent crime complex, informed by old and new ideas and practices? According to Garland and Sparks, the following features encapsulate the new complex:

1   High crime rates are viewed as a normal social fact and crime avoidance has become an organizing principle of everyday life.
2   Fear of crime is sufficiently widespread to become a political reference point, and crime issues are generally politicized and represented in emotive terms.
3   Concern about the victim and public safety dominates government policy, whilst the criminal justice system is regarded as limited in its impact.
4   Private, defensive and prudential routines are widespread and there is a large and growing market in private security.
5   A high level of crime consciousness becomes embedded in everyday life and institutionalized in the media, popular culture and the built environment.

Garland and Sparks also note that the new criminologies which have emerged stress 'increased social control and situational prevention, rational choice and disincentives, *and* incapacitation and punitive exclusion. In this new political culture, a criminology that disavows *emotive and punitive* policies, that echoes welfarist rationales and social solutions – such a criminology has little affinity with the values and calculations that shape government decisions' (Garland and Sparks, 2000, pp. 200–1; emphasis added).

It is difficult to argue with such a grand thesis and diagnosis of our 'late modern' times. However, taken *in toto*, the thesis distorts and downplays the importance of other countervailing developments occurring in contemporary criminological debates and policy developments in crime control. For example, the diagnosis underestimates the significance of the rejection of 'emotive and punitive' policies in the 'rational', evidence-led paradigm of the Crime Reduction Programme in Britain and the technocratic recommendations of the Foresight Crime Prevention Panel (DTI, 2000). We thus need to recognize the tenacity of the 'modernist' position that crime can be controlled and that high crime rates are *not* a normal social fact.

One final point. It is important to recognize that the history of crime control and prevention is not one of cumulative or linear progress. Rather, in the present historical context, there is a potent and volatile mix of the seemingly technicist, amoral techniques and moralizing, exclusivist and emotive strategies of crime control across many contemporary 'late modern' societies.[7] However, for criminologists further questions remain to be debated. What, for example, are the other possible futures of 'the social' and its potentially progressive role in new imaginaries of communal security and public safety? A focus on, and re-engagement with, the reconfiguration of 'the social' adds credence to the claim that the future of just and tolerant crime prevention and community safety policies is neither safe nor secure in the hands of either technocratic 'securicrats' or 'virtuecrats'. As a matter of urgency the future politics and practices of safety, security and control need to be resocialized and, perhaps equally significantly, rehumanized.

If we go back to our future imaginaries it is worth remembering the final scenes of Ridley Scott's film, *Blade Runner*, the visually striking and thought-provoking 'cyberpunk' vision of life in Los Angeles in 2019. The film is often used by criminologists to narrate a bleak post-liberal, post-social future characterized by criminalization, paramilitarization, privatization and dehumanization. But what is truly significant is that, even in this unnerving world, the complex debate about what it is to be human is not extinguished. The film ends with the 'death' of Roy Batty, the leader of the genetically engineered 'criminal' replicants, after a protracted battle with Deckard, the replicant hunter. As he dies, Roy reflects on his life, informing Deckard and the audience that: 'I've seen things you people wouldn't believe. Attack ships on fire off the shoulder of Orion. I watched C-beams glitter in the dark near the Tannhauser Gate. All these moments will be lost in time, like tears in rain. Time to die.' If even the hyper-techno, depthless *Blade Runner* can centre discourses about 'humanity' in its narrative, so should contemporary criminological debates about the future of crime control.

Notes

1   Garland (1996) has argued that there has been a challenge to traditional dispositional criminology in recent years from what he terms the 'new criminologies of everyday life', associated with such approaches as situational crime prevention, routine activities theory and ecological theory. In many respects it is difficult to disagree with this thesis. However, we prefer the term 'anti-social criminologies of everyday life', since it conveys more accurately the critique of, and opposition to, both modernist criminology and traditional criminal justice responses represented by such approaches. It is even debatable whether this 'new' thinking is committed in the long term to remaining in, or being associated with, the discipline of criminology. At the moment, however, a *rapprochement* between the anti-social criminologies of everyday life and mainstream criminology appears more likely than the establishment of a quite distinct discipline of 'crime science' or 'crime reduction'.

2   There is no scope for a detailed discussion of the key features of this approach here, but see Hughes (1998, chapter 4) and Chapter 2 in this book.

3   On the use of the term 'settlement' to describe crucial moments of compromise and consensus between competing elements in a specific policy field, see Hughes and Lewis (1998).

4   See also the recently (2000) established Jill Dando Institute of Crime Science in London, where research is aimed at crime reduction and evidence-led policy and practice focused on the crime event rather than on criminals and crime 'after the event'.

5   The crude contrast drawn here between the 'old' and 'new' criminology is inevitably somewhat problematic. Criminology, particularly in the United Kingdom during the twentieth century, has always been policy-oriented, pragmatic and theoretically eclectic (Cohen, 1974). Furthermore, 'sociological' criminology has never held a position of intellectual supremacy over more individualist psychological approaches. Bearing these caveats in mind, the general point made by Garland and Sparks (2000) remains apposite in alerting us to the broad shift from an aetiological discourse fixated with causation to that of a pragmatic, 'risk calculation' one. In passing, it is also important to note that the influence of sociological positivism on both criminology and its associated policy field may have been stronger in the United States than in the United Kingdom for much of the twentieth century.

6   See, for example, the following press report: 'The Big Brother of internet investigation agencies, America's E-watch, helps more than 800 of the world's largest corporations keep track of their reputations across cyberspace' (Wazir, 2000).

7   There is, of course, a danger in exaggerating the 'newness' of both crimes and controls in the 'late modern' security complex. Note, for example, the talk of a 'new medievalism' in which we see the growth of high-tech 'moats' to secure the castles of consumerism, and the rise of fortress-like cities and privatized 'gated communities' (Hughes, 1998, pp. 138–44; McLaughlin and Muncie, 2000). In many ways there is nothing new in living in a divided world of 'haves' and 'have-nots', both within and between different countries, best exemplified in the policing strategies of border control between 'the dreadful enclosures of the excluded and the gated denizens of the wealthy' (Reiner, 2000, p. 87). In such processes of exclusion, it is likely that the poor may be left to look after themselves without any need for an Orwellian 'thought police' for their resocialization or sophisticated means of surveillance. Nor should we lose sight of the growth industry around penal custody and exclusion across most of the world (Christie, 1993) in which the logic of expressive punishment sits alongside that of actuarial risk management. We continue to live in brutal times, with old crimes and punishments coexisting alongside the new reductive architecture of control and security.

References

Baudrillard, J. (1983) *Simulations*, New York, Semitexte.

Bauman, Z. (1998) *Globalization: The Human Consequences*, Cambridge, Polity Press.

Beck, U. (1998) 'The cosmopolitan manifesto', *New Statesman*, 20 March, pp. 28–30.

Bennett, T. (1997) 'Crime prevention' in Tonry, M. (ed.) *Handbook of Crime and Punishment*, Oxford, Oxford University Press.

Bigo, D. (2000) 'Liaison officers in Europe: new officers in the European security field' in Sheptycki, J. (ed.) *Issues in Transnational Policing*, London, Routledge.

Castells, M. (1998) *Into the New Millennium*, vol. 3, The Information Society.

Central Intelligence Agency (2000) *Global Trends 2015: A Dialogue about the Future with Nongovernment Experts*, National Intelligence Council Report, Washington, DC, CIA (http://www.cia.gov).

Chan, J. (2000) 'Globalization, reflexivity and the practice of criminology', *Australian and New Zealand Journal of Criminology*, vol. 33, no. 2, pp. 118–35.

Christie, N. (1993) *Crime Control as Industry*, London, Routledge.

Cohen, S. (1974) 'Criminology and the sociology of deviance' in Rock, P. and McIntosh, M. (eds) *Deviance and Social Control*, London, Tavistock.

Cohen, S. (1985) *Visions of Social Control*, Cambridge, Polity Press.

Cohen, S. (1996) 'Crime and politics: spot the difference', *British Journal of Criminology*, vol. 47, pp. 1–17.

Department of Trade and Industry (2000) *Just around the Corner: A Consultation Report*, London, Foresight Crime Prevention Panel (http://www.foresight.gov.uk).

Department of Trade and Industry (2001) *Turning the Corner*, London, Foresight Crime Prevention Panel Consultation (http://www.foresight.gov.uk).

Dixon, P. (1998) *Futurewise: Six Faces of Global Change*, London, HarperCollins.

Ekblom, P. (1999) 'Can we make crime prevention adaptive by learning from other evolutionary struggles?', *Studies on Crime and Crime Prevention*, vol. 8, no. 1, pp. 27–51.

Ekblom, P. and Tilley, N. (2000) 'Going equipped: criminology, situational crime prevention and the resourceful offender', *British Journal of Criminology*, vol. 40, pp. 376–98.

Esping-Anderson, G. (1990) *The Three Worlds of Welfare Capitalism*, Cambridge, Polity Press.

Etzioni, A. (1994) *The Spirit of Community: The Reinvention of American Society*, New York, Touchstone Books.

Farrington, D. (2000) 'Explaining and preventing crime: the globalization of knowledge', *Criminology*, vol. 38, no. 1, pp. 1–24.

Felson, M. (1994) *Crime and Everyday Life*, Thousand Oaks, CA, Pine Forge Press.

Felson, M. and Clarke, R. (eds) (1997) *Business and Crime Prevention*, Monsey, NY, Criminal Justice Press.

Felson, M. and Clarke, R. (1998) *Opportunity Makes the Thief*, Police Research Series Paper 8, London, Home Office.

Fishman, R. (1977) *Urban Utopias in the Twentieth Century*, New York, Basic Books.

Foucault, M. (1977) *Discipline and Punish*, Harmondsworth, Penguin Books.

Garland, D. (1996) 'The limits of the sovereign state: strategies of crime control in contemporary society', *British Journal of Criminology*, vol. 36, no. 1, pp. 445–71.

Garland, D. (2001) *The Culture of Control*, Oxford, Oxford University Press.

Garland, D. and Sparks, R. (2000) 'Criminology, social theory and the challenge of our times', *British Journal of Criminology*, vol. 40, pp. 189–204.

Giddens, A. (1998) *Runaway World: How Globalization is Reshaping our Lives*, London, Profile Books.

Goldblatt, B. and Lewis, P. (1998) *Reducing Offending: An Assessment of Research Evidence on Ways of Dealing with Offending Behaviour*, Home Office Research Study 187, London, Home Office.

Graham, S. (forthcoming) 'Spaces of surveillant-simulation: new technologies, digital representations and material geographies', *Environment and Planning D: Society and Space*.

Hobsbawm, E. (1995) *The Age of Extremes*, London, Abacus.

Hope, T. (2000) 'Introduction' in Hope, T. (ed.) *Perspectives on Crime Reduction*, Aldershot, Ashgate.

Hughes, G. (1998) *Understanding Crime Prevention: Social Control, Risk and Late Modernity*, Buckingham, Open University Press.

Hughes, G. and Lewis, G. (eds) (1998) *Unsettling Welfare: The Reconstruction of Social Policy*, London, Routledge/Open University.

Huntington, S.P. (1998) *The Clash of Civilizations*, New York, Simon & Schuster.

Kaplan, R. (2000) *The Coming Anarchy: Shattering the Dreams of the post-Cold War*, New York, Random House.

Kelling, G. and Coles, P. (1997) *Fixing Broken Windows: Restoring Order and Reducing Crime in our Communities*, New York, Free Press.

Leadbetter, C. (1999) *Living on Thin Air: The New Economy*, Harmondsworth, Penguin Books.

McLaughlin, E. and Muncie, J. (2000) 'Walled cities: surveillance, regulation and segregation' in Pryke, M. (ed.) *Unsettling Cities*, London, Routledge/Open University.

Mills, C. Wright, (1959) *The Sociological Imagination*, New York, Oxford University Press.

Mulgan, G. (1997) *Connexity*, London, Chatto & Windus.

Newman, G., Clarke, R. and Shoban, S. (eds) (1997) *Rational Choice and Situational Crime Prevention*, Aldershot, Ashgate.

Norris, C. and Armstrong, S. (1999) *The Maximum Surveillance Society: The Rise of CCTV*, Oxford, Berg.

O'Malley, P. (1992) 'Risk, power and crime prevention', *Economy and Society*, vol. 21, no. 3, pp. 252–75.

O'Malley, P. (2000) 'Genealogies of catastrophe? Understanding criminal justice on the brink of the new millennium', *Australian and New Zealand Journal of Criminology*, vol. 33, no. 2, pp. 153–67.

Palmer, G. (2000) 'The new spectacle of crime' in Thomas, D. and Loader, B. (eds) *Cybercrime: Law Enforcement, Security and Surveillance in the Information Age*, London, Routledge.

Pease, K. (1997) 'Predicting the future: the roles of routine activity and rational choice theory' in Newman, G. et al. (eds) *Rational Choice and Situational Crime Prevention*, Aldershot, Ashgate.

Raleigh, W. (ed.) (1912) *Samuel Johnson: Complete Works*, Oxford.

Reiner, R. (2000) 'Crime and control', *Sociology*, vol. 34, no. 1, pp. 71–94.

Rogerson, M., Ekblom, P. and Pease, K. (2000) 'Crime reduction and the benefit of foresight' in Ballintyne, S., Pease, K. and McLaren, V. (eds) *Secure Foundations: Key Issues in Crime Prevention, Crime Reduction and Community Safety*, London, Institute for Public Policy Research.

Rose, N. (1999) *Powers of Freedom*, Cambridge, Cambridge University Press.

Russo, G. (1997) 'Criminology in crisis and the social demand for crime prevention' in Newman, G. et al. (eds) *Rational Choice and Situational Crime Prevention*, Aldershot, Ashgate.

Scase, R. (2000) *Britain towards 2010: The Changing Business Environment*, London, Foresight, Department of Trade and Industry (http://www.foresight.-gov.uk).

Sève, R. (1997) 'Philosophical justifications of situational crime prevention' in Newman, G. et al. (eds) *Rational Choice and Situational Crime Prevention*, Aldershot, Ashgate.

Shearing, C. (1997) 'The unrecognized origins of the new policing: linkages between private and public policy' in Felson, M. and Clarke, R. (eds) *Business and Crime Prevention*, Monsey, NY, Criminal Justice Press.

Sherman, L., Gottfredson, D., McKenzie, D., Eck, J., Reuter, P. and Bushway, S. (1998) *Preventing Crime: What Works, What Doesn't, What's Promising*, Research in Brief, National Institute of Justice, Washington, DC, US Department of Justice.

Stenson, K. (1998) 'Displacing social policy through crime control' in Hänninen, S. (ed.) *Displacement of Social Policies*, University of Jyväskylä, SoPhi.

Wazir, B. (2000) 'Eating the greens', *The Observer*, 1 October.

Wilkins, T. (1997) 'Wartime operational research in Britain and situational crime prevention' in Newman, G. et al. (eds) *Rational Choice and Situational Crime Prevention*, Aldershot, Ashgate.

Wilson, J. (1974) 'Crime and the criminologists', *Commentary*, July, pp. 47–53.

Wilson, J. and Kelling, G. (1982) 'Broken windows', *Atlantic Review*, March, pp. 29–36.

Young, J. (1999) *The Exclusive Society*, London, Sage.

Lightning Source UK Ltd.
Milton Keynes UK
UKOW021449071111

181629UK00001B/99/P